42/23

].

TRICKS
OF
MEMORY

By the same author

The Socialist Myth
Peregrinations: Selected Pieces

TRICKS
OF
MEMORY

An Autobiography

PEREGRINE WORSTHORNE

Weidenfeld & Nicolson
London

First published in Great Britain in 1993 by
Weidenfeld & Nicolson
The Orion Publishing Group Ltd
Orion House,
5 Upper Saint Martin's Lane,
London, WC2H 9EA.

ISBN 0 297 81186 X

British Library Cataloguing in Publication Data is available for this title.

Typeset by Create Publishing Services Ltd, Bath, Avon
Printed in Great Britain by The Bath Press Ltd, Bath, Avon

LUCY

Acknowledgements

I should like to thank my dear friend Oliver Knox for much advice and encouragement; and Justine Oliver for her invaluable mastery of the word processor and many other assistances. My researcher Christopher Lloyd was also a great help.

For the chapter on Stowe I am particularly grateful to the headmaster for having given me access to the school records. That they should have kept all the correspondence, going back sixty years, about even such an unappreciative and unpromising pupil speaks a volume about how seriously the school cherishes its past.

Contents

Illustrations

All photographs appearing in this book are from the author's
private collection.

Foreword

Reading through this autobiography I am embarrassed to find how many people who played important parts in my life – relations, friends and colleagues – get no mention or none that does justice to the high regard in which I hold them. To some this will come as a relief. To others, who are hurt, however, let me explain the reason. In the interests of readability I have tried to compress my life into a coherent narrative, and this has meant ignoring individuals and incidents which do not lend themselves to this purpose. Also for reasons of readability I have tended to give greater prominence to public figures than to private ones. A better writer would not need to rely on dropping names. But after a long career in journalism the habit has become ineradicable.

One or two other omissions also require explanations. There is relatively little reference, for example, to books, in spite of the enormous amount of time I have spent reading them – much more time than I have spent doing anything else. Here, again, the reason is the same: a journalistic desire not to bore the reader. For although I love reading books, and have probably read on average two a week for the last fifty years, I am exceptionally bad at communicating this pleasure. As a matter of fact I did try to write a chapter about the books which have influenced me most, but the result was not worth printing. The same problem arose, to a far greater extent, when trying to write about music or pictures and, above all, about religion. When you have nothing worthwhile to say better, I concluded, to remain silent.

And neither is there any attempt to write a 'lessons of my life' final chapter to round off the story. This omission I do regret. It is a confession of failure to have reached the age of three score years and ten having learnt so little and forgotten so much. Like it or not, however, that is how it is. I now feel less confident about anything than I did once about everything. That is why punditry no longer appeals; in fact repels, and is conspicuously absent from these pages.

As for the life of journalism, I have tried to describe it as it was for me. My gift has never been to see things – people, issues, stories – in the round, but rather to see them from some unusual and, if needs be, distorting, angle. From that vantage point what I saw was never *the* truth; only if lucky, *a* truth. That was the best I could do. Objectivity in my experience was less an ideal to aspire to than a temptation to resist. The more research I did, the less likely I was to experience that indispensable flash of intuition. In other words, elaborate research never helped me to get to the heart of any subject. It merely served to blunt the edge of anything remotely interesting that I had to say. This is not something to boast about and I am not boasting about it. It is simply a subjective statement of what journalism has been for me.

Finally, why do I want to be the cartographer of my own calamaties, as any autobiographer must be? Perhaps Montaigne suggests the answer, 'Not to dare to talk roundly of yourself betrays a defect of thought', he wrote. Although this autobiography betrays lots of other defects, at least that particular one is not among them.

1

Childhood

I was born on 22 December 1923 at 81 Cadogan Square in Chelsea. There is no problem about remembering the house because it is still there and I pass it very often on my way to Sloane Square or thereabouts. From the outside the house is exactly as it was with the same bold number plate. Inside it is unrecognisable, having been turned into about ten apartments. My mother lived in this house on her own, except for the large staff of servants. Where my father was is not easy to discover. There were rooms allocated to him, but he never seemed to turn up to use them.

I remember little about my early childhood, and did not feel inclined to reminisce with my mother about it in later years, possibly because this would have involved raising the question of my father's absence. At no point during my childhood was my father's name ever mentioned either by my mother or by anybody else. Certainly I have no recollection of hearing or overhearing the servants, or my nanny, ever referring to him. He had become a non-person, whom my mother had simply written out of our history, almost immediately after bearing him two children – Simon,* the elder by two years, and myself.

Simon, of course, I remember very well. We were very close, and still are, although he now lives in Lancashire. We shared a nursery floor with a nanny and two nursery maids, and then, at about the age of six, with a governess called Miss Hart who was an early devotee of the Montessori educational theory. Not long ago she sent me a diary of this period in which she paints my mother as a typical society lady of the 1920s who rather neglected her two sons. About the neglect I would not like to pass comment

---

*Simon's birth was far more spectacular than mine. It took place in the middle of a private concert given by Paderewski, the world famous pianist who was also president of Poland at the time, in my paternal grandparents' house in Belgrave Square. Because Simon was due at any moment my mother arranged to sit near the concert room door, so that she could creep out and upstairs if the labour pains began, which they did. Later she was fond of recounting how gallantly she had stifled her cries of pain so as to avoid spoiling the maestro's Chopin mazurkas on the floor below.

3

since there is no way of telling at this distance. Certainly I don't recall feeling neglected but then I wouldn't have known what being neglected felt like. But if we were neglected it was not because my mother was a typical society lady. She was most certainly nothing of the kind. In retrospect I rather wish she had been since even at an early age I liked typical society ladies who always smelt good and gave little children such chocolates as they had not already lavished on their lapdogs. No, my mother was a serious young woman, already in revolt against her fate, i.e. having been born into the upper class. She certainly went out a lot. But I rather doubt whether her absences – so much deplored by Miss Hart – were because of any search for pleasure. It was much more likely she was searching for some useful role in the social service world in which she later worked with such satisfaction and distinction.

Miss Hart's diary expresses anxiety that Simon and I might suffer from an absence of maternal hugs. In support of this thesis – now a bit of a cliché but then quite psychologically advanced – she describes a scene in the hall of 81 Cadogan Square when the two little boys, attired in new mackintoshes, were reduced to hugging each other. As it happens, I do remember this incident very clearly, and it had much more to do with our delight in the texture of mackintoshes than in any frustrated yearning for maternal affection. In fact we were to ask to put the mackintoshes on even when it was not raining so as to be able to indulge this taste, giggling all the while out of embarrassment and guilt. Perhaps this is what Miss Hart objected to, believing that our mother's coldness – or alleged coldness – was sowing in her two young charges the seeds of a kinky perversion. If she was that sophisticated, and is still with us, and ever reads these pages, let me belatedly set her mind at rest. Neither Simon nor I have developed so far – and there is not all that much time to go – into rubber fetishists.

In my mother's autobiography, published about ten years before her death in 1991, there are very few references to me and only one that relates to my early years. 'Peregrine,' she writes, 'was nearly always antagonistic, even at the breast.' Again, there is no way I can either confirm or deny at any rate the last bit of this allegation. As to the general charge of early troublesomeness, I do feel entitled to put the record straight in one small respect. In the matter of enemas, yes, I did give my mother a great deal of trouble right from the start. But the trouble I caused her was nothing to the trouble she caused me. No reference is made to this in Miss Hart's diary. Possibly the subject was too delicate even for her advanced views. My mother had a passion for internal hygiene and gave instructions – or so I have to assume – that Simon and I were to be colonically irrigated – as the phrase was – by either nanny or governess at regular intervals. Every fibre of my being revolted against this outrage and neither nanny nor governess was able to carry out my mother's orders. So one evening she arrived to carry out the deed herself. In those days the arrival of the mother on

4

the nursery floor was no ordinary event. It was heralded in advance rather in the manner of a royal progress, requiring much preparation. Lying on my bed awaiting my fate, I could hear all the equipment being assembled, as if for an execution. 'Just relax,' said my mother in what was intended to be a reassuring manner. 'Be a good boy, there is nothing to worry about.' I won't go into detail. Suffice it to say that as the result of my non-cooperation, jets of warm water went shooting up to the ceiling and all over the walls and, worse, all over my mother who had so gravely under-estimated the difficulty of her task as to arrive in evening dress. As this memoir progresses there will be occasions when I will be happy to confess that I was entirely in the wrong and my mother, and many others, entirely in the right. But on this occasion it does seem to me that I was the innocent, not to say the injured, party.

What with the fraternal mackintosh-hugging and maternal enema-giving, or rather resisting, you will think that my childhood was very much less ordinary than it actually was. The trouble is that one only remembers the peculiarities, not the normalities. I only remember one other resident of Cadogan Square, for example, and that is because he was famous: Sir Samuel Hoare, a Tory cabinet minister. Miss Hart, being a progressive, did not approve of him. Nor did my mother, whose Tory sympathies even then were by no means deep enough to overcome the personal antipathy everybody felt, including his wife, Lady Maude, to this cold and un-attractive statesman. To me, aged five, however, he was by no means cold or unattractive and used sometimes to give my hoop an encouraging tap with his rolled umbrella when, returning from the Foreign Office, he found me playing on the pavement outside his house.

Possibly I am using these trivialities so as to postpone having to tackle properly the, for me, awkward question of my father's absence. In fact he can't have been absent all the time because my mother and he did not separate formally until several years later. And, as I say, he had his own quarters on the same landing as my mother. They had both married, I suspect, on the rebound and up to a point it was a marriage of convenience. She came from, or her English half came from, a grand English family – the Berties – without much money and he from a very rich and not ungrand Belgian family – the Koch de Gooreynds – quite eager to make the grade in English society. Neither was much above twenty when they married and they scarcely knew each other. My father had served briefly in the First World War, going straight from Eton into the Irish Guards, and my mother had been a nurse. When I got to know my father many years later he used to say that if he was in the dark about why he married my mother, he was even more so about why the marriage broke up. Apparently he came home one day to be met by a mutual friend, Wyndham Portal, who said simply; 'Priscilla has gone.' 'Where to?' my father asked. 'To nowhere in particular, just gone,' replied Portal ... and that was that. She never saw him again and, until very near her death, never allowed his name to pass her lips. Not that he had done anything wrong. That was the trouble. He shocked my mother by doing absolutely nothing whatsoever. She was shocked by his indolence, passivity, lack of interest. Even being a playboy was too much trouble. He was the eldest of four brothers and one daughter and they all inherited a quarter of a million pounds on becoming twenty-one – an enormous fortune in those days. His parents owned not one but two houses in Belgrave Square, the smaller having been built by his mother as a personal retreat. Presumably he gave my mother everything she wanted except the one thing she craved – a serious-minded husband with a job who would help her escape the life of idle leisure which she saw as a fate worse than death.

To begin with, she had encouraged him to become a politician and through a great-uncle, Lord FitzAlan, who had been Tory Chief Whip, had got him adopted as a prospective Tory member of parliament. With a political career in mind, he changed his name from Koch de Gooreynd to Worsthorne which is a village on an estate in Lancashire owned by my mother's mother. It was thought that the name Worsthorne would go down better with the voters than Koch de Gooreynd, and that may well have been right, although the difference was not sufficient to ensure his election. Possibly if he had become an MP, my mother would have had less reason to disapprove of his idleness. But he didn't and the only lasting result of his political ambitions was to saddle my brother and me with the name Worsthorne, a name which he himself renounced on separating from my mother, which my brother renounced when he inherited the Towneley property, and my mother renounced when she remarried, leaving me as its only bearer – or not quite, as this story will in due course reveal.

At the time Simon and I found it quite natural that we should not see our father. Children are like that. So limited is their experience that they tend to regard as normal anything that happens to them. In any case upper-class children at that time lived in nurseries where fathers, even when there was one, played no part. Not having a nanny – now that would have set us apart and prompted us to ask awkward questions. But not having a father, at least in those early years, gave us little, if any, cause for concern. For there was no absence of men in the house on whose backs we could ride. My mother had a butler and an odd job man, both of whom saw it as part of their job to be pestered by the two of us. Where the absence of a father did affect us was in its impact on our mother who felt the need to be more strict and stern than might otherwise have been the case. Untidiness was her bugbear and there were truly terrible scenes if chests of drawers or toy cupboards were not in apple-pie order. Every so often she would carry out an inspection. Master Simon always passed with flying colours. Not so

Master Perry who was duly chastised with a slipper, or even a hairbrush, an experience none the less unpleasant for being almost entirely painless. I have a feeling that my mother felt obliged to play the sergeant-major in this way so as to compensate for our fatherless condition. If so it was a sad error. For in trying to compensate for a missing authority figure, she succeeded only in depriving us of a soft and loving maternal figure. According to my mother's autobiography, she was at the time beginning to become active in the new Child Guidance Association, of which she was to become chairman. I do not know what their line on broken homes was in those days. All I do know, from my own experience, is that if children can't have both parents it is far better for the one they do have to concentrate on being a very good mother or a very good father, as the case may be, than to try and combine the role of both at the cost of being neither. If my mother had been softer, this would have brought out feelings of protectiveness in me that have never been properly developed. As it was, her attempt at hardness killed any sense of filial duty a son owes to a mother without inducing the kind of filial respect a son owes to a father ... without, incidentally, making me any tidier.

What my mother dreaded was that Simon and I should turn out as feckless as our father. In her book there is no category of human being more worthless than 'the idle rich'. In this she was wrong. There are many worse kinds of human beings. As well as being idle, my father was generous, kind, charming and intelligent – all important qualities which my mother tended to underestimate. If he had been around, life at home would certainly have been much more fun. On the one occasion when he was allowed to take us out from school, he arrived in a Rolls-Royce with a cocktail bar, thereby confirming our mother's worst fears about his contaminating influence. By then he was remarried to an enchanting Russian countess who loved spoiling children, and the two of them took the prep school by storm. Before the Russian countess there had been a white Rhodesian wife who bore him a son who did go to the bad. So possibly there was a case for keeping him out of our lives for as long as possible. But the lengths gone to really were extraordinary. Not only did our father become a non-person but so did his entire family, many of whom were fascinating and clever as well as rich. As children we did not even know of their existence. My paternal grandmother, Granny-Gran, I only saw once. Her solicitor contacted my mother's solicitor and it was agreed between them that on such and such a day the chauffeur would deliver us to Belgrave Square for lunch. It was a superb lunch of an elaborate richness which our mother would have regarded as wholly unsuitable for ten-year-olds – certain to give us bilious attacks. It was the first time, not surprisingly, I'd ever tasted gnocchi, seen footmen with white gloves or eaten veal with small onions and rich gravy. Dishes also came round twice

7

and we were urged to gorge to peals of approving laughter. But this glimpse of heaven was never repeated since Granny-Gran had broken the rule. Her solicitor had failed to mention that our father was to be present at the lunch and in the terms of the divorce my father had agreed never to see us without specific approval on each occasion.

For somebody who I say played no part in my childhood I seem to be going on about him; giving the impression, even, that he was the dog who did not bark in the night – a kind of brooding absence. This was not the case. Our early childhood life was entirely dominated by a world utterly removed from that of the Koch de Gooreynds. Christmases, for example, were usually spent with our great-uncle and aunt, Lord and Lady FitzAlan, at Cumberland Lodge in Windsor Park, a grace-and-favour mansion* lent to them by King George V who used to drive over from the castle, with Queen Mary, for tea. All I remember of these occasions was the sight of the king and queen descending from a Daimler, he in black with a bowler hat and she in the famous mauve. Their chauffeur, however, became a friend; much more than a friend, a hero. For it was he who showed me my first glimpse of a firearm. Then as now, the IRA were active and my Uncle Edmund had been Viceroy in Dublin where he took my father briefly as his ADC. Uncle Edmund was married to my maternal grandmother's sister, May. Catholicism hung over Cumberland Lodge like a great black drape. Mass was said every morning in the private chapel and much of the conversation had to do with ecclesiastical politics.

In fact Uncle Edmund, brother of the deceased Duke of Norfolk and uncle of Bernard, the new one, was to all intents and purposes the leading Catholic layman of the time. I never remember him wearing anything but the darkest of dark clothes, or without a heavy watch chain with a seal at its end which Simon and I, as a treat, were allowed to twiddle. The fast Edwardian age had passed the FitzAlans by. They were the last of the Victorian grandees, totally at sea in the world of flappers and suffragettes. Joyce, the young wife of Uncle Edmund's son, Boydie, created a sensation by coming down to dinner with painted nails. So great were the reverberations that they reached even the nursery wing where the nannies talked of nothing else. Quite soon, however, they had a far greater scandal to talk about: my mother's divorce and remarriage to a Protestant. In the grand old Catholic world of the period, of which this family was the very epicentre, my mother's divorce came as a truly terrible shock. Neither my mother nor Simon and I were allowed to darken the doors of Cumberland Lodge again. My grandmother, Aunt May's sister, was shattered and opposed the marriage to the very last moment and after. As children we did not know what was going on. Nobody explained why there were no

---

*Now a conference centre; I spent a weekend there in the 1980s when my friend John Vaizey was the Warden.

more Christmas visits to Cumberland Lodge, where the brandy snaps were the only luxury; no more visits to Arundel Castle where I got lost among the armour on my way to first communion; no more invitations to twiddle the seal on the end of Uncle Edmund's watch chain. All we knew was that the familiar routines were suddenly disrupted. So far as the FitzAlans were concerned, and indeed all the old Catholic families, our mother and her two boys had disappeared from the face of the earth, never to be spoken of, let alone seen, again. Henceforth, not only were Simon and I to be cut off from our father's family but also to a large extent from our mother's as well, with the exception of my maternal grandmother, Lady Alice, who increasingly took us under her wing.

What had happened was this. Our mother had met Montagu Norman, the Governor of the Bank of England. For a year or so we had noticed an unusually rakish Anthony Eden hat and stick in the hall as we came home from our London pre-prep school, and not thought anything more of it. Our mother had had gentlemen callers before, and all of them wore hats of one sort or another. In any case, the life of the grown-ups in those days was so remote – literally remote, all of four floors – that children had no way of knowing what was going on, except through the servants who in this case must have been unusually discreet. Then one day, travelling on the top of a bus down the Strand, in the charge of Miss Marshall (Mar), our mother's lady's maid, Simon drew our attention to a placard which read: 'Bank Governor to wed LCC Lady'. By then our mother represented Hammersmith on the LCC, and for some reason we knew that the LCC lady referred to was her. I don't remember the news coming as a particular shock. Children take things in their stride. If one's mother was going to marry a Bank Governor, and the first thing one heard about this was from a newspaper placard in the Strand, seen by chance from the top of a bus, then this must be all right because, if it were not all right, it would not be happening. Simon, being that bit older, was more excited than I. He must have known that our life would soon be changed out of all recognition. All that I knew was that Mar had promised to take us to tea at Fullers where the walnut cake was our favourite. I don't think Mar had been told about the engagement either. She bought the paper and read all about it over the crumpets and walnut cake, the news having in no way dampened our appetites. The story was on the front page in banner headlines with pictures of the affianced pair, my mother looking beautiful in a pearl necklace and Montagu Norman, twenty years her senior, every inch a cavalier to the tip of his Van Dyke beard. By the time we got back to Cadogan Square there were reporters outside the house and our mother had gone into hiding so as to avoid them. Simon had been right: life was never the same again.

Apparently our mother had met Norman about a year earlier at Laverstoke, a beautiful Georgian house in Hampshire which was the home of Wyndham Portal, the man who had broken the news to my father that his marriage was over. Portal and my mother were close friends, probably more. He had an invalid wife and my mother sometimes acted as an unofficial hostess both at Laverstoke and on his yacht which she had decorated. We called him Uncle Wyndham and spent long periods either at Laverstoke or, in the summer, at a castle he rented in Scotland. Having no children of his own he seemed to welcome our presence and we certainly welcomed his, since he was enormously high-spirited and generous, liking nothing better than to see children indulging themselves in all the things prohibited or rationed by parents or nannies. It was at his table that I first tasted smoked salmon and first drank a glass of champagne and was made to feel that enjoying them at my age, about ten, was a great achievement. He would tell his friends, behind my mother's back, that I was a boy after his own heart. Laverstoke was a dream house full of sunshine and great bowls of flowers and peaches and all the other luxuries. One weekend Montagu Norman had been invited there in the hope of persuading him to reverse the Bank of England's decision to cease using the nearby Portal paper mill for printing pound notes, and it was my mother's job to charm the governor into a change of heart. She didn't succeed in this. But she certainly did succeed in laying on the charm and this enormously distinguished middle-aged bachelor fell in love for the first time.

According to others present at the weekend the romance began on a walk in the woods when my mother's whippet escaped the leash and started to run riot with the pheasants. To my mother's amazement Montagu Norman, who hitherto had given no sign of athleticism, refusing all invitations to tennis, golf and so on, raced after the whippet and brought her safely back before harm was done; not only brought the dog back but made a courtly speech about how he hoped this would be the first of many services he might be permitted to perform. That somehow broke the ice which never formed again. For our mother this undoubtedly was the turning point in her life. She had found her *beau-idéal*. But for us it amounted to another uprooting. For Wyndham Portal, who had been a kind of surrogate father, was swiftly written out of the story, along with our father and Uncle Edmund. Henceforth it was Normans all the way, and if our mother's side of the family was very different from our father's, the Normans were different to both. Eighty-one Cadogan Square was sold and we moved into Montagu Norman's house, Thorpe Lodge, on Campden Hill. At least our mother did, and, up to a point, we did as well, but only up to a point. Thorpe Lodge was filled with rare panelling brought back by Norman from foreign parts and also with beautiful furniture made by his own hand. He had lavished on this house all the love of his hitherto lonely life and not unnaturally dreaded the prospect of having two young boys messing up the place. So even after the marriage it was quite a long time before we really took up residence. Beautiful as the house was in a William Morris kind of way, with an enormous garden and a vast music room, I never came to love it. It is today the headmaster's office of the Holland Park Comprehensive School and I sometimes take a look in for old times' sake and cannot resist a wry smile. For any damage Simon and I might have wreaked on his beloved house would have been as nothing to the vandalisation that has now become its fate.

Nor were Simon and I made to feel unwelcome only in London. We were not exactly welcome at Moor Place, his country home, either. In fact, Woodside, a lovely thatched house nearby was taken for us to stay in equipped with our own staff of servants. Again we took all this as normal. Boarding schools soon came to the rescue. Compared to the strangeness of boarding school, our rather lonely travesty of a home life seemed idyllic.

2

Ladycross and Abinger

I remember nothing about my first boarding school, Ladycross – then the leading Roman Catholic prep school – except the reason my mother took me away after, I think, only two terms. It was because I caught impetigo which she blamed on the primitive washing facilities. Impetigo in those days was a disgraceful condition to be found more often in the slums than at an expensive educational establishment. The signs were all too outward and visible: oozing sores on the lips and the face, made even more conspicuous by the dark blue ointment which was supposed to cure them if applied long and regularly enough. The washing arrangements at that time were indeed appalling even by the standards of the 1930s. They consisted of three great communal square baths filled with tepid water and surrounded by slimy duckboards in which some sixty or so little boys all splashed around together.

Although bad hygiene was the reason my mother gave for taking us away so precipitately, I now realise that there was a far more important motive behind her dramatic action. It was about this time that she decided to renounce Catholicism, in revolt against what she saw as its narrowness and intolerance, particularly in relation to her divorce and remarriage. Not only did she renounce Catholicism but she embraced Protestantism and accompanied the Norman clan to the beautiful Anglican church at Much Hadham. Our new stepfather, Uncle Mont, as we came to call him, did not attend himself. But his younger brother Ronnie, then chairman of the British Broadcasting Corporation, and his wife, Lady Florence, did, along with their five fine and beautiful children, two girls and three boys. Leaving theology aside, it is easy to see why my mother found more peace of mind in worshipping with the Anglican Normans in Much Hadham than ever she had among the Catholic FitzAlans at Cumberland Lodge. Early morning mass in the gloomy Cumberland Lodge chapel was cold and austere without music or hymns. Uncle Edmund used to serve, always in a dark suit, looking very stern and intense. To a child it was extraordinary to see this venerable and awe-inspiring figure, to whom so much subservience was paid in all other circumstances, kneel and bow in front of the priest, before handing him the water and wine and linen napkin, using very much the same gestures of humility which the servants, who sat at the back of the chapel, would be using to him in the breakfast room only half an hour or so later. There was nothing comforting, still less heartwarming, about mass at Cumberland Lodge. Nor should there be. For devout Catholics believe they are actually eating the flesh and drinking the blood of their Lord and Saviour, not merely commemorating an event that took place nearly two thousand years ago. Whereas for Anglicans the communion service induces holy nostalgia, for Catholics like the FitzAlans it induces holy terror. No wonder my mother preferred the church at Much Hadham, from which the congregation emerged looking happy and relaxed, to the gloomy procession that filed out of the chapel at Cumberland Lodge, led by boot-faced old Aunt May. Much Hadham, in those days, was one of those perfect English villages. Everybody had ruddy cheeks and from the Normans, who lived in the big house, Moor Place, downwards, they all played their allotted parts to perfection as in some idyllic English 1930s film. It was Harvest Festival all the year round with never a long face to cast a shadow over the sun that never seemed to set.

After early service at Much Hadham one Sunday, my mother drove to Ladycross to take us out and arrived at about midday to find lots of little Catholic boys pouring out of chapel, many of whose faces were pitted with impetigo. Did the Norman boys have impetigo? The very idea of those peach-pink skins ever being so defiled was inconceivable. It was all the fault of Rome. The speed of our removal was quite startling. Into the car and away ... out of the dark and into the light.

The light turned out to be Abinger Hill. If Ladycross enjoyed the reputation of being the best old-fashioned Catholic prep school, Abinger Hill enjoyed the reputation of being the best new-fangled progressive school. It was run on the principle of a little of what you fancy does you good which meant in my case that I did very little Latin or Greek and a lot of history and English – the easy options. Nor, compared to most schools of the period, was there much discipline. If pushed too far the admirable headmaster, G. J. K. Harrison, would give us a swipe with a golf club, turning corporal punishment into something more akin to a game than a torture.

A problem of being suddenly switched from one school to another was the need to buy a whole new set of uniforms in swift succession. Luckily for my mother's pocket, Abinger Hill did not go in for elaborate uniforms. Corduroy shorts, brown sack shirts, and sandals were the main new items required, but even buying these, so soon after kitting me out for Ladycross, struck my mother as inexcusably extravagant and I was sent with only one pair of corduroy shorts instead of three and so on, with the request to matron that I should be allowed to wear out my Ladycross clothes until it was at least established that my stay at Abinger was to be longer than my stay at Ladycross. It says much for the broadmindedness of Abinger that the headmaster and matron conceded to this request, attributing it more to eccentricity than to parsimony. Even more surprisingly, the boys forbore to notice the wrong togs. Abinger was an exceptionally civilised place.

Even after all these years, however, my mother's parsimony still surprises. For there was no shortage of money. With her it was a question of principle, not necessity. She was a stickler for turning off electric lights and not turning on electric fires, and there was never any question of lighting a proper fire in the drawing room before the evening. As for throwing extra logs on shortly before bedtime, that was deemed an inexcusable waste of wood. The more correct drill was to scatter the half-burnt logs into the four corners of the grate so that not a splinter was wasted after bedtime. This was long before wartime shortages. The war, when it came nearly eight years later, merely legitimised the trait, transforming it from a private vice into a public virtue. In retrospect it all seems rather comical. But at the time it caused me some distress. At Abinger I developed a passion for riding and sent an SOS home asking permission to buy riding boots. By return came a pair of my mother's cast-offs with ladies' heels and, naturally, very thin feet and pointed toes. Again the Abinger boys were understanding when I tripped painfully and unsteadily up to the stables in this unmistakably female footwear. But if they were understanding, I was not. Resentments were beginning to stir. My plea for riding boots was more than a childish whim and my mother's response had by no means done it justice.

Enough whines. I do not remember a day's unhappiness at Abinger Hill. Among my contemporaries were Nicholas Mosley, Edward Boyle, Derek and Julian Mond, Bamm Hoare, John Gale, Michael Howard, Billy Buckhurst and his younger brother Harry Sackville. The tone of civilised good humour was set right at the start of the first lesson, when the headmaster, in an effort to put the new boys at ease, read out an extract from one of Macaulay's essays. On coming to the end, he asked for questions. None of us had any except for little Edward Boyle who piped up as follows: 'Not really a comment, sir, but I just wanted to tell you that with that voice you could fill the Albert Hall.' Instead of finding this impertinent, the headmaster took the compliment at face value, beaming with pleasure, as if genuinely flattered. Never before had I seen a grown-up in authority take a child so seriously. Only servants took them seriously which was what made their company so enjoyable. On the right side of the green baize door grown-ups reacted with amusement or irritation but seldom with interest.

The name of only one other master sticks in my mind; Neville Bewley, who taught me English. One day after tea I found him in the school library with his familiar, a chameleon which changed colour according to its master's mood. It was dark purple, a sure sign of anger. The object of the anger was a new book by the fashionable young novelist, Beverley Nichols, not an author I had every heard of, my favourites of the time being G. A. Henty, Harrison Ainsworth, Stanley Weyman and Jeffery Farnol – not to mention the lesser ones like Edgar Wallace, 'Sapper' and Dornford Yates. Bewley explained that the novel was a cruel satire on Nelly Melba, the opera singer to whom Nichols had owed so much. 'Nichols is a little creep. Take his slime away, Worsthorne mi, and flush it down the plughole,' he cried. Needless to say I took the book away and read every word. Next holiday, when a friend of my mother praised the book, I was able to astound the company by my inside knowledge of Beverley Nichols's true character, thereby earning a reputation for bookishness which pride made me try to live up to.

An advantage of boarding schools is that they provide so many opportunities for out-of-class exchanges of this kind. Knowledge imparted by a master in class was public property, available to every Tom, Dick and Harry – like water out of a tap – and therefore not nearly so precious as the merest titbit of historical or literary gossip imparted personally which then became one's very own private treasure. So much of education is a matter of finding the right spark to set the flames of interest burning. No doubt my enjoyment of books would have been sparked sooner or later by something else, but unquestionably Neville Bewley's outburst against Beverley Nichols, which was a private confidence not shared with any of the other boys, started me off. I suppose this intense pleasure in exclusivity was a kind of childish snobbery, not unlike preferring, in later life, to be given a private viewing of a stately home, rather than having to go round as part of a crowd. The cricket coach at Abinger, who doubled as the classics master, also had something of the Bewley touch. Bowling in the nets one afternoon he said of some stroke of mine; 'That was almost worthy of my friend XYZ,' a well-known county player. I don't remember at any other school ever being so skilfully flattered as at Abinger. All the masters from Harrison downwards seemed to follow the principle, 'Give a dog a good name . . . '. My mother may have expected Abinger's progressive educational techniques to amount to something a bit more sophisticated than that. Mercifully for us, they didn't.

My time at Abinger did not entirely lack shadows. In my third year a Brazilian boy of my age, but almost a foot taller, began to befriend me. We would go for long walks in the wood and he was excellent company, very well travelled and knowing. Then one day he told me he wanted to share a great secret which he had never before confided to a living soul. Before he did so I had to pledge myself to secrecy by mixing my blood with his, which we duly did by both pricking our thumbs. The secret turned out to be that he was a murderer, having strangled a boy at a previous school. Nobody had suspected him. The boy was assumed to have hanged himself. At first.I did not believe him, and he did not seem to expect me to. Then a week or so later, he returned to the subject and produced an outsize Van Heusen collar which he claimed to have used to do the dreadful deed. Would I like him to show me how? The first time he took no for an answer, but on subsequent walks he became more insistent and actually tried to demonstrate his prowess by force. At this point I began to get really scared. What was I to do? To report him seemed out of the question. There was that blood oath between us. On the other hand it seemed unwise to refuse to carry on going for walks with him since this might rouse his suspicions as to my reliability. But what might he do on the next walk? Could my experience on the previous walk, when he had put the collar round my neck, have been a kind of dress rehearsal, or measuring my neck for size? Panic mounted. I had to run away.

How I got to Dorking Station, I have no idea. But I managed it somehow and caught the train to Waterloo. Then another kind of panic set in. What was I to tell my mother? Once away from the school I could hardly believe in my story myself. Could I have been dreaming? In any case, to put off the moment of going home, I went to the Pathé-Gazette cinema in Waterloo Station, possibly hoping that if I arrived home late enough my mother would be out to dinner, which she was. Nelly, the parlour maid, answered the door and I told her all. She expressed horror and told me to go to bed, when she would bring me something to eat, before telephoning my mother with the dramatic news. My mother came rushing home and was so horrified that she telephoned the headmaster there and then. Rather unkindly she began by asking him how I was, to which the headmaster crossly replied that at that hour I was tucked up and fast asleep. 'Oh no he's not,' retorted my mother, 'He's here beside me and you'd better come up right away to explain what's going on.' This he did, arriving at about midnight. As I feared, he did not believe me and believed me all the less when I mentioned quite innocently that I had been to the news cinema at Waterloo. Both he and my mother seemed to think that going to the cinema was a sign of non-seriousness. I could feel them relaxing. Something was on my mind, clearly, but nothing as serious as they had first been led to believe. Lulled by the security of home, I began to believe the same myself. But it turned out that I had not been wrong. The boy did have a record of violent assault in Brazil, where he had tried to kill a boy. By the time I returned to Abinger, he had been removed and the headmaster was almost embarrassingly apologetic for not having believed my story. But I could never get him to understand how a boy so terrified of being murdered as I was could have calmly sat through an hour of Movietone news before going home. Now that I am grown up it does seem a bit odd, but at the time it seemed the natural thing to do.

The names of some of my other more agreeable contemporaries have already been mentioned and most of them have changed astonishingly little, in spite of having used the ensuing half century to become distinguished scholars, authors and statesmen. Michael Howard* was the same judicious, slightly troubled authoritative figure then that he is now and when we meet, as we often do at the bar of the Garrick, I still find myself benefiting from his superior wisdom just as I used to do in the locker room at Abinger where we all gathered for elevenses to drink half a pint of milk through a straw. Nor have our tastes changed all that much. Just as it was his custom in the locker room to shake the bottle so as to spread the cream evenly and mine to suck out the cream first, now he drinks only a chaste glass of dry sherry while I indulge in a tankard of champagne. Also people went to him for advice then on roughly the same kind of subjects as they do now; in one respect even eerily so, given his subsequent distinction as a military historian.

When Mussolini invaded Abyssinia we decided to re-enact our own version of the infamous campaign in the woods. Not surprisingly there were many more volunteers anxious to play the part of the victim, the Lion of Judah, than that of the hated Italian bully. In fact no one was anxious to play Mussolini until Michael came up with the answer. Nicholas Mosley, son of Sir Oswald Mosley, should play him. Since Nick's political sympathies and general style were about as unlike his father's as is possible to imagine, this seemed a bit hard. Not at all, explained Michael. By playing Mussolini Nick would be at once demonstrating filial loyalty, a willingness to defy public opinion, and a Christian inclination to see good even in the worst of monsters. Having established his leadership qualities by solving the Mussolini problem, Michael proceeded to take command of both armies, thereby demonstrating at an early age the Olympian impartiality which in due course earned him the Chichele professorship at Oxford University.

Edward Boyle, on the other hand, did change. At school I remember him as anything but the saintly statesman which he was later to become. In fact he was a fat – in that respect he did not change – little boy who used to annoy me by continually drawing attention to my runny nose. He also had another disgusting habit which turned me against him. At the locker room elevenses ceremony he would pour milk into the great creases of his tummy and then float dead flies down a kind of fatty Cresta Run which started under his chin and ended up at his private part which acted as the finishing post. Edward went on to become a very wet Tory Secretary of

---

*Professor Sir Michael Howard, the military historian.

State for Education who won much popularity from the progressives by conniving at the destruction of the grammar schools, having already won applause from the same quarter for resigning from the government over Suez. I think I would have disapproved of Edward's public life pretty strongly had I not been prejudiced against him by his schoolboy conduct, but the memory of what he had once been certainly did not make it more difficult for me to dislike what he became.

Lots of Abinger contemporaries were killed in the war or have died subsequently. One was particularly close, Nigel Pearson, whose step-mother was Gladys Cooper. In spite of being taken out for lunch on one of her visits, I can remember nothing about the great actress, then at the height of her fame. Nor indeed can I remember much about any of the other famous parents who took me out: Paul Maze, the painter; Julian Huxley, the zoologist; Knickerbocker, the American journalist; Negley Farson, the British journalist. Their cars I can see as if it were yesterday. Lady De La Warr, mother of Harry Sackville, had a Humber Snipe which may have been a government car since her husband was then a minister. It was not that I was particularly interested in cars; only that I was wholly uninterested in parents.

Oswald Mosley did slightly impinge, being so very prominently in the news. But none of the other famous parents were given the time of day. I don't think I ever knew that the father of my friends, Derek and Julian Mond, was Lord Melchett, of ICI fame. Possibly some prep schools were snobbish. But I don't recall a hint of that vice at Abinger. The only parents I do remember well were Bamm Hoare's, again because of their car which had a back seat specially designed to carry rows of clothes from his dress shops. Having a father in the rag trade did not count against Bamm one little bit; indeed it was the least of his eccentricities since he was also addicted to eating dung. No other institution I have ever had any connection with – save perhaps the *Daily Telegraph* in its unreconstructed days – has ever succeeded so well in absorbing eccentricity without any fuss, as if it were the most normal and natural thing in the world.

3

Stowe

Towards the end of my time at Abinger the question was raised about which public school I was to be sent to. The choice, my mother told me, was between Ampleforth, Stowe and Eton, all three of which had offered places. Sensing my mother's suspicion about Catholic schools I rejected Ampleforth without much thought and in ignorance of a relevant piece of information which might have made me choose differently. Many of my Koch de Gooreynd cousins, and other relations of my father, were at Ampleforth at that time. Simon, being two years older, was already at Stowe where he was happy and well established. Like Abinger, Stowe had the reputation of being a progressive school, having only been started a decade or so earlier. There was also the additional advantage – at any rate from my mother's point of view – that the great founder-headmaster, J. F. Roxburgh, was a kinsman of Montagu Norman. On the other hand, the Norman family were all Etonians. My stepfather himself had hated Eton. But his younger brother Ronnie and all his children had triumphant careers there. My own father had also loved the place, but that, of course, was a black mark against it. By that time, my mother's hatred of the upper-class way of life had become pretty obsessional, and the way she referred to Eton left me in little doubt that it was part of that hateful way of life. 'You have to wear a stiff collar if you go to Eton,' she said. 'At Stowe they have far more sensible clothes.' In the event, I chose Stowe, largely so as to be near Simon, but also, I suspect, to please my mother.

It was a mistake. What parents so often overlook in choosing a boarding school is that the housemaster and house are just as important as the headmaster and even more so in the early years. It profits a new boy very little to have the most civilised headmaster if the housemaster is a brute, as mine turned out to be. The way I came to fall under the iron heel of Fritz Clifford of Grafton is such a perfect example of how the path to hell – and what a hell – is paved with good intentions, that it may be worth recounting

19

it in detail. Originally I had been intended for Chatham but there was no place there in the term my mother had set her heart on. 'Peregrine is growing up fast,' she wrote to Roxburgh, 'and I am therefore rather anxious for him to move on to public school as soon as possible.' Neither Roxburgh nor Harrison seemed to have been as impressed by my maturity as was my mother. In a letter to Roxburgh, Harrison wrote: 'He is young and small for his age,' a view confirmed by Roxburgh who wrote to my mother saying: 'Although Peregrine will be fourteen at Christmas, he is not big for his age. I saw him at Abinger.' (This meeting, of which I have no recollection, cannot have been an unmitigated success, since the very next day Roxburgh wrote unenthusiastically to Harrison, 'I only hope he is as nice a fellow as Simon.') From this quite lengthy correspondence it would seem that both Roxburgh and Harrison thought it a good idea for me to stay on at Abinger until January 1937 when there would be a place at Chatham. My mother was adamant, however, and it was she who first raised the idea of a vacancy 'at another house, say ... Grafton'. Roxburgh, in a letter this time marked 'Private and Confidential', wrote to Harrison asking him to have another go at persuading my mother to agree to a delay as 'I am desperately short of vacancies in Chatham. Please don't tell Mrs Norman that I have written.' It was to no avail. My mother insisted on my coming in January and formally requested a vacancy in Grafton: 'Perry is growing fast, mentally as well as physically ... I think it is time he mixed with older boys.'

So Grafton it turned out to be. Stowe, as everyone knows, was the seat of the Dukes of Buckingham. It was a magnificent place with superb grounds laid out by Capability Brown, and a wealth of temples, Palladian bridges, lakes and so on. Oh, what good fortune to be educated in such beautiful surroundings. Unfortunately Grafton must have been where the underservants were quartered. Not only was it damp and sunless, but also at least a mile away from Chatham, Simon's house, which meant that I scarcely ever saw him. Thus the whole purpose of my going to Stowe was undone from the start. Nor was my mother's reason for sending me there fulfilled either, or at any rate not in the early terms. She thought I would come under the civilising influence of J. F. Roxburgh for whom she, like so many other mothers, had developed a great admiration. Instead of J.F., I came under Fritz Clifford's influence, which was anything but civilising. His nickname Fritz derived from his hairstyle which resembled that of a Prussian *junker*, close-cropped and military. He ran the Officers' Training Corps and was a major in the Territorial Army. Long-haired boys with intellectual pretensions were his bugbear and the words of greeting he addressed me on arriving as a new boy were; 'Your first job tomorrow, my boy, will be to pay a visit to the barber in double quick time.' This concern with the length of my hair grew into such an obsession over the years that whenever I saw him he would make scissor-like motions with two fingers of his right hand, accompanying this gesture with the words; 'Clip, clip'. Right from the start our relationship was wholly adversarial. To the best of my recollection there was never a book in his study except a copy of the army manual, *King's Regulations*, which was his bible. A more unsuitable man to put in charge of small boys is difficult to imagine. In Noël Annan's admiring life of J.F., wholly insufficient attention is paid to how he can have entrusted a house to such a man. My own explanation is that Roxburgh was so confident of his own qualities as a headmaster that he did not feel it mattered all that much if housemasters were not up to scratch. Eventually it may not matter. Older boys can escape the confines of their house. But to begin with it can matter desperately.

Nor was Grafton the only problem. Possibly because of Abinger's adherence to the Dalton Plan, which did not force even required subjects, like Latin and maths, down an unwilling throat, I had passed into the lowest form of the school. Harrison did not think the Dalton Plan was in any way to blame. Writing to Roxburgh he attributed my 'disgraceful' results to 'excessive self-satisfaction'. Having been quite a swell at Abinger, editor of the school magazine for instance, it seemed an awful comedown to be among the dregs of the Lower Fourth. Very probably I made my dissatisfaction with both Grafton and the Lower Fourth a bit too obvious.

Class came into it too – much more than it is now comfortable to have to admit. Grafton was a very unsmart house, full of boys from lower-middle-class homes in northern England. This sounds a snobbish point to make. But there is no way of writing truthfully about schooldays in the 1930s without running the risk of sounding snobbish. Nicholas Mosley, in his autobiography, recounts a conversation he had with a friend at Abinger about their parents and the parents of some of the other boys. 'You and I, we're different, aren't we?' said his friend. Nicky writes that at first he did not know what his friend meant. 'I wondered, are we more clever? In love? Then I realised – he was referring to something which the grown-up world called class.' If upper-class boys were conscious of being different at Abinger, where they were thick on the ground, how much more reason was there to be conscious of this at Grafton where at that period I was the only one. At some earlier periods it might possibly have been an advantage to be a rare upper-class specimen in a house of what used to be called oiks; inspiring envy or even admiration. At Grafton in the 1930s it did the opposite. For the Grafton boys were a much less deferential lot than the sons of the rich cotton mill owners who used to come to parties at Dyneley in Lancashire where my grandmother, Lady Alice, lived. As the result of the post-First-World-War boom much wider sections of society were now able to afford to send their sons to public school. Indeed Stowe, and the other new public schools, had come into existence in response to this increased demand. Being new, they could not afford to be too choosy about whom they took, and just as they were happy to take Eton rejects so were they willing to take the kind of boys that no public school in earlier times would have accepted. Nothing in my life at home or at Abinger had prepared me for Grafton. Nor, judging by their reactions, had my Grafton contemporaries been prepared for me. It seems to have been a bit of a culture shock on both sides. The jazz singer George Melly, a contemporary at Stowe, was later to describe me as 'an exotic drifting past among the Brylcreamed heads and squat bodies of his plebeian fellows' and Colin Welch, reminiscing in *Harpers* about our schooldays, also gives rather the same impression.

> Nigh on fifty summers ago, in the glass fronted pavilion which served Stowe as a school shop stood a lissome youth, a shaft of sunlight gilding his fine chestnut hair. The tailor from Harrods with tape measure was in respectful attendance. Perry, for it was he, one elbow elegantly raised, was having the third fitting of a memorable tweed suit, too blue to be smoke grey, too grey to be powder blue, though perilously near it. A couple of louts, of whom I was one, surveyed this vision with Caliban-like scorn and guffaws. The other lout – I was too timid – picked up a half-dried cow-pat and lobbed it through the French window, where it broke over its victim.

That kind of teasing was obviously more than justified but there was much worse. Two examples will suffice, since this is not a horror story. The instrument of torture used in the first was a laundry basket into which I was stuffed. Then the lid was shut tight, and the basket propelled down a long flight of steep stairs, very fast, overturning several times on the way, like a plane looping the loop. The other brutality took place when one was having a bath, over the top of which was placed a row of soap racks to hold one down. Then the scalding hot tap was turned on quite slowly. The more one struggled to get out, writhing in pain and terrified of being scalded, the more general delight was given to the tormentors.

After a year of persecution I complained to my mother who, to her credit, took instant action. She wrote a letter to Roxburgh marked 'Secret', in which she requested a meeting as soon as possible. She suggested that it should be at noon the following day. 'I do not wish Simon and Peregrine or their respective housemasters to know I am coming down ... so I propose to come straight to your door at whatever time you say, leaving my car somewhere in your drive.' They met in the fog, and Roxburgh suggested that my mother should write to Clifford. He even gave her a draft of what she should write.

After receiving my mother's letter, Clifford wrote to Roxburgh to say that, 'I have had it out with Worsthorne what is at the bottom of much of his lack of success and unpopularity viz; that (1) he is prone to gossip in a malicious and unpleasant way about other boys, and that (2) he works on the principle that if one stands out for what one wants, other people give way. He has nothing to say for himself on these points (for a wonder!).' Then, referring to a remark of my mother's about 'obvious human difficulties' between himself and me, Clifford concludes, 'if Mrs Norman is hinting at pettiness on my part, I would like to assure her that I never have time to spare'.

Seemingly quite satisfied with Clifford's explanation Roxburgh proceeded gently to lecture my mother: 'The boys are of course allowed to rag in a mild kind of way before lights out. Very often a prefect or a housemaster will be talking to people at one end of the dormitory while the small boys at the other are having a friendly scrap. What happened to Perry was an extension of this system, which is in itself harmless.' He adds: 'In any place, Mr Clifford is a magnanimous person.'

Quite unsilenced by this, my mother returned to the fray:

Perry's morbid letter shows that he is going through an awkward stage, which often happens to young things, as Mr Clifford must know from his experience; but some suffer more acutely. Perry will, of course, grow out of it but I am anxious the growing out should bring no bitterness – which is why I hope Perry can be driven on a fairly light rein for a while until he is quite normal again ... please do not think that I am interfering. I should be as strict with Perry as anyone else when he is himself, but I do not think he is himself at the moment, and is likely to twist anything that is said to him, and exaggerate what to him is the truth.

Next day, 11 February, Roxburgh replied:

I am sorry that Perry has been writing so miserably. He is a friendless little boy. One sees him going about with chance acquaintances from other houses – I suppose because his own contemporaries in Grafton either do not interest him or do not like him. It is this friendlessness which is the base of his trouble. He misses the cheerful companionship which prevents most boys from thinking too much about themselves. Mr Clifford will, I know, by sympathetic and understanding ...

On the same day he sent a note to Clifford saying: 'I have assured Mrs Norman in general terms of our willingness to be forbearing and sympathetic as far as it is in the boy's own interest that we should be so.'

What is one to make of this correspondence? At one level it makes me blush even now to think of my childish problems causing such a lot of fuss – only a few months before the start of the Second World War. But at another level I am appalled by the complacency of both Roxburgh and Clifford. At no point did either try to take the measure of what was happening – 'friendly scraps' indeed. As for the idea that I was some kind of neurotic, friendless, unlovable loner, that was almost the opposite of the truth. I had lots of friends. But they were not the kind of friends who were approved of by the Grafton louts. In the end, I did 'grow out of it' as my mother predicted. But it was a horrible two years, far grimmer than anything I experienced in the war or at a later date. Neither Clifford nor Roxburgh knew what was going on as their letters make clear and not once did Roxburgh ever bother to ask my side of the case.

When I reminisced about my Stowe schooldays in 1977 in an article in *The Times*, a Major-General I. R. Graeme, presumably a Grafton contemporary, wrote to the then headmaster, in defence of Fritz Clifford. 'Stowe was unfortunate enough to have to endure Worsthorne's petty ways as a boy and now his slanderous article. He may have pleased himself by his insults but there are many old stoics who would willingly put him back in the laundry basket ... and this time keep him there.' Fritz himself reacted differently, demonstrating that streak of magnanimity to which Roxburgh had referred and of which I had previously no experience. Long since retired and now manifestly mad, he burst unannounced into my Fleet Street office, bowler hat on head – as had always been customary in the old days. When I jumped up, startled out of my wits by the apparition, he shouted, 'Sit down, my boy, no need to stand on ceremony. I am only old Fritz, poor old Fritz, whom nobody loves. I just wanted to tell you, no hard feelings. But you still need a haircut, clip clip.' Then, taking off his bowler, he sat down in front of my desk, remained silent for a couple of minutes, stood up straight, put on his hat, about-turned in a military fashion, and was gone. A little while later I read that he was dead.

The beginning of the war had made all the difference to Stowe from my point of view. For a lot of new masters arrived to take the place of those called up into the services. When I was working in the school library one afternoon, a small burly grown-up came in and, as was the custom, all the boys stood up. Instead of taking this mark of politeness as his due, the tubby stranger seemed taken aback, even angry. 'For Christ's sake,' he said, 'this is a library isn't it, not a bloody parade ground.' From then on John Davenport became my friend. Not long since down from Cambridge where he had won a half blue for boxing and a first in English, he was already a notorious London literary figure and drinking companion of Dylan Thomas. Barred from the army for reasons of poor health – bad heart, I think – teaching at Stowe was to be his war work. Apparently I approached him in the library that day and offered to show him around. He even remembered my words because he found them so unexpected coming from a sixteen-year-old. 'I don't know whether you are going to enjoy Stowe, but it looks to me as if we are going to enjoy you.' I certainly did. Whether he was any good as a classroom teacher I cannot recall.

Probably not, since he was wholly untrained for this role. Where he excelled was in private tutorials of an evening in his room along with a few other chosen boys: Colin Welch, Anthony Quinton, Frank Tuohy, and other kindred spirits, talking about history and literature. I remember going to his room shortly after our first meeting to get inspiration for an essay on some point of constitutional history that the rather uninspiring history master, Mr Fawcett, had set. The question had to do with the office of the Lord Chancellor, when did the office begin, or something like that. Davenport began to chuckle, then to shake with speechless laughter – a most unexpected response to a question about constitutional history. 'Don't know about past chancellors, dear boy, but at the Savile recently I put the present one on the mantlepiece for being such a little shit.' Nor was he boasting. The incident had happened. One evening at the Savile, not being able to bear Lord Maugham's conversation, a drunken John had lifted him up by the lapels of his jacket and deposited him on to the mantlepiece where he was left silently swinging his legs in time with the ticking of the clock.

John's knowledge of French and English literature was immense, as his famous post-war reviews in the *Observer* were to show. Not for a moment, however, did he ever patronise us or talk down. My debt to him was immense. From being an alienated schoolboy, unwilling to learn, I became a passionate reader determined to begin educating myself up to his intellectual and conversational level. The fact that such a sophisticated grown-up seemed to enjoy our company gave us all confidence. He also shared our hates: the duller boys and masters, particularly Fritz, and the awful school doctor, whom he abused as a 'second-rate provincial apothecary' for refusing to take his gout seriously. Occasionally John would invite us down to the White Hart at Buckingham for dinner. The bill, of course, was always presented to him and, being stony broke, he would pass it over to us with a lordly gesture, as if teaching how to settle up in restaurants was just another of his pedagogic duties.

It was John who first put the idea in my head that I might be able to win a scholarship to Cambridge. None of the other masters had ever encouraged such ambitions. In a letter to Donald Bevis, tutor of King's, dated 19 May 1941, Roxburgh wrote: 'I am sorry to trouble you further about the boy Worsthorne. He became eighteen at Christmas, and wants to go up in January '42. When will you be examining him? I wonder. In the Autumn or June? He is very immature, and the more time you can give him the better.' To Roxburgh's evident surprise, Bevis wrote back suggesting I take the entrance exam 'without further delay'. What Roxburgh did not know was that Davenport had written to Bevis – whom it turned out he scarcely knew – on his own initiative, months before, recommending me as possible scholarship material. He had also urged me to call on 'his old friend' Bevis if ever I found myself in Cambridge. Next holidays it so happened that my uncle, Ronnie Norman, was driving to Cambridge from Moor Place to have tea with G. M. Trevelyan and very kindly suggested that I might like to come too. Naturally I jumped at the honour for its own sake. But at the back of my mind was the idea of following up Davenport's suggestion that I call on Bevis at King's, which I did, saying that I was just passing by after having had tea with the Master of Trinity. John's example encouraged such effrontery. Whether it was this name-dropping cheek that persuaded Bevis to disregard Roxburgh's remark about my 'immaturity', I do not know. But it very well may have been.

Roxburgh, however, stuck to his guns. 'Thank you for your letter about Worsthorne. I doubt whether he will be up to taking your scholarship paper in December. He is a very slow developer as his brother was before him, and as I suspect his mother was in her youth. By December, he may have made more progress than now looks likely and, if so, we will send him in for the scholarship exams. Otherwise I shall be asking you to set him some papers of a less advanced kind.' In the event I did not get a scholarship to King's; only an exhibition to Peterhouse. But without John's encouragement, I would not have got anything at all, or ever have been allowed to have a go.

The trouble was, Roxburgh listened to his professionals, like Clifford, and distrusted his wartime stand-ins, like Davenport. Davenport had, for example, written a report on me for Roxburgh. It said, 'Worsthorne has all the passion of Belloc, without the erudition, and all the scholarship of Chesterton without the wit' – not a bad description of me then, or even now. Roxburgh requested elucidation. 'I feel I must send a line to raise a small query on what you say of Worsthorne. I have much enjoyed your account of the boy – as indeed I have enjoyed many of your reports – but I am wondering if there has not been a transposition in the reference to Chesterton. Will you look and see? If the text is correct as it stands, you must just forgive me for having misunderstood the point.' To this Davenport replied on the same day; 'Many thanks for your note. Yes, Worsthorne's report was a little over condensed! What I really meant to imply was that Chesterton's scholarship was non-existent!'

John never wanted to be a schoolmaster and left Stowe, by mutual agreement as they say, towards the end of 1941, as I did. He never fulfilled his promise as a writer and although there are many references to him in all the literary memoirs of the 1930s, 1940s and 1950s, only the odd piece of literary criticism remains, mostly in the *Observer*. But those of us whom he helped at Stowe will never forget him. In 1946 I saw him at a bus stop in the King's Road. He was reading Cyril Connolly's just published *The Unquiet Grave*, and looked shattered. It was exactly the book that he himself had always talked about writing. After the war it was all downhill for John and his conversation became ever more fantastical. In El Vino's one evening in the 1960s, shortly before he died, he told me that when I was next in Rome on no account to omit to call on his very good friend the Pope. All the journalists who heard him laughed behind their hands. I did not laugh. For it was that same vaingloriousness, before it had run wildly to seed, which had prompted him to urge a sixteen-year-old pupil to look up 'his old friend' the tutor of King's whom in truth he knew scarcely better than he knew the Pope. Having benefited so much from these delusions of grandeur when they still had some remote connection with reality, it seemed indecent to mock them now that they had become no more than the tragic ravings of a disappointed failure.

Other masters who were doing their wartime service by teaching at Stowe were G. Wilson Knight, the visionary Shakespearean scholar, and Martin Cooper who was later to join the *Daily Telegraph* as chief music critic. Martin Cooper was a convert to Catholicism with a beautiful wife who was even more Papist than him. Being a Catholic myself, this was a bond. Stowe itself was very low church and although most of the services were compulsory even for the half dozen Catholic boys, on Sunday morning we were allowed to go to mass in Buckingham – much the same arrangement as had applied at Abinger. At Abinger Simon and I were the only RCs and the delightful maths master, Mr Spofforth, would drive us to mass in Dorking in his old Morris Cowley. Not only was the drive itself, down the narrow leafy Surrey lanes, a welcome treat, but so was the bacon and egg breakfast in the priest's presbytery afterwards. Never before or since have I been so regular an attender at mass, sometimes even going to the length of inventing holidays of obligation so as to have an excuse for an extra outing. At Stowe, however, we bicycled to mass under the supervision of Martin Cooper, who made sure there was no backsliding. Not that he was in the least strict generally. In the classroom, where he taught French and German, he was a byword for civilised courtesy. Only in the practice of the Catholic religion did he behave like a martinet. This suited me well enough. For I, too, at that time was a Catholic bigot. Whether my bigotry had much to do with the moral or ethical side of religion, however, I am not so sure. I fear it was a bit of a pose to mark me out from the run-of-the-mill other boys – a bit like ordering my clothes from Harrods. If sent to a Catholic school, it could well be that I would have self-consciously championed Protestantism. Where the atmosphere was dedicatedly low church, as it was at Stowe, it meant giving tongue to Catholic apologists and historical propaganda mostly garnered from the copious works of Hilaire Belloc, Chesterton, Eric Gill, Arnold Lunn and Ronnie Knox. What made these authors so pleasurable was that they were telling me things that the other boys were not being told, such as that Queen Elizabeth I had inherited tertiary syphilis from Henry VIII. In my case, religion certainly acted as an intellectual spur and did this precisely because Stowe was not a Catholic school. But that was all it did. Of the spiritual and moral impact of religion I was sadly deprived. This was my fault, not Stowe's. Having cast myself in the role of defender of the true faith, I determinedly shut my ears and turned my back – sometimes literally – on all the school's moral and spiritual influences as coming from a tainted source. Scepticism and cynicism were pretty rife about school religion even among the Protestant boys but at least they put their heart and soul into singing the great Anglican hymns, and imbibed the beauty of Cranmer's prayer book and the King James bible; even on occasion benefited from the sermons and homilies. I, on the other hand, would sit and stand sullenly throughout, refusing to participate. When the other boys turned to face east for the creed, I would stare fixedly ahead and only open my mouth during the recitation to shout the word 'Roman' very loudly. Thus 'I believe in the holy Catholic church' came out as 'I believe in the *Roman* Catholic Church.'

Looking back I greatly regret my foolish obstinacies. I even deprived myself of the aesthetic experience of listening to the voluntary organ recitals which Dr Huggins, the music master – a job he combined with that of the local master of foxhounds – gave after evening service for those boys who wanted to stay on. Enthusiastic participation in one Catholic low mass a week in Buckingham scarcely made up for my total withdrawal from all the other parts of school life which bore witness to the beauties and glories of the Christian faith.

The war was not all bonus in the sense of introducing exciting new teaching talent. It also took teaching talent away, notably William McElwee, master of the History Sixth, who was to win the Military Cross and lose a lung in the Normandy campaign. This was a blow to me since he left for the army just at the time when I was due to join the History Sixth which, under him, had become not only the school's intellectual powerhouse but also its most exclusive social club, neither of which roles survived his departure for so much as a week. Nowadays Bill McElwee would unquestionably have been awarded a fellowship on going down from Oxford with a first; and very probably a chair shortly thereafter, so distinguished were his published works. Fortunately for Stowe such posts were incomparably rarer in those days than they are now. A. J. P. Taylor was a close friend of his, as was the great Lewis Namier whose pupil he had been. At Oxford Auden had loved him, without having his love returned, and wrote many of his early lyrics for him. Not that Bill McElwee was homosexual, or in any way encouraged homosexuality at Stowe. What he and his novelist wife Patience did encourage, however, was sophisticated gossip, particularly about masters and their wives but also about the boys, which at a boarding school cannot exclude homosexuality if the subject is to be given its full value and flavour. If at Stowe J.F. Roxburgh was king, then

McElwee was Prince Regent and Vancouver Lodge, a converted farm-house on the Stowe estate where he and Patience lived, a kind of alternative court where disaffection against the likes of Fritz was not so much encouraged as tolerated.

It was impossible to be at Stowe even for a term without noticing Bill and Patience. They would roar up to chapel in a vintage Bentley, the back seat of which was either strewn with dogs, guns and sporting bric-à-brac, or filled with two or three Sixth Form swells who clambered out looking immensely pleased with themselves, having just attended the Vancouver Sunday gathering. Noël Annan, who was just such a swell, remembers the first time he met Patience. She squeezed into the Bentley's back seat alongside him commenting: 'Have you got sharp buttocks or have I?' – unheard-of language from the wife of a master to a schoolboy in those days.

As luck would have it, my seat in chapel was just below the McElwee stall and at one Sunday service I met Patience's eye as I inserted the word 'Roman' in a loud voice during the creed. To my delight she smiled encouragingly, and on subsequent occasions our eyes always met at this moment until it became a kind of conspiratorial communion. Although amusing Patience, who turned out to be very high, had not been the original motive for my act of protest it certainly helped keep it going. Something else also brought me to the attention of the McElwees long before I had reached the Sixth Form; indeed while I was still struggling to climb out of the Lower Fourth. One of J.F.'s boasts was that Stowe, unlike less progressive schools, did not enforce compulsory games. This was in the prospectus which my mother had shown me at Abinger when we were discussing my further education. In fact the language was quite specific. 'We encourage boys to take up all forms of healthy outdoor exercise.' Armed with this document I asked Fritz permission to hunt every other Saturday, a concession which he refused on the ground that hunting was not the kind of healthy, outdoor activity which J.F. had in mind. Initially I took Fritz's 'no' for an answer. But after three or four terms of worsening relations, and perhaps emboldened by Patience's wink, I decided to chance my luck and appeal to Bill McElwee who was well known to be not only an enthusiastic rider to hounds – even sometimes to the point of taking classes in hunting gear – but also Fritz's arch enemy. For a relative new boy to go behind his housemaster's back to a Sixth Form master whom he had never met was more bold than tactful. But I was beyond caring and it worked. McElwee had a word with J.F. who rescinded Fritz's ban (this must have been when my mother was also getting at J.F. over Fritz). It also worked in an even more satisfactory way. Shortly thereafter I received an invitation to the famous Vancouver salon.

As one of the few non-seniors to be included in the salon I was very much on trial and therefore anxious to prove myself worthy; to win my spurs, so to speak, in the conversational jousting. Bill himself was a conservative in the sense of being sceptical of all forms of Utopianism. At the time that meant doubting the efficacy of the League of Nations and being quite clear about the fact that nothing would stop Hitler except brute force. He was also contemptuous about Russian communism. How on earth, he asked, could anyone be so stupid as to believe that a group of Marxist intellectuals could possibly turn barbaric Mother Russia, which had proved resistant to the reforms of Peter the Great, into a new Jerusalem? The very idea was preposterous. Belief in communism made no more sense than belief in flat-earthism. It flew in the face of all the evidence, not of science but of history; of how people actually behaved. 'Don't bother to read Marx,' he advised. 'It may or may not make sense in theory. But in practice it can't possibly work. Human nature, particularly Russian human nature, won't let it.' As for dreaming about equality, that too was dismissed as impractical folly. 'After turning society upside down in dreadful tumult and disorder, all they'll end up with is another form of inequality which may well be worse than the one which went before.' Such scepticism was entirely new to me. From my reading of Belloc, among others, I had taken on board the Godless side of socialism and rationalism, and as a result of overhearing grown-up conversation at home, was aware of something called the 'Red menace', but Bill was the first authority figure to suggest that socialism was not so much evil as stupid.

Even more startling than the content of the Vancouver conversation was the style. Conservative sentiments in those days were usually expressed by stuffy, pompous people who lacked panache. The atmosphere at Vancouver was utterly unstuffy and unpompous. The house was filthy beyond belief. If one shook out a rug, as like as not it would turn out to be one of Bill's recumbent retrievers. Patience's appearance was also quite extraordinary – huge sack-like trousers and baggy jumpers, with a slash of lipstick pasted casually on. Nor was there a hint of Wildean cynicism and decadence about the scepticism. Both Bill and Patience were religious, patriotic, and, in a way, strait-laced, in spite of their love of gossip. Only tea was drunk; never so much as a glass of sherry. The ideal way of life encouraged was that of 'renaissance man' – hunting and shooting in the morning and composing sonnets in the afternoon. Hoping to make a mark as an apprentice intellectual at my first visit, I said something about how boring and silly all the OTC drilling was. 'Not nearly so boring and silly as complaining about it,' retorted Bill. 'It's a duty to be endured, not whined about.' Bill was not an ideas man, any more than was his mentor, Namier, or his friend Alan Taylor – a frequent visitor to Vancouver. He believed that politics was about power and people. 'Take Fritz,' he would say. 'Nobody talks more about leadership and backbone and service. But what will he do when the war comes? He'll do nothing.' (Bill turned out to be right.) 'It's not opinions but character that count. Don't waste your time studying the ideals of the men in power. Concentrate on their actions. History is deeds, not words.'

How much of this talk I took in at the time is difficult to say. Probably very little. But the Vancouver salon left an indelible impression, and one of my many regrets is that I was never formally taught by Bill. Nobody at Stowe in those years can have failed to benefit, if only indirectly, from the Vancouver salon. Noël Annan, Robert Kee, Anthony Quinton, Nicholas Henderson, so many of the people who have given the description Stoic its distinctive meaning, came under his influence. Obviously the main influence was Roxburgh. But Bill and Patience also played an invaluable part. By and large Stowe was a second-rate institution, peopled by mostly dull boys and masters. A tiny minority of boys and masters – what would now be called the élite – formed the yeast that made the dough rise. That is the main lesson that I took away from Stowe. I learnt it the hard way. But it is a lesson that I have never forgotten.

4

James, the Butler

As a holiday base while we were still away at boarding school, Thorpe Lodge, our stepfather's house, just about worked. It was usually a matter of spending a few days there at the beginning and end of the school holidays, and since Uncle Mont was away at the Bank of England in the daytime, and we were in bed by the time he returned, opportunities for getting under his feet were relatively limited. His departure for the bank was punctually at 8.30 a.m. The car, a custom-built Black Lincoln, with a white roof built like a turret so as to accommodate the occasional ceremonial top hat, would arrive in the courtyard at 8.00 a.m., giving us children plenty of time to play around with all the American gadgets – a ritual much encouraged by our mother who was relieved to have found a polite way to get us out of the house during the somewhat tense half hour before the governor set off. In those days even ordinary Lincolns were rare in this country, and I once asked the chauffeur why the governor had chosen so unusual a vehicle. It was apparently because he could not abide the ostentation of a Rolls-Royce, and felt that a Lincoln was less conspicuous. That he was sincere in this belief I do not doubt. It was part of an almost neurotic desire to escape the plutocratic stereotype. On some days he even used the tube, travelling from Notting Hill Gate to Bank on the Central line. Nothing could have been more guaranteed to attract media and public attention. Hundreds of bankers went to work by Rolls-Royce; he could have been lost in the crowd. Only one, an instantly recognisable figure, went by tube, to the amazement of the other passengers.

At 6.00 p.m. he returned and a bowl of soup was brought up to him in his dressing room which meant that there was never soup for the guests at dinner – quite a sacrifice for my mother who loved soup. Before going down to dine he would walk along the corridor to our bedroom to enquire whether we had had a good day, what we had done, and so on, always ending up with the same final question: 'Had enough grub, boys?' While still at school we never once had dinner with our mother and Uncle Mont. His young nephew Mark, and his ravishingly brown and freckled newly-wed Virginian wife Toby, very sweetly used to take us out to dinner and the cinema. On one of these enjoyable occasions we saw *Showboat* which reduced Toby to tears. Never having seen a grown-up cry before, I attributed the phenomenon to the fact that she was American. Likewise America got the credit for her quite extraordinary generosity and sweetness which included taking us to dinner at Quaglino's without, in the manner of John Davenport, handing over the bill. In the nature of things, however, there was not all that number of relations or friends prepared to take two boys off our mother's hands and after a few days we would be sent north to stay at Dyneley, with our grandmother.

Not long before, she had unexpectedly inherited what remained of the great Towneley property which stretched from Burnley in Lancashire to the Yorkshire border town of Todmorden at the other end of the wild Cliviger Gorge which figures so romantically in Harrison Ainsworth's novel *The Lancashire Witches*. The house itself, Towneley Hall, a massive fortress dating back to the fifteenth century, had been bought by the Burnley Corporation and turned into a museum, which meant that the only available house on the estate for my grandmother to live in was the agent's rather charmless glorified Victorian villa, Dyneley, overlooking the gorge. Although the surrounding country was still rugged, much of its beauty had been tarnished by coal mining and the smoke-belching cotton mill chimneys – one of the reasons why so many of the old Lancashire families had moved south to less grimy climes. Strongly disapproving of absentee landlords, my grandmother had decided to reverse the shameful exodus. It was a brave decision. The Towneley estate was an oasis of old agricultural Lancashire in a great desert of industrial blight. Cliviger village, above which Dyneley perched, served the local mill and at the break of a summer's day the sound of clogs could be heard in the distance. My grandmother's smart friends could not understand why she wanted to go and live in such an outlandish place where there was no hunting and no social life, i.e. no neighbours of the right sort. She did not *want* to. It was a matter of duty. For six hundred years, since the time of Edward III, Towneleys had kept the flame of Catholicism burning bright in Lancashire, being cruelly persecuted at times for their fidelity to the faith, and my grandmother could think of no good reason not to continue honouring this ancient obligation. Moving north was certainly a great wrench. She loved the pleasures of fashionable life in the south and was a famous beauty. But no sooner did she inherit than she packed up in London and moved to Dyneley where she gave herself over to good works – the local girl guides, sitting on the county council and on the bench and reviving the Towneley Chapel in Burnley.

Unattractive as the villa was, it had one compensating blessing: James Burton, the agent's butler, who stayed on to see my grandmother in. In the end he did more than see her in. He remained with her until her death twenty years on and became an integral part of the family. What she would have done without James, I cannot imagine. Son of the agent's coachman and brother of his chauffeur, who also stayed on, he unobtrusively tutored her in Lancashire ways, acting as her ambassador to the local community and its to her. James at this time would have been about thirty, having served as a corporal in the trenches where he was badly gassed. Apart from the war, he had never been away from the Cliviger Gorge; not even to Manchester, let alone London. The arrival of my grandmother and her family revolutionised his life. Out went all the agent's heavy furniture and in came all my grandmother's beautiful things for which he suddenly became responsible. It was an exciting challenge which he took up with enthusiasm. A whole new way of life opened up before him.

So in a way it did for Simon and me. For James was the first male grown-up who from the start behaved as if he at least partly belonged to us. Unlike grown-ups on the other side of the green baize door, he was willing to talk about the trenches, or at any rate allow himself to be questioned about them. Among the officer class a stiff upper lip was still de rigueur, at least in front of children. None of my parents' friends who had served ever referred to it, except in general, non-personal terms. For them it was a one-off, uniquely awful experience which had nothing to do with what had gone before in their lives or what came after. For James, however, it was part of a continuum of rough experiences which had begun in a tiny cottage on the estate without running water or electricity where he and his five brothers and sisters had been born and brought up. Although life in the trenches had been hard, there was always plenty of food, and in James's reminiscences it merged not all that incongruously into what he remembered about life generally for a north-country working-class child in a mining area. So far as Simon and I were concerned his pre-war and war life were both equally strange and alien to anything in our own experience – all part of a foreign country about which we knew nothing. Although James was a grown-up, we did not need to be in awe of him or on our best behaviour. Being in service he carried a social handicap which levelled out the advantages he enjoyed through age and experience. So to a much greater extent than with other grown-ups we enjoyed with James a relationship of rough equality.

Possibly the reverse side of the same coin applied to him. With grown-ups from our social and educational background he would have felt ill at ease and buttoned up. But not with two young boys, although he would never have taken the liberty of sitting down in our presence. But at least he smoked which is more than he would have thought of doing in front of my grandmother or her friends. In each other's company neither he nor we had to watch our Ps and Qs so much as we did with the other grown-ups. His pantry was an oasis of naturalness in a still pretty arid world of social stiffness and inhibition. What we gained is easy enough to see: a grown-up who seemed to enjoy our company for hours on end and who laughed at our jokes as if he really found them funny; a grown-up, moreover, to whom we could say anything, however shocking, without provoking any rebuke stronger than 'Oh you are awful, Master Perry.' What did he gain, apart from our love and admiration which lasted until the very end of his life? I think he enjoyed our company even as children because we were the most accessible parts of a world he admired as being superior – better educated, better bred than his own. Such was the gap between the grown-ups of that world and his own that with them he could never have a proper relationship. But with us he could, and if he broadened our horizons, so we may have broadened his. Certainly living in my grandmother's house for so many years filled many gaps in his education, turning him into quite an expert on the care and maintenance of beautiful furniture, pictures, silver, objets d'art as well as wines – notably champagne.

On the minutiae of good manners, too, he was a walking encyclopaedia, having marked and inwardly digested all my grandmother's *obiter dicta* on these matters. When guests came to the house and behaved badly, or in ways that he regarded as bad, he made his disapproval clear, as Winston Churchill, among quite a few other notables, had reason to remember. Churchill's younger brother Jack had married my grandmother's sister, Lady Goonie, and when he came north to speak would sometimes stay overnight at Dyneley. On one occasion when something must have gone wrong with his arrangements, Winston arrived out of the blue – or rather, this being Lancashire – out of the grey, in a furious temper. Everybody was out that afternoon and it fell to me, aged about twelve, to answer the door. Rather brusquely, and without any preliminary courtesies, he demanded to be shown to a room where he could have forty winks. Walking away down the corridor after installing him, I heard a great bellow. What the deuce did I mean by putting him in a room where the bed was not made up? On James's return I recounted this tale and he was as indignant as I was. 'Mr Churchill is no gentleman,' James declared, a view then shared by many others. Later events that evening confirmed James in his harsh judgment. Of these I have only James's account since they took place at dinner after we had gone to bed. But I do not doubt for a moment that they did take place since James's extreme agitation in recounting them later that very night – stealing up to our bedroom to do so – could only be explained by something pretty traumatic.

Apparently at some point in the dinner Mr Churchill had grabbed a bottle of champagne out of James's hands, not to accelerate the replenishment of his glass, which James conceded might just be excusable, but rather to use the bottle to illustrate some point of naval tactics, scraping its base this way and that on the beautifully polished surface of James's pride and joy – the walnut-topped dining room table. This was worse than bad manners; it was vandalism. So James grabbed the bottle back. At first Mr Churchill refused to release his prize, and there was a battle of wills. 'Our eyes met, Master Perry. But I didn't waver. I stared right back. Then he gave me a wink as if to say sorry and let go.' What particularly shocked James was that Mr Churchill should have taken such liberties at my grandmother's table where there was no master to keep him in order. 'I couldn't have let him get away with it, Master Perry. I know it wasn't my place. But I had no choice.' It is difficult to exaggerate the amount of courage required in those days for a butler to defy a grandee statesman like Churchill in the face of whose wrath even field marshals were quite soon to quail. When, in 1990, Alexander Chancellor asked me to contribute to the *Independent* magazine series entitled 'Heroes and Villains', I had no hesi-tation in choosing James as my hero, very much with that story in mind. At the time of the incident, Simon and I were much more impressed by James having been gassed. But lots of soldiers were gassed. Only one butler outstared Winston Churchill.

When Mr Churchill became Prime Minister in 1940, James and I joined the Home Guard and we listened one night in our guard hut on the moors, over which we had been patrolling in search of German parachutists, to one of the great wartime speeches. Neither of us referred to our earlier experience of the great man, and I don't know whether James was even thinking of his. Probably not. Such was his respect by then for our wartime leader that the memory, if allowed to surface, would certainly have struck him dead with shame and embarrassment. But I could not help, a little wryly, thinking of mine. For the thunderous tones used by the leader of the free world to roar defiance at the axis powers were no different to those used only eight or so years earlier by an importunate house guest to snarl bad-temperedly at me.

For James, serving my grandmother was more a priestly vocation than a job – quite literally in one respect. At some point she persuaded the bishop to allow us to have mass said on Sunday at Dyneley itself. A Jesuit would come over from Stonyhurst College, the Catholic public school near Whal-ley, and it fell to James to prepare and lay out the famous Towneley vestments, altar linen and all the other clerical paraphernalia. Since James came from chapel folk who strongly disapproved of Catholicism, the imposition on him of this extra duty, wholly outside the traditional specifi-cations of an English butler, might have been expected to cause difficulties. But it didn't. James quietened any religious scruples he might have har-boured by treating his new sacristan duties as an extension of what his daily routine already required him to do. Nor was this altogether a pretence. On Sunday morning, for example, he would call me an hour before mass was due to begin. After pulling the curtains and discussing the weather, he would enquire what I intended to wear, and then, after ignoring my wishes, lay out the attire he thought I ought to wear, giving grave attention to every detail of apparel down to the colour of the tie and socks. Then there would be the matter of choosing the right pair of shoes from a rich array all polished to perfection by James's own hand. Since this degree of almost ritualistic attention was already being given regularly to preparing a teenage boy for the humdrum business of the day, it was not all that difficult for James to convince himself that there was nothing specifically holy about doing something very similar for a Catholic priest. Indeed he would lower his voice in the same way to ask the priest what colour vestment was required for mass that morning – white or gold for feast days and so on – as he had done only a few minutes earlier to ask me about the appropriate colour of my tie and socks. And even on the rare occasions when he was required to serve mass – there being no suitable Catholic around – there was the same kind of let-out for his non-conformist conscience. Not even the keenest and most suspicious Puritanical eye could have detected any more reverence in his mien while serving the sacred water and wine to the priest at the altar than when serving the non-sacred variety later in the day to guests at the dining room table. Finally, in the same way as he would make a point of studiously not eavesdropping on what was being said by the guests in the dining room, so would he turn an equally blank expression and deaf ear to what was being said by the priest at the altar. In these ways priest and Catholicism were subsumed into James's religion rather than he into theirs. The celebration of the mass became a new and challenging addition to all the other Dyneley rituals and ceremonials designed to honour and please my grandmother, in the organising and perfection of which he was proud to play a part.

Fitting priest, mass, and Catholicism into the Dyneley domestic rhythm was much less of a problem for James than a secular challenge which also occurred at about this time. Rear-Admiral Gordon Campbell, of Q-ship renown and one of the great naval heroes of the First World War, came to stay.* There was nothing unusual about that since he was the local MP (Independent) for Burnley and a great friend of my grandmother and mother. What was unusual was that for the first time he brought with him his Victoria Cross. James took the admiral's luggage upstairs in ignorance of what it contained and, while unpacking, came across this supreme

* Q-ships were merchantmen used by the Royal Navy in the First World War as bait to lure German U-boats to the surface. When the U-boat approached, the merchantman would then throw off its disguise and open fire. The Royal Navy crew on the Q-ships, led by Campbell, took suicidal risks. But many U-boats were sunk.

symbol of exceptional courage in the face of the enemy snugly nestling in the admiral's change of underclothes. Presumably he must have been going to some specially grand local dinner at which full decorations were to be worn. In any case, to James's consternation he suddenly found himself picking out of these most unsuitable surrounds an object more sacred by far to him than anything to do with the Catholic mass. I shall never forget his face when he came rushing into my room bearing the admiral's VC cupped in his two hands, in lieu of the silver salver which, had there been any warning, he would have wished to use instead. Nor is it to be supposed that I was any less overawed by the sight of this unique award than was James. With Victoria Crosses today being sold at Christies for a mere few hundred pounds, it is difficult to realise with what reverence they, and their holders, were then regarded, even by a teenager such as myself from a progressive public school. Although the mythology now surrounding the 1930s has it that all the young of that time were infected with pacifism, that is to get the period wrong. Yes, we read Siegfried Sassoon, Wilfred Owen, Bertrand Russell, Aldous Huxley et al, but their works were the merest surface scratchings of scepticism on the great rock of faith in empire, king and country which so many other writers – Kipling, John Buchan, Francis Brett Young, P. C. Wren, C. S. Forester, Dornford Yates and Sapper – continued to uphold. If one questioned these ancient verities it was rather in the same way as one questioned the existence of God, i.e. not supposing for a moment that the questioning had the slightest bearing on what would happen here in the real world. When James rushed in holding the VC in his trembling hands I could well have been reading, say, Aldous Huxley's *Antic Hay* and much enjoying his cynical mockery of conventional piety. But even if I had been, this would in no way have detracted from the instinctive reflex of jumping to my feet and standing to attention, so profound was the magnetic power of patriotism even in the decade famous, or infamous, for having spawned a generation pledged not to fight for king and country. The admiral went out that evening wearing on his chest the highest of honours and on his return, James, who had waited up, took the cross away to his pantry where it spent the rest of the night under lock and key in an emergency tabernacle put together for the purpose. The next day was Sunday, and James made it clear, even to my grandmother, where his priorities must lie. First and foremost came the polishing and the burnishing of the Victoria Cross, that supreme symbol of the heights of courage man could rise to when serving the gods of war, and only a long way behind in order of importance the Sabbath preparations required for worshipping the Prince of Peace.

About two years before the Second World War broke out, my grandmother was advised by her doctor to winter in temperatures warmer than any Lancashire was able to provide and, after visiting South Africa to stay with friends, decided to build three kraals – one for herself, one for James and one for the black servants – in the Transvaal, miles away from civilisation. As soon as they got there, James was stripped of his butler's uniform and all the other dignities of office, put into khaki shorts and long white socks and turned into a Jack-of-all-trades, including that of washing and cutting my grandmother's hair. What the blacks must have made of this strange English pair history doesn't record. On the face of it they were living cheek by jowl in conditions of great intimacy. Yet the social gap between them was such than I doubt if there were any exchanges much more personal than 'Good morning, m'lady' on his side and 'Good morning, James' on hers. When war broke out and they were forced to return to England for good, my grandmother soon became bedridden and James's many duties were perforce extended to include those of day and night nurse until her death. In the last few months, her health and temper had sadly declined and such strength as remained was spent on angrily throwing hot-water bottles at James's head – about the most uninhibited sign of affection he ever received.

When D. H. Lawrence wrote *Lady Chatterley's Lover*, it was his frank discussion of a sexual relationship between mistress and manservant that people found shocking. Nowadays it is probably the complete non-sexuality of the relationship between my grandmother and her butler that will stick in the gullet of some readers. Not for an instant would either of them have thought of the other in this respect, any more than a dog would think amorously of a cat. On his part there was a kind of feudal fealty that medieval knights felt for their lady – sexual love sublimated into a chivalrous desire to serve. What she felt was not dissimilar – a desire to be served by a man inspiring total trust. Between them there was an instinctive concordance of temperament which made her the perfect mistress for him and him the perfect servant for her. The right reverberations set up by the class differences of two individuals in those days were quite as powerful in their effect as those set up by gender or sexual attraction. Suffice it to say, James and my grandmother made a perfect class match, so complete was their rapport and so satisfactorily reciprocal their scale of values. Lancashire threw them together. For reasons of ancestral obligation she was determined to serve Lancashire and he happened to be the right Lancastrian in the right place at the right time to help her to do so.

Missing in that part of Lancashire since the exodus south of the Towneley family, was, quite simply, 'a touch of class'. The fact that the phrase is now as squirm-making to write as it is to read – rather as references to sex used to be – cannot be helped. Without an old family to occupy the high ground, topographically as well as socially, the area had fallen apart. Not only was my grandmother invited to take the chair on all the local boards and committees but to her house on the hill were brought all the local disputes and quarrels for resolution and unravelling. A judgment from Lady Alice carried so much more authority than from anyone else and when antagonists met under her roof they at least felt constrained into mutual politeness, if not agreement, rather as national politicians stop abusing each other in the presence of the Queen. To talk of Dyneley fulfilling the function of some tiny court may sound pretentious. But that is what it did, with James playing a central role as major-domo. How much was her doing and how much his is impossible to say since over the years people began to talk of Lady Alice and James as if they were a joint enterprise like Fortnum and Mason. Obviously Lady Alice was the ranking star. But it was James's supporting role that gave the performance its particular radiance.

Sooner or later, I suppose, the much talked about egalitarian society will find a better catalyst than class to animate and elevate a community. But having been lucky enough to see at first hand the good done by the return of class in Lancashire between the wars it is not surprising that I am more aware of the redeeming features of the old system than of the improvements wrought, at any rate so far, by the new.

When my grandmother died in 1950 James transferred his allegiance to my mother and served her no less devotedly. The demands she made were less dramatically out of line with what would now be called the job specifications of an English butler but in some ways even more beyond the normal calls of duty. As president of the National Association of Mental Health my mother felt obliged to do everything in her power to help its annual flag day which meant that she conscripted everybody on hand into collecting. James was given the job of rattling boxes in the local Kensington and Chelsea pubs. Mental health was not a cause that appealed naturally to his heart one little bit. Indeed he shared all the man in the street's – and still more the man in the pub's – prejudices of that period against 'trick cyclists'. Added to that he came from non-conformist stock and was therefore no more inclined to set foot in a pub than in a Catholic church. Yet on the appointed night, out he would set, a collection box in each hand, to trawl the pubs in search of contributions. Not allowed to come back until the boxes were full, he would have to go into one saloon bar after another trying to explain to the blazer brigade what mental health was all about. Not that he himself had much idea. But because it meant so much to 'her ladyship' – my mother had also become one by then – it meant a lot to him too and when the ribald drinkers refused to cough up he would give them the same stony stare as he had given that other imbiber, Winston Churchill.

If James had looked the part of a mental health do-gooder, the customers might have shown some mercy or not even have noticed his arrival. But he looked the very opposite. Six feet two, with iron grey hair and a military bearing, dressed in black and with a black trilby on his head, he was an imposing figure on whom all eyes – particularly female eyes – would automatically turn. This made him all the more of a butt for ribaldry when his true purpose was exposed. For James this was an annual penance that he uncomplainingly put up with until rescued, years on, by retirement. His last years were spent with Lily, his widowed sister, near Blackburn where I visited him in his terminal illness in the 1970s, driving over from one of the party political conferences in Blackpool. It was the first time I had seen him in bed and Lily had to struggle to prevent him from trying to stand up. In the course of reminiscing he talked about being in service with a degree of frankness never before vouchsafed. It wouldn't have suited everybody, he said. But it had suited him. Then he added, 'I always take the *Telegraph* to read your articles. Makes me feel quite proud.' This in turn made me feel proud. How difficult it is to explain our relationship. While the modern world is prepared to see the point of pretty well every other kind of human love, the one kind that it finds most difficult to understand or even tolerate – the one kind nowadays that dare not speak its name – is that between master and servant. Consenting adults can do everything else together except cohabit on a basis of inequality. This strikes me as very sad since the master-servant relationship suits more people than contemporary egalitarian philosophy is prepared to dream of. Indeed James embodied the concept of job satisfaction long before it was invented. Since his day domestic service has fallen into even sadder disrepute, to the point where only public school-educated children have enough social confidence to undertake it. Like so much of progress this has a bad as well as a good side. It is obviously a good thing that economic necessity should no longer force disadvantaged young people into service *faute de mieux* as it used to do. But it is a bad thing that people who might be happy as servants should close their minds to even considering such a station in life. If freely entered into, domestic service does not need to be humiliating. James exercised far more responsibilities, enjoyed far more power, was far more respected and admired, and had far more opportunities to develop his personality than would have been his lot in many other walks of life. Having him as a member of our family brought us many advantages over and above the advantages of what he did as a butler so superbly well. If we broadened his horizons, he certainly broadened ours, and if he sought to live up to our standards in some ways, we sought to live up to his in others. The more my grandmother and mother came to depend upon him, the more he was able, on the rare occasions when he chose, to make them dance to his tune rather than the other way round. In the beginning it was a matter of them giving the orders and him obeying. But nobody who watched their relationship develop would possibly suppose that this was how it ended.

Unquestionably domestic service in the bad old days lent itself to exploitation and there was bound to be a reaction against it. But there was always more to it than exploitation. More than any other institution – apart possibly from the armed forces – domestic service brought people of different social backgrounds, educational attainments, incomes, and even nationalities together under one roof, very often for long enough periods – in James's case for a lifetime – for deep relationships to take root and flourish. Paradoxical as it sounds, it was even a leveller of sorts, providing the only meeting ground for the great and the humble. It is no accident that the only intimate accounts of royalty's private, until recently, lives come from their servants who probably know them better than does anyone else. Obviously domestic service is never going to become the industry it was when it employed more people than any other. But with the pay and work conditions improved out of all recognition, as they have been, domestic service could at least give some under-privileged an opportunity to taste the good life, and at least some of the affluent an opportunity to get to know people worse off than themselves. Stratification today is no less alienating for being based on education rather than class, and on merit rather than inheritance, and any institution that might help to break down these barriers deserves respect rather than contempt. If domestic service did a good job of social mixing even in the 1930s – about the most snobbish decade ever – how much more of an integrator might it not be today, if only egalitarian prejudice did not stand so blindly in the way?

A final word about Dyneley. The house and estate eventually went to my elder brother Simon who in turn gave up a brilliant career at Oxford to go and live and work there. So completely did he identify with the place that he changed his name to Towneley and has given that name a long new lease of life by producing seven Towneley children, admittedly only one of them a boy, called Peregrine, not after me, but after his eighteenth-century ancestor, Peregrine Towneley. In recognition of all his service to Lancashire he was made Lord Lieutenant – the first Catholic Lancastrian to hold that office since the Reformation. James did not live to see my brother become Lord Lieutenant. But if he had, that too – and to a much greater degree – would have made him proud.

5

Cambridge and the Army

If my mother had been responsible for sending me to Stowe, Colin Welch, one of the small boys who had mocked me in the school tuck-shop a few years earlier, was responsible for the next big step in my education – Peterhouse, Cambridge. In spite of that inauspicious tuck-shop encounter, Colin and I became inseparable friends once we escaped from the divisive atmosphere of our respective houses into the much more civilised company of the Sixth Form from whom university scholarship candidates were drawn. In those days scholarship candidates to Cambridge were required to indicate three colleges in ascending order of preference, the idea being that the unsought-after colleges would have a chance of picking up talent rejected by their more famous rivals. Since at that time the only colleges that I had ever heard of were King's and Trinity, I consulted Colin as to which of the unknown ones might make the least embarrassing third choice, not for a moment expecting to have to go there. Colin, momentarily reverting to his tuck-shop mockery, would have none of this, rebuking me derisively for my snobbish ignorance. His first choice was going to be Peterhouse. Not only did it have the distinction of being the oldest and smallest college in either university (even Colin's broadmindedness did not extend beyond Oxford and Cambridge) but it also had the best historians in Butterfield and Brogan, and even – a point thrown in grudgingly and somewhat contemptuously for my benefit – quite a number of toffs because the Master, Paul Vellacott, had tempted them from Harrow where he had been headmaster. What is more, Colin added, with an uncharacteristic show of worldliness, Peterhouse, not having enough applicants, would be more likely to give us an award than King's, which always had far too many. 'It's something known as supply and demand,' he almost snarled.

One thing about Peterhouse at that time, which even Colin had not discovered in advance, was its very marked homosexual flavouring; quite as strong, if not stronger, than that of King's. This was all due to the Master, himself a homosexual, who liked to fill the college with handsome youths, again mostly from his own school. Another strong influx of homosexuals came from the wartime evacuation to Peterhouse of the Chichester Theological College, most of whose seminarists were conscientious objectors given to parading around the college courts arm in arm in green corduroys, waving lilies and screeching to each other in girlish high-pitched voices. Coming from Stowe, where homosexuality was also not unknown, none of this was much of a culture shock to Colin and me. Where did I stand on this matter? It is a difficult question to answer. For although compared to the seminarists, and to some of the Vellacott favourites, neither Colin nor I was homosexual, such romantic or even carnal feelings as we had were certainly directed towards our own sex rather than to the opposite, if only because there were no girls in reach. But this does not get the matter quite right either. For in those days one was not so much aware of being homosexual or heterosexual as of being repressed, and what struck one as odd and even shocking about the seminarists was not so much their homosexuality as their exhibitionism. All forms of sex were forbidden to the young in those days. At Stowe, for example, a boy would be sacked just as much for heterosexuality as for homosexuality. Even masturbation was fiercely prohibited. When sexual abstinence is the norm imposed on everyone regardless, different and even deviant individual sexual preferences fall into insignificance compared to the overwhelming reality of common deprivation. In a starving world the relevant difference is not between vegetarians and carnivores but between those who have food and those who don't. So it was then with sex. The difference that mattered was not between the forms of sexual indulgence but between those who dared to break the taboos and those who didn't; between the inhibited and the uninhibited, and in this respect the seminarists, say, who had bravely come out of the closet and the brazenly lecherous young womanisers, of whom there were a few, had more in common with each other than they did with the great majority of the rest of us for whom sex still meant repressing your feelings rather than giving way to them in any shape or form.

Looking back I am quite grateful for this protracted period of repression, both at school and at university, because all the energy that might have gone into courtship of girls went into friendship with boys and instead of looking into the eyes of a female beloved and whispering sweet nothings – and how much of the rest of one's life has been spent doing that? – one spent hours with friends talking intensely about poetry, religion and philosophy. If this was the result of sublimation then there is something to be said for sublimation. Never have I got such pleasure from romantic poetry as I did in those days when one read voraciously about what one was forbidden to do. Nor do I regret having to spend so much time in all-male company where relationships were quite different from those that arise in mixed institutions. Possibly the English public school education of that period rendered one marginally less able to develop deep relations with women in later life and turned a few into permanent homosexuals who might have been saved from that fate if they had gone to mixed establishments. But against that disadvantage must be set Britain's not negligible asset of having had a male political class – and we are talking about the years when the world was run by men – most of whose members had been subjected to an educational experience out of which they could only hope to emerge unscathed by developing skills, tolerances and sensitivities which made them, if not good lovers, at least good colleagues, good clubmen and, not unimportant, good parliamentarians.

If this digression does nothing to answer the question as to where I stood on the matter of homosexuality at Cambridge, it should suggest that such a question is not easy to answer. Certainly I had passionate attachments with a homosexual element. But since none of the partners was homosexual, or thought of himself as such, a more accurate description would have to be hetero-homosexual.

Shortly after I came up to Peterhouse another freshman from Trinity, whose parents were friends of my mother, called to ask me for a day's partridge shooting. We had a good day and did the same about a week later. He was a marvellous shot and for the first and last time in my life I enjoyed shooting. After these days in the country we would usually order dinner from the Buttery in one or other's rooms, such services being still just about available in 1943. Shooting by day and dining by candlelight in the evening, and talking and talking – under these ideal conditions friendship was bound to flourish. Work hardly impinged. We were really only filling in the time before joining up, which we were due to do long before being required to take any important examination. If anything interrupted our sporting life it was the Officers' Training Corps which took two afternoons a week, drilling and learning about the Bren gun. But even during these periods Tom and I were thrown together, both of us being in the squad made up of undergraduates seeking commissions in the Brigade of Guards, he in the Irish and I in the Coldstream. What is more we were both Catholics which meant, over and above attending Sunday mass together, also meeting afterwards at Fisher House, the Catholic chaplaincy where Father Gilbey regularly entertained us to drinks and lunch. Tom was very much part of the hunting and shooting set and also used to go out beagling, along with Father Gilbey, whose trim black figure in gaiters cut quite a dash streaking across the Cambridge stubble.

My own special set was much more aesthetic, although the two overlapped and at parties in the evening it was not all that uncommon to see some sporty fellow who a few hours earlier had been in tweeds or hunting coat, dance half naked with another man. One such later became Equerry to the Queen and on the rare occasions when I saw him in full court dress fulfilling his duties at the palace it was not easy for either of us to erase from our memories those earlier close encounters in rather more informal surroundings. This used to worry Tom, a very unsophisticated old Ampleforthian, much more than it worried me. In fact there was really no reason to be worried since the orgiastic element in these all male parties was minimal. My guess would be that ninety-nine per cent of those present went back to virginal beds, waking up the next morning with nothing more embarrassing on the pillow than a monumental headache. In our case this was certainly so. In so far as explicit homosexuality entered into our relationship at all it was as a subject for jokey conversation, since Tom found homosexuals who made passes intensely funny, rather as he had found grammar school boys who dropped their 'h's intensely funny. With him it was a matter of manners, not morals, and since at that time there were many more homosexuals at Cambridge than grammar school boys it was the camp antics of the former rather than the social gaucheries of the latter which gave him most amusement. *Etonnez-moi* was the order that some French king gave to his courtiers. If Tom had been king they would have had an easy time. For everything astonished him and I could keep him rapt in amazement at exploits of mine which did not provoke so much as the lifting of an eyebrow from less impressionable friends. For example he nearly went into a state of catatonic shock one day when I recounted to him something that had happened to me the previous evening. It had shaken me, too, as it happened, although in recounting it I pretended to have displayed much more sangfroid than had been the case.

As I was crouching at about 10.00 p.m. in my pyjamas in front of the gas ring in my sitting room fireplace, just about to fill up the hot-water bottle before going to bed, in walked Princess Marina, wife of the Duke of Kent and at that time about the most romantic person on earth, rather as Princess Diana is today but much more so since royalty had not yet devalued itself by foolish attempts at matiness. Imagine my horror at being discovered by this utterly unexpected apparition not only with my trousers down – or if not down then certainly not properly up – but, even more shaming, filling a hot-water bottle, than which almost nothing conceivable could have been more at variance with the man-about-town image that I was then beginning to promote, or allow others to promote on my behalf. The princess, for her part, was in full regalia, tiara and all, having just attended some grand function at King's where she had run into Alexander Poklewski, a Polish undergraduate whose émigré parents had been given refuge by the Kents at Coppins. Being a lover of parties, the princess had asked Alex where there might be an amusing undergraduate and he, taking me at my face value, had suggested that if anyone could be relied upon to have that kind of hospitality on tap, it was his good friend Perry. One would like the story to have a happy ending. But it didn't. The princess did not take off her shoes and tiara and have a ball regardless. She didn't say 'how simply too charming' and ask for a cup of tea which could easily have been provided given the boiling kettle which had begun to shriek its readiness just as she entered. She simply walked in, looked round, and walked out without a word. Tom loved everything about the story, particularly my discomfiture.

And so it went on for about two terms – an easy, undemanding, agreeable relationship with no strings attached. From him I gained such knowledge of the land and of nature as has ever come my way and from me he gained such knowledge of books and ideas as has ever come his. Then one evening towards the end of the second term and with the shadow of the army drawing ever closer, we planned a special dinner in my rooms. It was not a farewell since we were both going into the same bit of the army together. But it was, we thought, the end of something or other – an idyll of a kind, and it seemed fit and proper to commemorate whatever it was with the best food and wine that Peterhouse could provide, subsidised by some medieval college benefactor who, most unusually in that period, preferred to endow the kitchen rather than the chapel.

Such special dinners were not all that unusual. We were always thinking up excuses for a celebration, and this one did not promise to be much different from the many others that had gone before. But in the event it was. At some point Tom, very drunk – not of itself unusual – stood up to propose a toast: 'To Perry, whose friendship means more to me than anything else in the world'. Then raising a precious Venetian glass, he seemed about to smash it to the floor, in a manner made famous by Russian films. Horrified at the imminent loss of such a precious possession, I grabbed his arm and in the ensuing mêlée we fell to the floor with the glass crushed beneath us. Pouring with blood and drenched with wine we embraced, swearing eternal friendship. From then on, for some months, both in what remained of the Cambridge term and intermittently during our early army life, we had what I suppose has to be described as an affair. Certainly, we loved each other's company. Shortly after term finished I went to stay with my grandmother at Dyneley and one Sunday morning, while serving mass in the dining room – where the sideboard had been turned into a makeshift altar – I heard James on the telephone just outside taking down a telegram, the text of which he left by my place at breakfast. It read: 'Can't live without you. Please return to London. Love Tom.' Not unreasonably my grandmother wanted to know what was in the telegram possibly fearing bad news about my brother who was then serving in Italy, and rather than reading it out I handed it to her, adding – almost as much to reassure James as my grandmother – that Tom was the code name for my

47

commanding officer and the text code for an urgent summons back to barracks.

Tom's telegram gave a very exaggerated description of his feelings and was, in any case, partly a joke, humour never being his strong point. What he really meant was that life in London on leave, which at that time consisted for us of drinking at the Ritz Bar and going to nightclubs, was infinitely more fun when we did the rounds together – rather as shooting at Cambridge had also been more fun when we did that together too. I don't think I am playing down the sexual element unduly. It really wasn't all that important. What was important was being together, doing things as a pair; even, as it turned out, picking up the same girl one night at the 400, a fashionable nightclub in Leicester Square. I remember that evening well because it was indeed pretty memorable. By the time it took place we had both been commissioned – about which more later – and had gone to the 400 to show off our new uniforms. Tom had asked a beautiful Wren, also just commissioned, to dance and at about 4.00 a.m. we all three struggled back to Brown's Hotel where Tom and I were sharing a room. Disregarding the porter's prohibition, we took the Wren upstairs, only to be interrupted thereafter by a furious under-manager whom we very foolishly forced to beat a hasty retreat by waving our newly issued revolvers in his face. Why he didn't call the Military Police I cannot imagine and if he had, the game would have been up for the three of us. Instead he contented himself with a note of rebuke delivered next morning with our breakfast, along with three Fernet Brancas with the compliments of the management, perhaps correctly surmising that in our advanced state of intoxication there had been little likelihood of Brown's reputation as a respectable family hotel being sullied by any very grave impropriety.

That was the last of the high jinks and when some months later our paths crossed in Germany in 1944, he by then in the Guards Armoured Division and I in Phantom, we both realised it was a case of *autres temps, autres moeurs* and behaved accordingly, as we did many years later when dining together with our respective wives.

I hope this goes some way towards explaining where I stood at Cambridge on the matter of homosexuality. Without that extra physical element my friendship with Tom would have been less joyous and I would have missed an experience of human felicity quite different from any other. That this experience could never have happened in the way it did if Cambridge colleges had been open to girls I am pretty certain. Strict Christian moralists will find this a good reason for letting girls in: less homosexuality. But from the humanistic viewpoint, which favours broadening horizons of experience, I am not so sure. Ironically enough more of my generation, whose formative years were spent when the love of man for man dared not speak its name, may have actually experienced it in practice than have today's permissive generation who theorise so tolerantly about it without having the slightest first-hand knowledge of what they are tolerating.

Colin Welch seems to have entirely disappeared from this chapter in which he was meant to play a starring role. As the most recent senior scholar of Peterhouse he had to say grace once a week in hall and arising out of this honorific duty enjoyed more opportunities to get to know the dons than did a mere exhibitioner like myself. I envied him this privilege since they were an interesting lot. In order of appearance there was first Brian Wormald, the chaplain who had come to our notice while invigilating the scholarship exams which happened to have been taken in the Peterhouse Hall that year. Sitting on a high fender with his back to the fire he had never stopped swinging his legs. This was distracting enough, and made all the more so by the fact that his highly polished silver buckle pumps kept catching the autumn sunlight streaming through the tall white windows. What is more he wore an Anglican-type soutane with crimson facings which matched his crimson socks and an anguished expression which only the deepest kind of spiritual doubts could possibly justify. This, too, was very distracting as, on John Davenport's advice, I had been studying the Oxford Movement and was thrown off my stride by having an invigilator who reminded me so vividly of all the principal actors in that great religious drama. Mentioning this to Colin afterwards he commended me for my perception and confirmed that Brian Wormald was indeed about 'to pope' which is what he did shortly thereafter. Although at the time of the scholarship exams I had no intention of going to Peterhouse, still being intent on King's, the impression made by this singular chaplain, who was almost an identikit picture of everything I had hoped a don would be, played a large part in reconciling me to the change of plan.

In his initial encomium on the college, Colin had mentioned the presence there of both Herbert Butterfield and Denis Brogan, then plain misters but later to secure professional chairs and knighthoods and in Butterfield's case, the college mastership as well. Brogan sadly was away in America on war work but Butterfield was very much in residence and it was to him that I was sent for supervision. It has to be said that he did not look at all distinguished; not a patch on G. M. Trevelyan who was then the only other famous historian with whom I could compare him. Tiny, covered in cigarette ash and speaking rather fast in a strong Yorkshire accent, he seemed almost as shy of me as I was of him. At our first tutorial we talked generally about what I knew and in an effort to impress him I waxed lyrical about R. H. Tawney's recently published work, *Religion and the Rise of Capitalism* which was then my bible. More agitated than impressed by this enthusiasm Butterfield thrust a rolled up copy of *The Times* into the fire and tried to use this great burning brand to light one of the Will's Whiffs he chain-smoked, setting fire instead not only to his eyebrows but also to the quiff of grey hair overhanging them.

His teaching technique was always to sow doubt wherever certainty raised its ugly head. Thus if one arrived thinking, for example, that the great Reform Bill of 1832 had been a major step towards enfranchising the middle class he would point out, with a giggle, that there were more noblemen returned to the House of Commons after it had been enacted than ever there were before. Reforms, he insisted, almost never had the results intended. They sometimes did good and sometimes did harm but as much in the one case as in the other it was more a matter of accident than of design. His rule was that in all history 'ongoing imponderables' (i.e. chance) upset the best-laid plans. Thus if a statesman wanted to get from A to B – in international diplomacy, say – he would almost certainly end up at C and then, in an attempt to correct that position, get carried even further off course to position D. Crusading enthusiasm in a statesman, therefore, became a danger since the more eagerly and doggedly some objective was sought, the more likely it was that the opposite, or at any rate something completely different, would be achieved. At one supervision we got on to the Napoleonic wars and Butterfield said how much better it might have been if Britain had lost the Battle of Waterloo. If France had won it instead, the rise of Prussia would never have taken place which would have meant no German unification under the Kaiser and no Hitler. Thinking that he was joking I asked whether he thought the same kind of thing might apply to the present war. Might some historian of the future come to teach that the best result would be for Hitler to win it? To my indignation he did not reply that this was to take his logic to absurd conclusions. After pondering the question quite seriously, he said, 'In all likelihood this war, like every other, will have unintended consequences, many of which will be quite as shocking as those it was intended to avert.' In the event, of course, his prescience was more than justified although in 1943 this deep strain of pessimism about the war's outcome was not what anybody wanted to hear, least of all a young man about to enter the fray.

Fascinating as Butterfield was as a supervisor, he did not at this stage of my life impinge nearly as much as Dr Burkill who was in charge of college discipline. Years later I came to know him as a kindly man. But that was not how he appeared in 1943. For he was a stickler for applying the rule that required undergraduates to be in college before midnight and would punish any breach with draconian severity. In my case this led to the punishment of 'gating' which meant being confined to college for three days, a most unwelcome restriction which I took to be expressly and sadistically designed to prevent me going to Newmarket where the Derby was being run that year. Defying the ban I went to the race and, surreptitiously climbing back into the college in the small hours, found Dr Burkill lying in wait for me under the wall in a deckchair. This led to the much more serious punishment of rustication, i.e. banishment from the university altogether for the rest of the term which effectively put an end to the first part of my life at Cambridge, to which I did not return until after the war.

Leaving Cambridge prematurely did not of itself worry me unduly. But there was one bit of unfinished business. Having persuaded the Coldstream to accept me as suitable officer material and also persuaded them – an even harder task – to do the same for Colin, I had still not overcome Colin's doubts about whether the Coldstream was quite up our street or, more to the point, whether we were up its; doubts that were to prove all too well founded. Just as he had preferred the idea of an ungrand college to a grand one, so he preferred the idea of a line regiment to the Brigade of Guards. Nothing about me irritated him more than my almost automatic assumption that what was smart was best, that Eton was a better school than Stowe, King's a better college than Peterhouse and now the Coldstream better than some good county regiment. This was not a matter of me being snobbish and him unsnobbish, although perhaps that came into it a bit. It was much more a matter of him, from an astonishingly early age, having an imaginative understanding, almost Dickensian in its depth and breadth, of how much more fun was to be got out of the company of the ungrand than the grand, the dull than the brilliant, the plain than the beautiful, the stupid than the clever and, most of all, the unfashionable than the chic. That this was a prejudice goes without saying. But it was a most unusual prejudice and because Colin felt it necessary constantly to prove his point he had only to go into a pub or get on a bus for the company, however unpromising, to spark him off into the most marvellous flights of fancy and speculation about what might lie behind all those unremarkable exteriors. Passing some humdrum farmhouse Sherlock Holmes once remarked to Watson that 'more dreadful crimes were committed on such premises than in all the gothic castles ever dreamed up by the heated imagination of Edgar Allen Poe' or words to that effect. Holding that view about life in general and being a mimic of limitless invention Colin could and did make a funny story about almost everything that moved, a gift that would, I knew – and how right I was – be of inestimable value in army life. Hence my determination to have him by my side. Why he allowed himself to be persuaded to join the Coldstream I do not know. Perhaps he thought it only fair to let me have my way over the regiment since he had his over the college. In any case, persuaded he was and the two of us duly reported to the Guards' depot at Pirbright.

The timing of our arrival could not have been more unfortunate since it roughly coincided with the 'Montgomerisation' of the British army, i.e. the temporary transformation of one of Britain's more gentlemanly institutions into an efficient killing machine. Although this transformation – given the nature of the German challenge – was very much in the national interest it was certainly not in the interest of two eighteen-year-old Cambridge undergraduates coming straight from Peterhouse. In the higher reaches it meant replacing fat and unfit generals with lean and hungry younger men. But in the lower reaches, judging by what Colin and I found at Pirbright, it meant giving absolute power to a lot of sadists, most of whom were no more professional soldiers than we were. Far from members of the peacetime army being more than averagely aggressive or bloody-minded, most of the ones we ran into were more than averagely cosy and easy-going, having in many cases joined up for reasons more to do with shooting pheasants than shooting humans or, in the case of the other ranks, to escape irksome domestic responsibilities or wifely nagging. The influence of Monty changed all that. The army, which had previously been the place where rat-race types – people who came to be known half a century later as yuppies – were least at home, came to be the place where – for the duration – they were most at home. This was bound to happen under conditions of total war and Monty only exaggerated, and put his personal stamp on, an inevitable process. But our particular intake was unlucky enough to coincide with the peak period of this inevitable process when all the bullies, shits and sadists recently recruited from civvy street were not only officially tolerated but positively encouraged, to the point where any protest to a superior officer on the part of victims was automatically dismissed as impeding the war effort. It would be nice to report that the Brigade of Guards resisted these pressures more than other less well-favoured regiments. Unfortunately it did not. Excessively conscious of their sybaritical peacetime image, they leant over backwards – at any rate at that period – to prove themselves the most rigorously spartan training unit of all.

On the evening of our first day Colour Sergeant Craggs, a thickly set man of about thirty-five, arrived in our barrack room to introduce himself. He wanted us to know that he had only joined the Coldstream just before the war and was no more a regular soldier than we were. His job in civilian life, he explained, had been a boarding school housemaster. A long pause ensued while he glared at the expressions on our faces which ranged from relief to incredulity. Then came the *coup de grâce*. 'Borstal, ' he roared, 'F... ing Borstal, that's where I was a f... ing housemaster and life there for the poor little bastards was a piece of cake compared to what you lot have got coming to you here.' Our first day's training, designed no doubt to set the tone, consisted of bayonet practice. But this was no ordinary bayonet practice of the kind which Colin and I had done a lot of in the Cambridge OTC. For instead of the sacks we had to charge being filled with sawdust or straw they were filled with pigs' blood and, as if this were not enough,

Colour Sergeant Craggs and two corporals ran by our side splashing us with extra blood shouting all the while, 'Hate, hate. He killed your mate.' Most of the squad, having entered the army straight from school, were three months ahead in their training and therefore much more skilled at keeping out of trouble than we were. They reacted as required, bayoneting the sacks with a fine show of simulated rage. Only Colin and I, fresh from Cambridge, were reduced to helpless laughter. That evening, long after lights out, CSM Craggs and the two corporals decided to pay our barrack room an unscheduled visit. We heard them approaching since they were singing and clearly in rumbustious spirits, having spent a happy few hours in the NAAFI bar. Colin and I had the two beds nearest the door, over which the three of them proceeded to relieve themselves. Nor was this soaking any mere short, sharp shock. Because of the amount they had drunk it was an ordeal of almost limitless duration.

Next morning, to add insult to injury, great sport was made at barrack room inspection about the disgusting state of Welch's and Worsthorne's blankets. Henceforth, Welch and Worsthorne were inseparably coupled together as some kind of pantomime horse always good for a laugh. At another morning inspection CSM Craggs noticed white stains on one or other of our blankets – a sure sign to any sympathetic eye of a cadet who has been applying Brasso too assiduously rather than not assiduously enough. CSM Craggs did not possess a sympathetic eye. 'When you're not bed-wetting, you filthy details, you're wanking,' he bellowed for all to hear, eliciting from Colin, through clenched teeth, the brave and memorable response, 'I don't wank metal polish, Colour Sergeant. Do you?' If our drill had been up to scratch, perhaps things would have improved. But our drill was awful, mine in particular. There was no way I could call out the word 'halt' on the correct foot, and doing so on the correct foot made all the difference between the squad – or in some cases the whole company – coming to a standstill in good order and it collapsing pretty well into a heap on the barrack square. This inability of mine to be able to give the simplest parade ground order correctly angered my fellow cadets quite as much as the instructors since it meant that they were forced to spend the lunch hour doing extra drill which in practice meant giving me more opportunity to demonstrate my total unfitness to fulfil one of the basic requirements of a good Guards officer. That was not my only inadequacy. Although normally quite a good clothes-horse I could never get the battledress to look in the least crisp and well creased. This was not for any want of trying. I put the trousers under the mattress every night, but whereas for the others this produced razor-edged creases in the right places, it never did for me. Nor did my boots ever acquire the ideal sheen, or my webbing the right kind of colouration. If this inadequacy had only brought down curses on Welch and Worsthorne it would have been bad enough. But it also gave our whole squad a bad name which made our fellow cadets even more antagonistic. In this respect one particular cadet, Dukey Hussey, deserves a mention. Right from the start he chose to find our incompetence endearingly funny rather than provocatively perverse and being himself a model cadet, also a giant as well as a natural leader of men, his example naturally carried great weight with the others. What would have happened to us without Dukey's support and friendship I dread to think. On one occasion I really believe he saved my life. We were on an assault course in north Wales which required us to run up Snowdon carrying full packs and, in my case on this occasion, a Bren gun rather than a rifle. At some point on the ascent it was necessary to swing oneself across a deep ravine on a rope and there was no way that I was going to make it across with a Bren gun. Seeing me hesitating at the edge – in spite of being urged forward by an impatient CSM Craggs – he grabbed the Bren gun and carried it across himself, silencing Craggs with the kind of look that knocks the stuffing out of a bully as much as it puts heart back into a coward. After being commissioned in the Grenadiers, Dukey went on to fight gallantly in France where he lost a leg. Fortunately he survived, and is now chairman of the BBC. Nowadays when we run into each other at social occasions it is he who has to struggle around with the help of two sticks and occasionally it is my privilege to carry one for him – only a token physical act of reciprocity, his real gift, now as then, being to uplift the human spirit.

Three months or so later the regimental adjutant, Captain Cuthbert Fitzherbert – whose beautiful daughter Mary my brother was to marry – came down to Pirbright to tell us who had made the grade and neither Colin nor I, out of a batch of thirty, were in that unlucky number, unlucky only in that so many of the elect were either killed or wounded. The way he bore the tidings of our rejection was very civilised. Much as the regiment had been flattered by our desire to be commissioned in it, the colonel had decided, most reluctantly and after giving the matter considerable thought, that our undoubted talents might be put to use in some other army unit where originality of mind and eccentricity of manner could be given freer reign. With such a thick coating of sugar, the pill was relatively easy to swallow, and I remember feeling few regrets, except about the glamorous Coldstream uniform which I had looked forward so much to wearing and imprudently already ordered from the regimental tailors, Herbert Johnson. Colin, of course, was much relieved at the news and made haste to sign up with the Royal Warwickshire Regiment – socially about as far removed from the Coldstream as any regiment could be. I eventually opted for the Oxfordshire and Buckinghamshire Light Infantry which socially was the next best thing to the Coldstream and had the additional advantage of a very distinctive and stylish double Sam Browne which slightly made up for the loss of all those Coldstream buttons.

Although in retrospect it seems pretty shameful to have been so concerned about sartorial vanities in the middle of a world war, I don't think frivolity of this kind was all that unusual. Precisely because it was such a grim time one became fixated on such few silver linings as there were and, for unmilitary types like myself who got no pleasure from drilling, rifle shooting, map reading, weaponry, physical exercise and the like, the one advantage army life had over civilian life was the respectable opportunities it offered a male to play the peacock. In any case all regrets about particular uniforms were quickly subsumed in the general exhilaration of being any kind of a commissioned officer whose mere appearance henceforth required privates and NCOs to salute or, if marching in formation, to give you an 'eyes right'. Coming after months of organised humiliation it was wonderful to step on to the parade ground for the first time as an officer and receive a smart salute from CSM Craggs, rather than a shower of abuse. Not only did he give Colin and me a smashing salute but showered a new squad of cadets – our successors – with abuse for not being quick enough to do the same: 'Jesus f ... ing christ, can't you dozy details recognise an officer when you f ... ing see one,' an exact repeat of what he had shouted at us on our first day of drilling. All resentments against CSM Craggs were swept away by a wave of nostalgia, and in that instant the brutal bully of reality was transformed into a sacred monster who would be remembered more with wry affection than hatred. That is how it should be since CSM Craggs was soon to meet his maker against whose name he had so richly and repetitiously blasphemed.

Travelling by train from Pirbright to Waterloo was unadulterated pleasure; each successive salute a thrill, confirming our new status which still seemed too good to be true. The pleasure was soon to wear off, of course, as in no time at all a second lieutenant became much more aware of all the senior ranks to whom he must continue to defer than of all the junior ranks below who must now defer to him. Colin's mother, who met us at the station, also brought us down to earth with a bump. 'You two officers, never'. Even so it was a great day – a kind of milestone. Obviously being commissioned had happened to generations of other officers before. But like losing a first tooth or wearing long trousers for the first time or getting confirmed or, in my case many years later, being knighted, what excited was that something which you never dreamt would actually ever happen to you, well and truly had.

Something else also happened to me that day which I never thought would. Arriving home to Thorpe Lodge on leave after the passing out parade I found a telephone message asking me out to dinner. It was from Glur Quennell, the celebrated beauty and wit, who was then married to Peter. She had been a guest of another cadet, Henry Bentinck, at the ceremony and had apparently taken a liking to what she had seen of me. Or this was the impression my brother Simon had quite distinctly got over the telephone. The plan, which I was delighted to fall in with, was to pick her up at Felix Hope-Nicholson's home, More House in Tite Street, Chelsea. More House was no ordinary home. It was a period piece as was its owner – pure *fin de siècle*, Wildean, *Yellow Book* decadence with an extra touch of Catholic exoticism thrown in for good measure. Vast and dark, it contained many rooms filled with undusted treasures and people to match. Although Felix was homosexual himself he loved the company of beautiful girls who were no less fond of him. Just down from Christchurch, where his dandi-fied set of rooms had been an aesthete's mecca, he now presided over a much larger establishment in London dedicated to the same Walter Pater-esque ideals. Having been rescued from a disastrous short spell in the army by Harold Nicolson, Felix spent the rest of the war pretending it did not exist and while you were under his roof the pretence was so complete that even a bomb falling next door was somehow transformed into an excuse for 'madder music and for stronger wine' in the manner prescribed by Ernest Dowson. On my first visit to pick up Glur, lying around on *récamier* sofas were Mavis Wheeler (ex-wife of Horace de Vere Cole the famous practical joker, present mistress of Augustus John and present wife of Mortimer Wheeler), the utterly ravishing June Osborne (who later made a disastrous marriage to Randolph Churchill), Brian Howard, purportedly Evelyn Waugh's model for Anthony Blanche in *Brideshead Revisited*, Pauline Tennant, two deserters and other unmentionables. An officer's uniform in that highly sophisticated company did nothing to guarantee a friendly reception, although the double Sam Browne was generally regarded as quite cute and certainly looked fetching enough when wrap-ped around Glur's evening dress. Dinner at Rules in Maiden Lane was everything I had ever imagined a restaurant could be. No plush has ever been redder; no waiters ever more sedate and solicitous, no silver so burnished or napery so white; no candlelight mellower and no companion so flirtatious and enchanting. It was like a dream come true. After dinner, my head swimming with happiness, we returned to More House, and unlike on that earlier occasion at Brown's Hotel, when I had woken up the next morning not remembering what had taken place, this time there was no room for any further doubt.

After a short leave Colin and my paths separated and did not come together again until after the war. He went off to the Warwicks and I to a battalion of the Ox and Bucks stationed near Woodhall Spa in Lincolnshire. The quarters consisted of Nissen huts surrounded by a sea of mud, and my only clear memory is of endless route marches which I came to enjoy almost to the point of frenzy. Pirbright route marches, as part of a squad, had been hell. No sooner would we set off than my feet would burn with blisters, my equipment turn to lead and my heart sink. As an officer at the head of the platoon I experienced none of these difficulties. Quite the opposite. Instead of being the weakest link in the chain, I found myself by far the strongest with enough stamina to outlast the toughest of my NCOs. It was a heady time. Never before or since have I felt so strong. Sometimes we would do thirty miles a day, always making a point of returning to camp stylishly at the double. Joseph Conrad described youth as 'the feeling that will never come back any more – the feeling that I could last for ever, outlast the sea and the earth ... the triumphant conviction of strength'. Presumably athletes and sportsmen often have that feeling but before this army training it had passed me by. Looking back I worry about having selfishly and cruelly overtaxed my platoon, carried away by this astonishingly unexpected surge of physical energy and well-being. But I don't think I did and certainly Graham Leonard, a fellow subaltern very much my mentor then as now, who went on to become a great Bishop of London, never found cause to rebuke or restrain me. We would take our platoons out for week-long exercises, sleeping under canvas and talking long into the night. Another fellow subaltern of this period was called Pankhurst, an offspring, I think, of the famous suffragettes. He was an ardent admirer of Rupert Brooke and even now whenever I hear the famous lines:

'That there's some corner of a foreign field/That is for ever England'

I cannot forget the sound of Pankhurst's voice reading it before turning in, happily oblivious of how hackneyed it was and how sadly well it would shortly apply to his own fate. When today's modern authors, like Paul Fussell, write glibly about nobody having gone to the Second World War in the same chivalrous and romantic spirit as they went to the 1914–18 war, I wish that Pankhurst had survived to call them liars, although this is not a word such a good and gentle man would have ever used.

No sooner had I fully got into my stride in this energetic and outdoor life than it came to an abrupt anticlimax. On another of those souped-up assault courses I fell and wrenched my shoulder. The arm came out of its socket and refused thereafter to stay put, or not in any way that could be relied upon. For some time nobody took much notice, least of all myself. I was enjoying myself too much. But one night at dinner in the mess the matter was brought to the attention of the colonel, an officer of the old school, in an embarrassingly conspicuous manner. Although the mess was a Nissen hut, surrounded with mud – like everything else in the camp – at least some of the more essential proprieties were still observed, such as the loyal toast which was drunk in decent port from fine Georgian glasses. The colonel took the loyal toast seriously. It was a nightly ritual, soldier servants stood to attention behind our chairs, pulling them back when the colonel rose and pushing them forward again when he sat down. On this occasion, just at the peak moment when we were all upstanding, with our

glasses raised, my right arm escaped from its moorings and glass and
contents crashed on to the table. In itself the noise was only a minor tinkle
in no way sufficient to justify the colonel's explosion of wrath. No, what
caused the explosion, of course, was his assumption, not without some
justification, that I was drunk. Next morning he called me in for an
explanation which impaled me on the horns of a dilemma. If I mentioned
the disablement, my days with the battalion would be numbered but if I
didn't, there was no way of escaping the slur of drunkenness. Hoping to
fudge the issue I said that the disablement was very minor and had in no
way interfered so far with my military duties, a reply that tactlessly
overlooked his regular soldier's view that drinking the loyal toast was very
much a military duty, at any rate for any officer in the battalion of the Ox
and Bucks under his command. Shortly thereafter I was transferred to the
Regimental Depot at Colchester Barracks which had remedial facilities and
when these failed to work, was sent on sick leave so as to be able to have
treatment at the Radcliffe Infirmary in Oxford which at that time was the
only hospital with the necessary equipment. When the Radcliffe told me
that the treatment would take at least eight weeks, I got permission from
my regiment to go up to Oxford for a term since it seemed silly not to seize
this opportunity to improve my mind while they were patching up my
body. Magdalen College agreed to waive the rules and took me in right
away as a contribution to the war effort, assuming, I rather suspect, that my
injury had been suffered on active service – an illusion that I did not strive
too officiously to remove either from their eyes or from those of all the other
kind people in the town and university who, impressed by the sight of a
young officer in uniform with his arm in a sling, helped to make the next
two months for me – part of the period described by Churchill as 'the hinge
of fate' – most inappropriately self-indulgent and irresponsible.

6

Oxford and Active Service

Having suffered so recently from the restrictions inseparable from having rooms in college at Cambridge, I was determined to spend the uncovenanted blessing of my term at Oxford in lodgings where landladies could be cajoled into overlooking late night returns – and other breaches of the rules – rather more easily than could college tutors. Borys Villers, then an undergraduate at Christchurch, whom I had made friends with after meeting him at More House, came up with the dream answer. The set of rooms under him at No 7 Oriel Street had just been vacated by Auberon Herbert (whose sister married Evelyn Waugh) and he was sure Mrs Newman, the landlady, would accept me as a suitable, if temporary, replacement. Since No 7 Oriel Street, along with Mrs Clarke's No 8 next door, were two of the most fashionable Oxford lodgings, and had been the meeting places for many of the more legendary undergraduate parties of the period, this was indeed a piece of luck.

Another piece of luck was to find myself sharing a house with Borys who was an education in himself. Reading the portents his parents, rich Polish Jews, had emigrated to England in the mid 1930s, thereby escaping the fate of the rest of their family who were all to be destroyed either by the Germans or the Russians. Not that Borys ever spoke about these things. Inheriting his parents' prudence he realised that spreading gloom and despondency was not the best way to win friends and influence people even in wartime Oxford; perhaps particularly in wartime Oxford whose reaction to all the awful things going on in the outside world was to feel even more justified than ever in its inward-looking parochialism. This suited Borys to perfection. For if Oxford did not want to be reminded of all the horrors, nor – with much better reason – did Borys. Never can I recall more carefree months than Borys and I spent in Oriel Street in 1943. But this time it was not the carefreeness of ignorance – which is what Tom had embodied – so much as the carefreeness of knowledge. Borys knew why he

59

had good reason to be carefree. England was his reason. He loved the place and all it stood for and, what is more, felt at home there; more at home in a foreign country, whose language he had only just acquired, than ever he had in his native land. Half a century on it is difficult to make plausible what it was that impressed him so much because it was mostly those bits of England which post-war generations have been trying to get rid of – the old bits, of which Christchurch obviously was one. It was not so much its beauty that appealed to Borys as its antiquity, its changelessness, the fact that everything about it had withstood so well the ravages of time. Having himself just escaped from a dreadful whirlpool, he found Oxford's un-ruffled waters – yes, even its stagnant waters – a blessed relief. There were many signs of military preparation in the Oxford of those days – of which, I suppose, I was one – but it was the dogged determination of the elderly dons not to allow Hitler to interrupt their scholarly routines which really convinced Borys that Britain was invincible. While to the *Daily Mirror* and the other popular papers, Oxford's adamant refusal to come out of its ivory tower seemed to denote a weakness of warlike will, to Borys it signified a much more profound moral strength than all that Churchillian bulldog-breed rhetoric which left him cold. He rejoiced when he overheard shop-keepers and others asking, 'Don't you know there's a war on?' not because this suggested that so many people were taking the war seriously as because it suggested that at least a few people were not, or rather not in the officious way so much encouraged by the Ministry of Information. It was Borys's second term at Oxford and already he knew more about its history and geography than most of its residents pick up in a lifetime. Instead of being oppressed by the weight of Oxford's past – as so many English undergraduates even then affected to be – Borys welcomed it as a solid anchor in an increasingly turbulent present. For him tradition seemed more liberating than restricting. Although in theory, having just read Burke, I was aware of the case for conservatism, it was a different thing to find it embodied in the person of this strange new friend.

Borys's imagination had also been fired – as had so many other upper-middle-class central and eastern Europeans – by the idea of the English gentleman whose ranks he was now so eager to join. At first I put this down to snobbery but it was nothing of the sort. It was just another twist of his unsettling habit of admiring aspects of England which the English at that time were beginning to deplore. One of the things which he admired so much about the English gentleman was his refusal to take ideas seriously. An idea in Borys's book was only as good or as bad as the person holding it. So the style or manner in which it was held was far more important than the idea itself. According to Borys it was not so much parliamentary democ-racy that made British politics relatively civilised as the gentlemanly political class that made it work. If worked by England's political class even fascism would lose much of its viciousness just as liberalism had lost much of its virtue when operated by any of the eastern or central European ruling classes. Oswald Mosley, Borys insisted, was a case in point. His unforgivable sin was not to be a fascist but to be a bounder. The same could be said of the Kaiser and even Hitler. No more in the one case than in the other had the British gone to war for freedom or against tyranny. They had gone to war to uphold gentlemanly conduct against bounderism. This was no undergraduate-type banter. Borys was deadly serious about not being serious. For him the war was not so much a clash of ideas or ideologies or even morals as a clash between styles, with England's gentlemanly code having played a far more decisive role in eventually putting backbone into the forces of civilisation than any mere philosophical abstraction or even material interest. Thus what he had come to Oxford to learn was not anything to be found in books or lecture halls. It could only be discovered through friendships with the right kind of undergraduates, through living with gentlemen, rather as an apprentice in the old days learnt the secrets of a craft by living under the roof of a master.

It was very much a two-way exchange. For if Borys learnt a lot from us, we learnt a lot from him, particularly on the subject of women, about whom he knew a very great deal, not only through precocious first-hand experience but through the reports – leaked to him by his adoring and adorably eccentric mother – of a private detective she employed to keep track of the amorous exploits of his not-so-lovable father. Borys was no oil painting and his accounts of one successful seduction after another inevitably put the thought into our heads that if he found it so easy perhaps we could too. In any case the whole business was clearly something that could be approached much more lightheartedly than we had tended to assume. When Borys talked so easily about seductions this no more suggested a disrespect for women than did the awkward, embarrassed English way of talking suggest respect. In fact he loved women and the relaxed way he talked about them was rather like that of a great scholar who is so familiar with his subject that he can talk about it very directly and plainly, without fudge, jargon or circumlocution. No coach has ever had more attentive pupils.

His technique was to let drop that some woman of his acquaintance found one or other of us extremely attractive and would like nothing better than to receive an invitation to lunch. In my case, the woman in question was none other than the Vice-President of Magdalen's wife, whose charms I had indeed noticed at some college gathering without for a moment daring to think that she could possibly be interested in a mere undergraduate. After much pressing from Borys I plucked up courage and wrote her a letter. 'At the risk of seeming impertinent, I should so much like to invite you to luncheon here in Oriel Street where we try to keep a good table. If the

Vice-president would do me the honour of coming too, that would be an extra pleasure but I do not suppose for a moment that so busy and distinguished a man would be able to spare the time. Awaiting your reply with great trepidation, I remain, etc.' I know this is what I wrote because Phyllis, who arrived unaccompanied, never stopped teasing me about my sly hypocrisy. Her husband John was indeed a very distinguished zoologist who later gave the Reith lectures. Phyllis was about thirty-five and lived with her two young children in Hollywell Street, where I spent many happy evenings. Borys had been quite right. There had been no difficulty whatsoever. After the first lunch we had made love in front of the fire as if it were the most natural thing to do in the world. Afterwards Mrs Newman had brought us tea as if she too thought it the most natural thing in the world. And at drinktime Borys had arrived and he, not surprisingly, also thought it was the most natural thing in the world. I pretended to. But didn't really. For miracles are not the most natural thing in the world and winning Phyllis's favours always seemed to me nothing less than a miracle. Such was her unselfishness that she never allowed me to fall in love, while exercising no such restraint on her own emotions. For me it was a dream-like experience without a single shadow. But for her, locked in a loveless marriage, there were shadows, and on the occasions when we met after the war I could never avoid a feeling of guilt for having taken so much from her of lasting value and given so ungratefully little in return.

There were other girls as well. Unlike at Cambridge where girls seemed to play no part in our social life, at Oxford they were central to it. This was very largely the doing of Borys. He had made friends with a Columbian girl – whom he was later to marry – and through her met a lot of other South American girls who were at St Hugh's or one of the finishing schools which had sprung up at Oxford in those years. Being South American they were all good Catholics and even Borys had to concede that this put them, at least relatively, 'off limits'. One in particular, the most attractive of the lot, was such a strict Catholic that she would not even visit the rooms of any undergraduate not of her faith. Being a Catholic, this was not a barrier that applied to me but Borys, usually the most sanguine of men in matters to do with the heart, held out no hope whatsoever of the visits bearing any further fruit. Then one morning after breakfast he suddenly saw his chance. Our routine was to have breakfast, served by Mrs Newman, on our separate floors and then to meet to plan the day in one or other of our rooms. On this particular morning he arrived to find me scraping my uneaten plate of congealed bacon and tomato into the fire – a proceeding he regarded as most imprudent since if Mrs Newman smelt the burning she might in future take a far less tolerant view of our late night returns and other irregularities. A much less risky way of getting rid of unwanted breakfast, he explained, was to enlist the very willing cooperation of Mrs

Newman's dog, Sheila. Mrs Newman loved Sheila inordinately and one of the time-honoured conditions of residency at No 7 was to endure with good grace being woken up by the commotion surrounding Newman's early morning eviction from the marital bed to make room for Sheila. In other words befriending Sheila was the surest way to Mrs Newman's heart and because feeding Sheila titbits served this important purpose, as well as solving the problem of unwanted breakfasts, Borys quite rightly saw no possible reason for me to go on using the fire. It was at this point, in the hope of recovering the upper hand, that I let drop that Father D'Arcy had asked me to dinner that night. Father D'Arcy, provincial of the Jesuits and Master of Oxford's Campion Hall, was then at the height of his international fame as a theologian and philosopher. Borys did indeed fall silent. But this was less the silence of a snob overawed by the dropping of a famous name than of a conspirator suddenly put in mind of the makings of a perfect plot. Dinner at Campion Hall ended quite early and I was back at Oriel Street by about 9.00 p.m. where, to my astonishment, the unapproachable South American girl was waiting on the sofa with every sign on her beautiful face of both eagerness and admiration. At the time this seemed another miracle. But it was, as I should have guessed, a piece of devilry. Borys had told the obsessively ardent Catholic girl where I was dining and with whom and even hinted, for good measure, that it was my intention after the war to become a Jesuit myself. Sophisticated women may respond to diamonds, he explained next morning. 'But for well-brought-up South American Catholic girls there is nothing more aphrodisiacal than a touch or two of holy water.' Aphrodisiacal was overdoing it by a long chalk. But at least his plot helped break the ice.

Work was more of a problem, in the solution of which Borys was no help at all. For some obscure wartime reason Magdalen decided that I should read a weekly essay on political philosophy to C. S. Lewis who, accustomed to teaching Eng Lit, was not much interested and, being blunt to a fault, saw no need to avoid telling me so. This was shortly after Lewis had become internationally famous as author of *The Screwtape Letters* and sending me to waste his time may have been one of the more minor ways in which Magdalen colleagues took out their resentment at his success. His rooms I remember as very untidy and also filled with pipe smoke so thick that one could hardly see across them. This may have been on purpose. For quite often the great man would arrange to have his elder brother, Warnie, who looked not dissimilar, sitting in his customary chair and I would have got through my entire essay before realising that I had read it to the wrong brother. Not that this mistake made much difference because even when it was C. S. Lewis himself in the chair he scarcely ever bothered to make any comment. But this did not deter me from sometimes spending all night preparing these efforts, only one of which I have kept. It was on

Hobbes's *Leviathan* and I sought to take issue with the orthodox view that Hobbes was an authoritarian, and even a precursor of Hitler. Because of the abuses of fascism all arguments for an authoritarian state were then very much out of fashion, and Hobbes's more than most. This struck me as quite wrong and I contended that Hobbes's case for *Leviathan* sprang from an almost exaggerated respect for the individual. Whereas Locke saw individuals like so many sheep who could be kept in order by any old collie, Hobbes saw them as proud and glorious lions requiring an infinitely more masterful form of control. Then I went on to argue that liberalism in advocating weak government merely patronised the individual, by grossly underestimating his capacity for causing mayhem. It was a political approach fit only for eunuchs who, being impotent, did not need to be held down. For men and women with fire in their loins, nothing short of *Leviathan* would do. *Leviathan*, therefore, was not incompatible with the wild creativity of the free society, still less its enemy but rather its essential corollary – the reverse side of the same coin. I ended with a flourish: '*Leviathan* is a tribute to the spirit of freedom. At least it lauds a system of government which credits the subject with the strength of giants, not pygmies.' C. S. Lewis refused to engage. 'Sounds like an article in *Truth*,' he growled dismissively, before returning to his own work. *Truth* was an ultra-right-wing weekly and I don't think the comment was meant to be encouraging. In A. N. Wilson's sympathetic biography there is a quotation from a C. S. Lewis letter written at almost this very time. 'The great thing, if one can, is to stop regarding all the unpleasant things as interruptions of "one's own" or "real" life. The truth is of course that what one calls the interruptions are precisely one's real life – the life God is sending one day by day.' If Lewis really thought that I was someone God was sending him day by day then he certainly had an offhand way of receiving the gift.

These were strange times in which to be trying to study political philosophy. All the public prints were for ever extolling the virtues of freedom, or rather the four freedoms, and no speech, leading article or sermon was ever without the most slavish, uncritical references to democracy. Freedom and democracy, after all, were what the war was supposedly being fought for. Yet even the most desultory reading of the great political philosophers left one in little doubt that a good society required a democracy to be laced with aristocracy and freedom more than tempered by authority. Hitler, of course, had given a bad name to all forms of conservatism, the good as well as the bad. To talk about a ruling class was too much like talking about the master race and so on. If I had been reading the great classical texts of political philosophy at some other period – at a time, say, when politicians and serious journals had all become obsessed with national efficiency – I would probably have found good arguments in them for making me dissatisfied with that Zeitgeist too. That is what a university education is for: to stir you into wanting to look below the surface of things and since the surface in 1943 was so uniformly soft-soaped liberal that meant – at any rate for me – seizing on conservative insights which were all the more intellectually exciting for being forbidden fruit. Marxism provided the same order of intellectual thrill for those a few years older, and had I been their age, and gone to university when public discourse was dominated by bland conservatism, it might have done the same for me. But 1943 was rather special. Because of the wartime party truce there was no intellectually sharp political writing or orating either from the left or the right, just bland, high-minded Utopian waffle in which hope triumphed in every field over experience – the kind of stuff now appearing in the *Independent*. In 1943 the entire media, popular as much as quality, sounded like the *Independent* does today. Very few of my contemporaries were reading political philosophy – or anything else – at university at that time. Had they been, I am sure they would have reacted against that optimistic Zeitgeist as I did, not necessarily by becoming conservative but by becoming at any rate anti-Utopian, anti-wishful thinking and passionately hungry for a more realistic view of man and society.

As the Oxford term drew to an end, so did my course of treatment at the Radcliffe Infirmary, and I was declared fit to return to active service. But the army seemed in no hurry to get me back. The regimental adjutant wrote to say that I should return to London and await further instruction. But weeks went by and no further instructions arrived. I cannot pretend that the delay caused me any great concern since at that time London life seemed particularly jolly – at least on the surface. Living free at Thorpe Lodge meant that my lieutenant's pay went a very long way. The wartime regulation limiting even the swishest of restaurants to a maximum charge of five shillings also helped in this respect. Along with many other friends I found myself spending more and more time at More House where life was never dull. June Osborne was still living there and my other nightclub companions included Carol and Catherine Macmillan, with all three of whom I fancied myself in love. Carol and Catherine were living in a large house in Hyde Park Gate where I would collect them, waiting for hours – or what seemed like hours – in a large dark hall for them to come down. Occasionally Maurice, their elder brother, would sweep past looking incredibly glamorous in highly polished cavalry boots. These waits were not good for my morale – distant sounds of girlish laughter and merriment would descend from the upper floors, suggesting a private world into which there would never be much chance of gaining entry. How quickly confidence can seep away. At Oxford I had begun to feel cock of the walk. Then only a week or so later all the old shyness would come rushing back. When Carol and Catherine did descend they would often be accompanied by Daniel Sykes who seemed to fulfil the functions of a court eunuch. At the time I had no idea that he was addicted to drugs. All I knew was that he had the entrée to all the louche homosexual clubs – of which Carol was so fond – where his stylish piano playing seemed somehow to draw attention to my lack of any such social gifts. At dawn we would all three go to the Coffee Ann which was an all-night refreshment stall off Leicester Square much frequented at the time by Lucian Freud whose mesmerising presence also seemed to invite invidious comparison. In many ways I was far out of my league in this milieu. June Osborne had by then become the mistress of a famous writer and made no secret of her passion for Alistair Forbes who made no secret of his friendship with the Churchill family. Against that kind of competition I had very little chance. Felix Hope-Nicholson himself was the staunchest of friends and his often proclaimed love in no way prevented him from identifying with, and seeking to promote, my hetero-sexual romantic passions which he did not share. In some ways he was absurd. Second only to his obsession with pretty young men was his passion for genealogy, and when the two overlapped – as they did, for example, in the person of John Stuart – there was no restraining him.

After about three months of this hectic social life, my mother began to show signs of impatience at the dilatory progress of my military career. By then she was vice-chairman, and co-founder with Lady Reading, of the Women's Voluntary Services and therefore much involved in the war effort. In order to set an example to the Kensington neighbours – notably not followed by Lord Ilchester at Holland House – Thorpe Lodge's entire half acre of lawn had been dug up for vegetables and the cooking in the house also put on a war footing with bleak meals that owed not a scrap of fat, sugar, fruit or meat to the black market. Breakfast was always at 8.00 a.m. sharp, with no mercy shown to an unpunctual son who had returned only a few hours earlier from the Coffee Ann. Dressed in her smart green WVS uniform, which put my dressing-gown to shame, she would ask: 'Any word from the War Office this morning?' In any case, whether on account of this wholly justified moral pressure or because I was myself beginning to turn against the decadence of London life, which did not even allow me to shine, I leapt with enthusiasm at an army job offered in such an attractive way that I would have accepted it even without these other pressures urging me in that direction.

Standing before lunch, as a guest, at the bar of White's nursing a hangover, I got into conversation with a Captain Fitzwilliam of the Welsh Guards who asked me what I was doing. On being told of my predicament he clapped his hands and said that he had the perfect solution. I must join Phantom, for which he could tell at a glance I was ideally suited. Since my mother had told me only that morning that my face resembled nothing so much as two burnt holes in a blanket, this seemed to suggest that Phantom was no ordinary unit. After a good lunch Captain Fitzwilliam got on to the

War Office to fix up the transfer which came through with amazing speed, largely due to the Ox and Bucks showing an almost insulting readiness to let me go.

When I told my mother about the Phantom offer at breakfast the next morning her relief was slightly tempered by my inability to explain what Phantom did. All I could tell her was that its headquarters were in the great Lord John Russell's spacious Georgian home, Pembroke Lodge in Richmond Park, an address which struck her as much too comfortable and much too near London to be altogether serious. Still less did she like the sound of Captain Fitzwilliam whose job in civilian life as director of the Savoy Hotel did not encourage her nearly as much as it did me. In the event my mother had no cause to worry. For Phantom was a serious military unit which sensibly took the view that being comfortable improves morale much more than it impairs efficiency. It was one of several private armies which sprouted in the Second World War and its job at this particular period shortly after D-Day was to provide 21st Army Group HQ with speedier intelligence than that coming through the regular channels. A Phantom patrol was attached to each of the army group's divisions charged with collecting and transmitting upwards as much information on the course of the battle as the officer in charge could lay his hands on. All the technical communication side was taken care of by NCOs on loan from the Royal Signals and the officer's job – for which we were being trained at Pembroke Lodge – was to master codes and cyphers and develop an understanding of the kind of information which might prove useful – not unlike a journalist's training. As might be imagined from Captain Fitzwilliam's unorthodox method of recruitment, the officers, drawn from different regiments, were an amusing and agreeable bunch which included a number of dons, innumerable young Astors, and even one film star, David Niven.

Of the training itself I have very little recollection, and such memories as do come back tend to give the wrong impression. This is the difficulty of writing about army life, the great bulk of which is so monotonous that one tends to remember only the very occasional triumphs or disasters which are, by definition, highly unrepresentative. For example I can remember only one of the many exercises which formed part of our training and this only because it was quite unlike any other. The day had started at dawn, with my patrol leading the entire regiment towards Salisbury Plain. The patrol consisted of an armoured car filled with wireless equipment, operated by two Signal corporals, two despatch riders and my jeep and batman driver. After about two hours' drive I misread the map and led the convoy down the wrong road. The horror of that moment has never been forgotten. It was still dark when I realised that there was about a mile of military traffic behind me, all of which was going to have to turn around in a narrow lane. Although the colonel was relatively long-suffering, my own patrol

made little effort to disguise their extreme dissatisfaction at being com-
manded by such an incompetent nincompoop, and during the rest of the
day nothing seemed more important than that I should do something
equally remarkable – but this time creditable – to win back their esteem.
Being far too realistic to suppose for a moment that the balance of my
reputation could be restored by any act of conspicuous military prowess, I
realised that the only hope lay in some conspicuous contribution that night
to the quality of the patrol's rest and recreation. By the time dusk fell all the
various patrols had gone their separate ways and we found ourselves in
the thick of Savernake Forest. Then it was that I had a brainwave. My new
friend Glur had recently married Lord Cardigan, son and heir to the
Marquess of Ailesbury, whose great ancestral seat was situated in Savernake Forest. All that I had to do was find that house and the patrol could be
guaranteed a night to remember. Glur turned up trumps, as I knew she
would. Whether the hospitality would have been quite so good had her
new husband not been away in the Middle East is another question.
Fortunately he was away, leaving the way clear for Glur and the marvellously frisky octogenarian marquis to push the boat out. Even the musical
talents of the Italian prisoners of war working in the forest were roped in to
add to the general gaiety. Such glowing accounts of the revelry were given
on returning to Richmond that very soon they acquired the status of a
regimental myth in which the hero's inability to read a map was transformed from a curse into a blessing. Travelling under the command of
other officers might be safer. But only with Worsthorne was the arrival so
sweet.

Then a blur descends again. After the training was completed I was
posted to B Squadron which was stationed near Tilburg in Holland. But of
the journey out to the war I remember surprisingly little; less than I do of far
less important journeys in my life. Again it is only the picaresque detail that
remains at all vivid. At a transit camp near Dover, for example, I was asked
to serve mass by the Catholic chaplain and was acutely embarrassed to find
in the middle that I had forgotten the Latin responses, so long was it since I
had last been to mass. This was no sparsely attended service. It was in the
open, with a great congregation of all ranks very conscious of what might
lie ahead, and messing it up in these specially charged circumstances
seemed particularly unfortunate. The chaplain had made his request after
hearing my confession – something that I also had not done since my time
at Cambridge when I had chosen to endanger my immortal soul rather
than suffer the embarrassment of confession to Father Gilbey about Tom.

My arrival at B squadron coincided with a long lull in the advance as
plans were drawn up for the crossing of the Rhine. This was not as
frustrating for me as everybody else. In fact it was rather a relief since my
first job was to keep the maps up to date – a task greatly simplified by there

being so little need to move the flags. B Squadron was attached to General Crerar's Canadian army HQ where discipline was pleasantly relaxed, as was security, to a fault. Sitting at a desk on my first morning I noticed an officer enter. He went straight to the maps on the wall and started to study them intently, without any of the other officers looking up. That was unsurprising enough. Less unsurprising was the fact that the officer studying the maps, with his back to the rest of us, was in the full field uniform of a captain in the Wehrmacht. After a few minutes, unable to contain my curiosity, I tapped him on the shoulder and this was how I first met Milton Shulman. At that time he was an intelligence officer in the Canadian army and had decided to dramatise the deficiencies of GHQ security arrangements by seeing how long it would take before anybody noticed that they had a German officer in their midst. Apparently he had passed through all the checkpoints without a single challenge, until my tap on the shoulder, which hardly counted as a challenge. Milton was absolutely delighted with the success of his coup, news of which caused a great sensation and was talked about for weeks, without leading to many improvements in security – perhaps the first recorded evidence of that great journalistic talent which in later life so impressed Lord Beaverbrook.

My first taste of anything that could be remotely described as active service came when Major Peter Patrick, B Squadron's impressive and kindly commanding officer, sent me on a mission to recently liberated Brussels. This involved riding a motorcycle through miles of churned-up mud on impassable roads over broken-back bridges, in constant danger, not from the enemy but from the Canadian Military Police, many of whom spoke only medieval French and hated the English scarcely less than they hated the Germans. Although the human dead had been removed, there were still rotting corpses of horses and cattle lying around with their legs upturned. Absence of human dead should have made the scene less horrific than the great battlefields – Borodino, Waterloo, Sedan – one had read about in literature. But somehow it didn't, perhaps because the sight of dead and mangled animals is horrific enough to arouse pity but, unlike the sight of dead people, not horrific enough to dull it. In any case, in scenes of human bloodshed there is usually some redeeming irony – an inappropriately beatific expression on a dead soldier's face as if he had just seen a vision of heaven rather than of hell, or a fallen body twisted into some faintly indecent posture more suggestive of pleasure than of pain. Later I was to see more sickening battlefields but none that struck me as more irredeemably godforsaken than the one through which I bumped and slithered on the way to Brussels.

On arriving in Brussels I was able to find my aunt's house, 27 rue de Commerce, quite easily since I stayed there with my mother before the war. Expecting an enthusiastic welcome I was a bit surprised when Joseph, the butler, looked askance at the filthy bicycle drawn up at the kerb and, even more so, at its even filthier rider soiling the doorstep. I shouldn't have been surprised. For he had always been a stickler for protocol. But it had not occurred to me that four years of German occupation would make no difference. Madame, he informed me, had retired for the night and could not be disturbed. Perhaps I would care to return at midday the next morning; very much implied was the hope that by then I would be more suitably dressed. When next morning Aunt Adrienne received me she, and the drawing room, were exactly as I remembered them in 1937. Nothing seemed to have changed. Again I was amazed. Heaven knows, enough had changed in England which had not been occupied. Surely the experience of war should have shaken things up even more in occupied Belgium? In fact it had done the opposite, at any rate if my Aunt Adrienne was anything to go by. Whereas my mother, in common with most people of her background outside the pages of Evelyn Waugh, had seen it as her patriotic duty to give up all the old social conventions as a contribution to the war effort, my aunt had seen it as her duty to annoy the Germans by carrying on exactly as before. No doubt to some extent the two ladies were using the war as an excuse to do what they wanted to do anyhow, my aunt having always been a reactionary and my mother a progressive. But there was more to it than that. In wartime England a willingness to come to terms with the modern world meant a willingness to accept democracy. In eating in the kitchen, and never dressing for dinner my mother felt that she was somehow striking a blow for freedom, putting herself on the egalitarian side of the angels. In wartime Belgium adaptation to the modern world could quite plausibly be seen as putting oneself on the side of the Germans; even collaborating with them. Aunt Adrienne had insisted that Joseph lay her table exactly as it had always been and when we sat down to lunch that day there were innumerable knives and forks, and indeed innumerable courses, but all of the tiniest, token proportions with only a thimbleful of wine for every glass. Evidently my aunt gained enormous satisfaction from observing the old rituals, and wore exactly the same expressions of self-righteousness while doing so as my mother did when, with equal exactingness, she forced her servants not to use the silver and not to serve at table. At the time I was very much on my mother's side, and wrote to her that evening with very censorious impressions of Aunt Adrienne. My mother kept the letter and today it makes me blush. 'Unlike the rest of liberated Europe which is in a state of flux', I wrote, 'our Belgian relations are frozen as if in aspic.' Then putting the boot in even further I went on: 'If Aunt Adrienne represents Europe's old order, then oh how painful it is going to be to drag them kicking and screaming into the twentieth century.' So impressed was my mother by this letter, and by others from me at the same period, that she showed them to a neighbour, Norman Ebbutt, *The Times*

Berlin correspondent whom Hitler had expelled shortly before the war and some of whose anti-Nazi despatches the editor Geoffrey Dawson had refused to print. What he really thought of them I do not know. But he wrote me an encouraging letter, and for some months after receiving it all my further letters home were written as much in the hope of impressing him as of impressing my mother – both motives being more than sufficient to explain their progressive bias which did not represent my true feelings.

Back at B Squadron I became friendly with the administration officer, Captain Michael Oakeshott. He seemed to be amused by my company which was very flattering since he was much older and of senior rank. There was also something intriguingly different about him. On the first evening after my return from Brussels I told him about my experience with Aunt Adrienne and instead of looking shocked by her *ancien-régime* intransigence his face positively twinkled with delight. 'Sweet, sweet, sweet', he kept on repeating. Then there was the matter of my overcoat. Before coming out to Holland I had got my tailor to run me up one in fur, the sole purpose of which, I maintained, was to keep the cold out. Not all my fellow officers agreed. They seemed to think there might be a less utilitarian, even a show-off element involved – rather as had those mockers outside the Stowe tuck-shop. Just when the critics were on the edge of convincing Peter Patrick to ban the garment, Michael Oakeshott success-fully intervened on my behalf with a decisive quotation from the Duke of Wellington to the effect that 'dandies make the best soldiers'. What I had no idea of at the time was that Michael Oakeshott, in civilian life, was already a famous Cambridge philosopher; nor, I think, did anybody else. Certainly he never threw his intellectual weight around. The sweetest-natured offi-cer by far, Roderick McFarquhar*, was a communist, and after dinner in the evening we sometimes had informal debates at which I would try desper-ately to shine in an effort to show that being bad at map reading did not necessarily make one a complete fool. Although Michael used to giggle joyously he never took part. When I first got a patrol of my own he was deputed to show me the ropes and we spent a fortnight together swanning around Holland whose inhabitants welcomed us with open arms. This was still the Catholic south of Holland where Puritanism seemed to play no part. I suppose Michael must have been about forty which in those days seemed to me a great age. So when the girls chose his company rather than mine I assumed it was because they preferred to be safe than sorry. It was not only the full extent of Michael's scholarly renown that I ludicrously underestimated in those days. Equally ludicrous was my failure then to do justice to his virility.

Peter Patrick's fears that my various military shortcomings might prove

---

*Uncle of the distinguished sinologist of that name.

a liability in commanding a patrol were to prove, I believe, largely unfounded, not because the shortcomings did not exist, but because they
were more than made up for by the skills of those under my command. One
of the Signal corporals, for example, was a dab hand at map reading. Nor,
in the event, did it matter one jot that I couldn't change the wheel on the
jeep because the driver could. As for drill, there wasn't any. Another doubt
about my suitability to command had to do with my capacity to impose
discipline and here, there was a problem. My driver was constantly going
sick with clap. But I really don't think greater aptitude at learning all that
one was meant to learn at Pirbright and elsewhere would have helped me
solve that problem. One small triumph does stick in my mind. My patrol
was the first to report that the Allied armies had reached the North Sea.
Such was my excitement to get the news off that I made a mistake with the
code and the message had to be repeated. I remember standing looking
over the shoulder of the Signals corporal as he tapped it out, willing him to
do so faster. No doubt the message went straight into the field marshal's
waste-paper basket but none of my few journalistic scoops in later life,
which went straight on to the front page, ever gave me such a thrill.

Driving through the rebuilt Ruhr today it is difficult to believe that it
could ever have been the mountain range of rubble through which we
struggled in 1945, after the Allied bombers had done their best or worst.
Even more difficult to believe in the present climate is that we reacted to
these scenes of desolation with so much satisfaction. Such regrets as we
had were not about the human misery hidden in the ruins but about their
physical capacity to hold up the advance, thereby postponing Germany's
defeat. Occasionally one of the few inhabitants who had not fled would
look up reproachfully from her desperate burrowings, only to receive in
return a blank and stony stare. Time enough to feel magnanimity, we felt,
when victory was assured. Rereading my letters home at this time, I am
surprised to find expressions of concern about the consequences of blanket
bombing and can only assume that they were included to impress my
mother and Norman Ebbutt, both of whom shared the Bishop of Chichester's well-known squeamishness on this issue. My true feelings were
much more accurately reflected in a slightly later letter in which I described
the army order forbidding soldiers to fraternise with Germans as 'un-
necessary and gratuitously offensive ... as if we would ... '. By that time,
however, it was respectable again to speak vengefully about the Germans –
more than respectable, obligatory – since the Allied armies had begun to
uncover concentration camp horrors which temporarily invalidated all
appeals for Christian forgiveness.

In the event I did fraternise, as did we all; but not, I am ashamed to say,
for reasons that had much to do with Christian forgiveness. In the last

months of the war my patrol was moved to Hamburg, from which the Germans had just retreated, to help with the communications required to cope with mass German surrenders and refugees pouring in from the east. Much of the city had been destroyed. But the famous Atlantic Hotel on the lake had survived in full working order – rather as Claridge's survived the Blitz – and Allied officers moved in as fast as the city's rich burghers and their wives, plus dachshunds, moved out, leaving their possessions behind them. After months of austerity it was marvellous to be ensconced in a luxurious room with expensive scent still lingering on the pillows. I also seem to remember an ample supply of hot water and even capacious bathtowels. These quarters were certainly far above my station, being reserved for senior ranks. But one of the myths that Phantom had built up was that our reporting work required easy access to top brass and although this claim did not by any means always work, on this occasion it had. The dining room was a particular joy. The German staff simply carried on as before, with the kitchens augmented by army rations – mostly American as it happened. There were menus and table napkins and cut glass, with waiters in tail coats and all the frills; and access to the hotel's excellent cellar, all free. At first I did not dare order wine, thinking that this would be pushing a mere lieutenant's luck a bit too far. But encouraged by the wine waiter, who turned out to have been trained in the Savoy by Captain Fitzwilliam, I was soon ordering a bottle of Moselle every night. Not being part of a larger unit I knew nobody and, rather than dine alone looking into space, it seemed a good idea to read a book. As it happened, I had been carting a copy of Walter Pater's *Renaissance* around, given to me by Felix. Under dripping canvas its famous admonition 'to burn always with this hard, gemlike flame' had not set my spirits on fire. But sitting under the Atlantic Hotel's chandeliers, sipping Moselle, its seductively decadent charms were much less easy to resist. Greatly oversimplified, and devoid of its stylistic beauty, Pater's message was never to miss an opportunity to experience a new sensation, preferably if it was beyond the existing moral frontiers. Addressed to Oxford undergraduates in the 1880s this was rightly judged to be dangerously heady stuff. Addressed to an impression-able young officer of an occupying army surrounded by all the temptations of a demoralised and starving city, it was little short of diabolical.

What happened next cannot be blamed on Walter Pater. But had I not fallen under his spell in circumstances so ideally suited to practise what he preached, I doubt whether I should have risked getting so closely involved with the baroness. Ostensibly she was meant to teach me German and the lessons would take place in her tiny apartment. Payment was in tins of Spam, cigarettes and sweets for her young children who called me Onkel. The routine was as follows. First I would dine and have sublime thoughts while reading Pater. Then I would drive in my jeep to the baroness's flat through pitch black streets in defiance of the curfew and only return to the hotel in the small hours. Because of the ban on fraternisation the relationship was illegal and highly dangerous for us both, which was an added thrill, at any rate for me. If that had been all, there would have been nothing much to feel ashamed of. Plenty of other soldiers were carrying on prohibited affairs of this kind, also very often with baronesses, of whom there seemed to be a great many around. Unfortunately it was not all. After about three weeks of this idyll, my curiosity about the baron got the better of me. Where was he, I asked? The baroness did not know. The last she had heard of him was that he had been wounded on the eastern front, lost a leg or something. Very probably he was dead. Not that the baroness seemed to care all that much. At that time a British officer bearing gifts in the hand was worth any amount of German barons on or off the eastern front. Then one night at about midnight we heard footsteps falteringly climbing the stairs. 'That's the baron,' she whispered. 'Don't let him in. He'll kill me.' The approach was painfully slow, scarcely less for us than for him. Tap tap tap like Long John Silver in *Treasure Island*. Then came the knocking on the door and appeals to be let in. 'It's me, *liebchen*, it's me.' I opened the door and confronted him. He was a tall man with many days' growth of beard, in an iron-grey Wehrmacht officer's overcoat with a stick and only one leg – unarmed. By then I had buckled on my belt and taken the revolver from its holster. After a moment's silent staring, he drew himself up as best he could, about-turned as best he could and slowly tap tap tapped his way down the stairs and out again into the street. Instead of feeling disgusted with myself I felt like a hero and, most disgusting of all, was rewarded accordingly by the relieved and grateful baroness. It is a horrible story. The baron didn't come back while I was in Hamburg. Almost certainly he never came back because for a year or two into the peace I would receive letters from the baroness asking to join me in London. The boys, she would always add, sent their love to Onkel.

Loosely based in Hamburg my patrol would be sent all over the country to keep tags on the POWs and refugees, most of whom were desperately anxious to fall into British rather than French, American or, most of all, Russian hands. Whether they were right to trust the British in this way is another matter. Certainly the Cossacks were not. At the time, however, we found their preference quite unremarkable. For just as we assumed, with Kipling, that being born British was to win the first prize in God's lottery, so did we take for granted that foreigners were right to admire us. Perhaps their Anglomania was only simulated for our benefit, or not as general as I assumed it to be. Not speaking any foreign language, my conversations were limited to English speakers who tended to be the better educated types. Without any exception these people all had the same idealised picture of English civilisation and, in particular, of the English gentleman as Borys had. In their kind of rock-bottom circumstances, abstractions like freedom and democracy, so often on the lips of the Americans, or of liberty, equality, fraternity, so often on the lips of the French, let alone the slogans of Russia's Internationale, were so much hot air. What mattered was to fall into the hands of troops led by an English officer with high standards of human behaviour, i.e. an English gentleman. Again, lots of British officers didn't behave like gentlemen, me included as I have already recounted. But such was the myth's momentum that it carried on regardless of reality. Even more often mentioned than Churchill in this respect was Anthony Eden whose elegant style and appearance seemed to symbolise all the qualities which these lost souls were hoping to encounter. Field Marshal Alexander was another *beau-idéal* they had in their mind's eye – a very parfait gentle knight. What had vanished under the impact of Hitler and Stalin from their world was not anything so grand as the four freedoms – which had never existed – as individual decency, honesty, honour, and with these qualities the English ruling class were thought to be better endowed than any other. These conversations made a deep impression on me at the time because they were in such stark contrast to the kind of sentiments being disseminated to the troops by the Army Bureau of Current Affairs. Every so often bundles of ABCA pamphlets would come up with the rations, so to speak, all reading as if they had been written by Michael Foot or some other radical propagandist. Everything about the old order was traduced, especially the institutions responsible for training English gentlemen. In the brave new post-war Britain dreamt of by ABCA there was to be a new kind of leadership based on different values. Commenting on these pamphlets in a letter home I wrote: 'In these hell hole camps "modern" is not a word to conjure with. Hitler is modern; so is Stalin. Nor do their inmates like the sound of "waves of the future" since it is these that have battered them to pieces. Why do our politicians want to pull Britain up by the roots when seen from here its roots are its greatest blessing?'

Oddly enough I cannot remember where I was on the day the Germans surrendered; only the tune that was played immediately after the announcement on the forces programme: 'Don't Fence Me In'. But I can remember VE Day plus one, the first day of peace, because then it was that I first fired in anger the revolver that I had been carrying around on my hip for the last three years and fired it furthermore to kill. The fatal incident took place somewhere near Hanover where my patrol had set up camp. Feeling that the end of the war justified a more elaborate celebratory dinner than army rations would rise to, my corporal and I approached a local German farmer whose barnyard looked particularly well stocked and asked whether we could exchange cigarettes for some of his poultry, expecting, of course, the answer '*ja*'. But instead of responding with the expected deferential obsequiousness, the farmer, a great bull-necked ruffian, starting hurling Teutonic defiance. This put me into a rage and I drew my revolver, took aim at a range of about five feet, and shot his largest turkey stone dead.

No, I did not have 'a good war' in the sense that came to be given to that phrase. Never was my courage put to the test. Even that is putting too kind a gloss on the matter, as I did not look for an opportunity to put it to the test. Anybody reasonably healthy of my age who wanted such an opportunity could surely find it. So whilst I did not commit any specific act of cowardice, I cannot escape responsibility for omitting to commit any act of courage. In some ways this avoidance of danger – by accepting the soft option of Phantom, for example – was more reprehensible than some conspicuous act of cowardice. At least someone who was a proven coward had had the courage to put himself to the test before being found wanting which is more than I ever did. Asked once on the radio whether he regretted anything particular in his life, Enoch Powell memorably and movingly answered, 'Not being killed in the war', by which he meant that he had never been able to forgive himself for surviving while so many better men among his friends did not. Tragically many of my friends were killed too. My grief however was always tempered by a furtive feeling that their deaths slightly lengthened the odds against my suffering the same fate. My answer to the Enoch question, therefore, would have to be slightly different. One of the few great blessings in war is that no other activity is so superlatively good at sorting out the men from the boys and to go through all its waste and boredom, as I did, without discovering by the end in which category you fall, that really is regrettable, not unlike climbing the highest of mountains without ever bothering to look at the view.

Even so I have three campaign medals – more than some of the youngest of our contemporary field marshals – which I occasionally wear to public functions, not at all unhappy that younger men may credit me with glories that I did nothing to deserve.

7

A Glasgow Apprenticeship

Shortly after VE Day, I received a letter from Dr Burkill, my old Peterhouse enemy, asking whether I would like the college to apply for my early release from the army to pursue my studies at Cambridge. Apparently it had been decided that scholars and exhibitioners should be allowed to jump the demobilisation queue if their colleges wanted them back which, surprisingly in my case, Peterhouse did. But even priority demobilisation took a bit of time and I was still with B Squadron, back in Holland, when the news of Labour's landslide victory in the 1945 general election came in and then, shortly thereafter, the news of the atomic bomb dropped on Hiroshima. Of the two bombshells there can be no doubt that it was the first that caused our mess the most shock and horror. In fact the second, which saved the squadron from going out east, was greeted with relief. So, among a few officers, was the first. But only among a very few. To most it seemed the end of the world, or at any rate of their world. Next morning the entire squadron's communication system was jammed by my rich colleagues trying to instruct their stockbrokers in London to buy or sell or whatever it is rich people do in a panic. Looking back I think they were right to be in a state but not primarily for reasons to do with their wealth. Meeting them at Phantom reunions in years to come it did not appear that any of them had been reduced to penury by socialism. Rather the contrary. Because so much of their wealth had been in land, the value of which rocketed up after the war, they were probably better off by the time the Tories returned in 1951 than they had been in 1945. How the Labour landslide did hit them was morally, not materially. It was a vote of no confidence, if you like, in the old ruling class, a notice to quit, or at any rate to keep a low profile.

This aspect of the 1945 election result has been seriously underestimated in accounts of the period which all seem to suggest that it ushered in much less of a social revolution than had been either hoped for or feared, changing nothing fundamental. In terms of what Marxists regard as fundamental this may have been the case. There was no fundamental redistribution of wealth for sure. Nor did the outward signs of class predominance change much, even down to the absurd revival early in the 1950s of debutantes being presented at court. But compared to what did change, those continuities were superficial indeed. For what did change was nothing less than the Zeitgeist. Whereas before the 1945 election result the Zeitgeist was such as to make it possible for a hereditary upper class to feel secure and self-confident – or at any rate for its unthinking members to do so – afterwards it was not. I don't think this is hindsight on my part. In a letter home at the time I described how a grand fellow officer occupying the tent next to mine had reacted to the election news.

> Normally, his batman calls him in the morning with hot shaving water in a beautifully monogrammed silver jug from which he pours the boiling water into a beautifully monogrammed silver bowl, beside which are laid a pair of beautifully monogrammed ivory hairbrushes – a ritual never for a single day broken under the most unsympathetic wartime conditions even, to my knowledge, under bombardment. This morning – after the election news – instead of the silver bowl there was an ordinary 'officer for the use of' canvas one. Having shown an aristocratic determination not to allow Hitler to alter his habits, this most stylish of noblemen is obviously not going to meet the challenge of Mr Attlee and his socialist cohorts with comparable sangfroid. In the face of the foreign enemy he has not flinched from beginning to end; but in the face of the class enemy his nerve has gone before the battle is ever joined.

There was a lot of that kind of funk around at the time, and it continued pretty well until the high tide of Thatcherism towards the end of the 1980s. After the First World War, upper-class officers returned from the trenches with deep feelings of guilt at what had been done to the men under their command. After the end of the Second, thanks to the election, they returned much more worried about what the men were about to do to them. In the event, of course, they had little cause for fear. They were left with most of their privileges intact. But that was almost more demoralising than having them taken away. If they had been taken away, that would have been the end of that. They would have had to start again, find a new role. But their privileges were not taken away. What was taken away was the ethos of hierarchy that had made sense of those privileges. Everything about the class system was left intact except its raison d'être. To demoralise a ruling class, without dispossessing it, which was what the Attlee government did, gave post-war British society the worst of both worlds: those aspects of a ruling class which provoke envy and resentment and none of those which inspire awe and admiration.

But I am jumping ahead, anticipating an article along these lines which I was to write in an early number of *Encounter* in the 1950s. Not having any money to speak of myself, I was able to view the advent of socialism with relative equanimity. Only on returning to Peterhouse in Cambridge did I have occasion to realise that something unpleasant was happening which might affect me personally. Shocked to find that my college rooms were in a terrible state of disrepair, I asked the new Bursar, Air-Vice-Marshal Lockyer, himself just back from the war, if he could arrange for them to be given a lick of paint. To my surprise I got back a letter refusing my request on the grounds that the college had already exceeded its quota of repairs under some emergency regulations. I replied politely that in view of the college not being able to do the job for me I would get it done off my own bat and at my own expense, only to be told that since not all undergraduates could afford to do up their own rooms, none should be allowed, in his own words, 'the privilege'. This irritated me and I decided to get a painting firm in regardless. Before they started work I told them the situation and asked them to pretend to be my uncles doing the job for love in the all too likely event of the Bursar arriving on one of what he chose to call his 'little tours of inspection'. When he did arrive, puce in the face, asking what the hell was going on, this is what they did say. Naturally he did not believe them. But the situation had become too much for him. This was a challenge to which his service training offered no 'school' solution, and after looking up speechless as my uncles, on their ladders, proceeded with their labour of love, he retreated *pour mieux sauter* on another day.

This was the beginning of a long struggle which Colin, who had also just returned, and I waged with Air-Vice-Marshal Lockyer. Whatever we wanted to do he found some bureaucratic reason for opposing. The confrontations were all over small issues – like repainting a set of rooms – but cumulatively they got on our nerves. My pre-war scout William, for example, was quite happy, for a small tip, to bring me breakfast in my rooms as he always had in the past. That too was now against the rules. Exception was taken to my storing logs on the landing. All attempts to mitigate the post-war shortages were frowned upon on principle. At some point, exasperated beyond measure, Colin said to him, 'Don't you know that there is *not* a war on?' Although the witticism pleased us at the time it missed the point. For there was a new war on – Labour's war against inequality, unemployment, slums and the like, and this new war had to be fought with the same single-minded determination as had the old one. And who better to organise the fighting than the very people who had done such a good job in winning the just triumphantly completed earlier struggle, not obviously the chaps with martial skills so much as the staff and admin crowd. Historians have rightly dwelt on the achievements of the Attlee government, such as the National Health Service. But on the ground, from the worm's-eye point of view, one was much more aware of

Britain being turned into a land fit for the likes of Air-Vice-Marshal Lock-yer to lord it in. There was a rich irony in this. For the last thing the service vote had intended to bring about when they voted Labour was the perpetu-ation of bullshit and red tape. In fact that was probably what they had voted Labour in order to escape, having had more than enough of it during the six years of war. Instead, by opting for socialist planning, they got another dose.

Why the Peterhouse Fellows allowed the new Bursar to run the college like a military barracks is difficult to say. Partly, I suppose, because not having served for the most part in the armed services themselves, they were impressed by military rank; even as junior a rank as my own. The fascinating don who was my new supervisor, for example, Denis Mack Smith*, who had not served for health reasons, used to come to my rooms for the weekly tutorial, rather than the other way round. And the times would be arranged for my convenience, not his. If I was not ready to receive him he would sit patiently awaiting my pleasure. It was an absurd reversal of roles. Instead of my sitting at his feet he was sitting at mine. Another factor, I am sure, was the terror inspired by that election victory. Not only rich individuals feared for their privileges. So did rich institutions, like Oxbridge colleges, who thought it prudent to observe every new planning regulation to the letter. Nor was it only prudence that guided them into giving Lockyer his head. The historian Peter Laslett, Colin's supervisor, for example, was an ardent socialist himself. Whether Air-Vice-Marshal Lock-yer and his cohorts were the right instruments to build the new socialist Jerusalem was never considered, if only because in those days there were no others. If reactionary Colonel Blimp was deemed unacceptable by the country's new masters – as he was with a vengeance – then people like Air-Vice-Marshal Lockyer were the only alternative; very much a case, in my view, of out of the frying pan into the fire.

Not all the dons were prepared to knuckle under. Two resisters, in particular, spring to mind. The first was an historian from Dublin, Des-mond Williams, only slightly older than Colin and me, and the other, Eric Heller, a much older refugee from Nazi Germany, both of whom were to play a significant part, under the leadership of Herbert Butterfield, my old supervisor and the college's future Master, in turning Peterhouse into the bastion of conservative thought that it subsequently became. That was all much later, however. At the time the battle lines were much less ideologi-cally or philosophically grandiose. On the one side was an officious new broom of a Bursar determined to sweep the college clean of its familiar old cobwebs, and on the other a small, awkward squad, determined to frus-trate his tricks at every turn. Colin, poor chap, paid a heavy price.

It happened like this; he, Desmond and Eric – not I, to my great regret –

---

* Later the British authority on nineteenth century Italian history.

went up to London where they dined well at the Cavendish Hotel, then owned and run by the legendary Rosa Lewis, a one-time mistress of Edward VII. Dined well is a figure of speech because the food was always uneatable. Drink, however, flowed. More to the point, it was the kind of establishment where anybody harbouring burning resentments against a man like Air-Vice-Marshal Lockyer might expect to have them fanned into a furnace of fury. Not for nothing was it the favourite London retreat of Evelyn Waugh. In any case at about midnight a plot was hatched. Those were the days of the Jewish Stern Gang who were conducting a terrorist campaign against British soldiers in Palestine. No targets had been attacked here in Britain, or ever were for that matter. Might it not be fun, somebody suggested, to ring up Lockyer and tell him that a bomb had been put under his house outside Cambridge which would go off in half an hour. This is what Desmond did, in a thick Irish accent, with Rosa's cackling voice in the background. Nobody expected the victim to believe in so improbable a story. But such was Lockyer's self-importance that he did. After informing the police, he got the fire brigade to evacuate the house. Unfortunately the police traced Desmond's telephone call and within an amazingly short period of time came round to the Cavendish where they nabbed the three culprits.

No charges were pressed. In those days terrorism in England was not yet the serious matter it has become. But the college was not amused. Nor, naturally, was Lockyer. A scapegoat had to be found and because Colin was the only undergraduate of the three, with no academic career to be ruined, he was the natural choice. He was sent down and deprived of his degree.

Not being involved in this escapade I got my degree, a 2/2 in history, and went down voluntarily, if prematurely, unwilling to endure post-war Cambridge a day longer than necessary. My only regret was not being able to finish the course of lectures in political philosophy by one M. J. Oakeshott, who turned out to be my old Phantom comrade-in-arms. As I have already mentioned he had never given me any idea of his true identity during the war. So his appearance on the podium at my first lecture in cap and gown took me completely by surprise. Typically he only giggled when he saw me staring up at him from the front row. Just as he had made no fuss of his academic eminence in the army, so now he made no fuss of it back at Cambridge. After the lecture we went off together to have coffee at the Copper Kettle in King's Parade as if nothing had changed. But it had. Now I was a bit overawed by him, anxious to impress and since what he liked in the young was cheek and arrogance, my new respectfulness was the last thing to give pleasure. A few years later, after my marriage, he became our lodger in London. But by then it was in the company of my wife that he found the zest and the exuberance which in the army he had found in mine.

If there was an appointments board at Cambridge in those days it never occurred to me to use it. Nor would it have been much use if I had since for some years after the war there were no new jobs going. Every firm or organisation naturally gave priority to employees who had been with them before hostilities began. In any case I had no clear idea of what I wanted to do. It was at this point that I properly met my father, having not set eyes upon him since that early childhood lunch at Belgrave Square. It was at a Chelsea party and our mutual hostess, Hester Marsden-Smedley – a very gallant woman who had been a British agent in Belgium – not knowing that we were related, introduced us. 'Oh, Colonel Koch de Gooreynd,' she said, turning to my father, 'do you know Perry Worsthorne?' to which he replied, 'No, Hester, I don't know him but we have quite a lot in common.' Having been brought up to think of my father as at best a boulevardier and at worst a bounder I was taken aback to find myself talking to someone who was so obviously neither. He must have asked me at some point what I was doing and when I replied, 'Nothing' he was very sympathetic since that was what in peacetime he had always done himself. In any case, to be helpful, he must have mentioned meeting me to his younger brother Gerry, a senior figure in Panmure Gordon, the distinguished stockbroking firm of which my Koch grandfather had been chairman. Gerry, whom I had never met, kindly asked me to lunch, once again at White's which was where Captain Fitzwilliam had offered me the job in Phantom. It seemed a good omen and Gerry did indeed start sounding me out about working in the City where his contacts were unrivalled. It was a tempting idea. Gerry was an enormously popular social figure with a house on the Ditchley estate and a famous mistress, Laura Dudley, to whom he left his money, a good example of coals to Newcastle. Without the slightest difficulty he could have launched me into just those circles in the City where life is at its sweetest and most agreeable. In a way, given the Koch de Gooreynd background and the Montagu Norman connection, that was where I naturally fitted. So why did I reject the offer of help out of hand, almost rudely as if it were a bit of an insult? It certainly wasn't because I wanted to be a journalist or anything else, since at that time I had no such clear ambitions. Nor was it because I did not need to earn money; still less because I looked down on earning it. It was, I fear, something more frivolous than that: a feeling that a job in the City did not quite accord with the dandyish, devil-may-care reputation that I was beginning to cultivate. To be truthful I think I was rather tempted by the idea of a good job in the City but the thought of being able to tell my Bohemian friends that I had just turned one down was even more tempting. This was the first time, but not by any means the last, that I have caught myself doing and saying something that I did not particularly want to say or do simply for effect; for the pleasure of living up to an image of myself that pleased my vanity more than it met with my true feelings or wishes.

When I went home to Thorpe Lodge that evening and told my mother and stepfather what I had done, they were both much impressed, as I knew they would be. In temperament Montagu Norman was not really a City man at all, any more than he was in appearance. By then he had pretty well retired from being Governor, on grounds of poor health, and was increasingly giving vent to his true loves – art, music and poetry, and to his preferred style of life – informal and unconventional. For the first time the great music room of Thorpe Lodge was used for concerts, notably by my mother's friend, Kathleen Ferrier, and instead of dressing up for these occasions my stepfather would sometimes come down in slippers without socks on. Nor were his friends of the expected type. Sir John Reith, the former BBC Director-General, was one, as was the highly idiosyncratic banker/politician Lord Kennett, friend of T. E. Lawrence and husband of Kathleen Scott, the sculptress whose first husband had been Captain Scott of the Antarctic. Kennett came to dinner one evening when the new Labour government was in the midst of nationalising the Bank of England and I remember how passionately convinced both he and Norman were that party politicians could not be trusted to act responsibly as custodians of the currency. It was, both men agreed, the end of responsible economic management. Nor did they believe that Conservative governments would be less tempted to be irresponsible than Labour governments. So long as Churchill, whom they both loathed, was leader of the Conservatives, there would be no hope from that quarter. I remember being shocked by their distrust for Churchill whom they talked about far more censoriously than they talked about Mr Attlee. What they distrusted, of course, was his flamboyant character and his unprincipled friends and cronies – Beaverbrook, Brendan Bracken and even Harold Macmillan. Mr Attlee was at least respectable, and on balance a sober socialist was regarded as less of an economic menace than an erratic Conservative. One of my stepfather's reiterated themes of this period was the need for European Central Bankers to get together to impose responsible monetary control. In the political climate of those post-war years such talk, had it not been quixotically unrealistic, would have sounded sinisterly undemocratic. Today, of course, nearly half a century later it is the conventional wisdom even more among Labour leaders than among Tories.

Such a relationship as I had with my stepfather only really began at this period after I had told him of my turning down of the City offer in White's, a gesture which seemed somehow to convince him that I was an *homme sérieux*. To some extent I think this was because my decision pleased my mother so much. Her dread was that I might become a 'playboy', and although rejecting the City fleshpots was not enough to demonstrate a determination to make my mark in the world, it was unquestionably a move in the right direction. Henceforth they both took my career seriously and did everything possible to help.

Shortly thereafter Mr Martin, chairman of the Argus Newspapers in South Africa, came to stay and was prevailed upon to offer me a job. Precisely what the job would have entailed was never defined. Journalism would come into it, but more as a cover for doing other things than for its own sake. Smuts, a great friend of Norman – my mother and stepfather had just come back from staying with him at Groteschur in the Cape – was still Prime Minister and the idea seemed to be that he would somehow take me under his wing, rather in the same manner as Lord Milner after the Boer War had taken other young Englishmen under his wing in his famous kindergarten. My interest was very much aroused. It seemed a marvellous way of getting a foot into the door leading to the corridors of power. A career in journalism, as that is understood today, was not being discussed at all. What my stepfather had in mind by journalism was politics and government by another name, a different – not even a back door – entrance into the world of the establishment. Chatham House was another such door; so in a way was a certain kind of merchant banking. Everything seemed to be falling into place. This was indeed very much the life that I had dreamt of. Not for a moment did I think of quality journalism as something opposed to government or adversarial. Its relationship was more akin to what Phantom's had been to the regular army: a kind of annexe where the same purposes were pursued by people too unconventional or original to fit into regular moulds. Why on earth should any idealistic young man want to be adversarial if that meant throwing in one's lot – as in those days it did – with such obvious scum as Lords Rothermere and Beaverbrook or a 'hairy-heeled' – favourite adjective of my mother – social climber like Lord Kemsley.

Shortly before setting out for South Africa, however, I received a message to say the plan was off. The Argus company's journalistic trade union had objected to my appointment on the grounds that any available vacant job should be filled by returning South African veterans. Once involved in my future, however, my stepfather did not give up. Next to be approached on my behalf was Geoffrey Crowther, editor of *The Economist*, who, unable to do anything himself, passed me on to Donald Tyerman, deputy editor of *The Times*, who invited me to call on him in Printing House Square. As it happened I had already been to Printing House Square once before and had liked the feel of the place. It was either just before or early in the war when Geoffrey Dawson was editor and I had delivered a letter to him from Mrs Holland Martin, matriarch of another famous banking family, at whose country house, Overbury, my mother and I had been staying for the weekend. Just why the letter was so important I cannot remember. But it had to reach the editor by Monday lunchtime. Hence my value as a messenger boy. But I was not treated by Geoffrey Dawson as a messenger boy. He came out into his anteroom, where an open coal fire burnt, to thank me and shake me by the hand. In such ways were the bonds of establishment loyalty forged. Encouraging as Donald Tyerman was he also had no vacancy but strongly advised me to try to get some provincial experience. 'Come back to me when you have done two years on a provincial paper,' he said, 'and I'll see what I can do.' Not only did Tyerman say this but he followed it up with a letter of confirmation and a letter of introduction to Sir William Robieson, editor of the *Glasgow Herald*, who, when next in London, invited me to coffee at 11.00 a.m. at the Waldorf Hotel in the Strand.

Every detail of that interview is embedded in my memory. At no other time in my life have I ever so completely got hold of the wrong end of the stick. As I understood it Sir William was offering me the deputy editorship of his paper. This quite took my breath away. There was I without any journalistic experience or even ambition being offered this lofty position on a plate. True, the salary mentioned was pretty measly, only £6 a week. But one couldn't have everything – a top job and a high salary. Needles to say, I accepted with alacrity and promised to come north without delay.

In the event the post turned out to be sub-editor, not deputy editor, and an apprentice sub-editor at that, the lowest of the low. In keeping with my imagined status – but not my actual salary – I had booked myself in at the Central Hotel, Glasgow's grandest, which was only a stone's throw from the *Herald* office in Buchanan Street, where I presented myself at the appointed time, 6.00 p.m. on Monday. Finding the main door on Buchanan Street shut I went round to the back of the building where there was a squalid entrance guarded by a very surly porter sitting behind the glass panel. 'I am the new deputy editor, could you please show me to my office,' I said politely, only to receive a response which, although incomprehensible, so thick was the accent, did not sound in the least friendly or welcoming, let alone respectful. When eventually I found the sub-editor's room the full extent of my misunderstanding was immediately apparent. My job, as was swiftly made clear, was to make the tea for the other sub-editors. After about three months of doing nothing much more than this, I was put in charge of sub-editing the *Radio Times* which meant marking up the hours of the programme for the printer; the livestock prices and then, after about six months, the most humdrum news stories – fires, burglaries and so on. At first I thought there must be some mistake and that at any moment Sir William Robieson would summon me to higher things. But months and then two years went by and the summons never came. The great man would occasionally wish me a good morning, but that was all. Of writing opportunities there were none; not even really of rewriting since none of the big stories ever came my way or not until the very end of the two years. What I did not know at the time, and only learned later, was that I was a guinea-pig being used in an experiment.

After the war the Newspaper Proprietors' Association had decided the time had come to try to get more university graduates into journalism and had persuaded the *Glasgow Herald* to be the laboratory for the experiment. Naturally enough, the *Herald* journalists were not at all keen to see a lot of English graduates collaring all the good jobs and had stipulated that the apprentices, of which I was the first, should start on the very bottom rung of the ladder and stay there as long as possible, in the hope, presumably, that they would soon get fed up and push off. Years later, when an editor myself, I would tell job applicants that my determination not to give up and push off was a measure of how much I wanted to be a journalist and that if they were equally serious they would also be as willing to do a long stint in the provinces as I had been. This sounded good but was almost the opposite of the truth. The kind of work which I was given in the *Glasgow Herald* subs' room was of very little use to me in my subsequent career and if I had really been as keen a journalist as I later claimed to have been I would never had put up with learning so little for so long. In any case writing journalism is something you can't learn. You either have the knack or you don't. No, I stayed in Glasgow initially out of apathy induced by shock – the shock of discovering just how grossly I had overestimated my own importance – and then because my new life, so completely unlike anything I had experienced before, began to exert a certain almost masochistic fascination. Previously I had always been part of a group or crowd – boarding school, residential Oxbridge college, army mess – and now for the first time I was pretty well entirely on my own. But there were compensations – a complete absence of any peer group to conform to, or to put on an act for. For what is the point of putting on an act if there is no audience likely to be in the least responsive, still less appreciative. At work there were my fellow subs. But, to begin with, that was an exclusively working relationship. They never asked me to their homes or out to a meal. We ate black pudding and chips in the canteen together. But that was as far as socialising went. In time introductions from my mother began to bear fruit. But not for many months. This was my first and, to date, last experience of life without a club (or even a pub), without, that is, some warm patch of human solidarity in which to take refuge from self-doubt and depression, and it pleased me to find this deprivation surprisingly bearable, rather as it had pleased me, back in Woodhall Spa with the Ox and Bucks, to find that I could outlast my platoon on route marches.

After the first month I moved into a bedsit in Kew Terrace, near the university. From there I would travel at about 6.00 p.m. to the office by tram

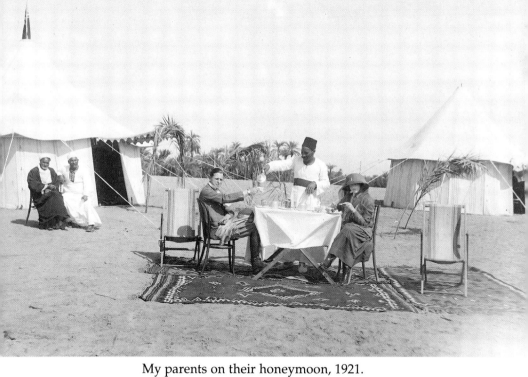

My parents on their honeymoon, 1921.

My mother, Priscilla Worsthorne, during the LCC election, which she won, being elected to represent North Hammersmith.

My father, Alexander Koch de Gooreynd, in the Irish Guards, 1918.

Left: My Koch de Gooreynd grandmother, Granny Gran, by Sargent.

Below left: My maternal grandfather, Major Robert Reytiens, ADC to the King of the Belgians.

Below right: My great aunt May (Lady FitzAlan).

Four generations: maternal great grandfather (Earl of Abingdon), grandmother, mother and my brother Simon.

Below left: James Burton, on duty at Lala Panzi, my grandmother's house in South Africa.
Below right: My step-father, Montagu Norman, and my mother on their way to Buckingham Palace in 1933.

As co-pilot to my brother Simon in the early 1930s.

With my brother Simon on holiday in Angmering.

Aged five and steering Uncle Wyndha[...] Portal's yacht.

While a boy at Stowe, drawing by James Bailey.

As Lieutenant in Ox and Bucks, 1944.

My brother Simon in the 60th Rifles, 1943.

Undergraduate again, outside the Peterhouse chapel, Cambridge, shortly after demobilisation, 1946.

Leader writer for *The Times*, 1953.

Press visit to Poland, 1960. Right to left: Richard Scott (*Guardian*), Polish journalist Krzy Ystof Klinger, who later became a Solidarity hero, Neal Ascherson (*Observer*), unidentified Polish official, and PW, all recovering from the shock of visiting Auschwitz. It was on this occasion that I am alleged to have said that I had not been so glad to see the back of anywhere since leaving public school – a flip remark that Neal Ascherson has never allowed me to forget.

and return by tram at about 2.00 a.m. along with other night workers, mostly prostitutes of an ugliness that excited more pity than lust. Clanging down Sauchiehall Street in the small hours on Saturday morning was a truly horrendous experience. The drunks, who had been lying moribund in the gutters since closing time, were by then just about coming to life again, in a foul mood and sparring for a fight. Finding a young, pink-faced Englishman sitting on the top of the tram was a sight for their sore eyes and instead of picking up the prostitutes they would pick a quarrel with me. On more than one occasion the tram had to be stopped and the police called – an eventuality I dreaded almost more than anything else because being questioned by a resentfully sober Glasgow policeman at this grim hour was scarcely less menacing than being threatened by a Glasgow drunk. In no time at all they would be making common cause, the one no less infuriated by being unable to understand me, or me them, than the other. It has to be said, however, that these misadventures came in very handy since they greatly amused my fellow subs when recounted over the black pudding at supper in the canteen; more than amused, almost endeared. Instead of being resented as a privileged English high-flyer I was soon taken pity on as a persecuted species in need of protection. Mr Anderson (Andy), the chief sub, a dear and good man, was particularly concerned and even deputed someone to accompany me home.

Eventually I found a way of avoiding trouble, at least in winter. I would wear my British Warm, a relic of army days. Initially I had refrained from doing so for fear that this mark of having held a commission would brand me as belonging to the officer class, not, in theory, the best way to avoid trouble on the top of a tram that also passed through the Gorbals. In practice, however, it did seem to do the trick. Most of the drunks had served in the armed forces and a British army overcoat served as at least some point of human contact. Instead of being abused as a class enemy and a f... ing Sassenach to boot, one was almost accepted as a former comrade-in-arms. It was quite extraordinary how quickly these Red revolutionaries could be deflected from drunken singing of the 'Internationale' by the opportunity to swap regimental reminiscences. Some of them I used to see quite regularly on the tram and got to know a bit. Everything about England they loathed, except for the opportunity it gave them from time to time to fight in a good war. As for the English king, they would like to cut off his head, until, that is, war came, when they would happily die on his behalf.

By day there was nothing to do but read, either in my bedsit or in the superb public library, devouring all the books that I ought to have read at Cambridge but hadn't. It was in the Glasgow Public Library that I came across the *Cambridge Journal* which Michael Oakeshott had just revived, with Desmond Williams – one of the anti-Lockyer resisters – as his deputy editor. It caught my eye on the periodical stand because of Michael's name on the cover. But once tempted to pick up the first number I soon became an addict and would eagerly await each new issue, one of which, in 1947, contained his famous essay, 'Rationalism in Politics'. No other piece of political writing has influenced me more. I read it over and over again, returning to the library day after day to do so. Much as I would like to be able to do justice to the article's subtle argument and style, that would be beyond my power. All I can do is describe its impact on me. It came as a most tremendous relief. Previously I had felt chary of politics because the subject seemed to require one to take sides between different doctrines, schools of thought, ideologies – Marxism, Utilitarianism, Idealism, Corporatism, Keynesianism and, in the aftermath of his controversial *The Road to Serfdom*, Hayekism, all of which seemed almost equally incomprehensible, a great swirling sea of conflicting currents into which I was unwilling to plunge. Rubbish, said Oakeshott. Listen instead to ancestral voices. Never believe in political abstraction. Grand designs, blueprints for the future, radical transformations, programmes based on social science or, worse, social engineering would never work out in practice. When it comes to finding the right answers in politics, he advised, one old-timer was worth a hundred whizz-kids. Then came the bit that reassured me most. According to Oakeshott, only the half-educated felt the need for ideologies or political doctrines, rather as only the stupid depended on a crib. Properly educated people had the good sense to allow habit, custom, hunch, or, in a word, tradition to guide them in the right political direction.

By properly educated Oakeshott meant people whose backgrounds had initiated them into the traditions and achievements of their civilisation, for whom the past meant more than an encumbrance, and most specifically not people whose only political knowledge came from mugging up on theories. Ideally one should have grown up in a political family and learnt the arts of government by watching masters at work, in much the same way as any other good apprentice craftsman learns his trade. Naturally this was music to my ears. Not only was history my favourite subject but much of my youth had been spent among people soaked in the traditions of our public life, notably Montagu Norman whose passionate distrust of theory – particularly Keynesian theory – was notorious. Far from my own inability to master complex theories being any longer a liability, ruling me out from an understanding of politics, it was, according to Oakeshott, an asset, almost the ideal qualification. No wonder I took to Oakeshott like a duck to water, and all the more so as his language, almost alone among contemporary political philosophers, was beautifully clear and wholly free of jargon.

In later years Oakeshott's indictment of what he called 'the Rationalist approach to politics' has, in my view, been more than vindicated by events.

Almost all forms of planning on a grand scale have proved disastrous. Utopian hopes about the United Nations were never fulfilled. Moral and sexual 'reforms', which seemed so marvellously reasonable to their supporters, now seem a good deal less so to their victims. Instead of the Rationalist belief that there are solutions to every problem leading to fewer problems, it has simply created lots of 'grievous' new problems – always described as crises – which people expect to be solved overnight.

Rereading that famous essay today it is quite incredible how much of it has proved sadly prophetic. The proof of its prescience, however, lay in the future. What appealed to me at the time was that it answered my own intellectual needs so amazingly well. Inadequate people respond to Marxism so warmly because, lacking any intellectual self-confidence of their own, they find it an all-purpose guide which tells them what to think on every occasion. Shameful as it is to have to admit it, I fear that something not wholly dissimilar drew me to Oakeshottism, the only difference being that while their intellectual weaknesses induced a taste for certainties, mine induced a taste for uncertainties. Being useless at science and baffled by technology the politics of hunch suited me down to the ground.

'Rationalism in Politics' was only one of a whole series of Oakeshott's articles that appeared in the *Cambridge Journal* in 1947, all of which I devoured. In some ways Burke had been saying the same thing. But Burke was illustrious and in any case writing about the French Revolution. Oakeshott, by comparison, was writing about the here and now, and I liked to feel that I had discovered him for myself. I cannot exaggerate the excitement his work engendered. It was not wholly dissimilar to the excitement Belloc and Chesterton had engendered at Stowe. Just as they had equipped me with a dismissive attitude towards Protestantism, so Oakeshott had taught me how to feel superior, not only to socialism, or even to what passed for Conservatism at that period, but, in effect, to the modern world. Almost accidentally I had found a focus for my future reading and eventually for my future writing. It was, as I say, an extraordinary relief.

After months of solid reading, with no social life to distract, my mother's social contacts did begin to bear fruit. One such caused me some embarrassment. It was for the wedding of the daughter of the Duke of Montrose on the Isle of Arran and my name was included in the Press Association's list of guests which duly arrived on Andy's desk. This was not helpful and it took a lot of late-night misadventures to undo the damage. Henceforth whenever a story came in about the aristocracy – i.e. pretty well every night – Andy would shout to whoever was subbing it, 'Watch out, they may be friends of Perry.' Many months later, after my social life had begun to perk up, high-life misadventures began to replace low-life ones as my passport to canteen popularity. There were not nearly as many of either variety as I liked to pretend but one in particular may just bear recalling.

In some connection or other I made the acquaintance of General Telfer-Smollett, a former GOC Scottish Command, and was invited to stay for the weekend in his ancient castle on the banks of Loch Lomond. The invitation, he explained, was not entirely altruistic. Being a widower he needed help with a difficult guest, none other than his old regimental friend, now Field Marshal Earl Wavell. There would only be the three of us since the field marshal hated house parties, did not suffer fools gladly and needed careful handling. My function, it was made clear, was to make myself helpful to the great man, to fill the gap in his life created by the absence of all the customary ADCs.

Arriving at the castle at about 6.00 p.m. on a blustery Saturday night I was led down miles of corridor to a room in a turret. At that time the castle had no electric light and the few gaslights on the walls did not make it easy to see where one was going. On the way to my room, long before the staircase to my particular turret – there were lots of others – a bathroom was pointed out. Returning there after unpacking, I found that the old-fashioned geyser only produced a very slow trickle of hot water and rather than wait twenty minutes or so for the bath to fill I went back to my bedroom in the turret. This was a mistake since on the return journey the gas lamp at the foot of the turret, the source of such dim light as there was, guttered out, plunging the whole long corridor into Stygian blackness. Thrown into confusion I must have groped in the wrong direction. In any case I lost my way. Five minutes, ten minutes went by and although I tried to follow the faint sound of water running in the distance, it never got any louder or nearer. Then it stopped altogether and I knew that what I had feared must have happened. The bath had overflowed. As ill luck would have it, the field marshal's bedroom was underneath this bathroom and slow as the trickle of water entering the great tub had been, its exit was evidently very much faster – positively flood-like. For in no time at all, a furious field marshal, oil lamp in hand, came charging down the corridor, demanding to know what the hell was going on. It was no good my trying to explain: 'Sorry, sir, I lost the way in the dark.' A field marshal's imagination cannot be expected to encompass behaviour plumbing such depths of incompetence, particularly when proffered by a young stranger in a dressing-gown, carrying a sponge bag and half blinded by having an oil lamp suddenly thrust into his face.

If there had been lots of other guests I could have got lost in the crowd. But, as I say, there were only the three of us. Never a talkative man, Wavell used his pre-dinner soaking as an excuse to dry up entirely at the meal itself. Our delightful and funny host, old General Telfer-Smollett did his best, telling anecdotes, reminiscing, as old regimental comrades are meant to do, anything to make the party go. But to no avail. Those few expletives upstairs had exhausted the field marshal's never very ample flow of eloquence. Left to myself I would have responded to our host's conversational sallies. But how could I react or laugh if the guest of honour chose not to do so? After dinner there was no let-up in his taciturnity. Should I make my excuses and go up to bed? Obviously I thought of doing that. But it somehow seemed *lèse-majesté* for a young man to retire in advance of a former Viceroy of India.

Although at the time I felt the weekend – which ended abruptly the following morning – could not have been more embarrassing I am now not so sure. For when the Chips Channon diaries were published a very much more relaxed picture of Wavell came to light and an even more relaxed one would have come to light if the diaries had been published in full. For on one occasion, apparently, when the great soldier was staying with Channon in Belgrave Square, he even relaxed to the point of pirouetting down the staircase in a ballerina's tutu. Heaven forbid! Compared to that, my Scottish castle encounter was not embarrassing at all.

Almost aggressively unamused by these kinds of stories was Alastair Hetherington, another graduate of about my age, who joined the subs' room six months or so after me. He, however, had previous journalistic experience, having ended his days in the army of occupation helping to edit a German newspaper. He also had the considerable advantage of being Scottish, with a father, Sir Hector Hetherington, who was Vice-Chancellor of Glasgow University. As his first task he was instructed by Andy 'to lick Worsthorne into shape', a task which he undertook with more seriousness than I thought strictly necessary, or at any rate desirable. The relationship got off to a bad start when he caught me using the hot water tap in the subs' washroom to make our communal tea. Initially I had done this one evening when the electric kettle packed up and then, because nobody ever complained, got into the bad habit. In any case the water from the tap was near enough to boiling and, as I explained to Alastair, the palates involved, hardened by other liquids, were in no state to notice the difference. 'Theirs may be, but mine is not,' replied Alastair primly. Shortly thereafter I was to blot my copybook even more seriously. As part of the licking into shape process Alastair used me to do various odd jobs, one of which was to check the ages of all the new peers and knights in some new honours list which Andy had given him to sub for the front page. I knew there was something wrong when I came in the following evening and saw Alastair's usually pink face flushed dark red. 'I only asked you to do one thing last night and you made a mess of it. You got the ages all wrong and the editor is furious.' What I had done was to look up all the years of birth in *Who's Who* without noticing the natal month – an omission that in some cases had resulted in getting the age a year out. As it happened, I had made them all a year too young and on discovering this, in an effort to alleviate the gloom, I hazarded a guess that there would be no complaints, certainly not from the two new dames. Alastair was not amused. 'If you take your duties as frivolously as that,' he said, 'you won't go far in journalism.' Alastair, of course, went on to become one of the youngest and most successful editors of the *Manchester Guardian*, responsible for moving the paper to London, and after that, head of the BBC in Scotland where our paths once again crossed in Glasgow. By this time, about thirty-five years later, I too had become an editor and Alastair, equally surprisingly, had developed into a bon viveur. In fact he invited me to dinner in a luxury hotel on a hill overlooking the Clyde where he proved the most generous and convivial of hosts, matching his guest's intake glass for glass.

Over the brandy, however, I got the feeling that I had been in the house before and in rather less jolly circumstances. Had it not once been the home, I asked, of Sir William Lithgow, the most hated shipbuilder on the Clyde? Indeed it had, and pulling aside the curtains we looked down on his old shipyards, now lying idle and disused. Dare I remind Alastair of a story, I wondered. Last time he had heard it in the *Glasgow Herald* canteen he had not been at all amused. Would perhaps the new reformed, or de-reformed Alastair enjoy it more?

Because Sir William had received assistance from the Bank of England in the 1930s he had invited me to stay as a very small token of his gratitude to my stepfather who was Governor at the time. Andy and the other subs were dead against my accepting. The man was a monster, a grinder of the faces of the poor. Worse, he was a teetotaller. I would have a terrible time, not a dram from morning to night. At the very least I must take a bottle of malt to fortify myself in my room, boss's orders. So obedient was I in this instance that when at dinner on the appointed night the octogenarian patriarch ended a long grace with the words, 'for what we are about to receive may the Lord make us truly grateful', above the 'Amen' from the other members of the family gathered around the table could be heard a resoundingly inappropriate belch, the source of which became immediately clear when the young English guest keeled over into the far from welcoming arms of Lady Lithgow. That, however, was not the point of the story. The point of the story was how well Sir William rose to the occasion. Instead of getting angry he made what in the circumstances, and coming from him, was a joke. 'It's not the Lord our young friend should be thanking for what he is about to receive but the devil for what he had so obviously already received in over-abundance.'

Next day all was forgiven and Sir William took me down to the yards which were already in trouble. Another remark of his sticks in my memory and this one I did not recount to Andy at the time for fear of giving him a heart attack. 'The Clyde has no future. The men are no longer interested in satisfying the customer. They are only interested in serving themselves.' Nor did I recount it to Alastair over our dinner thirty-five years later. Having abandoned priggery and Puritanism it was too much to hope that he had become reactionary as well.

Yet again I am conscious that these stories give a wrong impression of my Glasgow life, most of which was not in the least gregarious. As for a romantic dimension there was none unless Lady Lithgow's unwelcoming arms can be counted as such. For some reason shyness had resumed its sway. It took me months, for example, to summon up enough courage to invite the editor's redheaded secretary even to dinner, and this only after going through an almost nightly charade with a view to preparing her for this forwardness. The charade consisted of pretending that my fountain pen had run out of ink and asking her permission to refill it from the inkpot on her desk. Apart from a cursory nod of the enchanting head she gave me no other encouragement, and even a great number of cursory nods do not a green light make. Dinner at the Malmaison, Glasgow's grandest restaurant, went well enough but led nowhere. Instead of her being impressed by the Malmaison, I was made to understand that she thought it indecently above the station of a mere junior sub-editor to patronise such an expensive place which aroused in her breast more suspicion than warmth. Far from furthering the courtship the dinner set it back; indeed brought it to a halt, since the pen-filling charade, pretty transparent before, was now so patently so as to be embarrassing. It was her turn to ask me to her home which she never did. Again this may have had something to do with the Malmaison. Her first words over drinks before dinner had been that her father disapproved of the place. Why had I not anticipated this problem? With the benefit of hindsight the Malmaison, with its chic clientèle of Scottish grandees and their friends – even rich Glasgow businessmen did not use it in those pre-expense-account days – was so obviously unsuitable and therefore, of course, counter-productive. It was, however, the only Glasgow restaurant I knew, or wanted to know. If Colin had been around, he would have mocked me out of this ludicrous affectation, which made no sense either in terms of my income or my sub-editor status; pointed out that there were other less grand and expensive restaurants where one could have a much better time at half the price; restaurants with the added advantage of being places in which professional Glaswegians might feel at home.

Incorrigible in this respect, I committed the same mistake a little later, with potentially more serious consequences which were happily avoided through no new-found sensitivity on my part. I invited Oscar Hahn to lunch at the Malmaison. On paper he was much less obviously unsuited for the restaurant than the editor's Presbyterian secretary. He was the son of Lola and Rudo Hahn and nephew of Kurt, founder and headmaster of

Gordonstoun, a German Jewish family of great distinction and illustrious connections all over the world. Lola, born a Warburg, was a friend of my uncle Ronnie Norman who had urged me to look up Oscar, then working in Glasgow at Guest, Keen and Nettlefold, the famous steelmasters. What he had not told me was that Oscar, who was about my age, was working as a trainee engineer in the foundry, or that, as a result of polio in childhood, he was paralysed in both legs and only able to walk with the greatest difficulty. At the appointed hour he hobbled in tieless and in dungarees, appropriately dressed for the foundry but inappropriately for the Malmaison, and was duly barred entry. Not surprisingly this did not please him any more than did the thought of having laboriously to retrace his steps back to the street and on to another restaurant with most of his lunch hour already wasted. Neither then nor later a man to disguise his feelings he let me have it. 'What a bloody silly place to choose for lunch,' he muttered as we struggled up the restaurant stairs. Whether I counter-attacked by blaming him for coming out to lunch tieless and in dungarees I do not remember but it is certainly what I thought and indeed wrote to my Uncle Ronnie in a letter complaining about his ladyfriend's uncouth son. He must have shown her the letter since shortly thereafter she wrote in the most delightful terms, urging me to come to stay at their Scottish holiday house, Burnside, where she promised to make Oscar behave in a less curmudgeonly fashion. 'From what Ronnie tells me you are a friend from whose company our dear Oscar would benefit so much, as would we all.' Among her many gifts, Lola knew how to flatter, young and old alike, and this was only the first example of a skill which she went on practising, with unfailing success, to her dying day. I was quite won over.

One Saturday evening after work Oscar picked me up in his ramshackle car and we set off for a long night's drive to Burnside in the north of Scotland, overlooking the Moray Firth. To my relief and surprise he had arranged a superb dinner somewhere on the way, along with a back seat loaded with drink and sandwiches for further refreshment. No less of a surprise and relief was the agility he showed in mending a puncture, refusing to let me lend a hand in spite of his disability. By the time we reached Burnside both agreed that we had got each other completely wrong. He conceded that I was not the decadent dilettante he had written me off as and I conceded that my first impression of him as a boorish philistine was equally wide of the mark. Towards the end of his life I rather suspect that he reverted a bit to his original view of me just as I did a bit to mine about him. But that is a long way ahead in the story and there are at least forty years of close friendship to get through before that point is reached; forty years in which Lola acted as the 'governor', so to speak, keeping the sometimes stormy relationship on an even keel.

Why did she bother? Largely – at any rate to begin with – for Oscar's sake. Having succeeded, to an almost superhuman degree, in helping him to triumph over his physical disabilities, she was now determined to help him broaden his circle of friends who were then mostly scientists or other apprentice engineers. Educated at his uncle's school Gordonstoun – only a mile or two away from Burnside – where he had shared a room with Prince Philip, Oscar was a bit of a rough diamond very much in need of polishing and my role was to provide the polish. This sounds as if Lola was a scheming woman which was not the case at all. She simply loved her son and realised, being as intelligent as she was beautiful, that in England, unlike in her native Germany, being an engineer might cut him off from the more rewarding sides of their adopted country's social and cultural life. In Hamburg and Berlin the steelmaster Hahns or the banker Warburgs were at the heart of the artistic as well as the business and financial worlds. For Oscar to come into the same kind of inheritance here something more would be needed than a Gordonstoun education or even friendship with Prince Philip, and Ronnie Norman's journalist nephew must have seemed, not altogether wrongly, a promising catalyst to bring about this kind of transformation. In any case, for whatever reason, Lola treated me like a member of the family from the word go. Never shall I forget the warmth of her greeting when Oscar and I, in the highest of spirits – having stopped for refreshments all through the summer night – arrived at Burnside in time for breakfast that first Sunday morning. Burnside was just an ordinary square stone Scottish house, originally a manse, but the setting, over-looking the Moray Firth, was superb and the hostess took after the setting. Not only was the breakfast table laden with all the traditional Scottish and English dishes but many of the German ones too and also great bowls of apple purée as Kurt was trying out some new fruit diet. Seated around it, in addition to lots of Hahns and Warburgs, were also my Uncle Ronnie and Lola's other famous elderly admirer of that time, General Sir Neil Malcolm, a Gallipoli hero, and his Senior Wrangler son whom I was later in the day to find quietly masturbating over a glass of sherry in the library – a shocking enough discovery in any library but little short of earth-shaking in one where Kurt was wont to compose his famous school sermons.

On Lola's right there was a vacant chair which she insisted had been reserved for me. Not content with this signal honour she also protected me from having to join Oscar and his enthusiastically sporting father who were immediately setting off on some very long salmon fishing expedition on the Spey. How did she know that fishing bored me? She just did. She also knew that if she had not insisted on me spending the day with her I should never have dared say no to a day's fishing, thereby running the risk of branding myself almost as brazenly decadent as Willy Malcolm. Lola and I spent the day idling in the garden – another profoundly un-Hahnish thing to do. A passionate Zionist and one-time confidante of Dr Weizmann, Israel's first President, Lola wanted to discuss a recent *Glasgow Herald* leader about Palestine, then very much in the news. She had thought it 'very fine' and detected my hand – quite wrongly, of course, since, as I have said, throughout my two years on that paper I never contributed a single word. We must also have discussed education and in particular Gordonstoun's cult of physical fitness, about which I had strong views.

At dinner too, she seated me on her right, with Kurt on her left – an unheard-of honour for a young man. Food was always plain at Burnside. But for some reason even the plain-living make an exception when it comes to the luxury of fresh fish, even fresh shellfish, and on this occasion we all had not a half but a whole lobster. Having had little previous experience of coping with lobster, I was giving my full attention to cracking a claw when I heard Lola suddenly say, 'Oh Kurt, Perry' – and only she knew how to roll the two Rs so as to make the abbreviation sound important – 'has been talking most interestingly about education. He seems to think our Gordonstoun system leaves something to be desired.' At Burnside Kurt was God and not only at Burnside. His views on education were world-famous. Having had his German school, Salem, closed down by Hitler who then drove him out of Germany, he was a bit of a hero as well as a saintly guru. Lola admired her brother-in-law little short of idolatry; was high priestess at his altar and high priestesses do not usually give places of honour to heretics, still less positively encourage them to air their heresy. Even Oscar's shoulders, grown massive by reason of the double workload they had to carry, began to quake in horrified expectation about what his new friend might be about to say.

Surprisingly enough I was not nearly as frightened as I should have been. Such was Lola's gift of inspiring confidence that it never crossed my mind that she would have set me a challenge which I could not meet. If she thought my views on education were worth telling Kurt, then who was I to suppose otherwise? Fear of letting her down worried me much more than fear of provoking Kurt. As it happened, I don't think I did either. The gist of my spiel I remember well because in later years Kurt gave me many other opportunities to go over the same ground.

Of course education was about instilling moral and physical courage, I conceded from the start. No question at all about that. But to suppose that boys acquired these virtues through life-saving exercises on the Moray Firth or mountain rescue operations, as was the Gordonstoun assumption, was grossly to underestimate the scale of the problem. Almost anybody, even without benefit of a good education, would rise to these life-and-death challenges because they were so clear-cut and therefore so easy. Unfortunately, I went on, real-life demands for physical and moral courage were seldom as clear-cut as that. The Nazi experience was a bad guide.

That was not the form most moral challenges took. In normal life they were almost always in forms where it was by no means obvious what a man ought to do; and where it was all too easy to find seductively good reasons for justifying either course. In no field did this apply more than in the field of public affairs where almost all choices were between two evils, and the art consisted of choosing the lesser of two evils. For the mastery of that art, I went on, so indispensable for a ruling class, a different kind of education was needed; one that prepared a boy for the moral murkiness, ambiguities and ironies of life. It was not enough for a public school to set out to make a boy morally and physically brave. That might even be the easy part. The difficult part was to teach him not to oversimplify, not to believe that he had the answers, and above all not to believe that he could always tell the truth because so often there was no truth to tell. If only life was a choice between good and evil. Then it would be child's play, and a Gordonstoun education might well suffice. But in England most choices were not between good and evil and Kurt Hahn's educational methods, however desirable they might have been for German youth before the war, were quite unsuitable for British youth today.

It was an extraordinary attack to launch. The whole table was quite stunned and waited nervously for Kurt to react. Obviously they feared the worst. But I sensed that Kurt would be more pleased than angry, or at any rate more amused than angry. As far as I can recall he made a joke about my thinking that all Gordonstoun boys were as thick as Oscar or something like that. But immediately afterwards he took me aside and spent the rest of the evening talking tête-à-tête in a corner. Some people remember when they first discover a taste for gambling or for taking high fences out hunting or skiing dangerously, or first discover that they have a special gift for surviving these dangerous sports. In my case, that evening was when I discovered the kicks to be got from going as near to the conversational precipice as damn it, without falling over.

Not everyone has that skill, as became sadly clear not all that much later at another Burnside weekend, this time when Prince Philip was the guest of honour. It was shortly after he had taken up with Princess Elizabeth and Lola had invited me, and another friend of Oscar's, Gabriele Ulstein, to make up the weekend party. Highly intelligent, and from a German Jewish family no less distinguished than the Hahns or the Warburgs, Gabrielle should have fitted in perfectly. What Lola did not know, however, was that Gabrielle had fallen in love with Noël Annan, Fellow and later Provost of King's College Cambridge, whom she was shortly to marry and, as lovers do, had herself adopted some of the King's high Bloomsbury manner. Not only did she come down to dinner in clothes more fitted for Lady Ottoline's Garsington than for the Scottish Highlands, but she also expressed similarly unconventional opinions. In essence they weren't all that different

97

from my opinions but just as I had been certain that I was going to get away with them, I was equally certain that she wasn't. Next morning at breakfast one of the Hahns announced that there was a spare sleeper berth available that evening and did anyone want it? With one voice they all shouted, 'Gabriele', who was allowed no further say in the matter. 'There but for the grace of God go I,' was my somewhat unchivalrous reaction. Grace of God was plainly over-egging the pudding but equally clearly I did have some gift, not shared by everyone, which subbing on the *Glasgow Herald* gave me no opportunities to exercise. So perhaps the time had come to move on and even up.

Donald Tyerman, it may be remembered, had advised me to do two years on a non-Fleet Street paper and it occurred to me that if I were to reapply the very day on which these two years were up, he might be jolted into feeling some moral obligation to honour his side of the bargain or, as I perhaps shrewdly, if presumptuously, chose to call it, 'gentleman's agreement'. This I did, on the precise day, with much emphasis on my having fulfilled all the conditions laid down by him. The stratagem worked. He immediately wrote back and offered me a foreign sub-editing job on *The Times*. Being by then a bit more clued up about journalism I knew that this was a much better offer than it sounded on paper since the foreign subs' room on *The Times* was a jumping-off ground for future foreign correspondents. More promising still it was the place where Graham Greene had written his first successful novel, *Stamboul Train*, encouraging all subsequent occupants of his chair to see themselves as budding writers of genius. In a handwritten postscript to his letter offering me this job, Tyermen had scribbled: 'You have outwitted me this once but please don't make a habit of it. I won't.' Probably this tiny personal touch took ten seconds to compose. It made me ever after his devoted and grateful admirer.

No sooner did I decide to go south than several of my London friends started to follow in my footsteps up to Glasgow. I like to think I set a fashion. Colin Welch was even invited to replace me on the *Glasgow Herald*, which seemed to suggest that the experiment, of which I had been the guinea-pig, was judged reasonably successful. Roger Lubbock, another close Cambridge friend, also arrived in Glasgow at the same time on a Kemsley training scheme as did John Herbert, son of A. P. Herbert, on something similar. They were lucky. Instead of having to make their own circle of friends they were able to inherit one already made by me. Three families in particular must be mentioned because their kindness, first to me, and then to this second wave, was far, far beyond the call of social duty – John and Jean Baird-Smith, Hervey and Margaret Stuart-Black and last but not least the Colin Neil Mackays. Colin Welch actually met his wife Sybil in Glasgow at this time and got married and Roger also met his, the captivating Moyra Fraser, who was touring there as a leading dancer in the Royal Ballet before rising to ever greater heights as a star of stage and screen. Compared to mine, their Glasgow days were a piece of cake. Not that mine were all that awful. But living in a Glasgow bedsitter through two of the grimmest post-war years, working six days a week during the most unsocial hours among colleagues who, even when their suspicions were allayed, still took some time to get to know, on a job that offered absolutely nothing of interest to fill the boring gaps in what was, even at its best, a pretty lonely private life, all this, plus the greatest deprivation of all, a complete absence of family or intimates to complain to or consult, came nearer to what might deserve to be called a genuinely 'mettle testing' challenge than any other experience so far in my life; far nearer certainly than my shame-makingly cushy war.

8

A Chelsea Disaster

Having been away in Glasgow for two years, it was not easy to pick up the threads in London. Picking up the threads meant meeting girls and I did not know any. Those two years in Glasgow, as the reader will recall, were entirely celibate not by choice or even by necessity, but as the result of a new lack of self-confidence, very much at variance with my earlier amatory adventurousness. I say new lack of self-confidence. But it may not have been new. For the earlier amatory adventures, both in the army and at Oxford and Cambridge, had not really required much self-confidence. In none of the ones recounted earlier was I required to take the initiative or run any real risk of rebuff, and in most of them I had been greatly assisted by circumstances or by the presence of a friend, not so much egging me on as giving me vicarious courage. Obviously the circumstances of being a member of a liberating or conquering army made female friendship deceptively easy, as did being a young officer in uniform in wartime London. In Holland, too, there had been the extra boost of wanting to live up to Michael Oakeshott's immensely flattering idea of my romantic charms – another case of giving a dog a good name. At Oxford there had been my dear friend Borys who had made things easy by always assuring me that the object of my heart's desire – usually an older woman – was eager to respond. At Glasgow, however, I had been not only on my own, without a morale-boosting male supporter, but also without the adventitious advantage of a glamorous uniform or the power to dispense favours in the form of Spam and suchlike, as had been the case so markedly in Hamburg. Worse, my job as a junior subeditor on the *Glasgow Herald*, virtually a tea-boy, carried no status or perks such as might make me of interest to women; if anything rather the reverse. Once again, as at Grafton, I had found myself having to stand on my own two feet, without benefit of rank or class, and the going had proved threateningly hard.

So there I was back in London in a small furnished flat in Brompton

Square, for which I paid £6 a week, waiting rather hopelessly for something to happen. It is important to describe my frame of mind at this juncture, because without getting that right no sense can be made of the fateful events which were to follow. Sitting alone in my flat one summer evening, I suddenly heard my name called from the street below. Looking out I saw Adrian Earle, whom I had known at Oxford and not terribly liked, flanked by two attractive girls. Naturally I invited them all up and Adrian, on entering my tiny sitting room, immediately threw up his hands in horror. 'My dear Perry,' he shrieked, 'how on earth does a man of your quality find himself living in such poky quarters?' Then, turning to the girls, he gave an entirely fictitious description of my achievements ... coming man on *The Times*, war hero, and suchlike fantasies. 'What do you pay for this garret?' he asked, and on being told, fell into silent concentration. Then his face brightened. 'Tell you what, Perry, if I can find you a furnished house with servants which does not cost you much more than you are paying now, would you be interested?' Needless to say I did not bother to reply, assuming the question to be some kind of joke, and we all repaired to Adrian's small house in Ennismore Gardens Mews, just round the corner, where he was living with both girls, one of whom seemed to believe that I was all that Adrian had cracked me up to be – or at any rate behaved as if she believed it, which was quite enough to be going on with. Adrian's softening-up tactics had begun.

About a week later he rang to say that he had excellent news and could he come round at once to discuss my new housing arrangements which turned out to be an enormous mansion, 79 Elm Park Gardens, just off the Fulham Road. The house, he explained, belonged to the famous tank expert, Major-General Fuller who was prepared to let it very cheaply if the tenant was the kind of person who could be trusted to look after the precious furniture which included some truly valuable pieces – notably Thackeray's famous inlaid desk on which he had written *Vanity Fair*. On being told that the tenant might be myself, coming man on *The Times*, the general, or rather the general's wife, Mrs Fuller, had agreed to the let. What did I think? asked Adrian. 'Out of the question,' I replied. 'Even if the rent were very low I could not possibly afford it.'

'Don't be an idiot,' he retorted. 'You won't be on your own. I shall move in with you and the two girls as well. You will have the ground and first floors and I will have the second and third. We can let the attic and have a cook-housekeeper living in the basement. It's all arranged. All you have to do is sign the lease.'

Thus it was that within a month of leaving Glasgow I found myself sharing this enormous Edwardian mansion with a man who a few years hence would be sent to Wormwood Scrubs for extortion and blackmail. To begin with all seemed fine, at any rate on paper. A housekeeper, Mrs

Connolly, had been installed in the basement, albeit a mad one with a retarded son, and a tenant had been found for the attic, although she had not yet arrived. Nor could there be any possible complaint about my quarters which included a great panelled dining room and a red damask drawing room, all overlooking a beautiful garden. What with the rent from the attic, and Adrian's rent, my share in theory would indeed not be much more than the £6 I had been paying in Brompton Square. It all seemed too good to be true which, of course, it was. Entirely left out of account were rates, telephone, upkeep, cleaning, overheads and suchlike. Even if Adrian had continued to pay his share of the rent, and of the other outgoings, which he did not, the strain on my meagre finances would have proved crippling.

Right from the beginning I used to hear Adrian on the telephone referring to me in a grand voice as 'the landlord'. He would say things like 'I'll mention that to the landlord as soon as I can.' In my folly I used to take this as a mark of respect and draw satisfaction from it. Clearly Adrian knew who was boss, and there would be no question of my not being master in the house. When the lease was being drawn up the original plan had been to make us both co-equal tenants. 'No, no,' Adrian had demurred. 'Perry should be the sole tenant so that he can always feel free to kick me out if and when he wants.' Instead of smelling a rat I had felt reassured about Adrian's good faith. Clearly he had my interests at heart. Nor were my suspicions really aroused when buff envelopes addressed to me started to arrive with demands for all the obvious payments. In fact, seeing my name on such important documents made me feel grown up. My gullibility knew no bounds. I fear vanity came into it as well. My sub-editor friends from *The Times*, who were living in humble bedsits, would not have been nearly as impressed by the splendour of my quarters had I been co-tenant rather than landlord. My reputation went up by leaps and bounds. Something had to be done to re-establish my reputation for flamboyance – which the Glasgow interlude had dimmed – and all that red damask plus the presence of Adrian's girls were more than enough to do that. Fair is fair. However much harm Adrian did me in the end, he certainly reintegrated me into the London scene, more with a bang than a whimper.

Who was this extraordinary man? It is not an easy question to answer. Everything about him was mysterious; even his end. In about 1970, someone sent me a cutting from an Argentinian newspaper. It was in the death column and starkly said: 'Earle, Adrian, on such and such a date, in suspicious circumstances.' So far as one can gather, Adrian came from rich north-country banking stock, although his own parents were not themselves rich. The family is featured in *Burke's Peerage*, as is Adrian, born on 23 May 1922. After Winchester, Adrian went to Oxford, where I first met him just after the war. He was never an undergraduate, but somehow or other persuaded Worcester College to let him read for a PhD, without ever having taken a degree. Why he was never called up is a bit mysterious. Something to do with ill health, although he was six foot four and strong as an ox. His eyesight may have been the problem since he wore glasses. The subject of his thesis, which never got written, was Lionel Johnson, a minor nineteenth-century poet, who will earn a footnote in history as the man who introduced Oscar Wilde to Lord Alfred Douglas. Possibly Adrian chose Lionel Johnson as his PhD subject so as to be able to get in touch with Lord Alfred Douglas. Certainly that is what he did, and the two became close friends. Adrian used to invite the old monster to Oxford and exploit his notoriety to attract well-known literary figures to parties in his rooms, and to a dining club he formed. Harold Nicolson was a regular visitor, and became a great admirer of Adrian. Even Father D'Arcy came, as did Lord David Cecil, Elizabeth Bowen and many others.

Adrian had no money even then but could always get his hands on plenty of black-market booze, for which his friends were only too happy to pay. He had rooms in the most fashionable lodging house in Oxford, No 8 Oriel Street, next door to where Borys and I had lodged in 1943. What I remember about him was his social confidence. Few other contemporaries – unless they were called Cecil or Percy or Cavendish – would have dared to ask so many famous people to their parties. It was at one of these parties that he had offered me a cigarette from a very large silver case inscribed 'To dear Bosie from Oscar'. According to Adrian, Alfred Douglas had given it to him in return for literary services. Apparently Adrian would go round the country persuading booksellers to let him have copies of a biography of Wilde in which Lord Alfred had been libelled. When the booksellers demurred on the grounds that to sell the book was an offence, Adrian would plead that he was an indigent young scholar who needed it for research. Such was his charm that invariably the bookseller would succumb and bring up a copy from the basement where it had been hidden out of harm's way. Once out of the bookshop, Adrian would go straight to the nearest telephone box to inform Douglas of the name of the unfortunate bookseller who would soon receive a writ. It was always an open-and-shut case, and Douglas would receive his statutory £50 or so damages. Instead of being shocked by this squalid tale I remember being rather impressed. Obviously one would have preferred to have a contemporary who knew the high road to sophisticated literary circles, but better the low road than no access at all. And if famous figures like Father D'Arcy and Harold Nicolson gave Adrian their stamp of approval, who was I to try to be more discerning? Unquestionably, Adrian was what came to be known as a life-enhancer and in those grim and austere post-war times, that was really something. His girlfriend of that period, with whom he used to make love on the kitchen table, was the daughter of a lady-in-waiting to the Queen.

Today that may seem no great claim to fame. It probably happens all the time. But then it seemed the height of daring and sophistication. Even the rather dramatic end to that affair did Adrian's reputation with us no harm. When the girl in question refused to marry him, he threatened to send copies of their letters – including the bits in which she had waxed lyrical about the spring of the kitchen table – to her parents' friends, including the royal family. (Nowadays he would have threatened to sell them to the *Sun* or the *News of the World*, but this was still in the pre-Murdoch era.) Within no time an injunction arrived at Oriel Street, forbidding any such disclosures, along with a visit by four very tough young men from the Household Cavalry who came to collect the letters, if necessary by force. Adrian claimed to be highly amused. 'My dear, horsewhips were mentioned. Can you believe it? So very old-fashioned and common.'

Knowing Adrian, how did I come to share a London house with him? To enjoy him at Oxford was one thing. Everybody did it. Oxford and Cambridge were special; different. None of the moral rules applied. In tennis terms, Oxford was the knocking-up period of life. It did not matter how many services went into the net or whether slams were in or out. It was a self-contained world – or so we liked to think – where actions had no serious consequences. Countless contemporaries started to drink heavily at Oxford and Cambridge. They would pass out and be carried home in triumph as if they were fallen heroes on the field of battle. Forty years later one such died in a dosshouse of cirrhosis of the liver, and I was called to the mortuary to identify the body. Lying on the slab, his face had much the same expression as it used to have when we tucked him up in bed at Oxford, the only difference being that whereas then it had all seemed so funny, now it was so sad. Another friend at Cambridge used to collect whips which he would hang on the walls of his room. It seemed a great joke to have a friend who admired the Marquis de Sade – less of a joke when years later he was on trial for murder. Most of my contemporaries drew a clear line between university life and real life, and of those who did not, I was perhaps lucky to suffer no worse fate, bad as it was, than to find myself cohabiting in Elm Park Gardens with Adrian Earle.

The first intimation that something might be wrong was when some suits of my brother, Simon, disappeared. He had come to stay for the night to go to a wedding and changed into morning clothes, leaving two new suits behind in a cupboard. On returning after the wedding, the new suits were nowhere to be found. We searched high and low and no one searched more tirelessly than Adrian. When they did not turn up he said he would go down to the basement and ask the housekeeper if she knew what could have happened. Soon he returned beaming. The mystery was solved. She had sent them to the cleaners by mistake. At the time we believed his story. Implausible as it sounded, it was more plausible than the only other explanation: that Adrian had stolen them. That Adrian was unscrupulous we all knew. But that his lack of scruples encompassed petty theft still seemed out of the question. We had much to learn, and I was naturally an unwilling learner because the truth was so unwelcome. For months Simon would continue to ask whether his suits had returned from the cleaners, which of course they never did. Adrian had taken them round to a very well-known pawnbroker in Pimlico and raised a pretty sum – probably enough to pay a month or two's rent. This I discovered much later, in connection with another more serious attempted theft. Returning from *The Times* unusually early one afternoon, I found some removal men carrying Thackeray's writing desk down the stairs. 'What in God's name is happening?' I asked Adrian. 'Oh my dear, it's riddled with woodworm,' he explained. 'They're taking it away for repairs.' The look on the faces of the removal men did not confirm this cock-and-bull story and the game was up. The men were from the pawn shop, whose address I discovered, along with Simon's suits and much else besides.

Adrian confessed all and promised to make amends. He was expecting a large sum of money from his rich Aunt Lillian and there was indeed a letter which looked genuine enough to confirm these expectations. Of course I ought to have kicked him out there and then; indeed cancelled the whole lease and cut my losses. But by then the debts on the house were vastly beyond my means and I dared not despair of Adrian honouring some of his commitments. A showdown would have meant me going bankrupt, which was something a young employee on *The Times* could not expect to get away with without serious damage to his prospects; or if not going bankrupt, then appealing to my mother for help, which was an even more dismaying alternative. And there was also the matter of pride. Living at Elm Park Gardens had allowed me to cut quite a dash and I was deeply reluctant to have the whole façade of rich and stylish living exposed as a sham and me exposed as a sucker to boot. Something else of the greatest possible importance had also happened which made me reluctant to break up Elm Park Gardens. Claudie, my future wife, had happened. So when Adrian suggested that he should move into an upstairs room and leave his palatial quarters for me to let out as bedsitters, I agreed, believing this to be the best that could be made of a bad job.

Claudie was the tenant in the attic. About a week after moving into Elm Park Gardens, I had looked out on to the street and seen an extraordinary sight. Sitting on a handcart being pushed by Adrian was a young woman with a little boy, and a few suitcases. Apparently Adrian had met her a little while earlier in a damp basement flat and had offered her our attic which was at least airier and lighter, and so much better, as he put it, for the health of her five-year-old son. So as to clinch the offer, he had offered to come round to collect her things. Hence the handcart. For weeks I did not meet the new tenant and her child. So terrified were they by the picture of 'the landlord' as painted by Adrian, that they kept out of harm's way. Nor was I curious enough to seek them out. There was quite enough female company around already and in any case I used to get up very late, long after Claudie had left for work and her little boy for school; and come home in the small hours either from a late shift on *The Times* or from a nightclub, long after they had gone to bed. I was naturally aware that we had a tenant as I had watched her arrive from the window and her rent always arrived on time (unlike Adrian's). But as far as I was concerned, she was just 'the tenant' from whom Adrian would occasionally borrow, or more probably pinch, butter and sugar which were then still rationed. Then one Sunday morning when Adrian and I were having a late breakfast, she appeared in the dining room in tears. Her son David's tin soldiers had disappeared. Faced with such a crisis, all fear of the landlord was overcome. She appealed to me for help. Her little boy loved those soldiers and would be '*désolé*' without them. This was the first time I was to hear her French accent which remained with her to her dying day. Adrian went quite white, leapt to his feet and started pacing up and down the room. 'Of course we will find the soldiers for you,' he promised, and sure enough they were returned by nightfall. Never before had I seen Adrian show any sign of remorse or indeed any human emotion at all. At the time it was not so much Claudie I noticed as her dramatic effect on Adrian. Even his stony heart was reduced to pulp. After this meeting, Claudie ceased to be just 'the tenant' and swiftly became part of the Elm Park Gardens ménage or menagerie.

Her story was extraordinary, and even after forty years of marriage I never entirely got to the bottom of it. Born in Ismailia where her father worked for the Suez Canal Company, she spent very little of her childhood in France. All the photographs of the period show her half naked, either in the water or in the sand, brown as a berry with white bleached hair and enormous, sad brown eyes. When the photographs do not show her with her brother and two sisters, there is always a monkey on her shoulder. In 1939, when she was seventeen, the Royal Air Force arrived in Ismailia and she met Geoffrey Baynham, a young pilot, whom she married after knowing him only for a few weeks, not so much because she loved him but because she wanted to get away from her very domineering father. There are photographs of their honeymoon in the desert. Baynham had an enormous Hispano-Suizo car which is parked outside a large tent. Almost as soon as the honeymoon was over, Baynham was recalled to England, where he was to fight in the Battle of Britain, winning the DSC and bar. Claudie travelled to England on her own, flying to France, en route, where she arrived just after the collapse. At the military aerodrome where she touched down in transit, lots of French pilots tried to persuade her to stay in France rather than come on to England. Her loyalty, they said, should be to her country, not to her husband whom she hardly knew. What would she do in England which was bound to be invaded? She knew no English, and her husband would very likely be killed. Although much tempted, she pressed on to England where she was met by two Baynham spinster aunts who drove her down to their great rambling country house in the wilds of south Wales. The loneliness does not bear thinking about. Not only had this seventeen-year-old girl left home for the first time, but she had done so in circumstances which made all communication with her family pretty well impossible for the foreseeable future, ending up with total strangers, neither of whom spoke a word of French, in a climate and surroundings about as different to her native desert habitat as it is possible to imagine, with a husband away and, in all probability, never likely to return. As if all this were not enough, she was pregnant. There being no maternity hospital within fifty miles of Glensevon, it was decided that she should go to London to have the baby who was born, believe it or not, in the middle of an air-raid on Christmas Day, 1940. As soon as David was old enough to be taken back to Wales, Claudie joined the Free French and there is a picture of her with de Gaulle – captioned 'The Longest and the Shortest'. She was only five foot four. At some point she served in Algeria, returning from there in 1945 to learn that Geoffrey had gone off with the nurse who had looked after him in Rhodesia where he had been sent as a training instructor, having been shot down and badly wounded. He wanted a divorce, which Claudie willingly granted, on ludicrously disadvantageous financial grounds considering her husband's considerable wealth. That very roughly was how she and David came to be living in a damp basement in London when rescued by Adrian and brought to Elm Park Gardens: 'Out of ze frying pan into ze fire,' as she put it later, not entirely in jest.

Had life at Elm Park Gardens not been so disorientating, I would probably have never got to know Claudie. In those days I was bent on having a good time, drank a lot and moved in what might be called smart circles. Accusations of snobbery, which have been erroneously levelled at me subsequently, might then have had some justification. With every week that passed, however, the contrast between my conventional social life and my wildly unorthodox domestic life was growing greater and greater. Trying to make both ends meet, I had been reduced to packing the house with lodgers. My Abinger friend, Michael Howard, then a lecturer at King's College, London – and not quite as dignified a figure as he is now – had a room; so did my Stowe and Cambridge friend, Colin Welch, then working in the Colonial Office. In another room was the failed monk Peter Williams who acted as father confessor to us all, including Adrian Earle. In many ways Peter was a rogue, borrowing money from Claudie ostensibly so as to hear Eastern Mass at St Peter's in Rome but in fact for less pious purposes. But for all that, a holy man whose presence did much to hold the demons at bay. Nor was that all, there was also an incontinent female novelist who shared her room with her grown-up son, sleeping in the same bed in shifts and living on endless tins of spinach which they heated up on a bunsen burner; and a French marquis who gave me his clothes in lieu of rent. I still have his beautiful red velvet evening coat with a matching double-breasted waistcoat. Until very recently I used to cut a dash with it at grand diplomatic occasions – even sometimes at the French Embassy – and get a wry pleasure from remembering how it came into my possession.

One awful day, General and Mrs Fuller arrived on an unheralded tour of inspection of their beloved property and, looking up the well of the great staircase, saw innumerable heads peering down from every landing. Since taking lodgers was forbidden in the lease I had to pretend that they were all part of a family reunion. (Not that the Fullers believed me as the eventual legal proceedings made painfully clear.) Then things started going from bad to worse. The ceiling of the dining room fell in and someone sunbathing on the roof fell through the skylight, leaving a gaping hole through which the rain poured in. And more and more dust gathered since Mrs Connolly, the mad housekeeper, had long since given up the ghost, except to answer the telephone in such a manner that callers immediately rang off, assuming, not all that incorrectly, that they had got through to a madhouse. That was the least harmful of her telephonic habits. At one point our number got crossed with that of St Stephen's Hospital just down the road and urgent calls to the hospital were answered by Mrs Connolly who, accustomed to saying 'Yes, shir' to everyone, said it to them. Then she would put the receiver on the table and do nothing about it. Occasionally I would pass by and pick it up to find some furious caller still waiting to be put through to the emergency department. Out of the chaos even violence erupted. Late one night Adrian and I had a fight outside the house, about the key, which ended with Adrian banging my head, face down, on the kerb of the pavement until three front teeth were knocked clean out. Next morning at about midday he rushed into my bedroom to wake me up. As I came round and remembered the horror of the previous night I threatened him with the police. 'What? I can't remember a thing about last night and anyway, Perry, you must hurry and have a bath; a gentleman from *The Times* is here to see you. I will entertain him until you come ... hurry. I'll prepare some lunch.' It was always like that. In emergencies he was as good as his word. He did prepare some lunch for my distinguished visitor, Patrick Ryan, the assistant editor, who apparently lived close by and had looked in to ask me to write a fourth leader – a signal honour which drove all further thoughts of vengeance against Adrian out of my mind.

But increasingly I began retreating to Claudie's attic which became a haven of peace and quiet in a raging tempest. Whereas months or so earlier it had seemed the least comfortable part of the house, now it seemed the most comfortable. A comparable metamorphosis was taking place in my attitude to this occupier. Whereas initially her life and background had seemed so bizarre as to constitute something of a barrier, in my new and desperate condition it began to seem a bond. Claudie worked on a travel magazine called *Go* and would bicycle to her office every morning. The sight of that tiny figure pedalling down the street used to delight me and I began to make a much earlier start to my day for the pleasure of seeing her off; and to return home more promptly than had been my custom hitherto. We never went out together or did any of the conventional social things that couples are meant to do. It never occurred to me to take her to parties or to the nightclubs which were then my addiction. Nor did she introduce me to her friends, although we talked a lot about them – Reggie Hoare, with whom she had once shared a caravan, and Henry Bayne-Powell, whose role was to act as a kind of Professor Higgins in arcane matters to do with English class distinctions. Some of my friends also took her out – noticeably Michael Oakeshott. My own relationship with Claudie, however, was rooted in the peculiar soil of Elm Park Gardens, and there was never any question of trying to transplant it to less exotic climes. I say relationship rather than romance, because such was my immaturity that ideas of romance were for me inextricably bound up with punting up the Cam or high jinks at dances or necking at nightclubs, and Claudie and I were doing none of these things. Either she would share some squalid supper left for me by Mrs Connolly or she would put together some scratch meal with such remnants of her rations that Adrian had not pinched. Elm Park Gardens was visibly falling apart, and retribution approached. But Claudie remained wholly undisturbed as if the vicissitudes through which she had already passed had somehow traumatised her against anything short of total catastrophe. Off she would bicycle, smartly dressed and punctual, looking for all the world as if she had just taken her leave from some respectable bourgeois home.

I am trying to explain why I stayed on and on at Elm Park Gardens. Dread of facing the music, i.e. General and Mrs Fuller, was part of the answer but another part was a reluctance to send Claudie on her travels again. Elm Park Gardens had become her home, and its inhabitants her family, and 'the landlord', incredibly enough, her protector. A relationship even deeper than a romance had been formed which, like everything else about Elm Park Gardens, conformed to no ordinary pattern.

Then Claudie became pregnant. Perhaps we had assumed that since nothing ordinary ever happened under the roof of Elm Park Gardens, this could not happen either. It certainly came as a great surprise. Obviously we had slept together; but apart from that, our togetherness at that time was limited to Elm Park Gardens – scarcely a suitable place for babies. What happened next is acutely painful even to try to remember, let alone put down on paper. We decided to have an abortion. I don't think either of us considered getting married and having the baby. Claudie already had David whose welfare weighed very heavily on her heart. What is more our relationship at that time had not begun to reach that advanced stage. The thought of abortion was profoundly repugnant but it seemed the only answer. How we hardened our hearts to this dreadful deed I do not begin to remember. The moral atmosphere of Elm Park Gardens certainly helped. Nobody who knew Elm Park Gardens then could ever suppose that the permissive society only began in the 1960s. As for my Catholicism, it hardly came into the decision. Its teachings had gripped my intellect without taking possession of my soul. They proved no serious deterrent. I knew what we were doing was wrong, profoundly wrong. But this did not seem to matter. Even now I am not sure what this meant. Did it mean that deep down I did not believe abortion was profoundly wrong? Or did it mean that, under sufficient social pressure, I was prepared to disregard even the strongest pressings of conscience? In any case an abortion was arranged in Soho. I took Claudie there in a taxi. It was, she pointed out, our first outing. In those days abortions were illegal and the doctor in question, to whom we paid £50, looked the part, as did his squalid surgery. His words on our departure were chilling. 'If anything goes wrong, don't come back.'

They did go horribly wrong. Claudie haemorrhaged in the middle of the night and I had to dial 999. Not only did the ambulance arrive in a rush to take Claudie to St Stephen's Hospital, but so did the police to take me in for questioning. For hours they grilled me. Had Claudie had an abortion? Who had done it? Was I the father? Foolishly I denied everything, believing wrongly that an admission of guilt would send me, not the doctor, to prison. Temporarily allowed to go in the small hours, I rushed round to St Stephen's where they would not let me see Claudie, who was being prepared for an emergency operation. 'Come back at midday,' the nurses said. For hours I walked the street, praying that all would be well and gripped by guilt and fear – guilt for what I had done to Claudie and fear of disgrace for myself. When eventually I was allowed to see her she was lying deathly pale with her eyes shut, scarcely breathing. Kneeling by her bed, I prayed as I have never done before or since. 'Let her live, dear God, whatever happens, let her live.' A fortnight later she came out of hospital, and we got engaged to be married.

Discharging my responsibilities for Elm Park Gardens, which could now no longer be postponed, was every bit as difficult as I feared it would be. Unbeknownst to me General and Mrs Fuller had been using private detectives to collect evidence of all my and, more to the point, my lodgers' wrongdoings. It was a long list. Pretty well every shopkeeper in the district was owed money. Several public libraries sued for the return of scores of books, with most of which the lady novelist had decamped. Vintners were particularly vindictive, with some reason, since Adrian had ordered cellar-fuls of wine and spirits in my name, and sometimes – sublime cheek – in the name of my stepfather, Montagu Norman. Much valuable furniture from the house itself had been 'popped', in spite of my best efforts to prevent it, and the pieces which were still present were very far from correct, having received little loving care from Mrs Connolly. In a word, the house was a virtual write-off – not that the recriminations were reduced to one word or anything like it. My solicitor, whose firm had looked after my family for generations, said he could never remember such a squalid business in his entire professional career. Going through it with me in his panelled office in Henrietta Street, he nearly fainted clean away, as did I, with shame and embarrassment. Even Claudie was not spared. She was accused of acting in an obscene manner in front of an open window, to the shock and outrage of the neighbours, thereby giving the address a bad name. To the other charges there was really no defence. But this one I insisted my solicitor challenge hotly. I rather wish I had not since on my next visit he produced affidavits from a private detective to the effect that he had seen a naked Mrs Baynham standing on her head in front of the window and opening her legs slowly in a scissor motion on more than one occasion. How to explain to an elderly family solicitor, born in the nineteenth century, that my future wife was only doing her exercises? Rather than allow the case to go to court, my solicitor advised me to settle. The sum I paid was in the order of £10,000 which pretty well wiped out a small trust that I had inherited from my father. I never went back to 79 Elm Park Gardens. Nor did the Fullers ever return to their beloved home. The house is now no more. On its site stands a block of flats for gentlefolk in reduced circumstances from which many years later I took my father by ambulance, also to St Stephen's Hospital, where he died that night.

As for Adrian, he moved on to fresh prey, eventually biting off more than even he could chew. On 8 December 1953 he was charged with stealing from Lady Beaumont, former wife of the baronet, Sir Francis Beaumont, a fellow Stoic, although not at Grafton. The charges had a familiar ring: 'Theft of a guitar, a necklace, a recording machine, a quantity of dresses and bedding worth £500'. In evidence a detective sergeant said he recovered some of Lady Beaumont's property from a shop in Kensington Church Street, from pawnbrokers in the King's Road, Chelsea and from a house-boat on Chelsea Reach. For these offences he got nine months, with a further nine months for trying to extort money with menaces from Lady Beaumont's new fiancé. Peter Wildeblood, the journalist, who was in Wormwood Scrubs for a homosexual offence when Adrian arrived, de-scribed him in a book as a man of enormous superficial charm.

Then there was the Wykehamist blackmailer. He was immensely tall, and spoke in a high pitched scream. I had known him slightly at Oxford and he had attached himself to me as soon as he arrived, to the discomfort of the burglars, who had never met anybody quite like him before. He used to make outrageous remarks about them in French, which they rightly resented. He was, however, such an amusing raconteur that they eventually accepted him with reservation. He was undoubtedly one of the wickedest people I have ever met, but laughter is such a precious gift in prison that I was always glad when he came stalking towards me like a huge bespectacled crane.

At the time I, too, would have said that Adrian was one of the wickedest men I had ever met. Certainly he cost me dear. But that was before I had met Robert Maxwell and a few other giant-sized crooks, by comparison with whom Adrian was very small beer indeed; in hindsight almost endearing. For example, his last 'outrage' before leaving Elm Park Gardens for good was to steal my dinner. He must have nipped into the kitchen on his way out to his taxi, removed the pans and dishes out of the oven, and carried them off to wherever he was going – more the action of a rogue than of a monster. Infuriated as I was, it was difficult not to laugh. Yet he was malign, nevertheless. In terms of law-breaking he was obviously only a minor criminal. But law-breaking is not the only way to do the devil's work. After lunching one day with Harold Nicolson in the Travellers' Club, Adrian went off with the immensely valuable fur-lined overcoat of some Foreign Office mandarin. Nowadays if this happened at a gentlemen's club, suspicion would rightly fall on new members who are much less to be trusted than the staff, most of whom are old retainers. Not so in the later 1940s when it was felt to be utterly out of the question that any member, or guest of a member, could stoop so low. As a result all the downstairs staff were interrogated by the police and the atmosphere of the club poisoned for years: devil's work indeed.

Adrian was highly cultivated and well read. Quite possibly he was carrying in his pocket a copy of *The Waste Land*, every line of which he knew by heart, when he stole the coat or, for that matter, my dinner. These are deep waters, and just as it shook George Steiner's faith in civilisation to learn that concentration camp commandants listened to Beethoven and Mozart before turning on the gas ovens, so it shook mine to realise that a Wykehamist scholar could be a petty thief. How old-fashioned that sounds. It is no longer unusual for public school men to be criminals. Today there are probably more of them high up in the criminal classes than in the police force. Then, however, it was a rare and spectacular occurrence which challenged the whole social order.

So far as I was concerned, Adrian found the weak spot which led me into temptation in a way I like to think a bigger corrupter like Lord Beaverbrook – who tried – was never able to do. Adrian was just about as much of a devil as Britain's upper-middle-class market in evil would bear at that time. Those 'suspicious circumstances' in South America surrounding his death rather suggest that he may have done more serious diabolical work overseas. But even if he didn't, his achievements here at home should have been enough to earn him at least a humble place in hell.

9

Printing House Square

After getting married in Chelsea Registry Office, Claudie and I went for our honeymoon to the south of France, in search of sun. In those days there were no travel brochures or travel pages in the newspapers advising people where to stay and I decided to return to the only place I knew – the Grand Hotel, Beauvallon, near Ste-Maxime, a spacious Edwardian establishment where Simon and I had spent two happy summers, in the charge of a governess, so as to be on hand when our mother put into shore from Uncle Wyndham's yacht. This did not happen often but was worth waiting for when it did. On one particularly exciting occasion she caused great excitement on the beach by roaring up to the hotel pier in a swish motor launch, accompanied by 'Tom' Mosley who was then very much in the public eye, having just resigned from the Labour government over unemployment. Also with the party were Harold Macmillan, at that time a maverick young Tory MP and, most surprisingly, David Margesson, the stern unbending Tory Chief Whip – the only one of the three, incidentally, whom I remember being in the least kind to Simon and me whose entertainment was meant to be the object of the exercise. After whisking us off to an island for a picnic, the whole party returned to the hotel for tea, causing a further sensation. Not that Simon and I had the slightest idea what the fuss was all about. All we knew was that quite suddenly we were very much the centre of attention and after our mother's party had departed, something of their glamour still lingered on, guaranteeing us lots of flattering attention from the management and staff, warm memories of which may have tempted me to return there for our honeymoon. At least we would be known and given a warm welcome, which indeed we were.

But what I had wholly failed to take into account was the change in my circumstances between then and now and indeed the change in my country's circumstances. In pre-war days British visitors to France, thanks to the strength of the pound, were lords of all they surveyed. After the war they were limited to a £30 foreign currency allowance per head. Nor, in my case, was foreign currency the only problem. After the Elm Park Gardens débâcle there was an acute shortage of all forms of currency. In such circumstances the Grand Hotel Beauvallon was not a suitable place to choose for a honeymoon. Drawn up outside the entrance on the morning of our arrival was the manager, in a tailcoat, and his staff, all waiting to greet us straight off the Golden Arrow from Paris. Clearly the manager had set great store on our booking, hoping that we would prove to be the first swallows of a new summer season of returning English grandees. Imagine his horrified disappointment when he saw us trudging up the dusty drive carrying our own suitcases, having economised by coming by bus from the railway station instead of by taxi. At first the manager chose to look on the bright side of things, smiling knowingly as if this humble style of arrival was just some kind of English eccentricity. Nor did he allow himself to be cast down when, after one glance at the room tariffs, I said that there was no way our foreign currency could run to one night, let alone the fortnight we were booked in for. Not to worry, he replied, for special customers of our kind, ways round the currency regulations could always be found. Claudie was all for my coming clean right away, apologising and getting out there and then. But pride prevented me and only after the first week's monumental bill could not be settled did the manager's smarmy smile begin to crack. Hell hath no fury like a French hotelier about to be bilked. Our passports were impounded; further orders refused. Fortunately I had a friend in Paris, Charles Hargrove, then number two in *The Times* bureau, who eventually cabled the necessary funds, but only after an acutely embarrassing two-day wait in the course of which Claudie had plenty of opportunity to teach me a piece of rude French slang with which I was to become exceedingly familiar: *Jamais péter plus haut que son derrière.*

Departing as we had arrived, by bus, carrying our own luggage – but without the manager or staff to give us a send-off – we went just down the coast to St Tropez, still quite undiscovered, where Claudie found a small *pension* with individual bamboo huts in which the last few days of our honeymoon went swimmingly for the price of what one *citron pressé* would have cost at the Beauvallon. Getting back to London I made a joke of my Beauvallon folly, rather as I had already started making a joke of Elm Park Gardens. The story went down well at parties. But at the time it hadn't been in the least funny and had come close to ruining the honeymoon. Once again, chastening prickings of conscience about a serious character flaw, which might have led to reform, were too quickly and too painlessly eased away by that most comforting of all sounds: the laughter of friends.

For the first few months of our married life we stayed at Thorpe Lodge where my mother was living alone, my stepfather having died after a long illness. Claudie's son, David, was at boarding school and to begin with she and my mother got on surprisingly well. Far from Claudie's divorce and young son and unusual background casting shadows of doubt over my choice, they helped to confirm its wisdom. For, as my mother saw it, history was repeating itself. She too, when she had married Montagu Norman, was divorced with two young sons, and from a foreign background, not all that less strange than Claudie's. Also having herself been ostracised by her Catholic relations for marrying outside the Church my mother was all the more determined that Claudie and I should not suffer any such recrimination, least of all from her. As a result, the evening when I told her of my engagement to Claudie was one of the warmest and closest we ever spent together, my choice of bride further confirming her view that she and I were kindred spirits in rebellion against social and religious orthodoxy. Bringing downstairs an enormous jewel box, full of glittering gems, she asked me to choose an engagement ring and seemed very moved by the one I picked out which in my ignorance happened to be much the least valuable, a further indication, she implied, of how different I was from my playboy father.

Unfortunately, after a good beginning, relations between mother and daughter-in-law declined. The first indications of trouble came one summer evening when Colin Welch, who knew Claudie well from Elm Park Gardens days, was a guest. He must have arrived early while I was still dressing for dinner in my bedroom which overlooked the terrace where drinks were served. Claudie and my mother were already on the terrace and wafting up through my open window I heard my mother say, 'Oh Colin, since Perry's not down yet, do please mix us all a dry martini.' Innocent enough words if taken out of context. But more than dramatic enough to have me rushing to the window to see what was going to happen next. For there was a long background to Colin's relationship with my mother, dating back to outings from Stowe. She paralysed him with terror, turned his natural social gaucheness into behaviour little short of idiotic. Seeing Colin hesitate and knowing perfectly well that he hadn't the slightest idea of how to mix a dry martini, Claudie bravely volunteered to undertake the delicate duty herself, only to be told by my mother, quite curtly, that women always made a botch of cocktails. Everything had been prepared by James on a drinks tray behind my mother's chair and all Colin had to do was pour the gin and other ingredients into a beautifully polished silver cocktail shaker, which was still, in those pre-Ian Fleming days, the correct receptacle for the purpose. Whether Colin got the ingredients remotely in their proper proportions we shall never know. For in his agitation he forgot to screw the top on tightly and no sooner had he lifted the shaker, boxer-like, above his head in an acceptable imitation of what he had seen American barmen do in films, than a stream of frothy iced liquid shot into an arc over my mother's head right into her lap. But that was not the worst of it. No, the worst of it was that Claudie let out great peals of Gallic laughter, the like of which Thorpe Lodge had never heard before, interspersed with cries of *'quelle horreur, quelle horreur'*, which all too clearly indicated far more sympathy for Colin in his embarrassment than for my mother in her soaking.

Soon thereafter it seemed wise to move out of Thorpe Lodge and to start looking for more permanent accommodation, which, with a stroke of luck, did not take us long to find. Who it was who told us about Cardinal's Wharf I cannot remember but the house seemed, on the surface, everything that we could possibly want, or at any rate that I could want. It was, indeed still is, a perfect seventeenth-century gem on the south bank of the river opposite St Paul's, within walking distance, over Blackfriars Bridge, of *The Times*. According to legend, Sir Christopher Wren lived there while building his great cathedral so as to be able to keep an eye on its progress from the drawing room window. Catherine of Aragon had also stopped there to fortify her spirits on the way to meet her betrothed, Henry VIII, at Hampton Court. Its present owner, Malcolm Munthe, son of Axel Munthe, author of *The Story of San Michele*, was also a legendary figure, having been dropped into Norway during the war. Even before seeing the house I was sorely tempted, particularly as the rent was attractively low. Viewing it should have made us pause, but didn't. The day chosen was a summer Sunday when the river was looking so beautiful that one scarcely noticed that the house stood alone and isolated amongst acres of post-Blitz desolation, with a power station, very much on its best Sunday behaviour, as its only neighbour. After giving us tea in lovely china, Malcolm Munthe showed us around the house which was full of period furniture. The dining room, too, was ravishing with a ceiling hand-painted, or so we were led to believe, by Rubens. How could we resist such a temptingly romantic and stylish house – better than anything we'd ever dreamed of.

A fortnight later on a rainy Monday morning, it was a very different story. First, the power station was no longer on its best behaviour. Not only did it emit an ominous low hum, but, much worse, a steady stream of black smoke which coated everything with sticky grime. Rats from the barges, tied up at the wharf, were also a problem. The basement, which we had not been shown, was infested with them and at night they would invade our bedroom where they had the effrontery to climb up the drapes surrounding the four-poster bed in which Catherine of Aragon was supposed to have rested. Another minor nuisance came from the river pleasure boats which would slow down as they passed the house while the guides boomed on about Wren, Catherine of Aragon and, for good measure, the film star, Florence Desmond, who had been a previous tenant in the 1930s. According to the guides she liked a morning bathe in the river and would arrange for one of the wharf cranes to collect her from the first-floor bathroom window, dip her in the river and then swing her back into the bathroom again. Sometimes Claudie would be making her own ablutions in the same bathroom as the story was being told, in full view of at least the upper-deck passengers, who would wave and cheer, possibly under the impression that she was Florence Desmond.

Soon after we moved in Michael Oakeshott was appointed Harold Laski's successor as Professor of Politics at the London School of Economics and we were delighted when he asked whether he could lodge with us. At Cardinal's Wharf he was absolutely in his element. Even the rats did not faze him. In fact he was amused by their boldness and by Dolly and Daisy, the two rat-catchers who virtually lived under our roof, so never-ending was their task. Not that they set about it with any great vigour or conviction. 'Don't you want to catch the brutes?' Michael asked on one occasion after weeks of waiting for a single fatality. 'Oh no, dear,' they replied, 'we love the little buggers.' Love them we never did. But a grudging admiration could not be withheld. Reduced to abandoning all attempts to exclude them from making free with most of the house, we laid rolled carpets as thick as oak tree trunks across the base of the kitchen door, having previously blocked off all other means of rodent access. At least Claudie's kitchen, we thought, would be a high-security, no-go area. Not a bit of it. Next morning Dolly and Daisy were proud to announce that the little buggers had eaten their way right through it. 'Such a lovely hole, clean as a whistle,' they announced.

As well as Michael we had another lodger, Werner von Simson, now a distinguished jurist, who had come to England from Germany with the Hahns just before the war. Between them they kept Claudie company while I was away in the evenings at *The Times*. The river police would also put in a regular appearance, amazed to find anybody living in what was then a wilderness. Nor were the river police our only visitors. Cardinal's Wharf being such an interesting house, and so convenient for *The Times*, colleagues were quite keen to have a look. Whereas office socialising had been non-existent on the *Glasgow Herald*, it was pleasantly easy on *The Times*. Initially our guests were my fellow sub-editors, several of whom combined that job with scholarly or literary activities for which they later became well known. Quite soon, however, Cardinal's Wharf gave me an excuse to make contact with one of the god-like specialist writers who occupied the floor above the subs room. One morning Claudie and I came down to breakfast to find the famous Rubens dining room ceiling, for the care of which we felt personally responsible, flaking off. By good fortune there was a Rubens expert on *The Times*, Iola Williams, the museums correspondent, to whom I appealed for help. It took some courage to knock on his door. In those days doors on that floor were very much kept shut and an atmosphere of almost sepulchral stillness prevailed. Rumour had it that behind one of them sat the man who wrote *The Times* 'Hundred Years Ago' from memory. Iola Williams shared a room in those days with Patrick Morrah, Fellow of All Souls and constitutional expert. Always the soul of kindness Iola Williams agreed to come and look at the ceiling on his way to work next day. By then the flaking had got much worse and Claudie and I gazed at it in horror, waiting for the great man to pronounce on what should be done to save the masterpiece. What he would have recommended I shall never know because just as he was about to pronounced our cockney cleaning lady arrived, took one look at our glum faces, and burst out laughing. 'Lawks alive,' she said, 'there's no cause to worry about that, it only took him half a sec to put it up and he can do it again in no time.' Thereupon she danced around the room imitating her master splashing the paint on. Fortunately Iola Williams was not only museums correspondent but also music-hall critic and any irritation, under the one hat, he may have justifiably felt at being called out on a wild-goose chase, was more than made up, under his other hat, by appreciation of a bravura performance.

Sub-editing on *The Times* in those days was taken immensely seriously since the paper's reputation depended very much more on its factual accuracy than on its readability or entertainment value. It saw its function as that of providing decision-makers the world over with such information as they needed to reach the right ones. To later generations *The Times* of that period is chiefly remembered for having got Munich wrong, which it almost certainly did. But that memory does less than justice to the quite phenomenal amount of effort that went into getting thousands of little things absolutely right. I remember the words of greeting of Mr Donald Holmes, chief foreign sub, to this day. 'How is your Arabic?' he asked. 'None of our colleagues knows a word and we've got this despatch in from Khartoum which needs careful handling.' Needless to say I didn't and don't know a word of Arabic. But any draining away of confidence I may have felt due to my linguistic inadequacy was more than made up by the boost given to my morale being immediately accepted as a bona fide colleague, one of the team, somebody who could be assumed to be just as worried about getting the important despatch from Khartoum right as could the chief sub-editor himself. The despatch in question, giving the full list of the new Sudanese government, would not be regarded as at all important nowadays; indeed would never be sent, let alone published, any more than a full list of even a new French government is sent or published. But these were the days when there was a daily 'imperial and foreign page' in *The Times* and when a significant number of *Times* readers were still engaged in governing the Sudan. So they required their information to be accurate in all particulars. Apparently in an earlier despatch the names of important cabinet ministers had been garbled, causing *The Times* 'no end of embarrassment', as Mr Holmes put it, and my job was to prevent any repetition of this blunder. 'Go and have a word with the professor,' Mr Holmes advised. This was easier said than done since there were at least four professors and it took me a little time to sort out the right one, Professor Rushbrook Williams, who was an Arab expert, from Professor Lafitte, the social affairs expert, Professor Duncan Burn, industrial expert, and Professor Cyril Falls, defence expert. Nor, when identified, was Rushbrook Williams much help. The correct spelling of a Sudanese name, he explained, depended on whether the man came from the north of the country or the south. In his view *The Times* rulebook needed amendment in this regard, as, in its present form, no account had been taken of these important distinctions. Perhaps I should get on to a friend of his in the Colonial Office who might be able to help. All this, and more, took up a whole evening's concentrated work. 'Careful handling' was what Mr Holmes thought the despatch deserved and careful handling was what it received. Despite my best efforts, however, there was still a complaint from a retired colonial governor. The letters editor brought it down next day to Mr Holmes who asked me for a memo of rebuttal which, thanks to my new learning, I was able to supply in great detail. After reading my memo Mr Holmes's worried face was suffused with relief. 'That should see Sir XYZ off, Worsthorne,' he said, giving me a congratulatory pat on the shoulder.

After a few months in the foreign subs room I was transferred to the home news subs room under Mr Reginald Easthope who put me in charge of the social and court page, in those days an extremely important part of the paper also requiring great attention to accuracy and the correct spelling of names and, even more important, titles. On this page appeared all the deaths, births, engagements and marriages with their alphabetical order very much subordinated to order of precedence if there were a title involved. Thus the engagement of the Marquis of Zetland, say, would come above any commoner's engagement, however high in the alphabet that commoner's name might come. Births were a particular problem in these respects. At that time *The Times* printed a special complimentary section for all births that affected succession to a title. If the mothers had titles, even honourables, their inclusion was automatic but it fell to the sub-editor in charge to decide who else was to get a place. One would be telephoned by a Mrs Carruthers, who wanted to say that since she was the great-niece of the Duke of Wellington, her newly-born son, Charles, would be seventh in line of succession. Include or not include, it was a difficult question, requiring almost as much research as those Arabic names. Which lunches, dinners and dances to include in another complimentary section was also a source of headaches. Some hostesses went to absurd and embarrassing lengths to ensure my goodwill and, even more important, to punish its absence. Their anxiety for inclusion, of course, had nothing to do with a wish to economise. They would willingly have paid to be included and did indeed often offer to pay over the odds, and do other favours. What they were after was the social cachet bestowed by inclusion in the social columns of *The Times*, there being no more authoritative imprimatur of who was and who was not the genuine article. Being in charge of these columns was a great privilege and I enjoyed every minute of my three-month tenure. Other ostensibly more important jobs have come my way but few which carried more instant clout, or taught me more about the ways of the world.

Arriving at the subs table shortly after me was another new recruit, Roger Carey, straight down from Oxford where he had won a first and, rumour had it, just missed a fellowship of All Souls. Although he gave himself no airs and was thoroughly friendly, none of us was in any doubt that he was the highest of high flyers. The editor had even been heard to call him by his christian name in the lift and important people rang him up. Then disaster struck. One of Roger's jobs was to sub-edit *The Times*'s daily sermon which was contributed by a variety of bishops, some of whose Latin and Greek was not as good as his own. Cackling with laughter Roger would show me their mistakes and how he had corrected them, in the flattering belief that my knowledge of the classics was as great as his own. Sometimes he would disappear up to the floor above to show Dermot Morrah, a fervent Roman Catholic, just how philistine the Anglican episcopacy had become. Tact was not then Roger's* strong point, 'I am afraid, my lord, your admirable sermon contained a few schoolboy howlers which I am sure you will be grateful to see we have removed.' So long as Roger stuck to correcting their Latin and Greek, the bishops had to pretend to be grateful. After all he was only doing his sub-editorial duty. But unfortunately one evening, perhaps egged on by Dermot Morrah, he took it upon himself to correct the Archbishop of Canterbury's theology, and in an Easter sermon too; more than correct, rewrite. All hell broke loose. The archbishop stormed over from Lambeth Palace to see the editor, in those days W. F. Casey, a gentle, humorous Irishman who had no choice but to promise that Roger would be removed forthwith from his post. But that was not the end of the editor's troubles. For having appeased the archbishop by removing Roger, poor Casey had to face the wrath of Roger's father, a very prominent and famously irascible baronet and M.P. who arrived at *The Times* late one evening, bent on vengeance. The editor had still not returned from the Garrick Club, where he regularly dined, and it fell to me, Roger's colleague, to sit with the fuming father until he got back. At about 10.00 p.m., after dining well and long, in he walked, suspecting nothing, to be immediately confronted with Sir Robert whose language was most unparliamentary. Casey reacted superbly. Not for nothing had he begun life as an actor in Dublin's Abbey Theatre. 'Pray calm yourself, Sir Robert. You must not think ill of us. We all appreciated your son who is

* A deficiency long since rectified, as his BBC colleagues over many years have good reason to know.

indeed a most remarkable young man, as remarkable as any that has ever graced *The Times*. Therein lay our dilemma, Sir Robert. For a newspaper office is a stable of hacks. I am a hack. Young Worsthorne there is a hack. But your son Roger, Sir Robert, now he is a pure thoroughbred.' It worked like a charm and Sir Robert took his leave much mollified. Following him out I thought I saw Casey give me a conspiratorial wink which made me very proud to be a hack in such a stable.

Nothing in my journalistic life has given me more satisfaction than those months of subbing on *The Times*. The sense of corporate pride was quite extraordinarily uplifting. Here, I suspect, the rule of anonymity helped a lot. As soon as the cult of personality, which bylines encourage, enters a newspaper office concern for accuracy is undermined since no reporter or foreign correspondent becomes a star by attention to detail. Journalistic stars are born out of originality, colourful prose, prophetic speculation, downright invention, and writers with those kinds of gifts tend to resent sub-editors as pedants anxious to cramp their style. There were no such prima donnnas on *The Times* in those days. Sub-editors and writers were all part of the same choir. To be an anonymous *Times* man, that was sufficient glory which did not need to be augmented by a lot of fine writing or sensational scoops.

After about three months Donald Tyerman called me in to say that I had been appointed assistant foreign news editor under Ralph Deakin, a post which gave me a cubby-hole of my own. Why I had been deemed worthy of this promotion is difficult to say since, apart from the occasional light fourth leader*, I had still not been called upon to write a single word. The job of the foreign news editor was to make sure that foreign correspondents were in the right place at the right time and to commission and edit major feature articles about foreign affairs. Foreign policy was not our province. That was the responsibility of a senior leader writer, Iverach McDonald. Not that the outside world knew about this distinction and Ralph Deakin enjoyed a status which his basically nuts-and-bolts job did not altogether justify. He could not have been a kinder boss, taking me along to marvellous lunches at the Ivy and the Reform Club where he entertained ambassadors, foreign newspaper proprietors, foreign correspondents and suchlike. Sometimes when the guests brought along their wives, Mrs Deakin would come along too, much to Mr Deakin's embarrassment since she often let the side down. For Mr Deakin was not quite what he liked to appear. In the first place, as I say, he was not foreign editor. Nor had he been to university. What is more, unlike most of the rest of the staff, he came from a humble background rather than from the professional middle class. When on his own these peculiarities were not at all obvious. But when his wife was present she took a perverse pleasure in stripping away his veils of social

* One of these, on bedsitters, was found worthy of inclusion in *The Times* annual anthology. The selection was done by the great Peter Fleming who added to the honour by calling on me in person to ask permission.

sophistication. At the Ivy, for example, she would insist on ordering 'bangers and mash' which she alleged was what he would like to eat too, if only he did not feel compelled to pretend otherwise. Nor was Mrs Deakin the only cross he had to bear. Within the office itself he was also subjected to mild humiliation. At the afternoon conference it was his job to compile and read out the list of all the foreign stories of the day and the specialists seemed to enjoy nothing better than to show up gaps in his knowledge in front of the editor. Being insecure and vulnerable he could not take these corrections without bridling, which only made him look self-important as well as ill-informed. In many ways he was self-important and ill-informed. But he was also a passionately loyal servant of the paper, around which his whole life revolved. Yet even this virtue often took unfortunate, even graceless, forms, as when he told the wife of a foreign correspondent just killed in the Korean War, who had come to complain about her pension, that at least *The Times* two-column obituary had done her husband proud, as if a generous obituary was more than enough compensation for a mean pension.

Deakin and I would sometimes spend a whole afternoon pondering the headline for a major turnover article as it was still then called, in spite of having long since ceased extending over two pages. My suggestion for puns or for some catchphrase which took slight liberties with the text were never accepted. 'Better bore than mislead' was one of Mr Deakin's mottoes. Another, conveying the same message, was 'Look after the headline and the article can look after itself'. When we weren't perfecting headlines we were keeping tabs on the correspondents. One, John Marks in Madrid, took up more of our time than most because he was so often absent from the capital when some important story broke. The editor at conference often complained about this and eventually Mr Deakin asked me to look into the matter. Going through the back files I discovered a series of letters from Marks to Deakin justifying year by year his regular absence from the capital on grounds of what he called 'important regional developments'. Deakin, who admired and trusted Marks, never seemed to have asked what these important regional developments might be or why they never produced any copy. Being rather more cynical myself it did not take long to notice that they coincided exactly with the movements from province to province of the bullfighting season. Shortly thereafter John Marks produced his classic on bullfighting which enabled him to bear his dismissal from *The Times* with equanimity. Another of our jobs was the appointment of new correspondents. On what basis this was done was a bit of a mystery. It was no good anybody just applying. They had to be recommended. 'Who is he?' Deakin would ask, by which he meant not 'what has he done?' but 'who does he know?'. Writing ability seemed hardly to be considered at all. Nobody was ever asked to submit cuttings or anything like that. Richard

Harris, who became *The Times* China expert, was turned down several times before being finally accepted on account of Deakin discovering – at the Reform I seem to remember – somebody who knew him.

At the time this seemed to me an unlikely way to get the best man for the job, as well as being unfair to people without connections. Mr Deakin explained that although I was right in theory, in practice there was really no more satisfactory way, particularly in a small institution like *The Times*. In any case, what was meant by 'the best man for the job', he asked. Best in what sense? Did I mean some ideal best as judged, say, by an examination? That would be absurd since it would overlook one of the most important considerations: that any correspondent of *The Times* should be someone trusted by Ralph Deakin. Fitting into *The Times* was the first requirement and what better way of fulfilling that condition than through personal recommendation by people who knew *The Times*? Deakin quoted Admiral Fisher's famous dictum about favouritism being the father of efficiency. Fisher was equating efficiency with obedience to his orders. He wanted captains who, because they owed their advancement entirely to him, would be his slaves. That was not what Deakin wanted. He wanted people likely to understand what *The Times* was all about. In his view, favouritism was not so much the father of efficiency as of something far more important: institutional loyalty.

What Deakin was describing was not an old boy network, if by that is meant some public school closed shop. It was Deakin, after all, who appointed Louis Heren, born in the East End, as a foreign correspondent. Still less was it an aristocratic magic circle or an Oxbridge magic circle. Its roots lay deeper, in a suspicion of strangers. Having started as a messenger boy, Louis Heren was not a stranger. He was already at home on *The Times*. For Deakin *The Times* was his family and the correspondents his adopted children. 'Best man for the job.' The phrase made no sense. Being a correspondent for *The Times* was more than a job: love came in to it, on both sides.

Mr Deakin, by then, had indeed become sentimental, perhaps even, by today's tough standards, a little soft in the head. I think he sensed that both the times and *The Times* were changing in ways that would leave little room for the likes of him. Sir William Haley, a new broom from the BBC, had been appointed editor and had started throwing his weight around. At the afternoon conference Deakin announced that the Cairo correspondent could not cover a story in Cairo as he was on his way to Petra.

'What does he hope to achieve for us in Petra?' Haley demanded.

'A colour piece,' replied Deakin.

'We know the colour of Petra,' said Haley. 'Get him back.'

More and more Deakin would withdraw into himself, trusting his own little staff, including his secretary whom he sometimes took out to lunch.

Then one morning the news came that he had died of barbiturate poisoning, leaving a letter behind declaring a love for his secretary that he had never dared express. For months afterwards, as dusk fell, Mrs Deakin would take a position in Printing House Square underneath her late husband's office and slowly shake her fist up at the window where the secretary used to sit. In Mr Deakin's terms, however, the story had a happy ending. *The Times*'s long obituary did him proud.

Sometime before Mr Deakin's demise he had appointed me as number two correspondent in Paris, in succession to Charles Hargrove whom he sent to Bonn. Unfortunately just before taking up this post, to which Claudie was particularly looking forward, I went down with mumps which deteriorated into jaundice. Being ill in rat-infested Cardinal's Wharf was no joke. The family doctor was loath to travel to such distant parts and the only local one, a scruffy old Hungarian, spoke very little English. On his first visit he poured my sinister-looking urine sample down the bathroom washbasin, dismissing Claudie's protest at his lack of hygiene with the phrase, 'it ees not a septicus but an anti-septicus', an excuse which no more convinced Claudie on that occasion than it did when parroted by me in later years to justify my lazily using many hotel bedroom basins for roughly the same unhygienic purpose. Soon my condition became quite critical and I was carted off by ambulance to St Thomas's Hospital where I stayed for four months, under the care of a young doctor, Hugh de Wardener, who went on to become one of the world's leading renal experts. At first he was completely baffled by my exact kind of jaundice. That I had jaundice was clear enough since my skin had gone canary yellow. But it couldn't be the strain it seemed to be, he told Claudie, because that one could only be caught through living in rat-infested conditions which were unlikely to apply to me. Furthermore that particular strain had become rare to the point of non-existence, a bad memory from the days of Victorian slums. After Claudie had reluctantly and shamefacedly put him in the picture about Cardinal's Wharf, he became really interested. I cannot remember what my virus was called but it was sufficiently rare for doctors from other hospitals to want to come in to take a look. And the nurses, taking their cue from the doctors, also began to treat me as something special. Had I not been feeling so lousy, and so frustrated about the receding chances of taking up my appointment in Paris, my lot would have been quite enviable. How quickly one gets used to hospital life, particularly if you have an interesting disease which endows you with a kind of star status. Instead of being worried by new and alarming symptoms I rather welcomed them since they only served to deepen Dr Wardener and his team's interest. In the kingdom of the sick the seriously ill patient is king.

Dr Wardener did not take the traditional view that rich and fatty foods are bad for jaundice. On the contrary, he said, if the patient fancies such foods, let him have them. Likewise drink. Anything to keep your strength and morale up. When I told my mother this she was rather put out. I think she suspected the cause of my jaundice had been over-indulgence of one sort or another – too many of Claudie's French sauces, perhaps – and had seen it as heaven's warning that I should go on a strict diet. Even more to the point, Nellie, her cook, had been told to prepare a daily consignment of boiled fish and it was too late to change plans now. My father's reaction was quite different. Hampers of smoked salmon, grouse and champagne arrived from Fortnums. How characteristically irresponsible, sniffed my mother when she saw them. What I dreaded was that he and she would both arrive at my bedside at the same time. Fear of this gave me nightmares and worried me more than anything to do with the disease itself. Claudie and the nurses worked out an elaborate warning system which never failed, although there were some close shaves. My father would make a joke of my fears, offering to get under the bed or hide in a cupboard, as in a Feydeau farce, if the worst came to the worst. But for me it was anything but a joke. In my weakened state – at one point I weighed less than seven stone – the shock might well have been more than my heart could stand.

To begin with, friends would visit me regularly. But as the weeks stretched to months the visits became rarer. This was not because of any lack of willingness on their part. They suggested coming but I put them off. What was going on in the world of the healthy seemed so much less interesting than what was going on in the world of the sick. Every piece of hospital gossip brought to me by the nurses and doctors was eagerly received. But *The Times* office gossip, say, had lost all savour. Friends who arrived rosy-cheeked and bursting with health made me wince, not with envy but with embarrassment. I had to avert my eyes in exactly the same way as someone healthy averts his eyes when faced by offensive illness. Perhaps this is nature's way of consoling the sick. More likely, I suppose, it is a case of when in Rome do as Rome does. Hospitals have their own values, their own routines, their own horizons, and after a time a patient starts finding these natural and normal and those of the healthy world unnatural and abnormal. A preoccupation of mine, for example, which visitors could not reasonably be expected to share, was the colour of my urine. Nothing else occupied my waking or indeed dreaming hours more than this. Passing water was a matter of high drama. If the urine spurting into the bottle made a dark yellow froth, or a darker yellow than the time before, this meant that I was getting worse; a lighter froth, on the other hand, indicated improvement. On each occasion, of course, there was room for doubt. Perhaps the sun was shining brighter. Not wishing to rely on my own eye I would consult the nurses for a second opinion, and even the cleaners. Not that I cared all that much about getting better. After three months or so I had given up hope on that score. Concern about the colour had become almost an end in itself, like some piece of research whose original purpose the scholar has long since forgotten. Nor was it only the colour of my urine which required regular examination. So did the colour of my skin, and the colour of my tongue, not to mention the colour of my liver, slivers of which were occasionally extracted by Dr Wardener so as to enable him to know more about my progress, or rather lack of progress. With all these pressing matters on my mind I found the affairs of the great world a most unwelcome distraction and could hardly wait for kind visitors to be gone so as to concentrate again on the important business in hand.

So preoccupied was I with my illness that when Claudie gave me the marvellous news that she was three months gone in pregnancy I did not immediately realise that she could not possibly go on living alone at Cardinal's Wharf, amidst the rats and the grime. Fortunately my Cambridge friend, Roger Lubbock, now a London publisher, did. Giving Claudie a lift home after dark he realised for the first time how brave she had been to stick it out and immediately arranged for her to come and stay with Oliver and Patty Knox in Adam's Row where he was lodging at the time. Roger and Olly had been friends at Eton and then at King's and also in the navy, in whose service Roger had been a great deal more active (winning the DSC on motor torpedo boats) than had Olly who, for the most part, had been at Bletchley where his father, Dillwyn Knox, played such an important part in breaking the German Enigma code. Claudie's life was immediately transformed. For Adam's Row in Mayfair, next door to the Connaught Hotel, was a very different environment to the south bank; in the longer run my life was too since the Knoxs and the Lubbocks were to become our closest friends.

Possibly it was news of the baby on the way that jolted me into getting better. In any event, one morning, instead of there being a head of yellow froth on my urine, there were transparent Lux-like bubbles – the long-awaited sign of recovery. A fortnight or so later Claudie invited Dr Wardener to have a glass of my father's champagne and he called the nurses in to drink 'my health'. The phrase made me a little sad. I had seen Dr Wardener daily, often twice daily, for four months, in the course of which there had been some pretty darkish nights of the soul, and this relationship, so close and highly charged, was about to end. It was not unlike the drinks between old comrades the night before demobilisation which are as much wake as celebration. And just as old comrades promise to keep in touch in civvy street, so did Dr Wardener and I promise to keep in touch in the world of the healthy. But we never did. Our final conversation, however, has often come back to me. I asked him whether drinking might induce a recurrence of my jaundice and he pooh-poohed the idea.

'The hangovers may be worse,' he said, 'but that is all.' They certainly have been, and so far that has been all. Something else from that period also brings it back to me. John Raymond, a new friend on *The Times* – who went on to become a fine literary critic – gave me a beautiful edition of Gibbon's *Decline and Fall of the Roman Empire* to read in hospital. It is on my shelves now and few things fill me with more nostalgia than those pages still stained yellow by my sweaty jaundiced hands.

For convalescence Claudie and I went up to Dyneley where Simon lent us a cottage on the estate. It was the one where James the Dyneley butler had been born and bred, along with his brothers and sisters. Although now very comfortably and cosily done up, and ideal for the two of us, it was difficult to imagine how its far from large one bedroom could have housed that entire family. Rationing was still on but the Cliviger butcher, Mr Blackburn, whom I had known since childhood, sent up lots of liver – the one meat which I not unnaturally did not feel like eating. Anxious not to appear ungrateful I went down to thank him for his kind and considerate gesture, which prompted him to despatch further bloodstained parcels of this sickening offal. Fortunately Claudie was eating for two and it could well be that Mr Blackburn's misplaced generosity contributed greatly to the health and beauty of Dominique, our baby daughter who was born not all that long after.

In preparation for this great event it fell to Claudie – my state of health not being up to the job – to find a family home. My mother, who had generously offered to put up the then princely sum of £5,000, was very keen on Baron's Court, an area known to me only as an Underground station through which people passed, preferably as fast as possible. Pressed to explain her preference she said that lots of her social worker friends and colleagues lived there and loved it, which did not seem to us a conclusive reason for supposing that we would too. With the benefit of hindsight I now see that my mother had a point, as was often the case. We could probably have bought a great mansion in Baron's Court, with a large garden, for £5,000, or in some of the other locations she also favoured – Barnes, Wimbledon, Putney and Richmond. Our objections owed less to snobbery than lack of imagination. Nobody we knew then lived in those areas. Indeed few people we knew lived north of Hyde Park. My father still owned two houses in Belgrave Square and it somehow seemed quite wrong even to consider descending from Belgravia to Baron's Court in one plunge. That, of course, was just what my mother did want, for all the old familiar reasons.

In the end, after much searching, Claudie compromised by plumping for 41 Scarsdale Villas, not far from both Kensington High Street and Earl's Court Road, an area which was not fashionable in those days although it has since become so. (Our old house went the other day for three-quarters of a million – alas three decades or more after we had sold it.) By the time I came south from Lancashire, fully recuperated, Claudie had done all the hard work of doing it up, moving in and finding an au pair, as they had just begun to be called. Some might say I had it made. In fact that was what Claudie did say, or a ruder French version of the same. Even getting to *The Times* was easy, by District line to Blackfriars from Earl's Court Road Station, only a two-minute or so walk from the house.

As I had feared, the Paris appointment was filled but Donald Tyerman promised me the first available foreign post that fell vacant. He could not have been more sympathetic and suggested that I have a talk about salary and prospects with the manager, Francis Mathew, who had just been appointed to sort out the paper's somewhat straitened post-war financial circumstances. Francis Mathew came from an old Catholic family, as did I. So we both 'knew who the other was', and that was a help. Indeed not only did I know who he was but actually knew, through my brother Simon, two of his first cousins, both of whom were Catholic priests, David a bishop and Gervase a well-known Dominican theologian at Oxford. After quite a lot of Catholic gossip, the conversation got down to brass tacks.

'Capital idea that you want to work for *The Times* abroad,' he said. 'Newly married, no young children, just the kind of foreign correspondent we're looking for nowadays. Can't afford to cart nannies, nursemaids, that kind of thing, halfway round the world any more, can we?'

Not having thought of that aspect of our imminent happy event I had not yet told anybody on the paper about the baby on the way or indeed about my stepson already with me. Clearly this had been an oversight which needed correcting right away, lest I be accused of getting a foreign job under false pretences. 'As a matter of fact, sir, we are going to have our first baby quite soon.'

'First,' he exclaimed repeating the word several times as its implications began to sink in. 'Dear me, dear me, that puts quite a different complexion on matters. Extra travel expenses, higher housing costs; very, very different.'

At first, assuming he was joking or at any rate half joking, I replied somewhat in kind. 'Surely a good Catholic like you, sir, wouldn't want to encourage contraception?'

'Good God,' he said, blushing to the roots of his hair. 'I never thought of it like that. Encourage contraception. What a terrible thing. Don't tell David and Gervase will you? They would never forgive me.'

Henceforth Francis Mathew became a great support and when a few months later, after Dominique's birth, *The Times* sent me to Washington they sent us all first class with a nanny on the *Ile de France* and paid for us to spend a week en route in a suite at the Waldorf Astoria in New York. For my part I never did tell David and Gervase how near their relation had come to being the occasion of sin, although they, and Francis too, are now long past, I hope, having to worry about such things.

In the months before Washington I was made assistant diplomatic correspondent which meant occasionally standing in for the top man at the Foreign Office daily briefing. This was no run-of-the-mill briefing for all the press but a special personal briefing for *The Times* from the head of the news department, then the famous Sir William Ridsdale. First he would recount what he had just said for general journalistic consumption before showing one the telegrams themselves. The purpose of these meetings was to give the *Times* man an insight into the real reasons behind British foreign policy; reasons which were quite often different from those ministers were giving in the House of Commons. Ridsdale never made any bones about this. If British interests required a bit of healthy deception, then it was the Foreign Office's job to make sure that they received it. This did not for a moment mean that *The Times* should be an active party to the deception; only that they should be aware of the reasons for the deception. How could *The Times* make a sensible judgment about what was going on without knowing some of the subtleties that lay underneath the surface of events? Sir William didn't expect the *Guardian*, which took a black and white attitude to these matters, to understand, still less sympathise with reasons of state. But *The Times*, he implied, was a more sophisticated paper which could be fed on a stronger diet than soft soap.

Ridsdale was quite marvellous and in my experience there was nothing unhealthy about these special briefings which helped one to avoid being starry-eyed or quixotic about the subject of the day. If the *Times* man thought the Foreign Office was being unduly devious or that its deviousness was unjustified then it was easy enough for his copy to hint at that or for the leader writer to say so straight. This very often happened and the next day Sir William would give one his reasons for thinking that *The Times* had got the argument wrong. Thus was avoided the usual argument at cross-purposes which characterises so many exchanges between media and government. On no occasion do I remember Ridsdale ever trying to pull the wool over my eyes but rather trying always to remove the wool that journalists, in their innocence, pull over their own eyes. Usually I would go back to *The Times* with a much clearer understanding of the moral ambivalences affecting international relations and therefore able to write about them at a deeper, and incomparably more interesting, level than would otherwise have been the case. Yes, occasionally that did mean holding back and not getting on some moral high horse along with the rest of the press. But knowing when not to get on a high horse is quite as important a gift in responsible quality journalism as its opposite; even more important today when so few editors seem to possess it.

Occasionally the assistant diplomatic correspondent would also get a foreign assignment. My first one was to Finland as a member of a press invited by the Finnish government. That sounds a pretty humdrum assignment which, of course, it was. But it didn't seem so to me at the time. To be sent anywhere abroad for *The Times* seemed an immensely exciting challenge. It was now four years since I had begun a journalistic career without so far ever having had an opportunity to show my mettle. Now was my big chance. Never have I studied a subject so exhaustively – certainly not at Oxford or Cambridge. The weeks before setting out for Finland I went to the London Library and the Royal Institute of International Affairs at Chatham House – not yet the absurd organisation it has subsequently become – to mug up on the country's history. In those days reporters got their knowledge through reading books rather than through talking to experts or each other and I must have read at least a dozen. My colleagues on the trip were Richard Scott, grandson of C. P. Scott and diplomatic correspondent of the *Manchester Guardian*; Herbert Ashley, diplomatic correspondent at the *Daily Telegraph*; and the London editor of the *Scotsman* whose name I cannot remember, although he was far the most amusing of the lot. For them the assignment was pretty routine. They had done dozens of the same before. Only for me was it a kind of baptism of fire. The results were two 3,000-word turnover articles from 'our special correspondent lately in Helsinki', the first under the double heading 'Freedom of Finland: External Dependence As Price of Liberty at Home' and the second, 'Self Help in Finland: Struggle to Pay Reparations and Settle Refugees'. In the first article there was a small map by way of breaking up the density of the text; in the second, no illustration whatsoever. Rereading the articles today I am immensely impressed by the wealth of detail and density of argument. Nowhere in the daily or Sunday press today would such serious articles be allowed to appear. The articles contain one or two phrases which I remember having enjoyed writing, even after forty years, such as 'the Port of Petsamo is rendered ice free by the last flick of the Gulf Stream's tail', or 'Communism, the Finns argue, is a political philosophy that all civilized and healthy communities can afford to defy; Russia is a neighbour no small nation can afford to provoke.' My very much more experienced and senior colleagues did not produce nearly so much copy and in the case of Herbert Ashley such copy as he did produce turned out to be a straight plagiarisation from a Chatham House pamphlet whose author wrote a letter to the *Daily Telegraph* starting: 'Sir, I would like to say that I agreed with every word of your diplomatic correspondent's article which is not surprising as I wrote them all myself ... ' That was the end of Herbert Ashley. Donald Tyerman wrote me a memo which sent my spirits soaring. 'My hunch has paid off. May these be the first of many turnover articles from your pen which do the paper credit. Having watched you sail over your first fence, I look forward to you taking Becher's Brook [a reference to the impending American assignment] with the same sure step.'

Dominique was born, perfect in every respect, very soon afterwards and everything in my life seemed set fair. By now I did know what I wanted to do. I wanted to write articles. Before, I had vaguely hoped that that might be my forte. Now I knew it was, and approached what my mentor, Donald Tyerman, called my Becher's Brook with a thumping heart that betokened more confidence than fear.

10

Correspondent in Washington

In 1938 Simon and I had spent a summer holiday in North West Harbour, Maine, staying with some friends of my stepfather and mother, Eliot and Nancy Wadsworth. We had travelled out to Boston by boat on our own, aged thirteen and fifteen, which made us feel very grown up, a feeling further accentuated, on arrival in Maine, by the extreme lack of sophistication of our American age group, none of whom, for example, had ever heard of Oscar Wilde. Whether young Nancy, our hosts' delightful daughter, enjoyed being saddled for the summer with two such show-off English schoolboys seems rather doubtful. But her mother certainly did and we were taken the rounds from one clapboard ocean house to another as prize exhibits of British culture. It was a heady experience. Never before had we been made such a fuss of or so enthusiastically and generously indulged. Not only was this corner of Maine – Mount Desert, from which cars were still banned – one of the most beautiful spots in the United States, but the summer crowd we met – all rockribbed and ferociously anti-Roosevelt Republicans – could not have been more welcoming in every way. Even my total lack of athletic prowess was transformed into a virtue. 'Don't interrupt Perry, he's reading,' Mrs Wadsworth would say if her daughter's friends, all bronzed and muscular, sought to attempt or compel me into childish poolside frolics. Nobody has ever had a happier or a more ego-enhancing introduction to the United States.

In the event it was also more than that. For not only was Eliot Wadsworth a Republican, he was a very important Republican who had been Under-Secretary of the Treasury in the administration of President Herbert Hoover, whom he had introduced to my stepfather. The two became friends and I remember my stepfather showing us a telegram from President Hoover which read, 'Happy Birthday from the White House, Washington, to the Red House, London' (where Norman then lived), rightly assuming that it would appeal to our schoolboy sense of humour. Such early impressions have a disproportionate influence. This one meant that, unlike most of my generation, I first heard of Herbert Hoover in a rather endearing context, instead of as the wicked ogre responsible for the great slump and Depression. So not only had a blissfully happy pre-war holiday predisposed me in favour of Republicans but a connected experience had predisposed me to like Hoover, or if not like, at any rate to feel that I had some more intimate knowledge of the man than had the rest of the world who condemned him as the devil incarnate.

All this by way of explaining why I felt rather an odd man out in the Washington of 1951 where all my foreign correspondent colleagues almost without exception were unashamedly and brazenly pro-Democrat, as were all the British Embassy officials.* In those days for a British correspondent or diplomat to be pro-Democrat did not necessarily mean that he was pro-Labour at home. Even staunch British Conservatives were pro-Democrat. Churchill himself was pro-Democrat. FDR and the Democrats, after all, had brought America into the war, against strong opposition from the Republicans, most of whom were still, even in 1951, isolationists. Being pro-Democrat was, if you like, the consensus British view which nobody questioned. Possibly I would have felt tempted to question it anyhow out of perversity, rather in the same spirit as I championed Catholicism at a Protestant public school. But if that was a possibility it was transformed into a certainty by another spin-off from the Wadsworth connection which took place almost immediately after I took up my Washington post.

Eliot and Nancy Wadsworth, old-time Washingtonians, asked us to dinner at their immensely grand Tracey Place mansion. The dinner was in honour of Senator Robert Taft, then Republican congressional leader and an unreconstructed isolationist. Generous as ever, Eliot made sure that I had an opportunity to talk to the famous or, in British eyes, infamous man, responsible not only for isolationism but also for the recent Taft-Hartley

*The one exception was Jack Broadbent who occasionally stood in for William Hardcastle, the resident *Daily Mail* correspondent. Jack, a much older man, had for years been the *Mail*'s Westminster correspondent and was friendly with Christopher Soames who was the then prime minister, Winston Churchill's son in law and aide. In return for my help with his despatches about American politics – where he was happy to take my line – Broadbent would allow me to listen in to his nightly trans-Atlantic telephone calls to Soames in London. Even more valuable, he would take me along to Soames's hotel room in Washington and New York whenever he was accompanying the prime minister on one of his regular visits to the United States. All Broadbent's scoops came from Soames. When I queried him about the propriety of relying so wholly on a single source he answered: 'If you can get your information straight out of the horse's mouth, why waste time scooping up other men's droppings?'.

Another colleague, who became a friend, was Max Freedman of the *Guardian*. What I remember best about him was his hatred of his senior colleague in New York, Alistair Cooke, whom he accused of taking all the credit for the *Guardian* coverage without doing any of the donkey work. We also saw a lot of, and liked, Henry Brandon, who was then only a humble stringer for the *Sunday Times*. Because of his East European background and strange accent, he was rather suspect at the British Embassy which even excluded him from the Ambassador's circle of trusties. Ten years later the tables were turned when Brandon became President Kennedy's favourite British correspondent and a leading Washington social lion in his own right.

134

Act, denounced by trade union leaders as the slave labour bill. All it did, in effect, was to prohibit the closed shop, along much the same lines as Mrs Thatcher's trade union reforms did in Britain nearly forty years later. In that sense, far from being a reactionary measure, it was very much a forward-looking one, ahead of the times rather than behind them. But that is not how it was presented in the 1950s even in Britain's Tory press, then very much in the embrace of 'One Nation' thinking. 'Outlaw the closed shop', who but a neanderthal old-guard Republican like Robert Taft could ever dream of putting the clock that far back? Such was the spirit of the age.

Not that the senator talked about trade union affairs which in those days were regarded as an unfit subject for social conversation in polite Washington society. As always foreign policy was the topic and the senator spoke admiringly of Britain's role in the world. Seeing my surprise he explained that isolationism should not be confused with anti-Britishness. 'The more the US got involved in the world, the less Britain would count,' he said. 'You couldn't have *won* the war without America,' he conceded. 'But after Alamein you could have fought Hitler to a draw. That would have preserved British interests. Once America joined in, it became America's war, whetting America's imperial appetite – something which wasn't either in Britain's interests or in America's. American isolationism represented a much less serious threat to the British empire than did FDR's so-called policy of friendship, which would prove the kiss of death.'

It was a fascinating talk, at the end of which I asked him if I could report what he said, which seemed to me to cast new light on his views. He readily agreed, adding that they only seemed new because he had not talked to a British newsman for so many years. Next morning, as soon as I got to *The Times* office in the National Press Building, I told my chief, John Duncan Miller, what had transpired and proposed doing a despatch on what I regarded as an interesting little exclusive, only to be told, 'It is not the job of *The Times* newspaper to provide a platform for reactionary rant.' Although outraged at the time, I now bless Johnny Miller for that remark. For thenceforward I had a sense of mission: to provide precisely that platform. What Senator Taft had said had interested me; indeed enlightened me. After years of wartime propaganda about FDR and the Democrats, which continued long into the peace, Senator Taft's views had come as a breath of fresh air. Why shouldn't they be passed on to the British public? It was extraordinary, even disgraceful, that no British correspondent had tried to get close to him, and others like him. Clearly there was a gap in the then British coverage of American affairs which from then onwards I did my best to fill.

It was a pretty poor best. The number two job in *The Times* bureau did not amount to much more than being dogsbody to Johnny Miller who knew everybody – except, that is, the Republicans. While he was out and about, I looked after the shop in the National Press Building, rewriting agency copy and attending the daily State Department press briefings. Johnny Miller seldom went to Capitol Hill, or encouraged me to go there. Congress was then in the hands of the Republicans who were busy chasing communists, a pursuit judged by Johnny Miller as beneath his readers' attention.

How on earth Johnny Miller had ever been appointed *Times* correspondent needs some explanation. He had no journalistic training and came to the job straight from being director of the British Information Services in Chicago. Strange as it may seem today, very few of the regular stable of senior *Times* foreign correspondents in those days knew anything at all about the United States. That Washington had become a plum job was plainly true in theory. For that was where power lay in the post-war world. The trouble was, however, that so few mainstream journalists wanted to work there. The European capitals were still where they felt at home. After all, Churchill had been the first Prime Minister ever to visit America while in office. Nor was American history taught in the schools except in so far as it impinged on British history. In Cambridge it had just crept into the history tripos, although among my friends only Colin Welch read it, possibly under the influence of Denis Brogan who was a Fellow of Peterhouse. For the most part, we were all what has come to be called Eurocentric, and none more so than most of the high-ups on *The Times*.

Until the war this had not seemed to matter much. From 1920 to 1947 the *Times* correspondent had been a colourful figure called Sir Willmot Lewis, one of whose most steadfast working rules, according to *The Times* official history 'was to disregard instructions from Printing House Square – if indeed by any rare chance Printing House Square so forgot itself as to send instructions'. By 1947, however, Lewis was in his late sixties and becoming ever more eccentric. One of Britain's few senior journalistic figures who did know about America was Geoffrey Crowther, then editor of *The Economist*, and it was he apparently who recommended Miller to the then *Times* editor, Robin Barrington-Ward, largely on the urgings of Johnny's masterful wife Madeleine, daughter of a colonial governor, who was at the time contributing to *The Economist* from America, although she had no journalistic experience either, unless being an excellent hostess counts as such – which in Washington it does.

Madeleine was enormously tall, as was Johnny, and they made an imposing pair. Her first words to Claudie were unforgettable. 'Watch out, my girl. They all go impotent in this climate and you'll be lucky if he doesn't take to drink as well.'

In every social way Madeleine Miller was the ideal boss's wife, inviting Claudie and myself to her much-sought-after Georgetown parties where we met everybody who was anybody so long as they were Democrats. Dining with the Millers was also a must for visiting British politicians – second only to dining with Sir Oliver and Lady Franks at the British Embassy – but there again the only ones I remember meeting under their roof were up-and-coming Labour MPs such as Roy Jenkins and Anthony Crosland. Among the American journalist guests were Walter Lippmann and Joe Harsch; again not a proper Republican columnist was ever to be seen.

In many ways this was understandable. A Democratic administration, under President Truman, was making the news and what news it was. These were the years when the Cold War began – Marshall Plan, NATO, Russian invasion of Czechoslovakia, Berlin Airlift, the Korean War. Dean Acheson, Secretary of State at the time, described this period in his autobiography as 'In at the Creation'. No wonder Johnny and Madeleine Miller, with easy access to these gods, had no time for lesser mortals. In their position, I would have probably done the same. But I was not in their position. I was an ambitious, young and very junior foreign correspondent looking for his own furrow to plough, his own issue to latch on to, and this total disregard of the Republican Party struck me as sadly out of date. For twenty years, it is true, Republicans had been deservedly in the wilderness, first because of their opposition to the New Deal and then because of their opposition to the war against Nazi Germany. On both these historic issues they had been absurdly wrong. So during that period it had been safe to treat them as nutcases. But it was no longer safe. In the new circumstances of the Cold War, with communist Russia now the enemy rather than Nazi Germany, conservative America, i.e. Republican America, was bound to have a much larger – indeed leading – role to play. For whereas all the liberal elements in the Democratic Party had been united in their fight against the Nazis they were very far from united in America's fight against communist Russia. Certainly the Truman administration itself was staunchly anti-communist; as stalwart by then as could be. But that certainly could not be said about the party as a whole, which still contained large and influential elements who found it difficult to think ill of the Soviet Union. My point was that whereas liberal America was sufficiently united and dedicated to fight and win a hot war against fascism, it was not sufficiently united and dedicated to win a cold war against Russia. For that new and historic struggle something extra would be needed; some additional political strength and popular conviction and this could only come by harnessing the passions and, yes, the prejudices of conservative, even reactionary, America.

In arguing this case with Johnny Miller I drew a parallel with British politics of the same time. What chance, I asked, would a Labour government have of fighting the Cold War successfully if it had to rely only on the

Labour Party? Of course Prime Minister Attlee and Mr Bevin, his Foreign Secretary, were unswervingly anti-communist, as unswervingly anti-communist as were President Truman and his Secretary of State. But many in their party were not. Fortunately for Mr Attlee and Mr Bevin, however, they could rely on the enthusiastic support of a Conservative Party which had not been demoralised by twenty years in the wilderness. What is more, Conservative opinion was still a strong force in the land, particularly in the media. In America, however, as a result of twenty years of liberal democratic ascendancy, conservatives and conservatism enjoyed no comparable positions of prestige and influence – certainly not in the east coast media. Nothing, therefore, was more important, I argued, than to start taking right-wing Republicanism seriously again. Could not *The Times* set the other British papers – and the embassy – an example by doing this?

Not surprisingly, I suppose, my urgings fell on deaf ears. This was the period, it has to be remembered, when Senator McCarthy, a right-wing Republican, was at the height of his Red-baiting stunts, as were lots of other right-wing Republican congressmen and senators, including Richard Nixon. Against such an ugly background of Republican bad behaviour there was little likelihood of Johnny agreeing to my plea that *The Times* should take the American right seriously – except as a menace. Here again, on the subject of McCarthy, I was an odd man out. For unlike the rest of my colleagues I was not all that shocked by McCarthyism, as it came to be known; in fact rather more impressed than shocked. For it seemed to me that there was more than enough justification for a lot of Red-baiting in America's recent past. After all, at Yalta, the Democrats had grossly underestimated the depth of Stalin's evil, as a result of which Eastern Europe had been lost to the free world. Again, the same miscalculation had been made about Mao Zedong, widely regarded in Democratic circles as only an agrarian reformer, with comparably disastrous results for China. At home, too, internal security against communist espionage had been disastrously lax with the result that Russia had been able to develop its own atom bomb much earlier than would otherwise have been the case. Given all these Democratic blunders in the recent past, was it not understandable that the Republican opposition should look for scapegoats and, in a vigorous rumbustious democracy like America, was it not to be expected that this search would turn ugly? Eliot Wadsworth had often regaled me with stories of how he and his Wall Street friends had been mercilessly pilloried by congressional committees in the 1930s, charged with being personally responsible for the miseries of the slump. How fair was that? Had liberal America sprung to their defence? Of course it hadn't. So why all this liberal hullabaloo about McCarthy's unfairness to former communists? Far from McCarthyism being a sign of the sickness of American democracy, I argued, it was a sign that it was alive and kicking in a way that Britain's –

where no such awkward questions about fifth columnists were being asked – was not.

This was another of my *idées fixes* at that time: that Britain's relatively relaxed and civilised reaction to the recent defection of the two diplomats, Burgess and Maclean, was not so much an example of the superior maturity of British democracy as of the greater strengths of the British ruling class. In Britain popular anger and suspicion about the existence of communists in high places might well be just as great as it was in America. But whereas in America the political class was not authoritative enough to clamp the lid down, in Britain it was. Any British MP who dared to try to exploit that anger and suspicion in Senator McCarthy's boorish and ungentlemanly manner would not stand a chance. All sides of the House would gang up against him, not so much because he was a threat to freedom as because he was a threat to good behaviour. But in America there was no such all-powerful 'establishment' – this word had just been given a new lease of life in the *Spectator* by Henry Fairlie, about whom much more later – capable of imposing good behaviour from the top.

Needless to say, this point was not original. De Tocqueville had made it often enough. But it had been borne in upon me with great contemporary force when watching Dean Acheson get the works from the Senate Foreign Relations Committee. In polite Washington society in those days Dean Acheson was rightly revered. Never had there been a more perfect example of an east coast patrician – six foot tall with a ramrod back and bristling moustache and all the other accoutrements of a very superior person, a kind of American Lord Curzon. As the real author of the Marshall Plan and of NATO his reputation for statesmanship stood deservedly high. It is true that he had given the North Koreans the green light to invade South Korea in an unfortunate speech, but given all his subsequent achievements, nobody in polite society ever thought of holding this against him. On Capitol Hill, however, none of the rules of polite Washington society seemed to apply. To my amazement the senators did see fit to question Dean Acheson and go on questioning him about his Korean blunder, until the Secretary of State eventually lost his temper and snapped back: 'Gentlemen, would you mind putting up your hands when you want to ask me a question as I can't hear if you all speak at once like so many schoolboys.' In Britain such an Olympian rebuke from so famous an establishment figure would have been more than enough to silence rebellious MPs. Not so with the Senate Foreign Relations Committee, among whom all hell broke loose. The Secretary of State was roundly condemned by the chairman and ordered to withdraw his insulting comment. Next day the *Washington Post*, then as now the bible of polite Washington society, had a headline: 'Secretary of State Browbeaten by Senators' and Johnny Miller sent a despatch to the London *Times* on the same lines. But in truth the Secretary of State hadn't been browbeaten. He had tried to do the browbeating, to put the senators in their place, and instead been put in his.

Whatever else this was, it was not undemocratic, and much the same thing could be said, it seemed to me, about the McCarthy hearing. Incidentally, I remember at this time getting into a heated argument on this very point with a new Tory MP whom I met for he first time in a radio station in, I think, Austin, Texas. He must have been on a parliamentary tour and I must have been sent there by Johnny on a journalistic assignment. In those days the arrival of a visiting British journalist or MP was still rare enough to arouse some interest and we had both been asked to take part in an evening chat show. Inevitably the subject under discussion was Senator McCarthy whom the visiting Tory MP denounced in what was to become his usual heavy-handed way. Partly out of mischief I said that it was high time that the British House of Commons took the problems of communism in high places as seriously as the senator was doing. 'Instead of denouncing him you should take a lesson out of his book,' I told the MP. The MP took grave exception to my 'disgraceful' remarks, as he did, even more vehemently, to another point I also sought to make. Charging the Democrats with appeasement of communism, I argued, was a perfectly respectable drum for a Republican politician in the wilderness to beat. The Democrats were seriously vulnerable on this front. It was their Achilles' heel. True, the Truman administration had eventually had the wool pulled from their eyes about Stalin. But then, I said, so had Chamberlain eventually had the wool pulled from his eyes about Hitler. But this did not prevent his critics pillorying him almost to the grave for his folly. Then foolishly I started laying it on too thick. American politicians hungry for power after long years in the wilderness would be mad not to plug the anti-communist issue for all it was worth, I said. Had not Mr Churchill exploited the appeasement of Hitler issue for exactly the same purpose? This was more than the new Tory MP was prepared to put up with and he walked out of the studio, refusing to come on to dinner after the programme. Only on returning to London a year or so later did I discover the new MP's name. He was Colonel Edward Heath.

Another memorable encounter of mine at this time was with Senator Richard Nixon, at a party given by someone whom I had met at that Wadsworth dinner. In the eyes of the Millers Nixon had by then replaced Robert Taft as the bogeyman of American politics. They could not forgive him for the way he had brought Alger Hiss to book as a Russian spy. So far as they were concerned Nixon was the truly guilty man, not Hiss. Somewhat predictably, given my mood, I rather took to Senator Nixon who in turn seemed quite pleased to talk to a British foreign correspondent, possibly because in these early days of his career he had not previously met one. In the course of our conversation he told me of an exchange he had had a year or so earlier with Jack Warner, president of Warner Brothers, during a hearing of the House Un-American Affairs Committee in which Warner, after boasting of how many hundreds of anti-Nazi films his Hollywood company had made, was forced to confess that it had not yet made a single anti-communist one and had no plans to do so, in spite of the Cold War being then at its most critical stage. According to Nixon this was because the movie industry was riddled, not with communists, but with committed anti-anti-communists who, in present circumstances, were now more of a danger than the communists themselves.

Just as Taft's comments about the threat posed to Britain by American imperialism had given me food for thought, so now did this comment of Mr Nixon's. It was the first time I had heard the phrase anti-anti-communist. How was it that whenever I met a Republican right-winger, men dismissed by the Washington cognoscenti as retarded, something far more thought-provoking was said than ever was to be heard in the more fashionable Washington drawing rooms frequented by intellectual heavyweights like Walter Lippmann and James Reston of the *New York Times*? Once again I returned to the office with what I thought was a good idea for an article, on how Hollywood proposed to fight the Cold War or rather how Hollywood proposed not to fight the Cold War, only to be given another flat negative, coupled with a warning about the dangerous Red-baiting company I was getting into the habit of keeping. So far as Johnny Miller was concerned anti-communism was always 'hysterical', worthy only of absolute and unconditional condemnation. Up to a point he was right. Certainly by 1951 the Truman administration needed no lessons in anti-communism. Indeed it could hardly have been more anti-communist. The Truman Doctrine, in which the policy of containment was announced, amounted virtually to a declaration of war against Russia, albeit only Cold War. Moreover, vigorous security regulations, intended to weed out communists from government service, had already been introduced. So in those respects what needed to be done, had been done. But this was not Senator Nixon's rather more subtle point. For he had not pretended that there was any longer a serious communist conspiracy. The active communists in government had been weeded out. But that did not settle the matter. An awkward question still remained. Why were there still so many anti-anti-communists around in influential positions? If there had been as many anti-anti-fascists around in influential positions at the beginning of the war against Germany, would not the liberals have been the first to see that this constituted a serious obstacle to its successful prosecution? So why didn't they feel equally worried about the existence of so many anti-anti-communists in influential positions at the beginning of the Cold War against Russia? It seemed to me that the reason was obvious. Most liberal New Dealer Americans of that period did not hate communism in the way they hated Nazism. Whereas American liberalism required its adherents to feel whole-hearted, fierce hatred of fascism, it required only half-hearted, more in sorrow than in anger, opposition to communism.

There was a genuine problem here. In the 1930s many among what came to be known as the chattering classes had become accustomed to regard the communists as basically on the side of the angels, as an acceptable variation of the liberal tradition. They had had communists as their friends and were bound together, as Leslie Fiedler was to put it later in an *Encounter* article:

> not only by a passionate revulsion for war and the inequities of capitalism but more positively by certain tastes in books and in the arts, by shared manners and vocabulary, and especially by the sense of moral engagement that used to be called social consciousness. From this feeling of fellowship the great popular front organisations of the 1930s were forged; in the teeth as it were of the ordinary American voter who – immune to all this – identified not only the communists but also their liberal friends with free love, anarchy and other iniquities; and who were condescended to majestically by the enlightened, thus storing up a special resentment for the hour of disillusion.

About communism the mostly Democratic chattering classes had got it wrong and the mostly Republican red-neck know-nothings had got it right – hating communism and all its evil nonsense from the word go. So no wonder the know-nothings were in a vindictive and suspicious mood, only too pleased to see Senator McCarthy indicting all those patronisingly clever people for their appalling misjudgment. Not only did this seem to me natural and just in a democracy but also desirable. Even forty years later, after the full horrors of communism in the Soviet Union and all over the world have been exposed, many liberal Americans still could not stomach President Reagan calling the Soviet Union an evil empire. If they still found it difficult to think of the Soviet Union as evil in the 1980s, imagine how much more difficult it was for them to do so in the 1950s when Stalin, the heroic wartime ally, was still affectionately known as Uncle Joe? Such people were not remotely communist, still less communist spies. But they were not of the stuff out of which Cold War warriors could be made. Anti-fascist hot war warriors, yes; but not anti-communist cold war warriors. Liberal America had the will to fight an anti-fascist war through to the finish, that much was certain, since they had just done so. But it was not so certain that it would have the will to fight an anti-communist war through to the finish, unless – and this was the point I so much wanted to shout from the housetops – the country's right arm, i.e. the Republican Party, half atrophied through lack of use, was again brought into action.

Between Johnny and myself there was no meeting of minds, which made for an uneasy relationship; more so for me than for him since he was always very much the boss. He had the blue pencil and I had not. Nor were the differences only political. At our lunches at the bar of the National Press Club I would always order the same menu, chilli con carne followed by buttered pecan ice-cream, a combination of which I never grew tired. To Johnny, who loved soft shell crabs, clam chowder and Philadelphia German cheese on rye sandwiches, this was just another example of my incorrigible conservatism, an even more provocative example of which was my refusal to echo his constant demands to the London office for radical increases in our living allowances. This was slightly unfair on my part since by then Claudie and I were living rent-free in a Chevy Chase mansion lent by Marriner Eccles, a former governor of the Federal Reserve Bank. Admittedly we had to keep an army of black servants in the standard of life to which they claimed to be accustomed, i.e. wild turkey at least three times a week. But even this expenditure left us comparatively well off, and able to entertain on a scale which almost rivalled that of Madeleine herself. That, too, began to cause problems. In one of the gossip columns mention was made of this young English couple with the 'exotic' name of Peregrine Worsthorne whose hospitality was 'the talk of the town'. Madeleine, who read the gossip columns, was not much pleased and even less pleased when Claudie somewhat maliciously let on that her dire predictions about what happened to husbands in Washington had so far, in our case, proved unfounded.

Here the story takes a sad twist. Johnny dug his professional grave by going overboard for Adlai Stevenson, Governor of Illinois, whom the Democrats had nominated as their 1952 presidential candidate to run against the Republican choice of Dwight D. Eisenhower. It was a mad choice. Adlai Stevenson, a witty, refined east coast liberal, was about as unsuitable to lead America into the Cold War as would Clement Davies, Britain's Liberal leader in 1940, have been to lead Britain into the hot war. He never had a chance. Yet Johnny not only thought he ought to win but was convinced, right until the bitter end of the campaign, that he had a chance of doing so. By then his judgment had gone completely haywire. In his view General Eisenhower had lost all credibility and respectability by refusing to denounce Senator McCarthy's anti-communist witch-hunting and by choosing another 'rabid' anti-communist, Richard Nixon, as his running mate. Anyone who could choose Nixon as his running mate, Johnny insisted, could and should never make it to the White House.

With my chief taking this line in his despatches I felt a bit constrained in mine. Not that I had all that opportunity to disagree since Johnny did most of the campaign reporting. But I did spend some time on Eisenhower's train – this was the last of the whistle-stop campaigns before air travel took over – and even shook hands with the great soldier under whom I had served, in a loose manner of speaking, in the Second World War. There was nothing special about this encounter. Eisenhower used sometimes to wander down the press carriages, exchanging jokes with correspondents whose faces he recognised or, rather, with correspondents whom his aides thought he ought to recognise, one of whom was Eric Sevareid, the famous CBS pundit, whom I was, quite by chance, sitting next to. Naturally I jumped to my feet and Eisenhower, possibly sensing from my clothes that I was English rather than American, politely asked me my name. He had no idea what he was letting himself in for. 'Peregrine Worsthorne', as the gossip columnist had already noted, has an exotic ring to American ears and Eisenhower asked me to spell it out which, of course, I gladly did. Then one of his aides recalled that the first baby born to the Mayflower immigrants was christened Peregrine which prompted Eisenhower to quip that the name 'sure hadn't caught on' since he was 'goddarn certain' he'd never heard it before.

As soon as the illustrious candidate had moved on all the other journalists crowded around, anxious to know what he had been talking about. From then on, for about twenty-four hours, I became a person of consequence, and even Walter Lippmann, who was also covering the campaign, took me under his wing, which was not, as it turned out, quite as much of a blessing as I assumed it was going to be. For the night in question was one of those nights when Mr Lippmann was perhaps the least suitable person in America on whose lips to hang if one wanted to be well informed. It was the night Mr Nixon, Eisenhower's running mate for the vice-presidency, went on television, speaking direct to the American people in a bid to save his political career. A few days earlier the newspapers had been filled with stories about a secret fund which he was alleged to have accepted from a Texan oil man. Since the Republicans were making a great song and dance about the Truman administration's alleged corruption this was plainly potentially damaging and Eisenhower had ordered Nixon to come up with a plausible defence or else get off the ticket. Enormous tension built up all day on the Eisenhower train. He was speaking that night in Cincinnati. But Eisenhower's speech was not the story. The story was how he would react to the Nixon broadcast. Knowing Eisenhower's habits a bit by then it seemed likely to me that he would sleep on it overnight before announcing his verdict; in which case I would be only able to speculate about his decision for next morning's paper. Although Mr Nixon's speech attracted the largest viewership ever before recorded, sixty-eight million, it was pretty humdrum except for what became known as the Checkers Factor. After denying the charges Nixon said he expected the smears against him to continue. To forestall one, he admitted that he had accepted a gift from a Texan supporter. 'You know what it was? It was a little cocker spaniel in a crate that he sent me all the way from Texas. Black and white spotted. And our little girl Tricia, a six-year-old, named it Checkers. You know the kids

144

love that dog and I just want to say this right now, that regardless of what they say about it, we're gonna keep it.' Then came the perorations. 'Let me say this: I don't believe I ought to quit, 'cos I am not a quitter. And incidentally Pat is not a quitter. After all her name is Patricia Ryan and she was born on St Patrick's Day and you know the Irish never quit.'

As I feared, Eisenhower did not announce his decision that night and with a deadline approaching it seemed prudent to turn for advice to my new friend, Walter Lippmann. He was absolutely outraged by the performance which was, he said, the most maudlin piece of charlatanry he had ever heard. Even Dr Goebbels would not have stooped so low. Of course General Eisenhower could not keep such a cheap demagogue on the ticket, and so on and suchlike. In the event, of course, Eisenhower did keep him on the ticket, in response to popular demand. The broadcast had elicited tens of thousands of calls and telegrams of sympathy and not for the first time the great pundit, who initially had dismissed Franklin Roosevelt almost as contemptuously, got it wrong and I would have been wiser to take my cue from the black waiter in the dining car whom the Nixon broadcast had reduced to tears.

A few weeks before polling day we got a message from Printing House Square asking for two turnover articles, one on Eisenhower and the other on Stevenson, so that *The Times* could be prepared for either eventuality. Johnny spent a day writing the Stevenson piece, a labour of love. He included one of Stevenson's best cracks directed against Nixon. 'If you promise to stop telling lies about me, I will promise to stop telling the truth about you.' Days passed, however, and he had still not begun work on the Eisenhower piece. He would come into the office and stare for hours at a blank sheet of paper, looking sour and irritable. *The Times* began to get impatient, sending urgent reminders: 'Need Eisenhower soonest'. Still Johnny dithered. Finally, he conceded. Would I have a go? he asked. I think he must have realised by then that the Eisenhower article would be the one that eventually got used but even so he could not resign himself to writing it. When the news of Eisenhower's landslide victory came in he was shattered. I was not at his election night party because by then we were no longer on those kind of terms. But by all accounts it was a tragic affair. Not only did it mark the end of Stevenson's serious political career but also the end of Johnny's journalistic career. *The Times* never forgave him for misleading its readers so badly and after a period he gave up journalism altogether, moving on to the World Bank in Paris where at least he and Madeleine did not have to worry about inadequate living allowances. In fact he made a fortune in Sardinian land and died years later very rich in a lovely house in the South of France.

In the next six months or so I was to all intents and purposes in charge of the office which was a marvellous opportunity. Whether I acquitted myself well it is not for me to judge. But Felix Frankfurter, then the most famous of the Supreme Court judges, thought that I had. Writing to Leonard Miall, the BBC's first and most distinguished correspondent in Washington, he asked about the authorship of a long, three-thousand-word report that had appeared in *The Times* on the first session of the Eighty-Third Congress, the first Republican congress to share power with a Republican President for twenty years. Leonard Miall, who has kindly shown me the correspondence, replied that it was not written by Johnny Miller, who was away on holiday – a bit of a euphemism for a nervous breakdown – but by his assistant 'who rejoices in the exotic name of Peregrine Worsthorne. I don't know whether you know him ... he has been writing some splendid material in Johnny's absence but I heard today that unfortunately *The Times* is recalling him to write leaders.' Felix Frankfurter replied: 'My question about the authorship must have indicated my doubts that Johnny Miller could be the author of such a long ranged, balanced analysis of our politics. And I was pleasantly jolted by other despatches in *The Times*. You give the explanation. You know about the writ of Exeat. Why don't I issue the writ to keep Peregrine here?'

The writ of Exeat, as it happens, would not have been much good, since it allows one to leave rather than forcing one to stay – or that is what it did when I was at boarding school. In any case, I wanted to return to write leaders, having become more and more frustrated by being unable to get my message across in news despatches. In the event I was no more successful in getting it across in leaders either. In this respect Sir William Haley, the new editor, was as unresponsive as Johnny Miller. As soon as I got back to London he took me to lunch at the Athenæum to make his position clear. On no account was *The Times* going to start making excuses for Senator McCarthy. Having earned universal obloquy for making excuses for European fascism *The Times* was not going to make the same mistake about American fascism. My pleas that McCarthyism was at worst just another excess of American populism cut no ice. Still less did he like my idea that a bit more anti-communism would not come amiss in this country, and that the only reason it had not exploded here was that the authorities, including *The Times*, still had the power to damp it down for reasons which had much more to do with saving their own faces than with preserving the country's civil liberties.

After lunch I never saw Sir William Haley again. I wrote leaders, mostly on America, none of which were ever printed, or, if printed, only after being rewritten extensively by the foreign editor, Iverach McDonald, who was, in effect, my boss. After a few months of mutual exasperation and frustration Iverach called me in to say that it had been decided to offer me the job of Ottawa correspondent. Being a kind and good man Iverach spared no pains trying to convince me that this was promotion – rather than the equivalent of 'being sent to the Siberian salt mines' – even going so far as to arrange a lunch for me at the Garrick Club with Lester Pearson, then the Canadian Foreign Minister, and a much acclaimed world statesman who painted a glowing and flattering picture of how influential *The Times* Ottawa job, in the right hands, could now become. Sir Campbell Stuart, then a director of *The Times*, a Canadian himself, also invited me to dinner in his Highgate house *à deux*. I was a very lucky young man, he said, placing his hand on my knee. Canada was a country with a great future. Opportunity only knocked once and I would be mad not to seize my chance. Something warned me, however, that I was being conned. Perhaps it was a memory of my time in the foreign subs room when the Ottawa correspondent's copy had been the first to get spiked. Rightly or wrongly, I turned the job down. This decision was made easier to reach by my having been offered a much better paid leader-writing job by Colin Coote, the editor of the *Daily Telegraph*, entirely on the basis of a recommendation by Colin Welch who had been writing leaders for that paper for some time. Summoning up the courage to tell Iverach McDonald of my decision to resign was not easy. In those days working for *The Times* was more a vocation than a job. In the event I chose a bad moment to break the news. Iverach was standing in front of a mirror in his room straightening his black tie in a hurry to rush off to some diplomatic dinner and did not look round as I entered. Nor did he look round on hearing my news. All he said was, 'You are making a great mistake which you will regret for the rest of your life.' In a way he was right. Having once worked on *The Times* there was a sense in which all other kinds of journalism were a bit of a comedown. But in another way, he was quite wrong. About a quarter of a century after leaving *The Times* I visited Ottawa and met the very correspondent whom they had sent out there in my place. By then he had been there so long as to become something of a local legend. It was impossible not to shudder a little. How easily that could have become my fate.

11

From The Times *to the* Telegraph

The move from *The Times*, near Blackfriars, to the *Telegraph* proved quite a watershed not only in my professional but also in my social and even private life. Although *The Times* in those days was not far from Fleet Street physically it was a whole world away socially and culturally. The old chestnut about the butler saying, 'The press are here, my lord ... and also a gentleman from *The Times*,' still rang true. Certainly most of the senior leader writers – Captain Falls, Admiral Thursfield and all those professors – did not think of themselves as primarily journalists and those who did, such as John Pringle and John Midgeley, never thought of themselves, quite justifiably, as being in any way contaminated by the Street of Shame. On *The Times*, for example, we would write our leaders in longhand and take them down for typing to the editor's tall pre-Raphaelite secretary who would receive them reverently as if they were holy writ and type them out on a special machine reserved only for this neo-sacramental purpose. When on my first night on the *Telegraph* I tried to get the editor's zany secretary to perform the same service she managed to type the leader back to front, giving as her excuse that she had been quite unable to make head nor tail of it.

The accommodation, too, was markedly inferior. Whereas on *The Times* leader writers lived in spacious high-ceilinged rooms with coal fires, and took afternoon tea, served by uniformed parlour maids, in the proprietor's old private house, on the *Telegraph* my room was like a narrow cell and everybody ate together in a Hogarthian canteen. I remember Kenneth Rose, then an apprentice on Peterborough, putting his head round my door and expressing shock at the meanness of my quarters. 'My goodness,' he said, 'I should have thought you rated higher than that' – a comment containing barely enough flattery to disguise the sneer.

Kenneth Rose was right, as he always is in these matters. I had come down in the world; another case of landing up second best as with Stowe instead of Eton, Peterhouse instead of King's and the Ox and Bucks instead of the Brigade of Guards. But once again, as in all these instances – except possibly the Eton one – it all turned out for the best. For very soon the glamour of Fleet Street – and in those days it really did have glamour – took firm hold, a hold never loosened during the next thirty years or so. This had little to do with the work. Writing leaders for the *Telegraph* was much less glamorous than writing them for *The Times*. The glamour lay in the people; in the friends I made; in the social tumult into which I was swiftly drawn. Working on *The Times* had not affected the conventional way of life dictated by my background. Working on the *Telegraph* revolutionised it.

For example, I stopped lunching at Boodle's, a habit I never resumed. Coming out of the *Telegraph* office into Fleet Street on my very first day I ran into Henry Fairlie and John Raymond, two *Times* leader writers of my age who had also just left the paper for other things – Henry to become political columnist on Ian Gilmour's *Spectator* and John to become assistant literary editor on Kingsley Martin's *New Statesman*. They took me for a drink to El Vino's which I had never been to before. Standing at the bar were Derek Marks, then political correspondent on the *Daily Express*, Michael King, foreign editor of the *Daily Mirror*, and other Fleet Street giants – literal giants in those two cases – with all of whom Henry seemed on excellent terms, judged by their willingness to stand him drinks. Then we moved into the back room where we joined Philip Hope-Wallace's table for more drinks. The company there included Anthony Sampson, Patrick O'Donovan, Terry Kilmartin, the *Observer*'s literary editor, the writer and journalist Maurice Richardson and several others. The lunch break went like a flash. For the first time in my life the hours between one o'clock and three o'clock passed without any thought of food. Never before had I enjoyed myself so much. Thus began a lunchtime pattern which was not broken for many years.

Drinking at El Vino's, rather than lunching in Boodle's – which I had joined on coming of age – may seem a minor conversion compared to that of St Paul's on the road to Damascus. But on the scale of my life it was important enough. For me Boodle's had been part of a social ritual which included having my hair cut at Maurice Viane's (Charles) in Knightsbridge – very often sitting in the next chair to Anthony Eden who would be having his nails manicured, buying my suits at Adamson's in Sackville Street, my shoes at Hills also in Knightsbridge (with my own last); my shirts, always striped, at Drews in Piccadilly. It was to Boodle's that I had repaired immediately after returning from Washington to pick up the threads and hear the gossip. My proposer had been Dick Norman, a dashing nephew of my stepfather. Not only had Boodle's a shorter waiting list and a cheaper entrance fee than White's but also another even more important advantage over White's, at least in my mother's eyes: neither my father, nor any other

Koch de Gooreynd, belonged. Also, the building was very beautiful, with a bow window overlooking St James's Street in front of which all your friends passed by if after lunch you sat there long enough. Its disadvantage was that it contained no other journalists and, apart from Gladwyn Jebb and Anthony Nutting, pretty well no important politicians or civil servants who might be of interest to journalists, being full instead of landowners, many of whom were Lord Lieutenants like my brother, Simon. Not that the lack of journalists seemed a disadvantage to me at that time. Rather the opposite, since in those days I liked the place largely because, once inside, I could pretend to be – what at heart I still was – a man about town whose work was more an eccentric hobby than a necessary source of bread and butter.

Had I stayed on *The Times* that attitude might well have continued, although I am not so sure. For it was an attitude that made little sense. Nothing in the 1950s could have been sadder than the gentlemanly life which I was so anxious to cling on to. Turgenev wrote a sad short story called 'The Superfluous Man' about the fate of the Russian nobility after the tsar had deprived them of all the political and administrative duties which had earlier given some purpose and structure to their lives. Many of my friends at Boodle's in those days were superfluous men *à l'anglaise* who had also been deprived of their *raison d'être* by the post-war social revolution. For although the Tories were back in office, the climate was still highly unsympathetic to hereditary wealth and privilege. Upper-class young men took it for granted that just as their standard of living was lower than that of their parents – fewer servants for example – so that of their own children would be lower still, until there would be nothing left of the family fortune.

Naturally there were brilliant exceptions to this general air of decline and defeatism. My very dear friend, Oliver Knox, for example, also a Boodle's member, and two other old Etonians, bought an advertising company, Robert Sharp's, which did extremely well, and would have gone on doing well had it not suffered a grievous setback, entirely due to me. Thinking that I would do my friends a good turn I persuaded someone on the *Telegraph* to write a story about Robert Sharp's brilliantly original methods of recruiting bright young copywriting talents, one of which (the one we wrote about) was to invite applicants to spend a weekend at the Ritz where their wits were tested in a series of delicate social situations, the most delicate of all being a dinner party at which they were placed between a lady of quality pretending to be a tart and a tart pretending to be a lady of quality. Only those who could tell one from t'other were chosen. In my innocence I assumed that readers would be amused by this tale and that Olly Knox's company would benefit from such favourable publicity. I even expected to receive a case of champagne for my services. None came, not even a word of thanks. Nor was this surprising. The company was hauled

Sunday Telegraph editorial staff on the last Saturday in Fleet Street before moving to the Isle of Dogs in the summer of 1987.

Above left: Claudie, my first wife, when she came to lodge at Elm Park Gardens, 1949
Above right: Adrian Earle, the villain of Elm Park Gardens.

Below left: Claudie with my stepson, David Baynham, aged five. *Below right:* Claudie and Oscar Hahn, on holiday in Venice, 1960.

Portrait of Claudie by James Drew, 1965.

Friends. *Above:* Colin Welch, 1970; George and Pat Gale, early 1980s. *Below:* With Paul Johnson, 1970s; Henry Fairlie, 1960.

Giving my daughter, Dominique, away to her husband, Jim Keeling, outside the Brompton Oratory.

Jim, Dominique, Adam and Tom-Tom, the two eldest of my five beloved grandchildren, at Whichford Pottery.

Cartoon by Collett presented to me by my *Sunday Telegraph* colleagues on my retirement in 1991.

One of the last photographs of Prime Minister Thatcher in Downing Street, shortly before her departure, November 1991.

Portrait by my friend, Glynn
Boyd Harte, 1992.

t wedding to Lucinda Lambton,
May 1991.

Lucy Lambton, Clover and me at our beautiful home, the Old Rectory, Hedgerley, 1992.

before the disciplinary committee of the Institute of Advertising Practitioners and found guilty of 'bringing the advertising profession into
disrepute'.

Another very different exception was Bobby Buchanan-Michaelson –
not a member of Boodle's nor ever likely to be – whose father was an RAF
equerry to King George VI. When not jollying nuns into smuggling pack-
ages of contraceptive packets, under their habits, into Spain, he spent his
time thinking up other ways of mitigating hard times in relatively harmless
ways. One such was to persuade our mutual friend, Alex Poklewski – the
engaging ne'er-do-well undergraduate whose family lived with Princess
Marina at Coppins – to bamboozle the princess into using her influence
with the King and Queen to allow Bobby to invite young Princess Elizabeth
out to dinner and the theatre. Presumably in the hope of broadening the
princess's mind, permission was granted and the outing took place – the
first of that kind ever, I think. Understandably, Bobby milked the occasion
for all it was worth which in those days was a lot, including free meals in
perpetuity for Bobby and the rest of us in the lucky restaurant – L'Ecu de
France, I think – where the pre-theatre dinner had taken place. Unfortunately there is also a less than happy ending to this second example of
entrepreneurial spirit in action many years before the privileged classes
were expected to show any. As a result of being made a scapegoat for some
shady City dealings Bobby was sent to prison, which enabled him to claim
that his royal guest did eventually repay his hospitality, if only by putting
him up for several years at Her Majesty's pleasure.

For the most part, however, my friends did not fit easily into the 1950s.
Nor did a gallant war help. Rather the reverse since memories of past glory
made the new role of 'superfluous man' even sadder. In short they were a
depressed and depressing lot. Ernest Bevin at about this period made a
famous speech deploring the English working class's 'poverty of expectations', by which he meant their passive resignation to defeat in life. If he
had visited Boodle's in those egalitarian days he would have realised that it
was not only the working class that suffered from poverty of expectations.
Even more so did many of the post-war upper class, as a post-prandial
glance around the Boodle's saloon would have made depressingly clear.

So in a way the El Vino crowd did not have much to compete with so far
as I was concerned; still less as far as Claudie was concerned. She could not
wait for me to cut my links with a world in which she had never felt at
home. Claudie could not remember names and still less titles and got not
only bored but infuriated by the upper-class obsession with genealogy
which took the form, she alleged, of always asking: 'Who was his mother?'
The grander the person, the more certain Claudie was to forget who he or
she was and although some found this trait endearing, more did not. Nor
did she take to the Normans. Here I think she was mistaken, confusing
their joshing manner for rudeness and even arrogance. The Christmas after

our marriage, for example, we had spent at Moor Place in Much Hadham, one of the two Norman stately homes. At meals they would urge us to eat up. 'Come on, Worsthornes, you don't get food like this at home,' they cried, making a joke of our relative poverty. Claudie could not be persuaded to take this kind of heavy-handed teasing in good part. Nor were matters improved when all the Norman children received much more expensive presents than we had been able to give Claudie's son David. Never again would she agree to return to Moor Place.

Incidentally Claudie was not alone in finding the Norman manner difficult to stomach. Tommy Balogh, shortly after arriving from Hungary and long before he became a famous economist, was invited for lunch by my stepfather who thought he might make a useful recruit to the Bank of England. Any such possibility was soon knocked on the head when after lunch the young Normans, impeccably attired in white, bally ragged him into playing tennis, a game at which they effortlessly excelled – having won innumerable cups at Eton for this and other ball games – and at which he, dressed in grey flannels, cut the poorest of figures. Again there was no harm meant. So natural was their own physical grace that they did not even notice other people's humiliating lack of it. Many years later when Tommy Balogh had become Harold Wilson's recently ennobled economic adviser, I asked him if he remembered running off the Moor Place tennis court in a huff. He did. Whether that experience helped to push him into the arms of the Labour Party he refused to say. But having observed how he had arrived to lunch all smiles and charm, almost inviting seduction, and left all scowls and scorn, it does seem possible that it played a part.

In terms of social company I too was moving leftward, again thanks to Henry who knew far more Labour MPs than Tories. One evening he, Claudie, John Raymond and I were dining in a restaurant in Soho. At a nearby table was the great Hugh Massingham, the *Observer*'s political columnist, entertaining Aneurin Bevan and Michael Foot, both of whom stopped at our table for a drink on their way back to the House of Commons. I had often met important public men before in my stepfather's house but only in the way a child or youth is allowed to shake the great man by the hand and call him sir. Bevan was then front page news, being engaged in his fight to the death with Hugh Gaitskell for the leadership of the Labour Party. Here, however, was Henry, on the basis of equality, buying him a drink and even daring to lecture him about what he was doing wrong. At the end of the evening Henry's last train home to wife and family had gone hours ago and he came back with us to Scarsdale Villas where he burst into our bedroom the following morning bearing great armfuls of glorious fresh flowers which he had risen at dawn to collect from Covent Garden. No wonder Claudie fell in love with Henry. So, up to a point, did I.

As far as I can remember Henry stayed with us for the rest of the week and rather than let him go – not that he was showing any signs of wanting to – we invited his admirably tolerant wife Lizette and their three children to spend the weekend with us in London. The plan was that the two families should all join up with George and Pat Gale, whom Claudie and I had never met, for a picnic lunch in Virginia Water before going back to the Gales' house in Staines for dinner. George Gale was then Labour correspondent on the *Manchester Guardian* and had shortly returned from covering a Labour Party delegation to China, out of which arose *No Flies in China*, a book which debunked 1950s illusions about Mao Zedong's China as savagely as Malcolm Muggeridge's *Winter in Moscow* debunked 1930s illusions about Stalin's Russia. In the event the picnic, put together by Lizette, was not a success, not at any rate by my standards – too many children, not enough ice, melting butter, sliced bread. Nor did matters improve when we went back to the Gales' home in Staines. After drinking for hours, George growled something about sending out for fish and chips and got very angry when I said 'No thanks, George, not for me', fish and chips being my least favourite food, particularly after a sliced bread picnic. 'Why don't you like f ... ing fish and chips?' he roared. 'Too bloody snobbish, that's why', and much else besides in the man-of-the-people style which later came in so useful on his LBC phone-in programme. His beautiful wife Pat, however, sided with me and started screaming at George to mind his f ... ing manners. Henry took Claudie off to the pub until things calmed down which they soon did and at about 11.00 p.m. we all went out to some awful late night eating joint which made me regret the fish and chips. What the sleeping arrangements were I cannot remember; possibly because I don't want to remember. What I do remember is that Boodle's seemed a very long way, in another country to which it now seemed most unlikely I would ever persuade Claudie to return.

Henceforth things moved fast. What it was really like I cannot remember. There must have been leaders to write, books to read, conferences to attend. In retrospect, however, it seems to have been one long drunken party, starting daily with a lunchtime session at El Vino's and another, also at El Vino's, in the evening. Only a man of iron will could avoid these sessions because it was impossible to walk a step up or down Fleet Street without running into the inhabitants of my new country who would be heading off that way. If it wasn't Henry or George Gale, it was John Raymond, or if it was not Henry or John or George, it was Paul Johnson on a visit from Paris where he was working on a French magazine, *Réalité*, and also contributing articles on France to the *New Statesman*. Then there was Paul's friend, Hugh Thomas, who would arrive by taxi from the Foreign Office. Those were the regular temptations. But if they were not around that did not begin to mean that the coast was clear. Out of all the newspaper offices of Fleet Street at about the same hour, lunchtime and evening, poured hundreds of thirsty journalists, amongst whom there was always some kindred spirit, very often just back from exciting foreign parts, in search of a drinking companion. Nor was the company limited to journalists. George Gale's friend Kingsley Amis, then a lecturer in Swansea, was often to be seen and shortly after that fish and chip row at Staines he and his first wife Hilly were part of a group which went on to dinner one night at Quo Vadis. On this occasion it was Claudie who got into hot water for preferring to have her liver and bacon cut very thin at No 4, a preference which Kingsley, looking for trouble, condemned as bloody affectation. Presumably other more important matters were discussed – literature, politics, the arts. If they were, nothing said left much mark. I remember finding this a disappointment. Given half a chance I would have loved to discuss ideas. But we seldom did. Life was to be lived, not theorised about. In any case, such were our habits that they did not encourage abstract thought.

What did our group – for such we were fast becoming – have in common? Certainly not a political party or ideology. Henry, George and I were Tories but not of the same kind; John, Paul and Hugh Thomas were socialists, or thought they were. But these being the years of Butskellism – when both Labour and Conservative parties vied with each other to occupy the centre ground – ideology did not seem to matter. Certainly in our circle there was nothing similar to all the ideological debates – Trotskyists versus Stalinists for example – then raging among New York Jewish intellectuals. What we had in common, apart from a love of alcohol, was a hatred of cant which meant, in effect, a hatred of liberals like Mark Bonham Carter and other well-connected boobies. In only one respect was I an odd man out in this group. Everyone else seemed to be in love with Antonia Pakenham, then just down from Oxford. Attractive as she was, her personality jarred almost at our first meeting when she told me of her intention only to court 'the first eleven'. Such a remark, if made as a putdown to a pass, would have been memorably chastening; as it was, she threw it off with the heartless eye of a woman already loved to excess.

Henry, if not exactly the leader of our gang, was certainly its catalyst. Who was Henry Fairlie? In my new country this was not a question that anybody ever asked, much to Claudie's relief. It was years, for example, before I realised that John Raymond's mother was the famous light comedy actress Iris Hoey, and his father Cyril Raymond, a character actor then very much in evidence in all the Ealing comedy films. In Henry's case, however, it was a bit different since his father had been a journalist on the *Daily Express* who had collapsed and died in a taxi on his way home from El Vino's, than which no background could be more the stuff of legends – the equivalent at Boodle's of being the son of a Duke. It was when Henry recounted the story of his father's death that I first saw his face crease into what Philip Hope-Wallace once described as 'Henry's delinquent plough-boy grin'. One also knew that he had a hole in his heart which is why he had not served in the war; that he read history at Oxford, presumably only getting a second because he would have said if he had got a first. After Oxford he came to the notice of David Astor, then editor and proprietor of the *Observer* and a great talent-spotter, who took him on to write leaders. All went swimmingly at first until Henry began arriving later and later for work. Out of the kindness of his heart David Astor characteristically made an appointment for Henry to see a top Harley Street psychiatrist and, also characteristically, was much hurt and disappointed when Henry failed to keep it; but not so hurt and disappointed as to be deterred from persuading Donald Tyerman to give his ungrateful protégé a job on *The Times*.

Henry was always late for appointments, as much with prime ministers in Downing Street as girls in the Ritz, most of whom – until almost the very end – always forgave him, as had David Astor, who was only the first of a very long line of benefactors who let him get away with murder. In every generation there is one person who early on pre-empts the right to behave badly with impunity and in my generation that person was Henry Fairlie. Charm does not explain it, although he had lots of it. Nor does his wonderfully engaging rakishness. Certainly we envied him his conquests. But envy normally induces censoriousness rather than forgiveness. No, we indulged him because he was one of those rare people of whom it could truly be said that his private vices were essential to his public virtues. Alcibiades was the same, as was Charles James Fox, men for whom personal licentiousness and irresponsibility are the spurs which quicken and excite their imaginations to the point where, in Henry's case, he actually thought he had become the great statesman he was writing about, adopting his voice, his gestures and his whole persona. Claudie and I saw this over and over again when he lived with us. Never would his articles be full of such moral passion and display such sensibility and such authority as when sparked off by a night of reckless philandering and gross extrava-gance. Perhaps I am merely making excuses for Henry, or for all of us who never sought to rebuke or restrain him. One rebukes and restrains those who would be improved if they could be persuaded to abandon their bad habits. But what if the bad habits are the means to a valuable end, as they were in Henry's case, if great journalism can be so described?

Henry's most famous article, as it happened, was one in which I played a part since it arose out of an ongoing argument which the two of us had had on many occasions in El Vino's, beginning soon after my return from Washington, convinced that Senator McCarthy was a necessary evil; necessary in the sense that only a brutal battering-ram could ever break down Ivy League Washington's protection of well-connected communist fellow travellers in high places. Initially Henry disagreed with me, taking the view that in Britain at any rate parliament could do the job without recourse to populist demagogues. But as the years passed and the official obfuscations and prevarications about the Burgess and Maclean defections continued, Henry's doubts began to grow and in any case his beloved House of Commons happened not to be sitting when the government chose to announce officially, four years after their disappearance, that these two young diplomats, one a son of a former Liberal cabinet minister and the other an old Etonian, were indeed Russian spies. On the night of the announcement Henry and I, as usual, were sitting in El Vino's and he said that he was going to write about the matter. 'Do a McCarthy,' I urged. 'Just as McCarthy accused the Ivy League State Department and east coast liberal patricians of closing ranks to protect their own, why don't you accuse their equivalents here of doing the same?' Thus was the seed sown for the establishment article in which he accused England's unelected great and good – the Director-General of the BBC, the chairman of the Arts Council, and so on – of exercising influence, not so much through political pressure in the open as through behind-the-scenes social lobbying, word in ear, that kind of thing. The only person Henry mentioned by name was Asquith's daughter, Lady Violet Bonham Carter, who had seen fit to make a great hullabaloo about the popular press keeping a relentless watch on Donald Maclean's wife Melinda, on the grounds that it was an inexcusable intrusion on her privacy – a hullabaloo which looked pretty silly when the allegedly wronged lady did a midnight flit to join her husband in Moscow.

Henry's article caused a great furore and made him immensely talked about. But the dust soon settled and the establishment went on protecting its own as before: *vide* the continued charmed life of Anthony Blunt as keeper of the Queen's pictures and, for all we will ever know, many more besides. For one political journalist on the rampage in a highbrow small-circulation magazine could not begin to stir things up to the same degree as had a raucous, loud-mouthed American senator. That was my point. If you want to beat the establishment you can't afford to fight by Queensberry Rules. True, the senator's way of exposing the extent to which the American ruling class had been infiltrated by communists was contemptible and ran the risk of smearing at least relatively innocent men. But the British ruling class's way of covering up the extent to which it had also been infiltrated was equally contemptible and ran the scarcely less grave risk of leaving the guilty – or relatively guilty – untouched, the main difference between the two ways being that whereas the McCarthy methods were brazen and out in the open for all to see and condemn – as is right and proper in a democracy – Lady Violet's were discreet and quite hidden away from public scrutiny, as is not normally thought to be right and proper in a democracy. Although this thesis of mine had fallen on stony ground when first outlined over a fairly dry lunch with Sir William Haley in the Athenæum, it was some consolation that it had eventually borne journalistic fruit – albeit vicariously – after being sown in the much more receptive ear of Henry Fairlie over endless drinks in El Vino's.

Earlier I described Henry's journalism as great which is a big word to use without some attempt to justify it. What he succeeded in doing, I think, was to relate the colourful and intriguing activities of practical politics to some larger end. That meant he never judged what was going on at Westminster exclusively in political terms but also in terms to do with some larger conception of what he thought life ought to be all about. That is not an easy thing to do. Most politicians, and most political journalists, treat politics as if it were a separate activity, with its own values, morality and culture, rather in the manner of Machiavelli. Only a very few, while not ignoring its separateness, succeed in raising their sights to a higher level where politics merge with all the other worlds which go to make up a particular culture or even civilisation. In Henry's case that particular civilisation was made up of English gods, English destiny, English character, English morality, all of which grew out of English history and were usually summed up by Henry as 'the constitution'. Woe betide any politician who sinned against 'the constitution', which was tantamount, in Henry's book, to sinning against the Holy Ghost.

To me this was quite a new way of reflecting on contemporary politics; the humdrum politics of the here and now. For Burke to wax lyrical about the constitution in his reflections on the French Revolution, say, was one thing; but surely for a contemporary journalist to do the same, quite another. Not so for Henry. That mystical approach to parliamentary politics as something woven into the very texture of English life informed all he wrote. Whereas I was always tempted to see issues in ideological terms of right and left, he saw them in terms of which side of the question conformed best with his beloved constitution. Some socialist proposal – for progressive taxation, say – might find it easier to win Henry's approval, on the grounds that there was a good precedent for it, than might a new Tory regressive tax proposal which had been defended with arguments, never before heard in the House of Commons, culled from a German free-market economist. For my part I did not know enough history to react in this way; nor did I have Henry's confidence about what constituted Englishness. Lacking this knowledge and confidence I would get bogged down in dreary argumentation about 'isms' which could not begin to compare with Henry's deeper understanding of what was really at stake.

Again this comes back to force of personality. What is it about certain personalities that enables them to embody certain ideas? At the most grandiose level, de Gaulle and Churchill spring to mind. But in our own lives we all know such individuals. Henry was such a one for me. He embodied a certain idea of political journalism. His abysmal private life did not detract from that ideal but almost inspired it. Only by aggrandising, even ennobling, the importance and value of political journalism, and his own individual star role on the political stage, could he justify the self-ishness of his private life which often left his wife and children without the price of a pair of shoes or, far worse, the wherewithal to pay the children's school fees. He had to write like an angel so as to justify behaving like a devil. The lower he sank in debauchery the higher he aimed in his work. I would like to think that it was his high conception of journalism rather than his personal selfishness, that proved infectious with me. Even so, I was never in doubt, during those years of our intimate companionship, that the light of this Grub Street genius would not have shone so bright had not his black heart also cast such sad shadows over those who loved him.

If Henry was very much a son of Grub Street, John Raymond, another close companion, was what he called, a bit resentfully, a 'green room baby', i.e. a baby whose early years are spent in green rooms while their parents are performing on stage. Both his parents were too busy to be much at home during his childhood. When war came, however, work grew more difficult to get and they were unable to afford to send John up to Oxford, which gave him another grievance against them. After a comically undis-tinguished war in which he had never progressed beyond the rank of lance-corporal he somehow wangled a job – almost certainly through his parents' theatrical contacts – as *Daily Sketch* assistant dramatic critic, in which capacity he distinguished himself by walking out after the first act of Agatha Christie's *The Mousetrap* on the grounds that it was not worth reviewing, a conclusion much encouraged by his companion. Although our decision showed taste it was also notably ill-judged since the play is still running, while John's employment on the *Daily Sketch* ended the following morning. More strings were pulled to get John on the arts side of *The Times*, his principal duty there being to write vaguely cultural timeless leaders which could be held 'on ice' for use in emergencies. This proved a frustrating job. One such piece he wrote – it may well have been the only one – was on the Congress of Vienna, a beautifully crafted little essay on the art of diplomacy. Day after day, week after week, month after month it would appear on the list of leaders in type, and every so often the foreign editor would ask John to give it a new topical peg which meant writing into its first paragraph some reference to current diplomatic events. Here I was able to help in my capacity as assistant diplomatic correspondent. In spite of being 'renosed' more than a dozen times the leader never got printed, and John, whose main love was literature, took himself off impatiently to the *New Statesman* where his career swiftly flourished and he soon became almost as famous in London's literary world as Henry had become in the political. One particularly brilliant article, in which he analysed the anti-semitism of the novels of Buchan, was much acclaimed and talked about.

Through him I met C. P. Snow (who made John godfather to his only son), J. B. Priestley, Anthony Powell, Angus Wilson and many other literary giants. Just as, almost from one day to the next, my friendship with Henry had put me on christian-name terms with leading politicians, so now through John I began to feel equally at ease with the great writers. As an anonymous leader writer on the *Daily Telegraph,* my own name was still entirely unknown. Whereas their names on the stock exchange of journalistic reputations were at their peak, mine so far was not even listed. Where I scored, however, was in having a rich, civilised and worldly barrister friend, Billy Hughes, with a luxurious flat in Lower Belgrave Street where we were all made welcome to delicious dinners cooked by his resident cook-housekeeper Walsh: saddles of lamb, game, Scotch woodcock, vintage wines and all the other Edwardian luxuries which were then things more often dreamt about than tasted. In those days nobody else of our generation could remotely afford to have a resident cook or to live in Billy's gentlemanly man-of-letters style where the sideboard was always groaning with drinks and cigars and his bookshelves full of first editions and all the best new works. The atmosphere was more that of a set of college rooms or of chambers in Albany than of a mere flat. Never would he fail to put on a velvet dinner jacket for dinner and I do not recall arriving once when he was not sitting ensconced in a deep armchair reading some leather-bound volume which he would carefully replace in the bookshelves before offering one a long whisky and soda in a giant tumbler. Not even Henry took liberties with Billy* – or at any rate not until the evening got well under way. Nobody, however, dared get drunk, not because Billy disapproved of drink – far from it – but because the drawing room contained so many precious objects that we were terrified of knocking something over. On one terrible occasion Constantine FitzGibbon's wife, Theodora, started playing leap-frog with a Ming horse and that was the only other occasion I ever remember Billy losing his cool, or his sangfroid, as it would have been called. Billy was a barrister who in the course of his service in intelligence in Italy during the last stages of the war and in its immediate aftermath had met Iris Origo and her circle, and through her, Percy Lubbock (Roger Lubbock's writer uncle) and other famous American and British expatriates such as Bernard Berenson, Harold Acton and so on. Just how and why was a bit mysterious as was pretty well everything else about Billy's vaguely Brendan Brackenish background into which we never enquired. In a way this was a reciprocal courtesy. Because Billy was kind enough to

---

*The only man who tried to do so – by making a pass at his beloved Natalie Newton – was Anthony Crosland who got kicked downstairs for his effrontery. This was before Crosland became a reformed character under the redeeming influence of his second wife, Susan.

treat us as if we were much more important than we were – i.e. to indulge, even encourage, our delusions and fantasies – it seemed only right and proper that we should do the same for him and for his. Soon Billy became a member of our circle, regularly joining us at El Vino's where he was as mean as, in his own home, he was generous – a not unusual characteristic of rich people who will give you anything so long as they do not physically have to put hand in pocket.

It was at Billy's home that Paul Johnson first met the marvellous girl whom he quickly fell in love with and married. Getting fed up with always being the only female at our dinners, Claudie insisted one evening on bringing our new friend, Marigold Hunt, whom we had just met through Peter Waite, a director of Methuen – one of the many publishers, incidentally, from whom Henry had taken a large advance; in fact two, since he had managed to convince another Methuen director, John Cullen, that the first advance had not arrived. On that evening we only had drinks at Billy's before going out to one of the new bistro-type restaurants nearby where John, who became aggressive when drunk, caused an uproar by accusing the startled Italian waiters of having supported Mussolini. To begin with the Free French proprietor pretended not to notice. But in this mood John always began to believe that he was Winston Churchill – whom he did resemble a bit – and clambering on the table began to deliver a great growling oration in which not only the waiters but all the other diners were charged with being war criminals. Not to be left out of the act Henry then made a speech, also in a Churchillian vein, about the need to show magnanimity in victory and quite lost his temper when the French proprietor and the other diners refused to be placated by these kind words. By now it was getting late and Paul, who had been uncharacteristically well behaved throughout, invited us all back to where he was staying in Moore Street, Chelsea, with a masterful American mistress who had, as was customary in those days, been left behind. I seem to remember Claudie warning Paul that such a large and boisterous crowd, including Marigold, might not be welcomed at what was by then an unearthly hour. Nor were we. No sooner had the bell rung than a long, freckled arm shot out, seized Paul by his red hair and pulled him inside, before slamming the door in Marigold's face. Marigold was amused, as she had every right to be. For what we did not know was that taking advantage of all that restaurant tumult Paul had made an assignation for lunch the following day at the Ritz; an assignation which led swiftly on to marriage. So she at least could afford to be magnanimous in victory, the fruits of which have gone on giving pleasure ever since to all their many friends.

It was at about this time (1955) that I became involved with *Encounter* through the good offices of a close friend of Claudie's and mine, Margot Walmsley. Margot, then and now, was exceedingly kind and helpful and having just landed a coveted job on this immensely prestigious Anglo-American journal – which was beginning to fill the gap left by the demise of Cyril Connolly's *Horizon* – was determined that as many friends as possible should share in her good fortune. Exactly what she said to her American editor, Irving Kristol, I do not know. But it must have given a wildly exaggerated idea of my journalistic importance since he not only promptly asked me to lunch at Le Peroquet, a smart Leicester Square restaurant, but also at the same time commissioned an article, neither of which things his much better-known English co-editor, Stephen Spender, would in those days have dreamt of doing. Although *Encounter* had only been going for two years it had already published articles by Arthur Koestler, Bertrand Russell, Ignazio Silone, André Malraux, William Faulkner, and many other illustrious names, and the thought of something of mine appearing in that company seemed well-nigh incredible. The subject Irving suggested was anti-Americanism which was then greatly on the increase and giving the NATO alliance much cause for anxiety. On that subject I did have things to say although the proposed length of between five thousand and ten thousand words seemed a bit alarming given the fact that my normal length in the *Daily Telegraph* leader was about five hundred and even my occasional signed leader page features never more than thirteen hundred.

Once I sat down to write, however, ideas came bubbling up. That this was my most important challenge to date I was in no doubt whatsoever. All social life was cancelled. Every morning for about a month I would get up at 5.00 a.m. and work through to 9.00 a.m. And in the evening I would recharge my batteries by rereading all the books on America which I had studied in preparation for my Washington duties: Daniel Boorstin on the American Image, Bryce, de Tocqueville, Brogan, Sam Lubell on the Future of American politics, to name only a few. Within a few weeks the article was ready, all ten thousand words. It was published in the November 1955 issue, with cover page billing, under the title which I had given it, 'America: Conscience or Shield?'. The theme, as the title suggests, was that we were asking too much of America. If the Western world wanted to look to America as the ideal model of a free and democratic society then we could not also look to it to defend us effectively against communist totalitarianism. To do the latter effectively was bound to involve dubious practices which would endanger its moralistic image. In any case, I went on, America had never been as pure as myth would have it. So there was no cause to be disillusioned by such evils as McCarthyism which were as American as apple pie. There had always been that aspect of America, so why didn't the anti-Americans grow up and be thankful for small mercies. Having exaggerated the perfection of some mythically virtuous American past they were now exaggerating the ugliness of some mythically vicious present. In present circumstances – i.e. the Cold War – we should thank

God for the American warts since a Simple Simon pure liberal America, however satisfactory as a conscience, would be a pretty useless shield.

Irving Kristol seemed thrilled with the article's tone; much more so than his co-editor Stephen Spender, this difference reflecting the two men's rather different ideas about how best to fulfil *Encounter*'s basic purpose. Set up by the Congress of Cultural Freedom, which was an American foundation financed with American government money, its basic purpose was to rally free world intellectuals behind the Cold War by weaning them from their infatuation with Soviet communism. In Stephen's mind this meant primarily subjecting them to the same kind of intellectual and moral arguments which had converted him from communism to democratic socialism and who better to do this than the other famous converts such as Koestler, Silone and John Strachey. Making the case for democratic socialism: that was how Stephen saw *Encounter*'s political and even cultural function. Irving's ideas, however, were rather broader. Much earlier than most English intellectuals he saw that if the full intellectual resources of the free world, i.e. of Western civilisation, were to be persuaded to do battle against communism, conservative intellectuals – and not just free market ones – as well as those committed to democratic socialism needed to be brought into the act. In later years when it was admitted that the Congress of Cultural Freedom had received CIA money doubt began to be cast on Irving's motives for encouraging articles by conservative writers. Perhaps it was all part of some sinister Pentagon conspiracy. Nothing could have been further from the truth. Irving and his historian wife Gertrude Himmelfarb were genuinely interested in English conservatism; more than interested, fascinated. At our first lunch this had become obvious. He wanted to know about Michael Oakeshott, whose work he had only just begun to read. Stephen at that time had never heard of Oakeshott and if Isaiah Berlin, for example, had heard of him, he had not bothered to read him. (Still hasn't, I suspect.) Freddie Ayer had read him, only to declare that he was worthless. If Oakeshott was ignored or dismissed out of hand, what chances had a mere conservative journalist of getting his ideas taken seriously? *Encounter* under Stephen alone would certainly have been staunchly anti-communist. But it would not have used conservative intellectuals to fight the good fight unless they were so progressive as to be virtually indistinguishable from Gaitskellite Labour. Irving, however, was much more broadminded. Indeed, one did not necessarily have to be whole-heartedly in favour of democracy to get one's ideas into *Encounter* as the next article of mine he happily published goes to show.

It appeared six months after the first, under the title 'Liberalism versus Democracy', and addressed the question of what NATO should do if Indo-China or Italy, say, voted in a communist government which was then a very real possibility. My answer was clear: NATO should feel free to intervene to overthrow it. Democracy, I argued, was only sacrosanct so long as it safeguarded its country's liberties, as it had in Britain. British liberties preceded democracy, not the other way around. Democracy was primarily about sharing power, not preserving liberty, and was only acceptable as long as that sharing of power led to the preservation of liberty. Once it ceased to do that – as it would in Italy, for example, if the voters chose communism – it was no longer worth preserving. NATO was an alliance of free peoples, first and foremost, and if democracy, in any member state, should prove a Trojan horse letting in communist totalitarianism, then down with democracy.

Not only did Irving agree to print this piece but in an editorial at the front of the issue carrying it he wrote an editorial giving it a kind of blessing.

It seems to us that events, once thought to be transparent in their significance, have become intractable to the understanding, and principles once regarded as for all practical purposes self-evident, have become tantalisingly obscure. We are moved to these reflections by Peregrine Worsthorne's essay on Democracy versus Liberalism. Mr Worsthorne freely *confesses* [my italics] himself to be a young conservative and since he is on the staff of the *Daily Telegraph* he can claim almost a professional standing. But what has struck us most forcefully about his article was not all its conservative bias, but its freshness. There was a subject 'free election' which has been much to the fore, and which has given rise to certain perplexities; and here was the first article we had seen which had made a serious effort to get to the root of these perplexities. We do not say we agree ...

It was a surprising admission for those days. What it said, between the lines, was that in the post-war world where Russian communism had replaced German fascism as the principal threat, conservative thoughts about freedom were just as enlightening, if not more so, than democratic socialist ones. In subsequent numbers a long correspondence followed under the title 'Democracy, Liberalism and Mr Worsthorne'. Even at this distance I remember the thrill of seeing those words. In no other profession is the transition from being a nobody to being a somebody more swift and sudden than in journalism. 'Democracy, Liberalism and Mr Worsthorne' indeed – a Walter Mitty dream come true.

Then, a few months after this piece, I wrote a long study of John C. Calhoun, the conservative statesman from South Carolina, whose eloquent denunciation of majority rule also provided further grist for my anti-democratic mill. By this time the English weeklies were beginning to take notice and there were several articles about a 'new conservative voice'. Even the American *Time* magazine, then at the height of its international success, carried an item about me in their people and places slot.

Unquestionably the value of my shares on the stock exchange of journalistic reputations had begun to catch up with Henry's and John's, if not overtake them. I even got a fan letter from Bernhard Berenson, than which there could be no more reliable guide to the way the wind of fashion was about to blow, and an invitation – never taken up, alas – to go and stay with the Duke of Windsor.

Another less welcome approach was from Sir Oswald Mosley, the prewar fascist leader, who was then trying to re-establish himself in English social and political life. My Cambridge friend Quentin Crewe had invited Mosley and his wife, Diana, to a grand dinner and ball at Londonderry House (hired) for his first marriage party and I was sitting, quite by chance, at the same table as the Mosleys when two other guests, Harold and Dorothy Macmillan, arrived. The Mosleys didn't seem a bit worried. But everybody else was. The two couples had been close friends before the war but had not met since. Harold Macmillan was a senior cabinet minister at the time and it seemed unlikely that he could risk being seen to shake hands with Mosley who was still persona non grata in respectable society, banned from the BBC and so on. In the event, Harold himself ambled past without glancing at his old friend. Lady Dorothy, on the other hand, let out a cry of delighted recognition and sat down with the Mosleys. Presumably Quentin had warned them that the Mosleys would be fellow guests and they had worked out this sensible division of labour in advance. It was at the end of this party that Mosley invited me to fill him in about British politics over lunch the following week at the Ritz. A. J. P. Taylor was coming on the Monday, he said. So what about the Tuesday?

Arriving at his suite at the Ritz on the appointed day, I had an enormous glass of dry martini thrust into my hand. Already laid out on the luncheon table was the first course: a dozen oysters each. On learning that I didn't like oysters, he told the waiter to bring me some smoked salmon and to add my dozen oysters to his own dozen. Then followed a fish course and a roast partridge apiece, with excellent white and red wine. Only with the port and cigars, which had followed an enormous savoury, did we get down to 'work', as he put it. Unlike him, however, for whom this Lucullan feast was presumably a normal working lunch, I was by then utterly befuddled and can remember only one thing that he said. Asked by me how he can have stooped so low as to get married in Hitler's Berlin chancellory, with the tyrant as his witness, he replied quite seriously, 'It was the only place Diana and I could hope to get away from the attentions of the press.' Being by then quite drunk I could not refrain from letting out an enormous belly laugh as if to say 'tell me another'. He wasn't in the least put out, continuing to insist that a desire to protect Diana's privacy was indeed his only motive. In the end I did believe him. That was the trouble, really. Mosley was not so much evil as frivolous. Although I had several further lunches at the Ritz, and other enjoyable social meetings, I never again took him seriously. In convincingly demonstrating that he was not a monster he had succeeded only in showing that he was unquestionably a most appalling fool.

Another spin-off from *Encounter* were all the new people one met through writing for it. Among Irving's friends who stayed with him when passing through London were many of the New York intellectuals who were later to dominate the social sciences: Daniel Bell, Seymour Lipsett, Nathan Glazer, Edward Shils, as well as the famous literary critic, Lionel Trilling. In terms of scholarship and erudition I was completely out of my depth in their company. But this did not seem to matter. Having previously only read about English conservatism in their history books they were delighted to meet someone who embodied it rather more colourfully than most of the gloomy American conservative academics, such as Russell Kirk, then portentously rediscovering Edmund Burke.

In 1956 came the Suez crisis which was said to have been precipitated by a leader page article in the *Daily Telegraph* written by the new deputy editor, Donald McLachlan, known to our circle as Uncle Donald because his wife Kitty was the sister of Elizabeth Longford, mother of the Pakenham brood. This article criticised Anthony Eden, who two years before had succeeded Churchill as Prime Minister, for indecisive leadership, and called for 'the smack of firm government'. More telling than the words of the article was the illustration which was a shot of Eden emphasising a point in a speech by bringing his right fist down towards the open palm of his left hand but just stopping short before the point of impact. Rumour had it that this article so upset Eden that he seized upon Nasser's nationalisation of the Suez Canal as an opportunity to demonstrate his political virility. Whether or not this was so, it certainly pleased the *Daily Telegraph* proprietor's wife, Lady Pamela Berry, to think that it was because she was credited with having goaded Uncle Donald into writing the article. In fact she had nothing to do with it. Donald was the one senior member of the editorial staff over whom she never tried to exert any influence at all, if only because she could never take him seriously after hearing Malcolm Muggeridge compare him mockingly, and all too accurately, to poor cross-gartered Malvolio.

Having called for decisive leadership from Eden the *Telegraph* was clearly in no position to quarrel with his indignant reaction to Nasser's challenge, which sounded decisive enough. In any case Colin Coote, the editor, did not have any desire to criticise it. His own reaction was exactly the same as Eden's, seeing in the Egyptian dictator's aggression worrying similarities with Hitler's behaviour only twenty years or so earlier. Coote and Eden were of the same generation. Both had won DSOs in the First World War and both had been anti-appeasers in the years before the Second. My own reaction was rather different. I never accepted the Hitler comparison which struck me as wildly exaggerated. Nasser seemed to me more a colonial-type problem, justifying the despatch of a punitive expedition rather than the launching of an international crusade. Whether it was wise to do such a thing was obviously arguable. If the controversy had been about the prudence of using force I would have been very uncertain. But once the *Observer*, the *Guardian*, the Labour Party, not to mention John Foster Dulles and President Eisenhower started getting on a high moral horse, with lots of talk about the dangers of offending Arab nationalism and the rights of the Arab people to self-determination, I could not wait to have a go, not so much at Nasser himself for being an aggressive dictator as at them for being such liberal innocents.

In taking this view I was greatly helped by being plugged into the wisdom of Elie Kedourie – eventually recognised to be the greatest Arab scholar of his generation but then only an obscure academic – whom I had got to know through Maurice Cowling, my successor at the *Times*. Elie, an Iraqi Jew, was in no doubt about what would happen in the Middle East if the West proved a paper tiger and his nightmare scenario, which subsequent events entirely justified, had absolutely nothing in common with liberal dreaming. So far from a withdrawal of Western power over the Middle East setting the Arabs free to do wonderful things it would set them free to do horrible things, not only to us, but also to themselves. Elie had been brought up in Baghdad and he knew from first-hand experience just how awful those horrors would be. *Realpolitik* considerations – upsetting the Americans for one – might reasonably counsel against intervention, as might lack of military and economic resources. One could accept these arguments for inaction. But what could not be accepted, and had to be rebutted at every turn, were the moralistic arguments which were the ones being increasingly used. Truth to tell, I think I was always aware that the Suez operation was doomed without American backing, and if the opposition and liberal press had concentrated on these practical objections, I would have been tempted to say amen. But how could one say amen to a lot of claptrap about self-determination? The polemical temptation to let fly was irresistible. That Suez was a blunder nobody can deny; but it was not a crime. It was endearingly quixotic rather than shockingly Bismarckian. Never has liberal-bashing been more deserved or more enjoyable.

As the Suez crisis mounted, however, Colin Coote sent me off to New York to cover developments at the United Nations which was in a fever of outrage about Eden's decision to use force. On the day before the troops actually landed there was a meeting of the Security Council at which the United States led the attack. Anti-British feeling was running high. On that particular evening I had been invited to dinner at the home of Brian Urquhart, a senior UN official who also happened to be British, and I remember thinking that under his roof, at least, the Brits would not be given too hard a time. In the event such hopes proved unfounded. Presumably in an effort to demonstrate unmistakably where his new loyalties lay our host leant over backwards to be even more anti-British than were the rest of the mostly American company. At first I could not believe my ears. Urquhart had been a Second World War hero and it seemed incredible that he should be speaking ill of his own country in front of a lot of foreigners while British troops were actually going into action. When I remonstrated with him he was quite unrepentant. His first loyalty now, he insisted, was to the UN, not to Britain. In theory, of course, he was right. An international civil servant is in duty bound to subordinate his own country's interests to those of the world community as a whole. But however much I might have been prepared to recognise this high-sounding principle in theory, the spectacle of a fellow countryman self-righteously putting it into practice in front of a lot of admiring Americans filled me with patriotic disgust. I don't think this disgust had much to do with the fact that the UN seemed to me then, as it does now, an ill-conceived and ill-fated organisation. Even if it had merited loyalty I still think I would have found Urquhart's attitude disquieting. How could a man who little more than a decade ago had been proud to die and kill for Britain now find it in his heart to side with our enemies in another hour of crisis? For anybody of my or his generation to convert so rapidly and so completely, seemingly without any strain or sorrow, was unnatural, almost obscene. Rightly or wrongly, I lost my temper and made a scene, the full effect of which was marred by an unfortunate social detail. Urquhart, the perfect host, had kindly lent me some dry clothes to change into as I had arrived on foot during a torrential downpour. So instead of being able to get up from the dining room table and rush straight out of the house I had first to change back into my wet clothes, by which time any hope of making a dignified, let alone dramatic exit, had long since vanished.

Urquhart went nearly to the top of the UN ladder and retired only the other day full of honours: not least from Britain, many of whose great and good share his international values. Nevertheless I still think my disquiet was in order since any too sudden switch, even from a lower to a higher loyalty, has about it the whiff of betrayal which no amount of idealism can entirely extinguish.

A report of my reactionary boorishness soon got into a gossip column and New York hostesses being New York hostesses this did nothing but good to my social standing. Thanks to that flattering paragraph in *Time* magazine, I was already receiving a flood of invitations which this further publicity did nothing to dry up. Claudie and I had often visited New York during my tour of duty for *The Times*. Being there even as a very minor celebrity, however, was a sensationally different experience, particularly for anyone susceptible to social and particularly female flattery. One morning I received a marvellously funny letter from Claudie commiserating with me for missing the giant anti-Eden demonstration in Trafalgar Square. Apparently Paul Johnson, a fiery opponent of the Suez invasion, had retired from the field of battle to the Ritz Hotel where he persuaded the ladies' lavatory custodian to sew on a button which he claimed had been torn off by a fascist policeman. The letter went on as follows: 'Billy can't make up his mind which side he is on but that isn't news. Henry said to tell you that Dulles is far worse than Nasser. As for John, he is spending even more time than usual drilling his tin soldiers. Come back soon, you're missing a lot of fun.' I didn't come back soon. In fact I persuaded Colin Coote to let me stay on for a month in New York where I was also having fun – too much for my own good or anybody else's. Legend has it that the Suez crisis divided friends as nothing had done since the Spanish Civil War. It didn't divide our circle one little bit. True, Paul produced an instant paperback exposing all the iniquitous collusion between Britain, France and Israel that had taken place, which I reviewed scornfully at leader-page length in the *Daily Telegraph*, much to Paul's delight since the resulting furore enormously helped the book's sales which in turn helped to improve his finances to the point where he could afford to marry Marigold ... and live happily ever after. True, its effect on my marriage was not so favourable. But that was my fault, or New York's; certainly not Anthony Eden's.

12

A Romantic Attachment

Much has been written about the *douceur de vivre* of pre-First World War upper-class England. Even the *douceur de vivre* of inter-war England has also had its fair share of literary celebration, notably in Evelyn Waugh's *Brideshead Revisited*. By the time my generation came to adulthood, however, most of that style of living had pretty well vanished, except for the very rich. But fond memories of these grand old days still held our imaginations in thrall. Instead of forgetting about the old ways, almost all of which depended on a staff of now non-existent servants, we sought to maintain at least a pale shadow of what had gone before. This was not just nostalgia. There was also a practical side to it. For example, having inherited much of the grand dining room furniture from 81 Cadogan Square, Claudie and I felt pretty well bound to fit it into our much smaller dining room in Scarsdale Villas where it was wholly impractical. But once having furnished this imposing dining room we felt bound to think of it as the place where we ought to be eating, although in reality the dirty old kitchen was where we increasingly did eat, almost guiltily. If guests came we would say; 'You don't mind pigging it in the kitchen, do you?', the clear implication being that our real life fell far short of some ideal life to which civilised people still felt a duty to aspire. On special occasions we did use the dining room. But such was the inconvenience that these occasions were more trouble than they were worth. In the 1960s people started knocking their kitchens and dining rooms into one large and attractive combination, thereby reconciling the ideal with the real. But in the 1950s we fell uncomfortably between two stools: unwilling either wholly to abandon old ways or wholly to adopt new ones.

At this point the fault or lack of imagination was largely mine. At Dyneley, James had always prepared my grandmother's breakfast tray with meticulous and loving care the night before – Luneville china, Georgian silver, ornate pats of butter and so on – and I could see no good reason why our au pair girl could not make Claudie's and my breakfast tray look equally pleasing, particularly as we had inherited some of the same china. Claudie, whose formative years had been spent in Ismailia – 'in the desert', as she liked to claim – had no such hang-ups and not much sympathy, truth to tell, with mine. These were not easy times at home. Much as I loved the free Bohemian life of my fellow journalists, I still hankered after a more ordered and traditional domestic existence, and unconsciously blamed Claudie for not squaring the circle.

The *douceur de vivre* of New York in the 1950s, therefore, came as a most marvellous revelation. I am not talking about plutocratic New York which had always enjoyed the height of luxury, but middle- or professional-class New York, journalists, writers, academics and so on, all of whose homes seemed so incomparably more comfortable, elegant and – dare one use the word? – gracious than those of their London counterparts. When Americans like Henry James came to London at the turn of the century, they were enchanted by how much more civilised our social life was than theirs. In the 1950s it was quite the other way round. I felt I was entering a superior world – more sophisticated, better mannered, less vulgar, than anything I had ever experienced before. Compared to post-war London, where social life was in such a state of flux, it also seemed marvellously settled in its ways; even old-fashioned. New World, indeed! In so many respects New York in the 1950s had preserved more of the old social customs, courtesies and rituals than had my native city.

For example several people left their cards at the Knickerbocker Club on Fifth Avenue, where I was staying, a custom that had long since vanished in London. One of the cards was from Bill Buckley who had written on the back an invitation to spend a weekend at his house in Stamford, Connecticut. This invitation came as rather a surprise since on the only occasion when we had met, which had been in London some months earlier – at a party of Alistair Horne's – Bill's statuesque and swan-like wife, Pat, had had me thrown out on my ear. The row had erupted over Senator Joe McCarthy, in whose defence Bill had recently written a controversial book which went too far in exculpation even for my taste. I think I must have said something mildly critical about the book to Pat which provoked her to retort; 'I would have you know, sir, that Senator Joe McCarthy is one of the finest gentlemen who ever passed through my drawing room.' Assuming her to be joking or teasing I retorted, 'Good gracious, madam, how unfortunate you must have been with all your other gentlemen.' But she wasn't joking and my reply gave so much offence that it became a question of either Claudie and me leaving or the Buckleys leaving and since Bill was the guest of honour, whom Alistair had been at school with, the question brooked only one answer. So why this surprising invitation from Bill some six months later? The only explanation which seemed to make sense was that Bill had read that story in *Time* magazine which had referred to me as Britain's Bill Buckley and, on learning that I was in town, thought it a good idea to make contact, without connecting me with the rude stranger who had so upset his wife in London. Other things being equal I would have written back to make my excuses – anything rather than risk another humiliation when Pat – as formidable as she was glamorous – realised who it was that her husband had invited home for the weekend. But other things weren't equal. Bill by then had started a new right-wing weekly, the *National Review*, in the columns of which young conservatives were eager to write, and it seemed quite crazy for me not to seize upon this opportunity to make contact, particularly as our views on McCarthy were not nearly so far apart as my jocular remark to Pat had led her to suppose. In any case, I accepted the invitation.

Everybody was down at the swimming pool and the Filipino manservant suggested that I put on a swimsuit and join them. Now this really did present a bit of a problem. Whereas the prospect of meeting Pat again fully armoured in a well-cut English suit seemed just about acceptable, the thought of doing so in a pre-war swimsuit which exposed my spindly white legs and less than athletic body off to worst advantage, was much less so. In the event Pat could not have been more friendly, making no reference to our earlier encounter, and several of the other guests, such as James Burnham, author of *The Managerial Revolution*, were even less physically endowed for poolside socialising than I was myself. In retrospect the whole weekend was spent in lively political talk, whether around the pool, in Bill's superb library or on his sailing yacht where he seemed able to take the wheel and chart a course without these responsibilities in any way detracting from either his rhetorical flow or his dialectical brilliance. Previously I had always associated weekends of coruscating conversation and high living with Edwardian houseparties at certain grand English country houses – Garsington for example, presided over by Lady Ottoline Morrell – and it might be exaggerating to suggest that weekending at the Buckleys quite lived up to those legendary gatherings. But it certainly compared well enough with sliced bread picnics in Richmond Park or fish and chips in Staines.

In England in those days general ideas were no more discussed in El Vino's than they were in Boodle's – or at Oxbridge high tables for that matter. At pretty well all social levels people were too busy establishing their own particular forms of exclusivity and superiority, their own interlocking connections, to have much time for anything else; and the higher one climbed on the social scale the more stifling these parochial preoccupations became. Stately homes were particularly disappointing in these respects because so much time had to be spent admiring the heirlooms, hearing about the ancestors and the history – and thinking up intelligent comments to make about them – that there was never any energy left for the kind of talk I enjoy and can sometimes excel at. Not so at the Buckleys' where no time at all was wasted with any of these various kinds of English snobbery.

Bill, it is true, was no ordinary journalist, having inherited a fortune from a millionaire father and his home no ordinary home. But another much less glamorous journalist, who wrote for the *New Yorker*, provided scarcely less stunning hospitality, this time in the form of a dinner party which he and his wife gave in their small apartment in Gramercy Park. In terms of space the apartment was far smaller than Scarsdale Villas but somehow or other eight guests fitted comfortably into it and, in spite of there being no servants, gastronomic treats materialised on a perfectly laid table without any fuss or bother and as if such entertainment was nothing out of the ordinary. Nowadays, of course, this streamlined, self-service style of gracious living has spread to England but even today there is still something a bit self-conscious about it as if its practitioners were putting on a fashionable act. In New York in the 1950s, however, it already seemed an authentic domestic style, honed to perfection by long use over many generations, rather than something new-fangled learnt only yesterday from the pages of a colour magazine.

Other guests included Mary McCarthy, the James Thurbers and Dwight MacDonald, the doyen of political writers, and his wife, all important members of New York's literary journalistic circle whose equivalents in London Claudie and I would never have dreamt of inviting to Scarsdale Villas. On my left at dinner sat a largely silent woman of about thirty, introduced as Edith, who had recently been divorced, I gathered, from a famous novelist. It was a demure rather than a haughty or sulky silence, and more than excusable in the circumstances since James Thurber scarcely ever stopped telling unfunny stories at which Edith did not even bother to smile. Catching my worried glance, she said out of the side of her mouth, 'No need to bother to smile, the old bore is so blind he wouldn't notice if you put your tongue out.'

On my other side sat Mary McCarthy, then at the height of her literary fame, who had taken the trouble to find out who I was and what I did. Did I not agree, she immediately asked, that conservatism in America was a form of radicalism since it would involve pulling up the country's deeply liberal roots? Unlike English Tories, who wanted to keep the country as it always had been, American conservatives wanted to change their country out of all recognition. American conservatives, she went on, were fish out of water which explained why they were such a querulous, joyless, cranky lot, the mirror-image of so many English left-wing intellectuals of her acquaintance. Here Dwight Macdonald, who had just come back from working on *Encounter* in London, chipped in with some prime English examples. Unwittingly Mary McCarthy had given me the cue I needed to make a good conversational entrance. 'I've just been staying the weekend with Bill Buckley,' I said. Everybody was silenced, including James Thurber. Even Edith momentarily raised her eyes from the beautiful Delft china plate which had previously monopolised her attention. Bill in those days had a whiff of sulphur about him and here I was boasting about having supped with the devil. What was he like? they all wanted to know. Well, I answered, he wasn't at all querulous and joyless for a start. Seldom had I enjoyed a weekend so much as the one just spent under his roof. As for Bill being cranky, surely it was time people stopped assuming that someone was cranky just because he believed Alger Hiss to be guilty, Mao Zedong and Stalin to be monsters, and American capitalism to be incomparably better, both morally and materially, than Soviet communism. Then, warming to my theme, I asked how anyone in the least realistic could continue to believe in the United Nations or in a democratic socialism for the Third World. Such beliefs in the second half of the twentieth century, I said, would increasingly come to be seen as the merest superstitions. A new enlightenment was dawning, I prophesied, this time a conservative enlightenment in which right-wing encyclopaedists, such as Bill Buckley, would have as much fun blowing away progressive superstitions as Voltaire, Diderot and Condorcet had had in blowing away reactionary ones. The target for their clever and cheeky iconoclasm wouldn't be the American bourgeoisie, as had been the case in the Mencken era. Their target would be the American liberal establishment, whose long-overdue discomfiture would have ordinary Americans cheering in the aisles. 'Oh dear,' said Mary McCarthy, with a sweet and sour smile, 'you sound just like Rebecca West,' which was certainly a much less crushing putdown than my tirade deserved.

At the time Dwight Macdonald only guffawed but took up some of my points in a subsequent article. What is more he immediately made a point of meeting Buckley with whom he became friendly. Nor was that the only friendship to materialise out of my monologue. While holding forth I had been encouraged to notice a smile flickering across Edith's face and later she even spoke up – somewhat tangentially to be sure – on my behalf. 'From what Mr Worsthorne says Bill Buckley sounds much more fun than Michael Straight, and a good deal cleverer. Anyway, what a welcome change to have a millionaire intellectual on the right rather than on the left.' Being the only single man at the dinner it fell to me to walk her home to her apartment which was only a few blocks away, also in Gramercy Park, and she invited me up for a drink. 'After all that talk you must be thirsty.'

Her apartment consisted of an enormous all-purpose living room with a lighting system that left some parts dark while others were lit up – rather as in a stage set. In an instant there was a real log fire crackling in the grate of the central section which, on our arrival, was the only one lit, and a jug of whiskey sours – then my favourite drink – placed on a table in front of it. Over the fireplace hung an oil painting of a seventeenth-century Dutch interior, the glowing beauty of which seemed to transform this whole section of the room into its own likeness. Such walls as were lit up were solid with books – apparently the only possessions left behind by the famous novelist. Edith worked for the Museum of Modern Art and knew London where it turned out we had several friends in common, including John Davenport and Tony Lincoln. After about an hour she asked whether I would like to spend the night, doing so much in the same manner – somehow suggesting the enactment of traditional ceremonies rather than of familiar routines – as she had set the logs ablaze and mixed the whiskey sours. On receiving my affirmative reply, she dimmed the drawing room lights and turned up the ones in the sleeping quarters, designed to look like a ship's cabin with shelves under the bed. Next morning breakfast was laid in the eating section which looked over Gramercy Park. On a small glass table, suitable only for two, there was a beautiful platter piled high with finely sliced Ardennes ham, the like of which I had not tasted since before the war in Belgium. The *café au lait*, too, was perfect, served in large, round white cups. Nowadays such a *mise en scène* would make no great impression since the colour magazines, as I say, are full of that kind of thing. But at that time, more than forty years ago, it was a revelation and I was utterly enchanted.

During the month or so I lived with Edith in Gramercy Park we would meet in the evening near her museum and make our leisurely way home, stopping at bars on the way and on the last lap, by then often quite late, buying the food and wine for dinner. Never before or since has shopping been for me anything but a most time-wasting chore. With Edith it was all done so swiftly as to require no more than a momentary halt and the dinner itself would be on the table almost as soon as the front door was shut – no impatience, no cooking smells, no fuss and everything looking as good as it tasted. In Edith's case it wasn't a matter of riches making life simple. She wasn't at all rich and had no domestic help. She made life simple by exercising astonishing skill. A couple of poussin would be tossed into a pan along with a knob of butter and a few herbs and in a moment there they were on the dining room table golden and fragrant. Just as she simplified domestic life, so she did the same for all the other sides of life, including the emotional. My living with her seemed to present no complications: no change of plans, no explanations, no embarrassments, no inconveniences and, above all, no telegrams or anger. Over her own life she seemed absolutely sovereign, never requiring anybody's consent or permission. How could somebody be as free as that? I was free because I was miles away from home, temporarily released from the myriad ties and duties which at home pin one down. But she wasn't thousands of miles away from her natural habitat. This was her natural habitat and still she was free to do exactly as she liked.

At weekends we would go to stay with her friends, writers, journalists, museum people, all of whom seemed to have hideaways in the country on lakes or in forests. Very often Edith would only ring up on Saturday morning to ask if we could come and there never seemed to be any problem. The spare room was never full, drink and food had never run out. Whether our hosts really wore identical tweed jackets with leather on their elbows I wouldn't like to say but that is certainly how I remember them. Also inescapably associated with that time is a certain sort of richly aromatic Virginian pipe tobacco which all Edith's male friends used to smoke sitting on their porches under the stars. One hideaway I remember was little more than an extended lakeside log cabin which the host had converted with his own hands. But once inside it was perfectly comfortable as is almost any booklined room if warmed by an open fire. Gadgets help, of course, deep freezes and suchlike which were not yet cheaply obtainable in England. But what helped more than the presence of American gadgetry was the absence of European pretension. Just as it would not have occurred to me then that a log cabin could be made habitable, so it would not have occurred to Claudie that a one-room apartment could be given almost as many dimensions as a three-storey house. It was not that Edith and her friends had more money than us but more imagination, or rather imaginations less shackled by memories of some ideal pre-war way of life that had long since vanished for ever.

In Edith's case, however, there was something else: a truly impressive boldness. One day I got a message from London asking me to write a series of articles on Eisenhower's America. Clearly this would involve a lot of travel. Without a moment's hesitation she threw up her job at the museum so that she could accompany me. Travelling with Edith was another revelation. Everything always worked like clockwork. Cars were hired, hotels and air tickets booked and appointments made. Life, it seemed, did not have to be a nerve-racking hassle. Most novel of all, she simply assumed that everyone I wanted to meet, however important, would be only too happy to oblige. To a surprising extent she was proved right. For example, finding ourselves in San Francisco she telephoned the Governor of California in his mansion to say that an editor of the London *Daily Telegraph* was passing by and could he drop in to pay his respects about noon. Back came the message that the governor would be mighty pleased to see such a distinguished visitor. There must have been something about Edith's quiet, cool voice that always did the trick. The governor then was Pat Brown, father of Gerry Brown, and he received us by the mansion swimming pool, serving cans of iced beer. Apart from the presence of two uniformed sheriffs, with pistols hanging from their enormous hips, it could have been anybody's home and even the slight air of formality imparted by the armed sheriffs did not survive for long since the governor soon sent them bowling off downtown to fetch the hamburgers. Great care was given to which sort of hamburger we all wanted, with the sheriffs writing down our complicated details in their notebooks normally filled, presumably, by more incriminating information. Off they sped downtown, siren wailing, and in no time returned with armfuls of hamburger boxes, but no relish or ketchup. So back they had to go.

I remember nothing about the conversation over lunch, but I do remember the sheriffs making such a botch job of serving the ketchup, when it did eventually arrive, that lots of it got smeared over their hands and even their pistol handles. 'Go get cleaned up, boys,' ordered the governor, as soon as lunch was over. 'You look as if you'd been in a bloody shoot-out.' Although the *Telegraph* in those days paid its journalists badly, it made up for its parsimony on the home front by allowing us to live like kings when on foreign travel. Accordingly Edith always took suites in the grandest hotels where she informed the manager in advance of his good fortune at having such a distinguished English guest under his roof. Not only would the hotel manager have been informed but so would the newsdesks of the local paper and radio station who would send reporters to interview me on arrival. Their presence impressed the manager that I really was a VIP, just as the manager's deference to me, and the size of the suite, infected the reporters with the same illusion, with results that were rewardingly visible on next morning's front page and that evening's local news bulletins.

At that period most of the American media were referring to Eisenhower's America as philistine, complacent, conformist and materialistic. A bestseller called *Organisation Man* by William Whyte had been published which alleged that a new generation of Americans had sold their souls to one or other of the great American corporations in whose ranks they would remain for the rest of their working lives, cautiously ascending the hierarchical ladder rung by rung. According to this book America's old entrepreneurial and pioneer spirit had been replaced by a longing for security to the point where the only question beginners asked prospective employers was about their pension prospects. Another fashionable book of the period was David Riesman's *The Lonely Crowd* which suggested that Americans were so much putty in the hands of Madison Avenue.

In my despatches to the *Daily Telegraph*, however, I was giving a much more up-beat impression of Eisenhower's America. Certainly Americans were prosperous and contented, also not unduly bothered about the rest of the world, that much was unquestionable. But it was not, I argued, a selfish prosperity and contentment. For example, when we arrived of an evening to stay with various friends of Edith who lived in the much maligned

American suburbs, either the host or hostess, and sometimes, both, was invariably at some community meeting or charitable committee, the details of which all too often occupied the family's attention at suppertime. NATO and suchlike did not get a mention but the local church and its various good works certainly did. All the outdoor activities, too, were very far from being the self-indulgent hedonism depicted by the media. One lot of Edith's friends had taken me for a weekend's camping in the mountains in the course of which a child got seriously lost. Fortunately the father was a member of the local mountain rescue team whose courage and training were in no way inferior to those instilled by Kurt Hahn into his Gordonstoun pupils. Even golf and tennis were serious affairs with children eager to practise day and night. All this struck me as grounds for praise rather than for criticism. Eisenhower, I argued, personified great innocence and great strength which was a peculiarly American combination. His was not a charismatic high-profile style of leadership of the sort that the media could mythologise but it was ideal for the purpose of recharging the country's batteries after decades of slump and war, and if more storms did lie ahead, American morale would be all the stronger for having enjoyed, under Ike, the sleep of the just.

It says something about the mood of the period that *Time* magazine thought my pieces sufficiently unusual to run a story about them under the title, 'A Tory-eye View of Eisenhower's America'. At the time I felt worried lest I had allowed my personal happiness with Edith to affect my professional judgment. But I don't think I had. The Eisenhower years still seem to me to have been good for America, some of the best ever, and Ike himself a good President, one of the best ever.

Before returning to New York, Edith took me to Boston, her home town, where we stayed at the Ritz Carlton. At dinner she ordered for herself a steak tartare which the head waiter prepared at our table, mixing the herbs into a pile of raw beef with what seemed to me disagreeable lasciviousness. Surely, I thought, she can't eat that, but she did, licking her lips at every mouthful. Steak tartare was one of Oscar Hahn's favourite dishes, and the sight of him wolfing it down was pretty disgusting. But the sight of Edith, so pale and ethereal, doing the same was even worse. Unfortunately, there had been an earlier off-putting experience of a more intimate kind, too unsavoury to mention, which the sight of the steak tartare suddenly brought back to the surface of my mind and, after a month of enchantment, the spell was broken. At first I struggled to disguise this sad reality even from myself. But it would not go away. In any case, with the Eisenhower series completed, there was no further excuse for me to stay any longer in the United States. Before catching the plane home, however, I must have said thoughtlessly and irresponsibly something about how wonderful it would be if Edith came to live in London, never thinking for a moment that she would actually do anything so wildly unsuitable. I should have known better. She always did what she wanted to do and having been the fortunate beneficiary of her impetuous disregard for obstacles, it was only to be expected that some time I would be the victim of that self-same trait.

Two months after my return home a letter arrived at Scarsdale Villas bearing a New York postmark. Claudie handed it to me at breakfast and asked me who it was from. I had to lie, my first face-to-face deception. In the letter Edith said she was coming to London and would like me to find her a furnished flat to rent. Claudie must have guessed from my face, and from my unconvincing response to her enquiry, that something shameful was afoot. A wise and honest man would have cabled back a firm refusal. Instead I wrote to say that I would arrange the flat but she would have to understand that there was no possibility of our meeting except occasionally. Undeterred she went ahead with her plan, and in due course took up residence in a flat in Eaton Square which belonged to some friends of mine who were abroad for a few months. To my relief she seemed quite self-sufficient and in no way upset by my infrequent appearances. Her many London friends had rallied round and she seemed quite happy. Then the roof fell in. Claudie must have been away for a day or two which meant that I could take Edith out to dinner and stay the night in Eaton Square. At about 2.00 a.m. there was a great banging on the bedroom door and four policemen burst in, accompanied by the caretaker whose key they had used to gain entrance. The police inspector in charge said they were acting in response to complaints by neighbours that the premises were being used for immoral purposes. To my indignant protestations that there must be some mistake, they answered that the flat had been kept under surveillance and men had indeed been seen coming and going at all hours of the day and night. Edith remained quite remarkably calm, getting dressed with the same easy grace that she always brought to this activity as to every other. Yes, she had received lots of men friends in her flat. But their visits, she insisted, had been respectable and innocent. 'Like that of this gentleman,' sneered the inspector, pointing at me as I drew up my trousers. 'No, not like this gentleman,' retorted Edith coldly. 'Oh, isn't he a friend then?' asked the inspector with more sneers. And so it went on, hour after humiliating hour. Finally, after taking endless statements, they withdrew. No charges were ever laid. But, as I was to discover later, Edith's London life had indeed given the neighbours all too many grounds at least for suspicion. For good or ill London is not a place where you can do as you please. Naturally word about the vice squad raid got back to the flat's owners who were horrified and asked Edith to leave. Soon afterwards she went back to New York, resuming her civilised life about which there has never been any further hint of scandal. Years later, I read in the *New York Times* that she had married a well-known professor.

My own life, however, was more seriously affected. Somehow or other rumours of the vice squad raid, and my involvement in it, also reached Claudie whose suspicions had already been aroused by the New York postmark. I don't think she ever forgave me. And in a way this implacability was justified. For as well as being unfaithful by falling in love with Edith emotionally and physically I had also been unfaithful by falling in love with her free and easy New York way of life; with her stylish apartment, and with her marvellous ability to smooth over difficulties – in none of which accomplishments Claudie was even prepared to try to excel. On every count I was guilty. In London it had been up to me to untie the knots and solve the problems and I had lamentably failed to rise to that challenge. So long as Edith was in charge, as she had been in the US, our relationship had done nobody any harm. Only when the onus began to fall on me was the damage done.

By a stroke of luck the Paterson family roared into our lives at about this time, creating a welcome distraction. We met them through an old friend of mine, Kenneth Bradshaw, who rightly thought I might be interested in buying the lease of their palatial flat in Airlie Gardens, next to my old home, Thorpe Lodge. The lease was going cheap because Jim Paterson, an up-and-coming director of Alcan, was moving to Ghana at short notice to set up a large aluminium works there. With the benefit of hindsight it now seems mad of me to have moved out of freehold into leasehold property but such was the charm of the flat in question that this is what we did (more later about the folly of that move for which I was never forgiven). At the time, however, it seemed a good idea, at least to me. The flat was on two floors with a vast drawing room letting on to a splendid communal garden of over an acre. The Patersons, a golden couple from Montreal, could not have been more helpful in the move, and, out of the kindness of their hearts, left all their curtains and carpets behind for nothing. They also suggested that perhaps Claudie and I would like to visit them in Ghana for the summer holiday. In our somewhat tense domestic circumstances this seemed a good idea and we accepted.

At the time I knew absolutely nothing about Ghana except that it had just won its independence from Britain, the first African colony to do so. Had it not been for the Patersons' invitation, it would no more have occurred to me to go to Ghana for a holiday than to the moon. Nor was my editor, Colin Coote, whom I approached with a view to getting help with air fares and expenses, any better informed. Where was Ghana? he asked. When told it was the former Gold Coast, in other words the white man's grave, he looked surprised that one of his leader writers should volunteer to go to such an outlandish place; surprised but also relieved, and from his manner I gained the distinct impression that by doing so I was doing the *Telegraph* a service well beyond what he regarded as the normal calls of a leader writer's duty. Not only would the paper pay for my air fare and expenses but he suggested, almost apologetically, that it might be a good idea for me to stay on there as a correspondent for a while after the holiday was over. Walking me to the door he actually put an avuncular arm around my shoulder rather as a commanding officer might do to a young subaltern who has offered to go on some mission for the regiment which nobody else was anxious to undertake.

As for my own thoughts, they were not all that different from Colin Coote's. Africa was a continent that had entirely failed to stir my imagination. If we had been going to India, I would have been thrilled. Shades of Rudyard Kipling. But apart from Rider Haggard's *King Solomon's Mines*, which I had read as a child, and Evelyn Waugh's *Scoop* which I had read later, no writer had done for Africa what Kipling had done for India. About the exploits of Stanley and Livingstone, Cecil Rhodes and Milner one had heard vaguely, and about the Boers, too. But these men were all white and even they had seemed somewhat peripheral figures about whose lives an educated Englishman need not bother to learn more than the barest outlines. In this respect I may not have been wholly representative of my generation. For when, soon after I was born, my father and mother split up, he had gone to live in Africa which henceforth became in my young mind part of the outer darkness into which my mother had consigned everything about him. But not, I suspect, all that unrepresentative. Most of the jokes about Africa in *Punch* in those days, for example, were still of half-naked fuzzy-wuzzies enjoying a good boil-up of Christian missionaries. Moreover black Africa had no history, no art, no literature or architecture. Normally I did a lot of reading before visiting a new country. But about Ghana there was nothing much to read. Such preparations as had to be made involved filling our bodies with vaccines rather than our minds with knowledge. Only in one respect may this have been an advantage. Had I done a lot of research I might have risked infection from the fashionable wisdom of that period, fostered very largely in the columns of the *Observer*, which encouraged one to take the prospects of African democracy seriously, particularly in Ghana which was going to be a model of parliamentary government setting an example for all the other African colonies about to become independent. A knowledge of Africa based only on *Scoop* and *King Solomon's Mines* certainly did not encourage those kind of illusions.

How can one do justice to the sheer excitement and joy of post-independence Accra? High and low were having the time of their lives, dancing and drinking from morning to night. Bliss was it to be alive and to be young was very heaven. The Patersons lived in a great palace of a colonial house with dozens of servants in flowing white robes who padded about silently on bare feet. Every night was party night with black guests, mostly politicians, and white guests, mostly businessmen, mixing for the first time on terms of equality, or not quite equality since in those early days it was very much a question of white businessmen sucking up to black politicians in the hope of winning all the various concessions and contracts up for grabs. On one occasion the Speaker of the Ghana House of Commons came to dinner wearing his wig, adding greatly to the general hilarity.

After a few days in Accra we found ourselves eating, drinking, dancing and talking with Africans as if the colour bar had never existed. Exciting as this was on a personal level, I am not sure that it helped us to see public affairs clearly. Because the colour bar had for so long created artificial divisions between the races, its removal initially created an almost equally artificial feeling of unity. Everybody felt so relieved to discover that differences of skin pigmentation did not matter that they were tempted to ignore the really profound differences of history, culture, religion and custom which obviously did still matter. After the Paterson dinner parties, Jim would say how marvellously impressive he had found the particular minister or official who had been that night's guest of honour. This, I thought, was to go from one extreme to the other. Having in the old days grotesquely underestimated blacks, the new fashion was to overestimate them equally grotesquely.

Nobody could have been more absurd in this respect than Barbara Ward, the former journalist and foreign editor of *The Economist*, whose husband, Sir Robert Jackson, was then one of the many distinguished advisers in Accra working for Dr Nkrumah, the country's first President. She was a friend of my mother and gave a lunch for Claudie and me at which she fawned on a perfectly dreadful Ghanaian minister who fell from grace shortly thereafter as a result of ordering a golden bed from Harrods. For my own part, I found the new intimacy made possible by the breakdown of the colour bar more worrying than reassuring, particularly when discussing politics. After the third whisky and soda on the Patersons' verandah, African ministers were often sufficiently relaxed, which they would never have been in the old colour bar days, not to feel the need to pretend that Ghanaian politicians had much resemblance to their Westminster counterparts. It was on one such evening that I first became aware of a whole new dimension to African politics, new that is to me, one never mentioned in the columns of the *Observer*: juju superstition. We had been arguing far into the night the pros and cons of Dr Nkrumah's arrest of forty-three members of the opposition. Had there indeed been a plot? Was the government justified in refusing a trial, and in suspending habeas corpus? We seemed to be at cross-purposes, getting nowhere, until a ministerial guest put an end to the discussion by saying, 'Anyhow, the President couldn't afford to take any risks; the witch doctors had told him there was trouble in the air.' I did not ask him to elaborate. I doubt if he would have even if I had. This was the first time the minister had been entirely serious, the roll in his eye being replaced by an iron glint. I think we both realised that there was no meeting point. The reality behind the African spirits was beyond my comprehension, just as the reality behind the rule of law was beyond his. We both knew the words but in neither case did we know enough to make further argument worth while.

Another high-level ministerial exchange, in much less agreeable circumstances, also remains in my mind. After a month of holidaying in Accra we rented a car and African driver to tour the country. In those days there were no hotels; only official rest-houses, some more comfortable than others. Thanks to Jim Paterson's ministerial friends we were given a pass entitling us to put up at the ones reserved for VIPs. All went well for the first week. Although the rest-houses were not luxurious they were comfortable enough and the welcome friendly. Not so at one in the remote Northern Territories, miles away from civilisation. After driving a whole day through thick rainforests we came to a lake, with the rest-house built out over it on tall stilts. No sooner had our car approached than a posse of servants ran out in front of it, brandishing sticks and shouting threats, or what we took to be threats, since the driver turned the car round and started to make back off into the rainforest at full throttle. My inclination was to indulge his instinctive reaction of wanting to turn tail and flee. But Claudie, braver than either of us, would have none of it. This was the only rest-house for hundreds of miles and having spent much of the day driving through the rainforest to get there she was not leaving until at least we had eaten and had a rest. How she made her determination clear to the driver, who spoke little English, I do not know. But she did and back to the house we went, scattering the furious servants who once again tried to bar our way. Up the steep stairs she clambered, with me in her wake, only to be confronted at the top by the enormous figure of Mr Welbeck, one of the few ministers we had not met nor wanted to meet because he was notoriously anti-British and bloody-minded. 'What the hell do you think you are doing here?' he shouted. 'This guest-house is for ministers only. Would you think of breaking into Chequers where your ministers like to take their ease?' Less flummoxed by this analogy than I was, Claudie stood her ground, showing him our all-purpose VIP pass. 'All right,' he said, with the worst possible grace, pointing to a verandah overlooking the lake, 'eat your chop there and shove off at first light.' Getting to the verandah meant passing through the room where Mr Welbeck's cronies were slouched over a table laden with half-empty bottles of beer and whisky. What they were up to was not clear but their furtive glances suggested activities rather less respectable than those for which Chequers is intended. Nor was the verandah exactly a reassuring haven when we got there since in the shallows of the lake below we could just discern the backs of sleeping crocodiles. The ministerial party soon resumed their carousing which went on for the rest of the night, with only occasional lulls for whispering which we found much more disturbing than the drunken singing. Try as we might to laugh off our predicament as something out of Evelyn Waugh's *Scoop*, the literary work that really sprang to mind, all too unmistakably, was Joseph Conrad's *Heart of Darkness*.

Shortly thereafter Mr Welbeck also fell from grace. In his case the offence was to conspire against Dr Nkrumah rather than to use public money for a golden double bed. Possibly it was this conspiracy into which Claudie and I had blundered. If it was, then we got off lightly, bearing in mind those crocodiles waiting down below.

On our journey back to Accra we spent a few days in Kumasi, capital city of the Ashantis, where we called on the Asantaheni, the ancient king whom the British had stripped of all political power. Even for a deposed monarch his palace was surprisingly, dismayingly modest, a small tin bungalow with chickens scrabbling around the porch. Even the historic 'stool' – i.e. throne – which took pride of place in the living room seemed much like any other domestic stool. In fact there were no outward signs of any sorts that to a western eye denoted a royal residence, except for a few old photographs in silver frames of former Asantaheni posing with members of the British royal family. Yet such was the old gentleman's natural dignity and authority that we had no difficulty in treating him deferentially as one of the Lord's Anointed. Neither evidently did his former subjects, a dozen or so of whom we had noticed squatting outside amidst the chickens, patiently awaiting an audience. It was all most strange. The sense of majesty was unmistakably present, in spite of there being no trace of any pomp or ceremony, unless a young boy in a dirty white robe bringing in mugs of tea can be so described. How was it, I kept asking myself, that this frail and bent old king, so completely deprived by the British of all visible and tangible symbols of monarchy, nevertheless seemed authentic, while the government in Accra, so richly endowed by the British with symbols of democracy galore – mace, bewigged speaker, and suchlike – seemed such an obvious sham or fraud? More to the point, why had the British decreed that this ancient monarchical institution with such natural authority be consigned to the dustheap of history while the new parliamentary government, headed by an increasingly megalomaniacal and spirit-haunted Dr Nkrumah, which carried no conviction, should be the wave of the future? When the Asantaheni came to the door to bid us goodbye, the petitioners rushed towards him hoping for favours which he had just explained to us were no longer in his power to grant. It was a touching picture, evoking some mythical age of African innocence; an age no more imaginary than the democratic one, hailed by the *Observer*, Sunday after Sunday, as about to dawn.

Next day we called on Dr Appiah, a leading opposition MP whose marriage, across the colour bar, a few years earlier to the daughter of Sir Stafford Cripps had caused quite a scandal. In a way, as a leading member of the Ghanaian opposition, Dr Appiah was as much a figure of the past as was the Asantaheni; indeed rather more so since while in Dr Nkrumah's one-party state there was some kind of future for the Asantaheni there was going to be none for the likes of Dr Appiah, except in prison. Why were the British doing Dr Nkrumah's dirty work for him? Dr Appiah wanted to know. The bulk of foreign aid from Britain, he insisted, was being used, either directly or indirectly, to consolidate Dr Nkrumah's one-party rule, either by providing him with sums of money – beyond an opposition party's wildest dreams – to buy votes or by subsidising grandiose projects like four-lane highways and stadiums, which served only to build up his prestige. Also, by seconding high-level former colonial officials to work for the new independent government, Britain had provided Dr Nkrumah with a far more highly horse-powered political machine than any available to any opposition party entirely dependent on local talent. In any case, he went on, the presence of these ex-colonial civil servants helped to white-wash the regime. Nobody, for example, believed that the Ghanaian civil service could be corrupt so long as British officials were happy to grace its ranks; or that the Ghanaian police were being used for political intimi-dation so long as British officers were in charge: or that Dr Nkrumah was controlled by his astrologer as long as he could boast among his advisers such well-known English liberals as Barbara Ward and her husband. In primitive African communities, there were, he said, only two genuine means of limiting abuse of power: fear among those on top that those underneath would refuse to obey their orders, and sheer inefficiency. The continued British presence, without in any way strengthening parlia-mentary democracy, simply served to remove these two natural brakes. It helped to give Dr Nkrumah an efficient and reliable police, army and civil service with which to impose his will.

On getting back to London I incorporated many of Dr Appiah's cogent criticisms in a pessimistic article for *Encounter*, which was ferociously attacked by all the usual Labour Party experts who dismissed its argu-ments as the blimpish ravings of a reactionary fascist. Little did they know that much of it drew upon the wisdom of a disillusioned black socialist married to the daughter of an erstwhile hero of the Labour left.

Arriving back unexpectedly one evening in Accra we found the Pa-tersons away for the weekend, and in their short absence the house had completely gone to pieces. Of the army of servants there was no sign apart from the sound of loud music emanating from their separate quarters at the back. Eventually the Nigerian major domo, much the worse for drink, did appear. But Claudie refused his offer of assistance and said she would prepare the supper herself. I still remember the shriek when she opened the enormous fridge and found inside layer upon layer of dead rats, with their long tails hanging down over the edges like the fringes of a roughly woven black shawl. We never discovered what the rats were for. The major domo later gave some cock-and-bull explanation to Rosalie who swallowed it whole for much the same kind of self-deceiving reasons as Barbara Ward and most of the other whites, including Jim himself, swallowed lots of other cock-and-bull stories about more important matters.

I fear the *Encounter* article on Ghana, which appeared shortly after my return, caused the Patersons some embarrassment as they were assumed, quite wrongly, to share its critical views. This is always a problem. If a journalist causes embarrassment to his host he is guilty of biting the hand that fed him. On the other hand if he writes something that benefits his host he can be accused of singing for his supper. Apart from embarrassing the Patersons my article, as I say, infuriated the African experts, many of whom, including the *Observer*'s Colin Legum, wrote outraged letters of rebuttal. In the midst of this furore Margot Walmsley, who was by then *Encounter*'s assistant editor, rang one morning with a marvellous piece of news. Apparently the Duke of Edinburgh's private secretary had just requested six copies of the magazine to be sent round immediately. 'It must be your article,' Margot said. 'He's probably going to Ghana or something.' Unfortunately, as we found out later, it wasn't my article that had aroused HRH's interest but a much livelier one on London prostitution by my old friend and Stowe contemporary Wayland Young called, famously, 'Sitting on a Fortune'.

On my return to Fleet Street I found myself writing leaders on the death throes of the Fourth Republic as one French government after another failed either to suppress Algeria's struggle for independence or to reach an accommodation with it. Almost every week there were votes of confidence in the Chamber of Deputies and quite often these required me to rewrite a leader from home late at night. It was on one of these occasions that Henry Fairlie, after dining well, decided to play a practical joke which very nearly involved me and the *Telegraph* in making terrible idiots of ourselves. At about midnight the telephone rang at home and Henry, disguising his voice and describing himself as Mr Snails, assistant night editor, said that the French government had fallen and would I wish to rewrite my leader? The man's voice was a bit odd and the name Snails not familiar. But that was not all that suspicious since leader writers did not know all the night staff. In any case such suspicions as I might have had were swiftly allayed when Colin Coote, to whom I immediately telephoned to give the news, seemed to know about it already. Again, if I had been on my mettle, I would not have necessarily found this reassuring since one of Coote's character- istics was always to claim prior knowledge of everything any colleague told him. So without further thought I hurriedly rewrote the leader and telephoned it over in good time to catch the last edition. No sooner had I got back to bed than the telephone rang and this time Claudie answered it. It was 'Mr Snails' wanting to know when the office could expect the new leader. On being told, furiously, that the leader had already been sent, 'Mr Snails', i.e. Henry, was so pleased to hear of the success of his hoax that he prematurely let his guard down, and Claudie rumbled him, just in time for me to warn the real night editor of what was going on.

Having to cancel my rewritten leader was embarrassing enough. But only when I got to the office on the following day did I learn of the wider and near disastrous ramifications of the hoax. For Coote, after hearing from me, had immediately rung John Wallis, the *Telegraph* man in Paris, who was also in bed at home, there having been no crisis to keep him late at the chamber on that particular night. The conversation must have gone something like this: 'Coote here. What do you make of the government's defeat?' Taken entirely by surprise and not wanting to be caught napping (probably quite literally) John Wallis did not ask 'what defeat?' but excused himself from further talk by saying that he was in the middle of writing a hurried despatch with only a few minutes to go before the last edition's deadline; a despatch which he then sat down to write, on the basis of the editor's say-so, there being no time for him to check the story out. His despatch simply said: 'After a surprise vote last night, the French government resigned. Note to subs: take voting figures from Reuters.'

Had not Claudie rumbled Henry, this despatch, plus my leader, might just conceivably have got into the paper. Even as it was, Coote, John Wallis and I had been made to look perfect fools. Naturally Coote wanted to know who was the perpetrator of the hoax. Possibly I shouldn't have named Henry. But by then pretty angry and frightened myself, I did so. Further complications then ensued. For only the day before the hoax Coote, at the instigation of the proprietor, Michael Berry, with whose wife, Pamela, Henry was friendly, had offered him a plum job; an offer now, needless to say, withdrawn. Although this was not the first occasion when Henry bit the hand that fed him – or was about to feed him – it was the most spectacular example to date of a pattern to be repeated over and over again right until the bitter end. For me the episode also set a bit of an unfortunate pattern, being the first of several occasions when my name was associated in Michael Berry's mind – in this instance somewhat unfairly – with goings-on which he rightly felt did not exactly augment his paper's reputation for dignity and decorum.

Coote, however, seemed to bear me no grudge, rightly recognising that his folly was rather greater than my own. In fact not long after the unfortunate episode he despatched me to Paris to write features on France's Algerian crisis which ended with General de Gaulle returning to power. On this assignment Claudie also came with me, this time to help with the language in which I was shamefully deficient in spite of having bilingual parents and, of course, a French wife. My excuse is that when I was very young my mother and grandmother always spoke French on the frequent occasions when they wanted to talk about something unsuitable for my innocent ears, thereby associating the language in my mind with a secret world far beyond my reach. At a slightly older age I could have been put off by my mother's habit of wincing, on the few occasions when I did speak French, at my grammatical errors. Such little French as I do speak, however, I speak with a very good accent; in fact so good an accent that Frenchmen are misled into supposing that my command of their language must be better than it really is. It was precisely this illusion which caused me to do less than justice to one of the more fascinating journalistic opportunities of my life. At the height of the Paris crisis Claudie and I were asked to lunch by François Bondy, editor of *Preuves*, France's equivalent of *Encounter*, to meet some French intellectuals, including Camus. General de Gaulle had returned to Paris from Colombey-les-Deux-Eglises and was ensconced in a hotel. Tanks were on the street and it seemed all too possible that the army generals who seized power in Algeria might be about to do the same in Paris. Clearly a historic moment in the history of France was fast approaching. Who the other French intellectuals, apart from Camus, at the lunch were I cannot now remember. One, I think, was Bertrand de Jouvenel and another Raymond Aron, both of whom did speak excellent English, as I had been assured did most of the others. 'Don't worry,' our host had said. 'For Perry's benefit it will be an English-speaking lunch.' To begin with all went well. Most of the conversation was in English and I was learning a lot. Passions ran high. There was much melodramatic talk of taking to the hills if the army seized power. Only Camus, a *pied noir* himself, had any sympathy with the rebel generals who were fighting to keep Algeria French, declaring rhetorically that forced to choose between justice and his mother (i.e. French Algeria) he would always choose his mother. Then I made my mistake. I said something or other in French, like '*très intéressant*' or '*c'est vrai*', but in an accent so natural and authentic that as one man they all relapsed thankfully into their native tongue, thenceforth speaking so rapidly and excitedly that I was unable to understand a single word. Afterwards Claudie told me the gist. But when privileged to attend such a lunch at such a time, it was unbearably painful to have missed so much.

In those days the *Telegraph* office was in the Place Vendôme, a stone's throw from the Crillon Bar where at lunchtime Sam White held court, dispensing champagne and, more precious than champagne, inside information. He never doubted for a moment that not only would de Gaulle soon be back in power but, once back, would betray the *colons*, as indeed he did. Gladwyn Jebb, our ambassador, was not nearly so well informed nor, incidentally, so generous with his champagne. My job was not to send news but colour pieces and also unsigned leading articles. Oh what fun it was. Public gloom: private happiness. Claudie and I wanted the crisis to go on for ever. Pretty well everybody craves drama but does not get nearly enough of it in their own lives. Drama, however, is one thing a journalist can rely on getting, even after working hours. For example one evening after telephoning over my stuff, we ran into Michael and Jill Foot, also in Paris for the fun. Michael was very pleased with his piece for that day's *Daily Herald* in which he had written that all the Coty perfumes would not be enough to sweeten the stench of what the French army was doing in Algeria – a jibe at the expense of the then French head of state, President Coty. Waiting for his return at the hotel where we were all staying was a senior member of the Sécurité who presented him with a deportation order under a clause in the French constitution which prohibits insults to the head of state. Deporting Michael Foot was almost certainly one of the Fourth Republic's last effective acts. He was on a plane back to London at first light the next morning.

Returning to London, where there were no tanks on the street, was a bit of an anticlimax. Here the central questions of politics were all to do with the economy and about these matters I had no strong views. Nor indeed did the editor except after lunching, which he did regularly, with his old friend Robert Boothby. Donald McLachlan, the deputy editor, was equally ignorant, as were all the other leader writers of that period. The proprietor himself did know about economics, having studied the subject at Oxford under Roy Harrod. Before the war he had even written a good book generally sympathetic to the views of Maynard Keynes. But since he did not attend the editorial conference this was not much help; in some ways indeed it was a disadvantage, tending to lock the paper into economic attitudes which, however relevant to Britain's pre-war problems, were not necessarily relevant any longer. The nearest thing to an economics guru we did have was Eric Francis, an expert on the gas industry about which he wrote with great authority. But when consulted on broader economic issues he would give his views so tentatively and apologetically that an ill-informed leader writer like myself came away with his mind more confused than clarified. The only colleague with strong, clear and consistent economic views was Colin Welch, a monetarist long before monetarism became fashionable, but he didn't attend our editorial conferences either, having been sidelined into starting the Peter Simple column. Usually economic subjects were left to the end of the editorial conference and allotted to whichever leader writer had not succeeded in coming up with some more interesting topic. 'Sorry, Worsthorne,' the editor might say, 'I'm afraid you've picked the short straw today.'

One such occasion has remained in my memory. It was when Peter

Thorneycroft's entire Treasury team, including Enoch Powell, resigned in protest against Harold Macmillan's insistence on increasing public expenditure. With the benefit of hindsight one can now see that this was the first shot in an economic battle that was to rage on in British politics until Mrs Thatcher, twenty years or so later, eventually won it. None of this, however, was apparent to me, or to Coote, at the time. Because the Conservative Prime Minister, already known as 'Supermac', had dismissed the resignation as, in a famous phrase, 'a little local difficulty', our leader took roughly the same line. When in doubt always support a Conservative government, was Coote's sensible enough rule and since on all economic matters I was never not in doubt, my politico-economic leaders make very painful reading today. Fortunately I was soon sent on my travels again, to cover Harold Macmillan's famous 'Wind of Change' tour of Africa.

The next four weeks were marvellous fun. The tour took Mr Macmillan, who was accompanied by his wife, Lady Dorothy, first to Ghana and Nigeria on the west coast, then to the Central African Federation, ending up in Cape Town where the speech itself was made. So newsworthy was it expected to be that the popular papers sent some of their most famous bylines, including René McColl of the *Daily Express* and Sydney Jacobson of the *Daily Mirror*. Normally the *Daily Telegraph* news editor would have insisted on giving such a plum job to one of his own top correspondents, rather than to a 'mere' leader writer, and it was a signal honour that he had not objected to me. Reaching Accra a few days before the Prime Minister's party I was able to set the scene rather more fully than most of my rivals, thanks to having better contacts. My report of the Prime Minister's arrival also had an extra edge to it since it was the only one to make the point that he was the first Prime Minister ever to visit Britain's African colonies ... 'just in time to say hello before bidding them a fond farewell', as my first despatch put it. I also made much of the fact that the welcoming crowds lining the street were very much smaller than the Ghanaian authorities had planned for; so much smaller as to be almost insulting. This caused a furore, provoking the Ghanaian minister of information to publish a wholly unconvincing denial. At a reception in Government House a few days later I ran into Barbara Ward who said she had not been at all surprised by the low turn-out for the British Prime Minister since Dag Hammarskjöld, the UN Secretary-General, on a recent visit, had not done any better, to which I could only reply that *Daily Telegraph* readers were unlikely to find this unfortunate comparison quite as consoling as she did.

At the end of the Ghanaian leg of the tour, Mr Macmillan and Lady Dorothy invited members of the British press party in for drinks, as was to become a regular custom in the following weeks. In those days journalists did not meet prime ministers nearly so often as they do today, and tended to be overawed on the rare occasions when they did. John Wyndham, his private secretary and close friend, took us all up in turn to meet the two of them, possibly in alphabetical order because I was last in the line. This short wait gave me time to think of whether, on shaking hands with Lady Dorothy, I should refer to my earlier fairly close friendship with her daughter Catherine in the course of which I was quite often their guest at Pooks Cottage where the Macmillans lived during the war. Indeed on one occasion I had been snowed in there – an episode referred to in a letter Lady Dorothy wrote to Harold who was then minister resident in Algeria (Alistair Horne came across it in Macmillan's papers when writing his official life.) Nor was Macmillan himself a complete stranger since he was one of my mother's friends who had called in at Beauvallon from Uncle Wyndham Portal's yacht. In a private social gathering I would have mentioned these connections. But to mention them on this occasion, very much in front of colleagues, might this not seem like showing off or, worse, stealing a march – establishing, so to speak, a special relationship in the hope of receiving an extra ration of news? So horrifying to me was this thought that I said nothing, only referring to these matters on the last such gathering of the tour by which time no one could suspect me of trying to win unfair advantages.

At some point in these evening gatherings the Prime Minister would sit us down and say a few words. It was almost always a memorable performance. On this occasion he struck a mournful note which was one of his favourites. How sad it was, he said, that Britain was giving up her African empire just at the time when technology and resources had made it possible for us to transform the continent. During the thirties, he went on, Britain could do very little for Africa. Even if we had the money, the technology was not there. We had the political power, but not the physical means to put it to good effect. Now, just at the very moment when imperialism had the means to translate its high-sounding paternalistic words into actions, to do all the good it had promised, it was coming to an end. Foreign aid, he said, was no substitute. Nor was there much hope that black Africa would be able to modernise itself on its own. Fate was cruel. Freedom was coming to Africa at the wrong time. Having had all the humiliation of being bossed about by whites, the blacks, poor innocents, were bent on kicking us out just when they ought to be begging us to stay.

At the time, incredibly enough, none of us saw anything odd about these musings coming at the end of a day in the course of which the Prime Minister had made many upbeat speeches about Ghanaian independence. If this really was the time for the white man to pick his burden up, why on earth was the British Prime Minister going around the continent urging him to lay it down? Nowadays some bright Conservative journalist would have certainly asked that question. Why didn't I? Partly so as not to appear impertinent. But also because in those days such a question would have seemed irrelevant. Imperialism had been ruled out by the spirit of the age or Zeitgeist with which it was pointless to argue. In public a Prime Minister could no more appear sceptical about the Zeitgeist than could have a Victorian Prime Minister appeared sceptical about Christianity. That much we all simply took for granted. So instead of taking our leave of the Prime Minister shocked by his cynical fraudulence we felt touched that he should share with us his private musings; musing which we, like him, understood had no bearing on the real world and were for the ears only of a few trusted friends among whom we were honoured to be momentarily numbered.

Ghana and Nigeria were not the real point of the tour, having already won their independence. Its real purpose began only when we reached Salisbury, capital not only of Southern Rhodesia, still dominated by the white settlers, but also of the new Central African Federation which included Northern Rhodesia and Nyasaland where there were no in-tractable white minorities. Not unnaturally the blacks of Northern Rho-desia and Nyasaland wanted to see the break-up of this new federation which they saw as an extension of white domination and a barrier to their own eventual independence. Equally naturally the whites were deter-mined to keep the federation intact precisely because it was an extension of white domination and it was the Prime Minister's impossible job at least to give an impression of accommodating both desires. In the event he did not try very hard and even before arriving in Salisbury had subtly let it be known where his sympathies lay. He did so in several ways but the most characteristically feline was a remark made in answer to a question at one of those evening gatherings, this time in the palace of the Sardano of Sokatoo, the colourfully robed hereditary ruler of Northern Nigeria who had been entertaining the Prime Minister in a right royal fashion. One of us asked Macmillan, rather mischievously, whether he was looking forward to his visit tomorrow to Salisbury where he would be the guest of Roy Welensky, the Federal Prime Minister, a former heavyweight champion boxer and railway worker who was known to be highly suspicious of British policies. 'Roy and I,' Macmillan replied deadpan, 'are old friends. But it has to be said that as a Highlander myself I have felt agreeably at home with the Sardano who reminds me so much of one of those feudal chiefs who were heroes of my youth. Oh yes, I like Salisbury well enough – so charmingly suburban. But the Sardano is such a splendidly old-fash-ioned gentleman.' Whoever leaked this remark to the Rhodesians I do not know. But its unmistakably offensive gist appeared in all the Rhodesian papers in time to guarantee the Prime Minister a frosty welcome when he touched down at Salisbury airport on the following evening.

This putdown of Roy Welensky gave us all in the press party a welcome new angle for that night's story since the tour so far had been frustratingly lacking in rows and controversy. As a result of this frustration nerves were beginning to fray. René McColl, for example, had whipped himself into a frightful tantrum on the plane because his arch rival on the *Evening Standard*, Anne Sharpley, had scooped him with an exclusive account of Lady Dorothy's visit the previous day to the Sardano's harem. Nor was his temper smoothed on finding her colourful report reproduced in full in the main Salisbury newspaper. In any case it had been a long flight and we were all anxious to get back in touch with our London offices, my impatience being particularly keen as I had some good material gleaned from John Wyndham on the plane.

After hurriedly checking in at the Meikles Hotel reception desk I was handed a message which read: 'Mr Worsthorne rang. Will ring back later.' Assuming this to be a garbled message from my London office I impatiently asked the black clerk to check with the exchange for the correct message, explaining that it couldn't be from Mr Worsthorne since I was Mr Worsthorne. No, insisted the exchange, there was no mistake. Exasperated I stormed up to my room, only to hear the telephone ringing as I entered. It was the exchange again asking whether I would take a call from Mr Worsthorne. 'I am Mr Worsthorne,' I shouted before banging the phone down. A moment or two later it rang again, and the voice on the line said, 'Jeremy here, Jeremy Worsthorne.' Thus it was that I came to meet my half brother, a son of my father by a Rhodesian wife, about whose existence he had never breathed a word. Much later that night, when I had finished my work, we met for dinner at a smart Salisbury nightclub. As a celebration Jeremy ordered champagne which was very slow in arriving. When he remonstrated with the head waiter, there was much whispering and it soon transpired that no champagne or even dinner would be forthcoming until many unpaid bills were settled. My expenses for this Rhodesian leg of the journey must have been exceptionally heavy, although 'paying off half brother's debts' was almost certainly never listed as the excuse. That was the one and only time I ever met Jeremy. However, he did try to keep me abreast of his news. Some six months after I returned to London a cable arrived, reading: 'In dire danger of civil imprisonment. Please send £500 urgently.' I rang my father who, greatly embarrassed, said he would deal with the matter himself. Whether he sent the money I do not know. For having never referred to Jeremy before, he never referred to him again. I had another surprise during this Salisbury visit, also thanks to my father. Spending a day on the racecourse I was pulled up with a jolt to hear the announcer giving the names of the runners in 'The Worsthorne Cup'. Apparently my father had been quite a major figure in Rhodesian racing and also in Rhodesian politics as I discovered on visiting Parliament House, where he had sat as an MP, even forming his own party. On these matters, however, he was no more forthcoming than he was about Jeremy.

Clearly something traumatic must have happened to him in Rhodesia. That he lost a fortune there we do know, but I fear the loss may have been more important than that since after those relatively active days he completely let life pass him by.*

Exciting as all the Central African Federation developments were at the time, they seem very small beer now. I remember interviewing Kenneth Kaunda, who had that day been released from detention, in his tin shack of a house just outside Lusaka and being greatly impressed by his 'almost Gandhi-like air of saintly simplicity'. About Roy Welensky I wrote that his bluff and forthright straightforwardness, reminiscent of Ernest Bevin, was not likely to commend itself to Harold Macmillan 'unless such personal incompatibilities are somehow reconciled by the mysterious workings of the attractions of opposites'. In Blantyre, capital of Nyasaland, there was a small demonstration outside Macmillan's hotel in favour of Dr Banda who had not yet been released. Desperate for a good action story, we all greatly exaggerated the amount of force used by the local police against the demonstrators, which by African standards – or indeed by any contemporary standards, including Britain's – was absolutely minimal. One of my colleagues even compared the white police officer in charge to the SS. So outraged by our allegations were the colonial authorities that they set up a court of enquiry in Blantyre under Mr Justice Southwell before which, months later, we were all subpoenaed to appear. It was not a pleasant experience. The whites were in a lynching mood and some of the reporters, whose reports had been particularly vile, were chucked out of Blantyre's only decent bar, than which there could be no greater mark of disfavour or indeed, for a foreign correspondent, sterner punishment. At the court of enquiry itself, which went on for days, we were all cross-examined mercilessly by counsel who had no difficulty in establishing – at any rate to the satisfaction of the public gallery – that the alleged Blantyre bloodbath had been nothing of the sort. The poor *Daily Mail* man was given particularly rough treatment by the judge and never recovered from the experience. I

*His last years were spent in a tiny two room flat in Chelsea. It was in a block built by Chelsea Council for gentlefolk down on their luck, near the site, strangely enough, of the infamous 79 Elm Park Gardens. Apart from the visit of one or two loyal friends – notably Diana Royds – and the much loved Ciechanowski family, he lived the life of a recluse, only going out to shop, collect his library books and his old-age pension. Claudie did what she could to make his life more comfortable but so fierce was his independence that there was not much anyone could do. Shortly before his death he wrote me a letter, the only one from him I ever received. 'I have done nothing with my life', he wrote, 'but possibly my example spurred you on to do something with yours. It pleases me to think so. It is too late now for us ever to talk – this note will have to do instead.' Claudie and I arranged for him to be admitted to St Stephen's Hospital on the evening of 12 November 1985. He was uncharacteristically crotchety and once installed in the ward despatched Claudie to buy him sliced bread for the following morning's breakfast, a previous experience having taught him that the regular hospital toast was uneatable. By mischance Claudie brought him back a loaf sliced too thick and he lost his temper. Having taken philosophically so many far worse disappointments, this one apparently was the last straw that broke the camel's back. In the event, there was no breakfast since he died in his sleep later that night.

got off fairly lightly and in his final report, which contained witty pen portraits of us all, the judge even said he had enjoyed my performance in the box. After he had retired, and was living in England, he visited me in my *Sunday Telegraph* office and asked for a job on the paper, saying that presiding over that court of enquiry all those years ago had given him a taste for journalism. This came as a surprise since in court he had definitely seemed more repelled than attracted.

On the plane to Johannesburg for the last leg of our journey I sat next to the *Observer*'s correspondent, Anthony Sampson, who already knew South Africa well, having spent several years there brilliantly editing *Drum*, the only white-owned magazine produced specifically for blacks. As a result of this experience he had unrivalled contacts with black politicians, including Nelson Mandela, and was a mine of information about what was going on in the townships and in English-speaking white political circles. While listening to him, however, I was struck by a revealing omission in the list of people whom he thought I ought to try to meet, and was kindly offering to introduce me to. Although the list included Alan Paton, Nadine Gordimer, Helen Suzman and several opposition white leaders, and a few black politicians, absent from it were the names of any Afrikaner politicians and journalists. At a party given for us by the British press councillor on the evening of our arrival, there was the same absence of Afrikaner politicians and editors – not a single Nationalist MP or journalist from any of the papers supporting the ruling party. Neither were black journalists thick on the ground but at least of them there were the statutory two or three.

There was nothing surprising about this. Relations between the two white communities have always been lacking in mutual understanding, as South Africa's whole history demonstrates. What did surprise me, however, was the degree to which my colleagues seemed to feel no obligation on this trip to transcend these ancient barriers of incomprehension and suspicion. On the second day of our visit, for example, the Afrikaner head of the South African Bureau of Information invited us all to a *braaivleis* and out of the whole British party – which by then must have comprised at least thirty reporters – only I and a single American reporter, Bob Manning of *Time* magazine, bothered to turn up. Not only was this boycott exceptionally rude, but also professionally irresponsible since, like it or not, the Afrikaners were running the country whose affairs we were due to report. From my point of view, however, their absence was a godsend since it threw into relief my presence. The host made an emotional speech which ended with him proposing a toast. 'Let us *not* tonight drink to absent friends,' he said, 'but rather to our non-absent friends whose courtesy and goodwill we shall never forget.' Taking their cue from the toast, the other guests, all Afrikaners – for the Boer-English hostility was mutual – for once dropped their guards and opened their hearts.

It proved a fascinating occasion. For the Afrikaner journalists present were incomparably more interesting than their English-speaking counterparts of the night before – highly educated, erudite and, of course, intriguingly different. One, in particular, stood out: Piet Cillier, editor of *Die Burger*, with whom I spent most of the evening. No other journalist of any nationality has ever impressed me more. He didn't defend apartheid, but explained it in terms which made so much of the outside world's condemnation seem at best facile and at worst hypocritical. One of his points I have always remembered. 'What you have unfolding in South Africa is a true tragedy – an irreconcilable struggle not between right and wrong but between right and right. The blacks are in the right, but so are the whites. Outsiders, therefore, shouldn't try to pass moral judgment. For passing moral judgments on a tragedy is as cruel and unhelpful as rubbing salt in a wound.'

Another guest at the *braaivleis* was a Nationalist MP who suggested that I lunched with him and a few of his colleagues after Macmillan's Wind of Change speech which was due to be delivered at the parliament building in Cape Town in a couple of days' time. In the event the speech was something of an anticlimax, the basic message being so wrapped up with polite waffle that few in the audience got it. Certainly my host at the lunch he gave for me in its immediate aftermath had not got it; nor had his colleagues or, if they had, they were far too polite to show any resentment. Far from it. They all said that they had expected something much worse. On the basis of this lunch I wrote a despatch saying that the speech had been surprisingly well received in South African government circles, causing less of an Afrikaner outcry than had been expected. Unfortunately the accounts of my colleagues in all other papers were very different. Not having talked to any Nationalist MPs they simply assumed that they were outraged, and reported accordingly. In the end, they and not I were proved right since after reading about their anger in the playbacks of the British press, ministers thought they might as well live up or down to what the rest of the world so obviously expected of them. So, I was left with egg on my face: the only reporter in the whole wide world to underplay the impact of the Wind of Change speech. Too much first-hand knowledge for a journalist is a dangerous thing. Far from stealing a march on my colleagues by actually taking the pulse of the Nationalist MPs, I had succeeded only in appearing uniquely ill-informed.

A happier consequence of the *braaivleis*, however, was an exclusive interview with Dr Verwoerd, arranged by the host as a reward for what he regarded as my outstanding courtesy. It took place the morning after the Macmillan speech at Groteschur, Cecil Rhodes's old home, with its famous view of Table Mountain. When Smuts had been Prime Minister my mother and stepfather had stayed there several times, always returning uplifted by its simple beauty. To my surprise there were no guards on the entrance, and a complete absence of any other security arrangements. My taxi just drove straight in and dropped me at the front door which was wide open. At first I thought it must be the wrong address. Surely the most hated man in Africa, the villainous architect of grand apartheid, would not risk being exposed to all his enemies. Assured by the taxi-driver that it was the right address, I rang the bell. Answer came there none. I rang again and again; still no answer. Eventually, the door being open, I stepped inside and then banged it shut, hoping to attract attention. But still no one appeared. The house was bathed in silence with no signs whatsoever of domestic or any other kind of activity. Tiptoeing through the hall and drawing room beyond I came upon another door opening on to the garden where at last I found Dr Verwoerd sitting alone in a wicker chair, in the middle of the lawn, reading the bible. If he had been shattered by the Macmillan 'bomb-shell', the look of serene calm upon his face certainly belied it. Almost immediately one of his daughters came out of the house, carrying coffee. (On my return journey the taxi-driver explained that the Verwoerd family, on principle, employed no black servants.) Was there a wind of change blowing through Africa? I asked. Yes, indeed, he replied beaming. But that was not the only wind of change blowing. Far more significant than the wind of change blowing through Africa was the wind of change blowing through Britain about Africa. That a few thousand African nationalists should be calling for independence and 'free-dom' was nothing new. The novelty was that so many English conservatives were prepared to listen to them and give them what they wanted. It was quite erroneous to suppose that African nationalism had become infinitely stronger; what had happened was that British nationalism had become infinitely weaker. It was not so much that Africans had found a new faith or new leaders as that Britain had lost her old faith and her old leaders. The blacks themselves had not become more serious. It was the British who for the first time were now prepared to take them seriously. Take the very phrase itself, wind of change, he went on. 'A memorable phrase. A most memorable phrase that will rightly go down in history. But who coined it?' he asked. Not one of the African leaders. It was made in Britain, which was rather as if in 1776 the American nationalists had left it to Lord North, instead of to George Washington, to forge their inspiration. 'No, Mr Worsthorne,' he concluded, 'please tell Mr Macmillan when next you see him, it is the British, not the Africans, who are the wind of change blowing through this continent.'

I did try to do so at the last of those intimate gatherings on the eve of the British party's return home. But Mr Macmillan was so busy inveighing elegantly against Dr Verwoerd's closed mind that he did not listen. Eventually

I wrote four major leader-page articles for the *Daily Telegraph* about the 'Wind of Change Tour' which were later published as a successful pamphlet. Anything in it that remotely stands the test of time was garnered from the despised Afrikaners, to whom my colleagues never bothered to speak.

13

Starting a Paper

One morning in the summer of 1960 a letter arrived from the chairman of the *Yorkshire Post*, Colin Forbes-Adam – whose sons had been friends of mine at prep school – offering me the editorship of the paper in succession to Sir Linton Andrews who had held the post for many years. Because of the size of Yorkshire and its importance to Conservative Party fortunes, the *Yorkshire Post* in those days was more than a provincial paper. All the London clubs took it and it was widely read at Westminster. On one occasion before the war, when it was the first British paper to break the silence about Edward VIII and Mrs Simpson, it had even won international fame. So it was a flattering and tempting offer. The salary too was an inducement since it was considerably more than what I was earning at the *Telegraph*. Mention was also made of a Rover car and an expense account, neither of which were available at the *Telegraph*. My inclination was to accept, particularly after being assured by the board, at a meeting in the paper's Leeds office, that a guarantee of complete editorial freedom would be written into a three-year contract. Claudie, however, had understandable reservations about going to live in Leeds. For not only had we just moved into a new London flat but Dominique had just started at the French Lycée.

In an effort to make up my mind I consulted Colin Coote who strongly advised me to postpone a decision. The *Telegraph*, he said, also had exciting plans in the pipeline affecting me which he was not free to disclose there and then but would be writing to me about them just as soon as possible. Later that day – presumably after he had told Michael Berry of the *Yorkshire Post* offer – I got a handwritten note offering me the deputy editorship, and a signed political column, on the new *Sunday Telegraph* which the company was planning to launch and the same salary as the one offered by the *Yorkshire Post*. His note also laid great emphasis on my being able to play a crucial role in the creation of a new national newspaper. Wholly carried away by this prospect, I immediately wrote to Colin Forbes-Adam refusing the editorship of the *Yorkshire Post*.

It turned out to be a foolishly precipitate act. For Coote had written to me in these terms without first consulting Donald McLachlan, still deputy editor of the *Daily* and editor designate of the *Sunday*. Presumably Michael Berry had said I was a writer worth trying to keep in the *Telegraph* stable and Coote had rightly concluded that in view of the *Yorkshire Post* offer this required some immediate action. Coote despised McLachlan, even to the point of usually mispronouncing his name, and would automatically have taken 'McLufflin's' acceptance of me as his deputy for granted. Not surprisingly McLachlan did nothing of the kind. Nor did he like the idea of a signed column since he disapproved of signed columns. It was all very awkward. Unable wholly to renege on Coote's offer, McLachlan did the next best thing. He allowed me the title of deputy editor without any of its powers or responsibilities and also a signed column but one with such a circumscribed scope as to be painfully unsuitable to my particular bent or information. As for being in at the creation of a new Sunday newspaper, that also proved an idle promise since the only part I was allowed to play in the planning was to suggest Nigel Dennis as a book reviewer. At the time I was more bemused than bitter. For weeks I carried Coote's handwritten note around in my pocket, naïvely believing that somehow or other its existence would eventually guarantee my rights. The idea that such a distinguished figure as Sir Colin Coote, DSO, would not find some way of honouring his word seemed quite simply incredible.

Having now been an editor myself, I know all too well how easy it is to say or write things to staff members, into which they read more than was intended. No doubt Coote's letter was an example of this. In his mind he was not giving me a specific job description so much as a rough idea of the kind of work I could look forward to on the new paper. But by the time his letter – probably only one of several written about staffing matters in quick succession – had reached my desk it had been transformed, in my imagination, to something more akin to holy writ. Looking back I can see it was all a cock-up and in no way a conspiracy. Coote had meant only to be encouraging; and McLachlan probably felt that he had done more than could reasonably be expected of him to honour undertakings for which he was in no way responsible. According to their own lights both men had done nothing wrong and I had nothing to complain about. But, of course, I had. From the *Yorkshire Post* had come the offer of an executive post of real power which I had turned down for what I had wrongly assumed was a better executive post of real power on the *Sunday Telegraph*. Almost thirty years later an executive job of real power on the *Sunday Telegraph* did materialise. But it was to prove a long and frustrating wait.

Donald McLachlan, before joining the *Daily Telegraph* as deputy editor, had been deputy and foreign editor of *The Economist* and before that the editor of *The Times Educational Supplement*. Originally, however, he had been a highly successful schoolmaster at Winchester and it was this job that suited him best since he was much more of a schoolmaster than a journalist. That is to say, his enthusiasm for ideas was distinctly puerile. One could imagine him being a star performer at a gathering of sixth-formers who would find his zaniness stimulating and provocatively original. But in the company of worldly-wise journalists it tended to fall very flat indeed. Even his hospitality had a schoolmasterish rather than journalistic scale to it, particularly in the matter of drinks. One would be offered the choice of a glass of sherry before lunch or a glass of claret with it. It was over one such lunch at Brooks' Club that he explained to me his ideas for my column. What he wanted was a weekly unsigned political article containing at least one piece of hard news. Anybody can write a viewy piece, he declared. What the new paper needed was a political writer who could tell readers what was really going on at Westminster. On the question of signing the piece I stood my ground and insisted on Coote's promise being honoured in at least this one particular. Apart from pleasing my authorial vanity, signing an article meant that one got invited to repeat its contents on radio or television, thereby earning quite a lot of much-needed extra money. As to the exclusion of views and opinions, I reluctantly agreed. It seemed a pity since views and opinions had by then become my forte. According to McLachlan this was the wrong path for me to follow. Given my social connections, I was ideally placed, he said, to become the best-informed political journalist in England, even rivalling Randolph Churchill who was then making a great reputation for inside knowledge by recycling high political gossip gleaned at the bar of White's for next day's *Evening Standard*. Leave opinions to the hacks, he argued. You have access to the Tory grandees. Exploit your assets.

Reluctantly I agreed to have a go, possibly tempted by McLachlan insisting on the *Telegraph* reserving me a regular luncheon table for two at the Connaught Grill where he wanted me to do all my entertaining. Why the Connaught Grill? I asked. 'Because it's the best and most expensive food in London and VIPs feel that if they have been lunched there, at least they owe you a good story in return.' Unfortunately it didn't work out like that for me. The VIPs came to lunch. McLachlan was quite right about the drawing power of the Connaught Grill. But they seldom, if ever, spilt any beans. The trouble was that my heart was not in the job of asking questions. It somehow went against the grain. I would do it, of course, out of professional duty; but without the necessary eagerness and enthusiasm needed to attract a revealing response. At the time I liked to flatter myself that this was because my mind was on higher things, on ideas, political philosophy and suchlike. More probably it was a form of snobbery. To show too much curiosity was rather common, conduct unbecoming in a gentleman, and the last thing I wanted to be taken for was a nosy parker. Montagu Norman, under whose roof I had spent my formative years, detested reporters and would go to great lengths to avoid being questioned by them when they waited for him outside our house. On one such occasion, aged about ten, I let the side down by revealing to a reporter what my stepfather ate for breakfast. He kindly blamed the reporter, not me, railing against him as 'a low and impertinent fellow'. No wonder in later life I was almost neurotically determined never to be taken for that.

Unlike the politicians, most political correspondents of that period had not been to public schools or Oxbridge and therefore felt ill at ease when interviewing people whom they would then have regarded as their social and educational superiors. As a result, they were embarrassingly deferential. That was not my problem. My problem was too much pride rather than too much humility. It was not so much a fear of embarrassing or demeaning the VIP that held me back from asking impertinent questions as the fear of embarrassing and demeaning myself.

In any case, for whatever reason, my political column in the *Sunday Telegraph* seldom lived up to McLachlan's expectations and on the very few occasions that it did this was entirely by courtesy of Lady Pamela Berry, my proprietor's wife, who presided over London's last and best political salon. At this time Pamela was in her fifties, still strikingly handsome and something of a legend, particularly in the *Telegraph* office where she had a reputation for imperiously demanding menial services from the journalists whom her husband employed, particularly the foreign correspondents. She would ring up the Paris correspondent, for example, asking him to take delivery of a hatbox, things like that. Or so it was rumoured. So I rather feared the worst when one morning this alarming figure, whom I had not met, came on the telephone asking me to do her a favour. 'Dean is coming to lunch, Mr Worsthorne,' she cooed, 'and I was wondering if by any chance you could help me out. Michael has just rung to say he was held up and it would be such fun if you could take his place.' Dean was the great Dean Acheson, Truman's Secretary of State, and Michael, of course, my boss. If this were a menial chore then I was happy to undertake it.

This was my first visit to the Berry house in Barton Street which turned out to be very different from the kind of residence newspaper proprietors are supposed to inhabit: entirely ungrandiose or pretentious and full of a highly personal taste and style, without any of the tell-tale signs of having been done over by some fashionable and expensive interior designer. Arriving early as requested, I found Pamela busy mixing dry martinis which she asked me to try. (Another chore willingly undertaken.) The reason I had been asked, it soon transpired, was that Harold Macmillan, whom Pamela at that time loathed, had complained to Michael about one of my articles, thereby prejudicing her hugely in my favour. Soon the beautiful L-shaped drawing room began to fill up. Dick Crossman, whom I had not met before, arrived early and was very complimentary, in Pamela's hearing, about something I had written in *Encounter*. Others present were Christopher and Mary Soames, Hugh Gaitskell, Virginia Crawley and David and Evangeline Bruce, David then being American Ambassador in London. When Mr Acheson arrived I was talking to Dick Crossman and Pamela beckoned us over to meet the guest of honour, introducing me first. That, I was to learn, was always her way. Under her roof, journalists – at any rate those in favour – were given preferential treatment. Lunch was served at a large round table which not only facilitated general conversation but also allowed enough room at the centre for a most ravishing display of Lalique glass. Beside each place were two half-bottle decanters, one for red wine and one for white, for the guest's individual use. Anybody's spirit would rise when sitting down at such a lunch table and when the first course turned out to be eggs florentine, a favourite dish, mine almost exploded with pleasure and excitement.

The topic of the day was the new President Kennedy's abortive Bay of Pigs invasion of Cuba. Pamela set the ball rolling fast and furiously by saying; 'We are all terribly worried, Dean, about your new young President. Surely General Eisenhower would never have tolerated such a fiasco – much worse than the mess poor gaga old Anthony made at Suez.' 'Don't be silly, Pamela,' chipped in Crossman. 'Suez was a conspiracy; the Bay of Pigs only a cock-up.' And off we went. By the time Acheson could get a word in edgeways the rollicking tone had been set. This was no occasion for elder statesman guff. If he was going to make any conversational mark at all he had to take the gloves off. Precisely what he said I cannot remember. But it gave me enough material for exactly the kind of article McLachlan wanted. Next Sunday's effort started as follows: 'Informed American sources in London tell me that President Kennedy did his level best to stop the Bay of Pigs expedition which had been set in motion by his predecessor. Unfortunately there comes a point in the planning of such an operation when the bureaucratic machinery of a superpower cannot be put into reverse in time to avert disaster, any more than can a supertanker, once set on the wrong course by an earlier skipper, be saved from the rocks by the most determined new pair of hands on the wheel.' The rest of the article was an apologia for Kennedy and an indictment of Eisenhower, all attributed to this unknown source. I suppose it was a useful article, enabling readers to know the kind of things that were being said in high Washington circles.

In the course of the next year or so I went to lots of Pamela's lunches and dinners which seldom failed to provide good copy of this kind. How could it be otherwise, given her assets? Pamela was very special, being the daughter of F. E. Smith, later Lord Birkenhead, one of Churchill's closest friends. In her youth she had listened to these giants exchanging political confidences as if doing so were the most natural thing in the world. She did not have to drop these names. They came as naturally to her lips as did her own. Having been privy to so much of the highest political gossip of those great days, the present lot of Tory ministers, many of whom she had grown up with, could not possibly be so cruel as to start denying her the same diet of indiscretion now. In any case, they wanted to maintain the old traditions. If a free-and-easy, no-holds-barred knockabout was good enough for giants like Churchill and Birkenhead and semi-giants like Duff Cooper and Oliver Stanley, who were such small fry as Harold Macmillan, R. A. Butler, David Eccles, Quintin Hogg and all the other present lot of Tory ministers – still less her old Labour friends, like Dick Crossman and Frank Pakenham – to want to improve on it? There was always a challenge in Pamela's eyes. 'Be as witty and outrageous as Duff and Oliver used to be, I dare you to.' All her younger guests, journalists, writers and dons, as much as politicians, felt the challenge. Our hostess had been intimate friends with most of the famous names of the 1930s: Evelyn Waugh, the Mitfords, Harold Acton, Somerset Maugham and many others, and we, a later generation, struggled valiantly not to seem and sound too inexcusably dull by comparison.

Frances Donaldson, in her memoirs, describes Pamela as a hardened Tory. I don't remember her as that at all. She loved the theatre of politics and any performer, quite as much on the left as on the right, could hold her attention and command her admiration if they were good enough. Ideas bored her, except in so far as they could provoke quarrels. That was my role at her parties: to be the reactionary grit in the oyster. Years later, during the Vietnam War when Walter Lippmann, who had just turned against it, was the guest of honour at one of her lunches, she called on me to tell the great man why I thought L.B.J. should drop an atom bomb on Hanoi. It was pure mischief. Lippmann, who until then had been on his usual Olympian high horse, was forced to descend into the heat and dust of polemical battle. Again I got an excellent article out of the resulting ding-dong, full of lurid details about L.B.J.'s iniquities. Pamela had not meant to do my dirty work, or to be helpful to me professionally. She was merely doing what came naturally. But like all good partnerships, ours was based on complementary interests. A good row enlivened her party as much as it did my column.

Although Pamela's salon alleviated the difficulties of writing a McLachlan-type column, it did not solve them. The Friday deadline would approach and more often than not I would still have no exciting story to tell in spite of all those expensive lunches at the Connaught Grill. Such was my desperation that I began to take purple hearts in the hope that they would give me inspiration. Instead of doing that, however, they only took my appetite away which made the Connaught lunches even more unrewarding. Eventually McLachlan relented, and it was agreed that my column might take any shape or form I chose. I remember our conversation very well. The concession was made with many warnings about how I was choosing a lightweight assignment in place of a heavyweight one. Did I not realise, he said, that in the world of professional journalism a free-ranging personal column was not taken seriously; no more than in the world of professional bakery was the role of putting the cherry on the cake? I did not accept that then, and do not now.

A column putting current controversies into historical perspective or illuminating them from a fresh angle or introducing new arguments does the reader just as much service – and to many readers, gives just as much enjoyment – as one purveying new inside information which is very often no more than the latest gossip. Ideally, of course, a column should contain both elements and very occasionally this is what I succeeded in doing. But more often than not I got my ideas from reading books which I found a far more useful and rewarding activity than lunching with most politicians, Richard Crossman being the outstanding exception. Very little is new in politics. Everything has been debated before. So on pretty well every topical subject there exists a mass of illuminating earlier writing waiting to be reworked by any journalist curious enough to take out a few volumes from the London Library. It helped my being a conservative columnist because the great conservative writers of earlier periods had been out of fashion for so long that their ideas were wholly unfamiliar to contemporary readers. Reworked by me, therefore, these ideas seemed startlingly fresh and original. If a liberal journalist on the *Observer* or *Guardian* had produced rehashed versions of John Stuart Mill on liberty, say, or John Morley on compromise, their columns would have caused no stir since most educated readers had been brought up on these famous works. But my rehash of the reactionary thoughts of, say Sir Fitzjames Stephen, John Stuart Mill's great opponent, was a very different matter. They really did cause a stir, so utterly unacceptable were they to the reigning liberal Zeitgeist. One week when a bill to abolish capital punishment was before parliament I wrote a particularly bloodthirsty column in defence of the gallows along very much the same lines as one I had read by Sir Fitzjames Stephen in a back number of the *Saturday Review*. Donald McLachlan called me in to protest. The piece, he said, was a particularly bad example of my besetting sin of 'intellectual sensationalism'. 'Will you never grow up?' he asked in his most schoolmasterish manner. Perhaps I should have come clean and confessed that the most intellectually sensational bits were thinly disguised borrowings from the more mature work of an immensely distinguished eminent Victorian, who was also the uncle of Virginia Woolf. But I didn't, preferring to be found guilty of puerility than plagiarism.

Another useful reactionary writer was Mosca whose monumental study of *The Ruling Class* down the ages provided me with masses of ammunition for firing salvos at contemporary egalitarianism. A great work by Pareto demonstrating the iron laws of oligarchy also came in useful, most particularly by enabling me to explain rather earlier than some why the trade unions had deteriorated from being democratic organisations run in the interests of their members to bureaucratic organisations run in the interest of their bosses. Countless other writers were also conscripted to my cause – de Maistre, Charles Maurras, Mallock, Burckhardt, Taine – none being more useful than Nietzsche whose famous diatribe against the tyranny of the weak gave bite to many a column critical of the welfare state. As I say, I was lucky to be a conservative columnist at a time when there was no one else regularly ploughing that same furrow. Like Dr Johnson's woman preacher, one did not have to do the job particularly well. It was surprising and shocking enough to be doing it at all.

Fashions in ideas are not unlike fashions in clothes. They come round in circles, rather like a stage army. Just as a dress designer can provoke startled oohs and aahs by rediscovering a long-forgotten style from a century before, so a political columnist can do the same by giving a new lease of life to an old doctrine. Intellectual sensationalism indeed. All I did was to express ideas – the case for colonialism, for example – which a hundred years ago were conventional wisdom in any reasonably well-educated conservative home.

McLachlan eventually became resigned to this kind of column. But he was never happy with it and continually nagged me to spend more time talking to contemporary politicians, civil servants and sages. Frequently he drove me down to Nuffield College, where he was a Fellow, so that I could pick the brains of the master, Norman Chester, and the psephologist David Butler, then at the beginning of his life's work. The evenings were always interesting but I never came away excited to have found the germ of a fresh thought that I could work up into a column. Rather the opposite. If any such germ did for a moment materialise, it would be swiftly smothered by a mass of complicated qualifications. So it has to be in any discussion involving experts. If my job had been to write long features on some particular area of public policy, then these evenings would have been immensely useful. But it wasn't. It was to write the centrepiece article on the leader page of a new Sunday paper and anyone who has ever seen people opening their Sunday papers around the breakfast table will know that long, serious, specialist articles on public policy are not what even the most highbrow reader wants at that particular time. But neither do they want unserious or unintelligent articles. Ideally they want instant intellectual stimulation without having to think too hard or too long. The obvious answer is articles that confront received opinion; think the unthinkable; point out the unacceptable consequences of actions which on the surface seem so eminently sensible and desirable, i.e. paradoxical articles. Bernard Shaw, Oscar Wilde, G. K. Chesterton and more recently Malcolm Muggeridge and A. J. P. Taylor were masters of this genre. So were Dean Inge and H. L. Mencken. The point about a paradox is that it hooks the reader. Take, for example, Oscar Wilde's 'I can resist everything but temptation'. Conventional wisdom has been stood on its head. An early column after McLachlan had released me from only writing on subjects about which I had inside information began with the statement: 'In the long run Communism, being so hateful, will do less harm to free societies than the far more insidiously dangerous doctrine of liberalism' and this at the height of the Cold War on the leader page of a leading anti-communist newspaper. Another article began: 'If the Tory Party is really serious about full employment, then the only way to achieve it is by reintroducing direction of labour.' Or: 'Government is not so much about the choice of priorities, as Aneurin Bevan said. Almost always it is about the choice between two evils.' Or: 'Capitalism will destroy the class system far quicker than socialism.'

For me confronting received opinion was much more than a convenient journalistic technique. It was also the natural inclination of a conservative journalist during a period of liberal ascendancy. Thus to journalistic opportunism was added the extra push of ideological conviction. The formula seemed to work. Ralph Thackeray, the new paper's features editor, used to refer to my pieces as 'Perrydoxes'. Donald McLachlan, I suppose, was right. Paradox *is* a form of intellectual sensationalism. But whereas he thought this was a vice, I preferred to think, and still prefer to think, that it was a virtue.

Apart from writing this one column a week, another duty was to take charge of 'To The Point', a collection of very short leaders, each not more than a hundred words or so long, which, it was hoped, would attract more attention than the much longer-winded editorial pronouncements in the *Sunday Times* and the *Observer*. The intention was to sum up the main issues of the day in a few pithy sentences – ideally an epigram. McLachlan canvassed almost every member of the editorial staff with his new concepts. 'Imagine, at dinner, you are sitting next to Lady Bloggs, and she turns to you and says, "Oh, Mr so and so – *do* tell me what you thought of the budget [or Rhodesia, the latest moon shot, the Beatles or anything else in the news]." You turn to her, and in a few brilliantly polished phrases encapsulate all that needs to be said on the subject.' In his book *The House the Berrys Built*, Duff Hart-Davis writes: 'Like many of McLachlan's ideas, this one sounded good at first – and everybody was exhorted to submit Points for publication; but since the extra payment offered was derisory, and most of the Points were never used anyway, enthusiasm soon waned. Besides, the fallacy underlying the whole operation quickly became apparent – that leaders as short as those tended to be not so much memorable as jejune. Irreverent calls were soon heard for the column to be renamed "Beside the Point".'

As well as encouraging all the staff to try their hand writing 'To The Points', McLachlan also recruited three bright young freelances whose job it was to come in on Friday evenings and Saturday mornings to do 'extra research'. One of these was Geoffrey Howe, then an up-and-coming young barrister and aspiring politician. Another was Bernard Donoughue, a very bright postgraduate at the LSE, who went on to head Harold Wilson's think tank, and the third, a young art historian, James Joll, who went on to become something big in Agnews. I would dread their arrival, never being able to think of anything for them to do. For extra research was the least-needed ingredient for a good 'Point'. Bernard Donoughue was a help since he had an original and quirky mind with, in those days, a witty right-wing bent. Geoffrey Howe, on the other hand, would bustle in carrying a briefcase stuffed with material more suitable for a Bow Group pamphlet – where in due course it appeared – than for an epigram. James Joll was an eminently civilised presence but I don't recall him opening his mouth, let alone putting pen to paper. Brushing aside my complaint that we were wasting these young men's time, and our own, McLachlan insisted that simply having young high-flyers around was a good investment for the paper which would bear dividends eventually when they arrived at the top of their respective trees.

Another high-flyer he recruited was a young man called Michael Wolf who used to produce masses of research on penal reform. Although an agreeable fellow, with a delightful wife, he was no good as a journalist and soon left to find his proper level as an assistant to Edward Heath. In the end the only reliable 'To The Pointer' turned out to be Douglas Brown, formerly a senior *Daily Telegraph* foreign correspondent whom McLachlan had appointed foreign editor. He and I shared a room and became great friends, having much in common over and above our shared frustration at being part of an editorial set-up which deprived us of all responsibility worth the name. For on the *Sunday*, as on the *Daily*, news and comment were rigidly separated, with news coming under a managing editor, Brian Roberts – formerly night editor on the *Daily* – and only comment and features coming under McLachlan. This meant, in effect, that Douglas Brown – like me, a McLachlan appointment – was no more foreign editor than I was deputy editor. Douglas did not even have a column of his own. From time to time he would write excellent features, either on the Catholic Church, of which he was a devout member, or on South Africa where he had served for many years. But more often than not, his most valuable service to the paper was to give McLachlan's endless flow of zany ideas such a frosty reception that they withered on the branch.

One that unfortunately didn't wither on the branch was the office lunch for senior executives every Saturday, attended by Michael Berry, editor-in-chief of both papers. In theory this made a lot of sense. On the *Daily*, Michael, like his father Lord Camrose before him, was a remote and Olympian figure who inhabited his own palatial quarters on the fifth floor. Most of the staff had never set eyes upon him, let alone met him, his arrivals and departures being shrouded by commissionaires and other lackeys over-eager to protect him from any potentially embarrassing encounters. I don't suppose he welcomed this protection and probably accepted it only so as not to have to break a tradition laid down by his father. But the new *Sunday*, McLachlan reckoned, having no traditions, would give Michael Berry a welcome opportunity to turn over a new leaf. In a way McLachlan was right, since Michael, to everybody else's surprise, readily agreed to attend the lunch. So far so good. But if the purpose of the lunch was to break down barriers between the editor-in-chief and his staff, it failed utterly. This did not surprise me. Even after being very friendly at lunches and dinners in his own home, once back in the office he was always as remote as ever. So it was after the Saturday office lunches. During them he was affable and courteous. Immediately afterwards, though, down came the barriers again with a bang. What his presence at these lunches, however, did succeed in doing was to inhibit their other purpose which was to enable the journalists to talk seriously about next day's paper, all our energies being required to think up intriguing subjects of conversation which might tempt Michael to join in. Basically financial gossip was the only reliable bait. Unfortunately, our first City editor, Nigel Lawson, could not be relied upon to provide it, being far more interested in stuffing himself with Searcy's grouse and lobster than in feeding his editor-in-chief's insatiable appetite for details of the latest City dealings. After attending one or two of McLachlan's Saturday lunches Brian Roberts, the managing editor, sent a characteristically rude message to say that in future he would wish to be excused, having more useful things to do than waste his time at such pointless gatherings – a feeling which all of us shared but lacked the courage, or the ruthlessness, to express. In time, even the standards of the catering went down as Searcy's, noticing that Michael Berry much preferred cold beef to grouse and lobster, adjusted the menu and also, I trust, the price.

That the paper got off the ground at all must have had something to do with the enormous reserves of goodwill felt towards anything associated with the *Telegraph* name. Also, in Brian Roberts it had a production man of remarkable forcefulness who made up for his abysmal ignorance about what should go into newspapers by knowing everything about how to get them out on time. Another tower of efficiency was the features editor,

Ralph Thackeray, whose ruthlessness in cutting the gold out of good writing was at least equalled by his ruthlessness in cutting the dross out of bad. The news editor, George Evans, also made a most valuable contribution, being equally trusted by Brian Roberts and Donald McLachlan, who very soon were barely on speaking terms. Desmond Albrow, the deputy features editor, was another major asset. Lapses of taste or accuracy which had evaded less discerning eyes could never pass through his hands without detection. Most important of all there was Michael Berry himself who not only had most of the genuinely good ideas, like publishing the Denning Report on the Profumo scandal in full and serialising the incomparably revealing diaries of 'Chips' Channon, but also made most of the successful appointments. It was Michael, for example, who picked Alan Brien as drama critic and the largely unknown Nigel Lawson as City editor. The book section of the paper under Anthony Curtis was also first class, boasting not only my nominee Nigel Dennis* but also Rebecca West.

Donald's own contribution is more difficult to assess. He certainly encouraged young writers, even if this did often involve sending them off on wild-goose chases. More important he had the independence of mind and spirit to be utterly underwhelmed and unintimidated by the stifling *Daily Telegraph* ethos which even as rebellious a journalist as Malcolm Muggeridge – when deputy editor of the *Daily* – had not found easy to defy. It was McLachlan, for example, who gave a column on the *Sunday Telegraph* to Claud Cockburn, the ex-communist editor of the *Week* – an appointment that Michael Berry would not for a moment have allowed on the *Daily*. In the event, it was a boring column, in spite of being telephoned to the office from a pub in Youghal where Claud Cockburn – very much a spent force – then lived. Nevertheless, carrying any kind of regular column by so notorious and disreputable an old scoundrel gave the new paper a certain something. Another McLachlan innovation was a rag-bag column called Mandrake, edited by the much-married Bobby Birch of *Picture Post* fame. Again it was not a particularly good column since Bobby laboured under the illusion that anything unusual – i.e. Dervishes Dance in Shepherd's Bush, say – must be interesting. For a *Telegraph* paper to have such a lighthearted column at all, however, was innovation enough.

The trouble is that only somewhat back-handed, ironical praise can possibly do justice to Donald McLachlan. The old story about him wanting to appoint Peter Utley as television critic is quite true. His reason, given to me, was that Peter, being blind, would not have his judgment of programmes affected one way or the other by the pictures. One just about

---

* In the 1950s while I was still on *The Times*, Alan Pryce-Jones, the editor of the *TLS* had asked me whether I would like to 'cut my teeth' as a book reviewer on two first novels, *Cards of Identity* by Nigel Dennis and *Under the Net* by Iris Murdoch. In his covering note he said, 'only two hundred words each if they are no good'. In the event, I am glad to say, each got half a column of enthusiastic praise.

knew what he meant. But as a serious suggestion it was pretty nonsensical. For those of us working on the paper, and being subjected at first hand to his eccentricities, day after day, it was not much fun. But by the time the raw McLachlan spirit had been purified and processed by its passage through the hands of Ralph Thackeray and many others, its impact on the reader – which is all that matters – may not have been so much maddening as intriguing, giving the paper a certain idiosyncratic character all its own. If that was the case, then there was method in his madness.

Perhaps aware of the unfulfilling nature of the duties he had assigned to me, McLachlan generously encouraged me to undertake foreign travel, an opportunity for which arose fairly soon after the new paper began. Out of the blue, in October 1962, the Americans announced that air reconnaissance by U2s had discovered Russian nuclear missiles stationed in Castro's Cuba, only ninety miles away from the coast of Florida. Washington's reaction was seismic. Short of actually going to war, Russia could not have done anything more hostile or challenging. For America and Cuba were already locked in deadly combat, and for the Russians to place nuclear missiles in Castro's Cuba in the middle of the Cold War was no less provocative for the Americans than it would have been for the British if the Germans had placed them in De Valera's Ireland in the middle of the Second World War.

Initially the European and even British response was incredulous, not to say sceptical. It was assumed that there must be some mistake. Although Mr Khrushchev, the rumbustious Russian leader, was known to be foolhardy, surely he could not conceivably have done anything as foolhardy as that. That was the view, even on the pro-American right. The left went even further. They suspected that it was all a CIA fabrication to justify a further American, or American-backed, invasion of Cuba – a second, more successful Bay of Pigs. Although I knew in my bones it was not that, I secretly prayed that it was; anything rather than having to accept the fact that the world was faced with the imminent threat of a thermo-nuclear war.

To allay these suspicions President Kennedy sent Dean Acheson to Paris and London on a secret mission to show President de Gaulle and Prime Minister Macmillan the photographic evidence of the missile emplacement. Both statesmen were convinced beyond a doubt of its genuineness, as were the experts. Shortly after Mr Macmillan had seen Dean Acheson, a few journalists, including myself, were summoned to Downing Street to be shown the photographs. The dark blobs meant nothing to me but from the expression on the briefing officer's face there could be no doubt in my mind that they were indeed the real thing.

After the Downing Street briefing I returned to the office to tell McLachlan the news and he suggested that I should catch the first available plane to Washington so as to be able to write about the crisis from there. From then on events moved with incredible speed. Russian tankers, all too visibly carrying new missiles on their decks, were found steaming towards Cuba. Next President Kennedy threatened to turn them back, if necessary by force. The situation could not have been graver. The whole world sat glued to their TV sets watching the tankers steaming ahead, knowing that it was only a matter of hours before they would reach the exclusion zone specified by President Kennedy, at which point would come the moment of dreadful truth.

After leaving McLachlan I took the Central line tube from Chancery Lane home to pack a bag and say goodbye to Claudie and Dominique. (In those days we were not allowed to put taxis on expenses.) Oddly enough I don't remember this farewell as being highly charged. Possibly this was because neither of us believed that the worst could happen. But I don't think it was that. I think it was rather that the worst, in these circumstances, was so uniquely awesome as to rule out all ordinary human emotion. Since this was going to be no ordinary war, it seemed inappropriate to show the emotions normally associated with ordinary wartime partings. As for the appropriate emotions for a parting on the eve of a war that might cause the end of the world, there were simply no precedents or traditions to guide us. Fear was too ordinary; so were tears; even dread somehow seemed inadequate. In the event, what took over at any rate for me was *excitement*. After all, this might be a drama to end all dramas.

Before catching the plane to Washington I had to go back to Bush House in the Aldwych to take part in a broadcast which I did every week for the BBC Overseas Service. John Freeman, then at the *New Statesman*, was a fellow panellist and I remember getting very steamed up when he criticised President Kennedy for overreaction – a view then very common on this side of the Atlantic. If the Russians tolerated having American nuclear missiles so near their borders in Turkey, he argued, why should not the Americans tolerate having Russian missiles so near their borders in Cuba? My answer was that the Americans had placed them in Turkey openly, with the Russians' tacit acceptance, whereas the Russians, by placing them in Cuba secretly, had broken all the unwritten Cold War rules. The two acts, I insisted, were not comparable and John Freeman had no business clouding the issue in this irresponsible way. It was a good debate, as debates with John Freeman always were.

From Bush House I did take a taxi to Heathrow, judging this to be part of a foreign assignment when domestic economies no longer applied. In those days we were also allowed to fly first class, and even more champagne flowed than usual. I don't think this was the old stiff-upper-lip syndrome, or even the eat, drink and be merry for tomorrow we die one either. It was rather that the possibility of the whole world going bang, with everybody being blown up together, somehow made fear irrelevant, out of date, anachronistic. We had gone beyond fear. If everybody was going to die, then nobody was going to die because death involved leaving the living behind and there would be no living left behind.

Probably I am rationalising after the event. I have no idea what the other passengers were thinking and even no clear recollection what I was thinking. All I do know is that the atmosphere was much less grim than in the days preceding the Second World War, and this was certainly not because people had any illusions about what was at stake.

The atmosphere in Washington was extraordinarily subdued. From the moment of announcing the exclusion zone President Kennedy and his small team of advisers had gone into purdah in the White House, making no appearances and issuing no statements. This unprecedented hush lasted for several days during which there was nothing much to do except wait and pray and hope for the best. I think we all knew by then that if anybody was going to flinch from this eyeball-to-eyeball confrontation, it would not be President Kennedy. How we knew that I do not know. But we did. Somehow or other the total public silence from the White House had succeeded in communicating determination more effectively than any number of official communiqués.

I was staying with old friends, Phil and Cherie Geyerlin. He was then in charge of the editorial page of the *Washington Post* and a friend of President Kennedy. But even well-connected journalists like Phil had no idea what was going on. Then came the sensational newsflash. The tankers had turned back and we all began to breathe again. Weeks before the crisis began Phil and Cherie had arranged a dinner party, all thought of which had been expunged from their minds if only because two of the guests, the brothers McGeorge and Bill Bundy, were part of the presidential team who had been immured in the White House. At about 6.00 p.m. on the day the crisis ended, I was sitting with Phil in his study when the telephone rang. It was McGeorge Bundy himself calling from the White House. He wanted to know whether he and his brother Bill and their respective wives were still expected for dinner. Phil, a hard-bitten American journalist and ex-American marine, almost broke down. It was a bit like unexpectedly hearing from one of Wellington's aides-de-camp only a few hours after the victorious conclusion to the battle of Waterloo.

What a memorable dinner it turned out to be, not because it was so extraordinary but because it was so ordinary. At about 8.00 p.m. the front doorbell rang and Phil and I let the Bundy brothers in. 'Hi, Mac, hi Bill,' cried Phil, slapping them on the back. 'That was one helluva ball game' – a good enough salutation for the victorious heroes of a baseball match but somehow inadequate for two men who had just played crucial roles in the most potentially deadly confrontation in human history. Never before had the contrast between the august imperial responsibilities wielded by high Washington officials in their public lives and the extreme simplicity of their private lives struck me so forcibly. As far as I can remember Phil Graham, proprietor of the *Washington Post*, and his wife Katharine were also there, as was Stewart Alsop.* Released from the tensions of the last few days the Bundy brothers disclosed fascinating details about how the fateful crisis had been managed. But here again another feeling that I have often experienced before in Washington returned more forcibly than ever: the inadequacy – at least to English ears – of even Wasp-ascendency demotic English – 'the fat lady sure sang', for example – for the discussion of high politics, almost as unsuitable as is any kind of an American accent for declaiming Shakespeare. After the other guests had gone to bed, Bill and Mac stayed behind for a nightcap which consisted of cold beer from the fridge in the kitchen. By now it was quite late and I remember holding forth about how the Cuban missile crisis would go down in history as the first – and hopefully the last – thermo-nuclear war. For if an act of thermo-nuclear war could be defined as the confrontational deployment of thermo-nuclear weapons to alter the balance of power, then this, I argued, is exactly what had just taken place, albeit without a shot being fired – not unlike one of those medieval wars when opposing armies rushed about making lots of noise without actually being joined in battle.

As happens late at night after a good party this thesis was given far more serious attention than it deserved, allowing me to feel that I, too, had made a personal contribution to the Cuban missile crisis, if only by being the first to appreciate fully its unique importance. That is what makes Washington so exhilarating. Even a journalist is made to feel involved in the making of history. Yet all the ceremonial trimmings associated with such privileged proximity were missing – drums, fanfares, footmen, balls, chandeliers. Perhaps it was always thus. Late at night even victorious Augustus must have sometimes relaxed. But surely not to the same degree. Late twentieth-century Washington is certainly special in this respect. For one of the ironies of history is that technology made available unprecedented concentrations of military power just at the very moment when American democratic egalitarianism had produced an unprecedentedly informal ruling class to inherit it.

The White House itself was quite another matter. Never have I been present at a more impressive occasion than President Kennedy's press conference in the immediate aftermath of his triumph. It was his first public appearance since he had gone into seclusion for the duration of the crisis and the great auditorium was overflowing with newsmen from all over the world for once more anxious to pay homage than to ask questions. When the President strode in from the wings everybody stood up and cheered. Many were in tears. Perhaps it was only in our imagination that the

*Stewart Alsop later wrote a famous article in the *Saturday Evening Post* about the Cuban missile crisis, in which he divided the team of Kennedy's advisers into 'Hawks and Doves' – categories first formulated in the course of this dinner.

President seemed to have grown in stature. As I put it in a star-struck despatch, 'before the crisis he had been glamorous Prince Hal; now he was every inch a king'.

Little of what came to be called the Myth of Camelot has survived the test of time. But to me his handling of the missile crisis seems even more heroic today than it did then. For we now know that if the President had succumbed to the urgings of the American high command to take the Russian missiles out by invading Cuba, the Red Army general on the island would have used them to hit back with or without Mr Khrushchev's authorisation. On the other hand, if Kennedy had demonstrated insufficient resolution, and not threatened to turn the Russian tankers back, if necessary by force, his own generals might have themselves felt obliged to press the button, also off their own bat. Arguably the choices facing Kennedy during those terrible days were the most difficult and frightening any statesman has ever been called upon to make. In the end he got the balance between toughness and restraint absolutely right.

Years later friends have often teased me about having fallen for the Kennedy hype and it is true that my language did sometimes go overboard. Not satisfied with comparing him to Henry V on this occasion I soon found another opportunity to hail him as 'the Emperor of the West'. But unlike some of my other journalistic exaggerations – comparing Harold Wilson to Lloyd George, for example – the Kennedy ones do not make me blush with embarrassment. For Kennedy *was* special. It is now thirty years since that presidential press conference but I can still remember the excitement we all felt as that golden figure stood at the lectern, arms raised, acknowledging the cheers. Then, when silence eventually fell, there was a long pause and we all assumed that he was collecting his thoughts to say something momentous. Instead a rueful grin spread from ear to ear and he quipped; 'Gentlemen, long time no see.' His seclusion in fact had only lasted a week. But far more eloquently than any high-blown oratory this colloquialism, combined with the grin, made us understand how for him that dreadful week must indeed have seemed like an eternity.

In addition to my column, and writing 'To the Points' I had one other duty on the *Sunday Telegraph* and that was to commission the occasional article from famous authors. McLachlan used to say at the Wednesday conference; 'Oh Perry, why don't you ask Einstein if he would do us twelve hundred words on space travel?' or 'What about a piece from the Pope on abortion?' – ideas so far beyond our reach as to be easy to ignore. But occasionally he had good ideas. It was his, for example, to get Kingsley Amis to do a three-thousand-word review of the bible as if he had never read it before. To my objection that Kingsley might not be anxious to undertake such an onerous assignment, McLachlan replied, with a rare lapse into realism, 'Offer him a thousand pounds [now nearer to ten thousand pounds], that might tempt him.' It did. For that princely sum, said Kingsley, he would even agree to review the collected *oeuvres* of John Wain.

Another of McLachlan's ideas was to get Evelyn Waugh to write about the French army which had recently been causing so much trouble in Algeria, also for an enormous fee. A few months earlier, as it happened, I had been taken by Pamela Berry to lunch with the Waughs at Combe Florey in Somerset, on our way back from a big political meeting in Jeremy Thorpe's West Country constituency. We often did these kind of trips together. In return for my allowing her to tag on at my side on journalistic assignments, she allowed me to tag on at hers when visiting grandees – an arrangement that satisfied her craving to be part of the journalistic action as much as it satisfied mine to be part of the higher social whirl.

On this occasion Evelyn Waugh could not have been jollier or more welcomingly hospitable, using a tongue-tied young Auberon to pour out bottle after bottle of excellent pink champagne. Only one thing was slightly wrong. Waugh insisted on calling me by my father's name, Koch de Gooreynd. Not that this mattered at the time. In fact I was flattered that the great writer even knew that much about me. In any case, emboldened by this earlier experience, I wrote to Evelyn Waugh outlining the article McLachlan had in mind and offering to visit him again in the country if he were at all interested in hearing more details of the project. Back by return post came a postcard suggesting that I should either meet him for a drink at the St James's Club or invite him to dinner in London at any place of my choosing. Although I had by then pretty well given up using Boodle's I had kept up my membership and this seemed exactly the right kind of opportunity to put it to some good use. So on the appointed evening I sat in the saloon there waiting for my distinguished guest. These being the Pinfold years my expectation was not unmixed with trepidation. But because our first meeting had gone off without mishap, it seemed not wholly unreasonable to hope that my luck would hold out a second time.

At 8.00 p.m. I heard a vague rumble which at first I thought must be my imagining. Only when the rumbles grew so loud as to leave no further room for desperate wishful thinking did I rush out in the hall. There, standing four-square in the middle, was Evelyn Waugh, puce in the face, shouting abuse at the hall porter. No sooner did I appear than he turned his abuse on me. 'Is it not the custom, sir,' he bellowed, 'when one gentleman invites another to dine with him in his club for the host to take the elementary precaution of first joining that club?' Since by then I had known the hall porter for twenty years I turned to him in amazement. 'But he didn't ask for you, sir, he asked for a Mr Koch de Gooreynd and I told him that we didn't have any member of that name.' Not a good beginning. Once in the dining room upstairs things got no better. He ordered a dozen oysters for his first course and another dozen for his second which some-how suggested a continued determination to make life unnecessarily awkward for his by now severely shaken host. Quite suddenly, however, the mood changed. Indeed his conversation at dinner could not have been more interesting and convivial, and he even agreed to write the article. The worst must be over, I thought, but it wasn't.

Downstairs in the saloon he asked for a glass of port of which he took only a sip before starting to bellow once again. 'I don't think this is the quality of port which Lady Pamela Berry would wish me to be offered.'

By this time other members of the club were pricking up their ears and I felt bound to demur. 'But it isn't Lady Pamela who has offered it to you,' I said plaintively.

'Good God,' he cried out, rising to his feet. 'I had no idea you were paying for this out of your own pocket.' Then pulling out his wallet, from which white five pound notes fluttered all around us – and around the legs of the other members – he hauled me off to White's next door where we sat happily on the fender drinking brandy and peppermint until at about 1.00 a.m he asked me to take him back to the St James's Club. In the taxi, he apologised for having been so difficult, saying that he was in a bad way because of the drugs he was being forced to take. Next morning his agent, A.D. Peters, rang me in the office to say that Mr Waugh greatly regretted that he would not be able after all to write the article since he had already accepted to do something similar for the *Daily Mail*.*

McLachlan's editorship did not last very long. In 1968 it was announced out of the blue that he had resigned. None of us was exactly flabbergasted. His eccentricities were getting worse and worse, the circulation was falling and it had been only a matter of time before Michael Berry was bound to lose patience. What did take us by surprise, however, was what happened next. Determined never again to have another viewy intellectual in an editor's chair – one had proved more than enough – he chose as McLa-chlan's successor Brian Roberts, the archetypal production man, which meant that the paper went from one extreme of having an editor with too

---

* This is how Evelyn Waugh described his evening in a letter to Ann Fleming: 'I went to London for a night to see a civil young man who says he is the editor of the *Sunday Telegraph*. He signed his letters "Peregrine Worsthorne". I said "an unusual name". He said: "Yes, my father chose it when he stood for parliament. I should be called Koch de Gooryend". Then to make it quite simple added: "He called my brother Towneley". "Like the Towneley marbles?" "Yes, he owns them". Confusion of elderly party. Well, this man of mystery proposed to send me abroad for a treat. We drank heavy and I behaved rather like Randolph in his braver moments, calling for more & better wine, until I said: "I presume Michael Berry is paying for this?" "No, indeed, I am, out of my wages". So then I felt I had behaved badly & could only atone by giving a lot of wine to the mystery man, so I took him up the street to my club and we drank heavily and I woke next day with the vague but persistent impression that I have promised to go to the war in Algiers for him. Not at all what I wanted. My French is not up to jolly evenings in paratroop messes nor are my stiff old limbs in any condition to dodge terrorists.' (*The Letters of Evelyn Waugh*, edited by Mark Amory.)

many ideas to the other of having an editor with no ideas at all, very much a case, in my view, of out of the frying pan into the fire.

I remembered Donald's last Saturday night on the paper with some sadness. Douglas and I took him out for a drink after the first edition had gone to bed. He was as tiresome as ever, advising me to do a stint in the City office so as to broaden my horizons. What valedictory advice he gave to Douglas I cannot remember but in all likelihood it was equally off-beam. In the taxi going back to the office, however, he suddenly burst out laughing. 'I have just thought of something,' he said. 'Yes, you're both quite right, my editorship was a failure' (we hadn't said anything of the kind). 'But it had to be, don't you see. It was the only way for a Sunday offspring of the immensely successful *Daily Telegraph* ever to make its individual mark. Better for the new paper to be an interesting failure than a successful clone.'

Getting back to the office very much later than promised we ran into Brian Roberts, his designated successor, on the stairs. 'Unreliable to the bitter end, McLachlan,' he snarled out of the side of his then toothless mouth. (The first thing he did after taking over as editor was to get himself a new pair of false teeth.) Douglas and I were outraged. 'Say what you will, Perry,' said Douglas, 'we are going to miss that lunatic.' We did.

14

Indiscretions

'Peregrine Worsthorne was a nice man. It was impossible to recruit him; he was a great snob, a very sociable man. I was many times at his parties, where the cream of society gathered, such as Reginald Maudling, the trade secretary at the time.' So said Michael Lyubimov, a KGB agent in London during the 1960s, in an interview in Moscow with the *Daily Telegraph* in 1992. I don't recognise Michael Lyubimov's description of our life. Claudie and I used to give one big party a year which was all we could afford. Michael Lyubimov came to one of them – he was in London five years – and wrongly assumed that it was something we did every week. He was a popular guest, propositioning several of the lady guests, notably the beautiful Pat Gale who arrived at a restaurant where we were dining after the party with a graphically memorable description of 'ten feet of Russian tongue trying to lasso my tonsils in a taxi'. Much more often than he came to us Lyubimov would give me luxurious lunches at the Ecu de France in Jermyn Street where, over the aperitifs, he would go through the motions of asking abstruse questions about NATO weaponry. Rather than lose face by admitting that I had no inside information on this subject I would trot out whatever I had read in the previous week's *Economist*. Then, both our duties done, we would have a jolly lunch. As for Claudie and me entertaining 'the cream of society' that was absolute nonsense. Just possibly Reggie Maudling may have been at one party but I rather doubt it since we were never at all close; and even less close after an incident at the dramatic Tory Party conference which coincided with the Prime Minister, Harold Macmillan's sudden resignation, through illness. Reggie, one of the contenders for the succession, was my guest for dinner in the main conference hotel and had just lit up a fat cigar when a television crew started filming our table. To my disgust, instead of boldly continuing to puff away, he furtively hid this symbol of affluence under the table and never forgave his host for telling him in no uncertain terms that anyone frightened of being seen smoking a cigar in public was wholly unfit to head the great party once led by Winston Churchill.

No, our friends continued to be very much the old Fleet Street gang, some of whom, by the end of the 1960s, were beginning to show signs of wear and tear; and none more so than Henry Fairlie. In the first place so unreliable had he become that no British newspaper was any longer prepared to take the risk of employing him. There had been a famous occasion, for example, when he simply failed to turn up at some big conference in Paris, which he was due to cover for the *Daily Mail*, preferring to spend his generous advance on throwing a party at the Ritz. Worse, he had fallen badly into debt and on one occasion was even sent to prison overnight for ignoring a court order over unpaid bills. Like so much else to do with Henry, even this squalid episode was somehow turned into the stuff of legend. For not only was the arrest made immediately after he had finished performing on the BBC radio programme *Any Questions*, but Cardinal Heenan, one of his fellow panellists, was so shocked to learn of his troubles that he there and then coughed up £100 towards the repayment – not enough to stop the mills of justice grinding altogether but more than enough to cheer Henry on his way. Nor was that the end of the cardinal's kindness. He also rang Henry's magnificently long-suffering wife Lizette to break the bad news that her husband was on the way to Winchester jail, only to be taken aback by her surprisingly cheerful response: 'Oh thanks, at least I'll know where the old so and so is sleeping tonight.' Legend has it that even the prison governor fell victim to Henry's charm, arranging for the repeat of the *Any Questions* programme to be relayed at lunch in the communal dining room the next day so that Henry should not miss it. When the cardinal was heard on air commending Henry for the soundness of his views on something or other, the other inmates broke out into spontaneous cheers, or so Henry always claimed.

There was one disaster, however, that could not be redeemed by Henry's unique panache. His son was sent back home from an expensive boarding school as a result of Henry disregarding repeated warnings about unpaid fees. Much could be turned into a joke, but not that. As so often is the case, the final straw turned out to be the least of Henry's offences. He was found guilty of libelling Lady Antonia Fraser and rather than paying her the £12,000 damages, he fled to the welcoming arms of a mistress in the United States from whence (the US, I mean) he never returned.*

Another member of the gang, John Raymond, also pretty well disappeared at about this time, albeit less spectacularly. Always a heavy

---

*He died penniless in 1990 in Washington. During his last years he lived and slept in a small office at the *New Republic* where he was a contributing editor. American benefactors among his generation had by then lost patience. But among discerning young journalists he remained an inspiration to the end.

drinker he started on week-long benders from which he would return badly bruised and beaten up. Ten years earlier his bad habit of addressing strangers in pubs in the angry style and manner of Churchill pouring wartime scorn on Hitler and Mussolini had usually provoked more laughter than blows. Judging, however, by the black eyes and broken ribs he was now getting, unwilling audiences were becoming far less indulgent. His work at the *New Statesman* was also going badly. Having for years put up with John's heavy drinking, which he strongly disapproved of, Kingsley Martin, the editor, was suddenly faced with an additional challenge to his tolerance. John was received into the Roman Catholic Church, and if there was one thing Kingsley Martin hated more than alcoholism it was Catholicism. After the reception ceremony in Farm Street – at which I was one of the witnesses – Father D'Arcy paid John a great compliment. The conversion of so eminent a man of letters was, he said, 'a red letter day for Rome and a black letter day for Canterbury'. Kingsley Martin, however, took a different view. His tolerance, he said, just stretched to having a Catholic on the staff or an alcoholic, but he was damned if he was going to have a Catholic who was also an alcoholic. Fired from the *New Statesman*, John wrote reviews for a time for the *Sunday Times* but henceforth it was tragically downhill all the way to an early grave.

From the gang's point of view, Billy Hughes's fate was scarcely less sad. He got married to a woman who completely cut him out of our lives. Presumably she thought we led him into temptation, or encouraged sides of his character which she did not like. It was a bad blow, particularly to Claudie for whom over the years he had become a kind of older brother. From one day to the next we never saw our dear old friend again except as a somewhat embarrassed stranger at other people's parties. In a way the inexplicable desertion of a friend is even more hurtful than a death since to the pain of loss is added the humiliation of rejection.

Much more worrying, however, than anything else was the state of Claudie's health. One evening I returned from Fleet Street to find her lying on her bed semi-conscious and unable to speak. The doctor could find nothing wrong and next morning she seemed recovered. About a week later she had what seemed like an epileptic fit which again left her semi-conscious and unable to speak. This time she was taken to hospital for tests for a brain tumour. But the tests revealed nothing. Nevertheless the fits continued. They would come on suddenly and I would only know that something was wrong when, instead of replying when spoken to, her eyes would simply fill with fear. Back into the hospital she went for more brain scans which were always negative. At some point a specialist suggested that the trouble might be psychological rather than physical. Much against her will Claudie agreed to visit a psychiatrist who shocked her by suggesting that she might be suffering from a neurosis caused by an unhappy marriage. Most of his questions, she complained, had to do with me rather than her. After a while she lost faith in this man, but not before he had planted seeds of suspicion in her mind about the cause of her illness which were never wholly uprooted. Months sometimes went by without what Claudie came to call 'one of her attacks'. But just when we had put them out of our minds, I would see that frightened look on her speechless face and know that another attack was on its way. Yet still the neurologist could find no cause. Eventually even our close personal friend Professor Roger Gilliatt, who took her under his wing at the Middlesex, came to the reluctant conclusion that the cause might indeed be psychological. Under his influence Claudie admitted herself to the Maudsley Hospital where my mother was a governor. Her experiences there were grim. Put in a ward for the mentally unbalanced and treated as if she were round the bend, it was a miracle she did not become so. At some point, however, she was examined by Mr Murray Faulkner, an Australian brain surgeon – one of the dearest and greatest of men – who immediately after the examination rang me in my office to say that he was having her moved from the Maudsley to Barts for an urgent operation. There was no doubt that she did have a brain tumour, and he could not understand how it had taken so long to diagnose. The only doubt was whether or not it was malignant. Claudie did the journey between the two hospitals by ambulance, 'on the bell', an experience which she described to me very vividly when I visited her just before she was taken down to the operating theatre. Uppermost in her mind was the relief of having escaped from the mental ward and from the attentions of specialists trying to prove that she was mad. Even the prospect of major surgery, from which she might not emerge alive, was better than another day of that hell.

Thanks to Murray Faulkner's skill she did survive. The tumour proved non-malignant. For two days Claudie was in intensive care and I was not allowed to see her. By the time I was allowed to visit she was sitting up in bed, impatiently waiting to send me off in search of a wig – an urgent new worry now taking precedence over everything else. Fortunately a dear friend, Martine Burnaby, who had excellent contacts with fashion magazines, was able to get one without delay, free. She brought it along for a fitting, along with dozens of turbans and every other kind of glamorous headgear – also all complimentary. I wish someone had taken a photograph of Claudie trying them on. For never can I recall her looking happier or more radiant.

Once back home Claudie's happiness did not last. Possibly because of the drugs she was taking, she would fly into terrible rages. Unfortunately, when I was the target – which happened more and more often – she had reason to be angry. Before her long illness I had become close again with a pre-marriage love. But whereas then Claudie had accepted this relationship, now she was increasingly resentful. Knowing what she had been through I should have mended my ways at least until she was fully recovered. But I did not. In fact my behaviour in this respect grew worse since my relationship with this old flame had deepened during Claudie's long spells in hospital; so much so, indeed, that she had left her husband to come and live nearby in London. After about three months, unable to stand the bitter criticism any more, I walked out. It was an unforgivable thing to do. Claudie was clearly still very far from well. But I somehow convinced myself that she would be better off without my provocative presence.

First I went to stay with my old love. This was thoughtlessly misleading. For not only did it give Claudie the impression that I was leaving her for my old love but my old love got that impression as well. This was only a quarter true. Primarily I had left because the atmosphere at home had become so unbearably painful. So to correct this false impression I moved into the Beefsteak Club which in those days still had very cheap bedrooms – £10 a night. Then my cousin, Elizabeth Jane Howard, came to the rescue. At that time she was married to Kingsley Amis and living in a large house in Maida Vale where I was invited to lodge. This arrangement lasted for about six months and Jane and Kingsley could not have been kinder. In those days their marriage seemed enviably happy and one of their hospitable home's many enjoyable rituals was a gregarious communal breakfast around their enormous double bed at which all present would compete to read out the silliest lefty *bêtise* in the morning newspapers – a marvellous way, incidentally, to cure a hangover and get the adrenalin stirring for a good morning's work. From time to time Claudie would ring me during these breakfast sessions and Jane, intending to be protective, would say I was not available. I hated those moments, being able to imagine all too well Claudie's hurt and humiliation. Her letters, too, broke my heart. Once we had lunch together to discuss some problem about Dominique's education and the sadness was unbearable. It was a miserable six months during which I was racked with guilt. Nor was it only guilt about the pain I was causing Claudie. For there was also the pain I knew in my bones I would in the end cause the other lady in my life from whom I had received so much, by going back home.

At one point I thought of following Henry to America and indeed was offered a column on the *Washington Post* by its proprietor, Philip Graham, whom I had met earlier at that Washington dinner. Michael Berry – always infinitely responsive to his staff's personal problems – also offered to help by sending me on a long trip round the world. In the end, after months of indecision, I did go back home, the promptings of my own conscience being much reinforced by the moral counsel of our very old friend, Kenneth Bradshaw.

Whether these personal troubles, which continued after my return home, had any effect on my work is difficult to say. Certainly it was during these years that I began committing indiscretions, of which by far the most notorious was using a four-letter word on television. Although it was not the first time this four-letter word had been used on television – Kenneth Tynan had already done so – it was the first time it had been used by someone not yet associated with being outrageous. What is more my use of it was on a programme, *Nationwide*, which went out at 6.00 p.m. while children were still watching. Asked by the chairman, Michael Barratt, how I thought people would react to the news that the minister of war, Lord Lambton, had resigned after being caught in bed with two tarts, I gave a long reply which included a lot about never underestimating the strength of the British non-conformist conscience. Then I paused and almost as an afterthought said, 'Of course I may be wrong, the public probably won't give a ... well, there's only one word for it, isn't there ... won't give a fuck.' Suggestions that I had planned to use the word are quite untrue. In fact I had planned not to use it, in spite of having been urged to do so at El Vino's by both George Gale and Philip Hope-Wallace. So why did I change my mind? Spontaneous bravado, I fear; a sudden irresistible temptation to throw caution to the winds.

Because this was not the last item, I left the studio before the end of the programme and therefore did not hear Michael Barratt make a formal apology for my bad language on behalf of the BBC. In fact I rushed off to a dinner at the Royal College of Physicians, where I was due to make a speech, happily oblivious of the storm about to break around my head. Rather the opposite. I seem to remember feeling pleased with myself, having mistaken the unusually friendly smiles of the programme's television crew as I left the studio for approval of my performance rather than commiseration for my impending plight. Even the sight of reporters and cameramen waiting in Harley Street after the dinner at first seemed more gratifying – could my speech really have been as newsworthy as all that, I thought – than worrying. Only when I caught the import of the questions did the penny begin to drop. 'Do you regret using a four-letter word on television, Mr Worsthorne?' With the benefit of hindsight I can now see that I should have apologised then and there. Instead, still gravely underestimating the seriousness of my offence, I made a joke. 'Not at all, it was exactly the *mot juste.*'

Next morning the gaffe was front page news in most newspapers – except the *Daily Telegraph*. On my desk awaiting me at the *Sunday Telegraph* was a letter from the editor, Brian Roberts, which said: 'In view of your disgraceful conduct on the television last night you are suspended from your duties until the proprietor has determined your future.' Angered by the tone of this note, I immediately went to see Roberts who was almost literally speechless with rage. 'Go back to your room,' he spluttered, 'and stay there until the proprietor calls you.' Instead I went to the *Telegraph* pub next door in search of sympathy which, to my dismay, was not forthcoming. It was only then that I began to realise that there was something really wrong. For my colleagues did not want to know me. It was not that they turned their backs, or did anything actively unfriendly. But there was an unmistakable coolness, as there was on the staircase and corridors returning to my room – the same reluctance of colleagues to catch my eye.

Just before lunch came the summons upstairs to the fifth floor to see 'Mr Michael'. This was the first time I had ever been into his office which was an imposing panelled room with windows opening on to an artificial lawn. He was sitting behind a vast desk and looking very stern. 'What an individual says on television is his own business,' he said. 'But when the individual holds a senior post on the *Telegraph* it is also my business. You have let the paper down; shocked many readers.' There was, he said, no question of my being sacked. That would be an absurd overreaction. But it would be best if I did not write my column for a week or two and did not do any more broadcasting for six months.

In effect Michael could not have been kinder and I got the distinct impression that the purpose of the punishment was more to appease Brian Roberts than to discipline me. Just as I was leaving the room, however, I remembered that I was due to appear the very next day on *Any Questions*, advance billing of which was already in the *Radio Times*. 'Do you want me to cancel that appearance?' I asked, adding that I would have to put out a statement explaining why. There was a long, frowning pause as Michael pondered this unexpected complication. Then his brow lightened. 'What time does *Any Questions* go out?' he asked. Eight thirty p.m., I replied. 'Let's amend the rule,' he said with a wintry smile. 'Don't do any broadcasting before 8.00 p.m., by which time the children ought to be safely in bed.'

Surprisingly, Lady Pamela was far more worked up about the incident than her husband. She wrote the angriest letter I have ever received, accusing me of having let Michael down. 'Everything you are in journalism you owe to him,' she wrote. 'And all you do in repayment is to bring the *Sunday Telegraph*, which is his own creation, into disrepute.' Another letter came from Desmond Wilcox, then head of BBC television features, saying that in view of my 'solecism' he did not think it would be a good idea to proceed with a major new talk series which he had been discussing. It was a charming letter, in its way, and marvellously auntyish:

When we lunched, you may remember, I advised you (humbly and for what it's worth) that a proposition, featuring Peregrine Worsthorne, in a more worthwhile role than that of occasional interviewee on magazine programmes, would need your cooperation in the matter of how often and when you appeared – and what impression you created.

Since then there has been the furore about what might best be described as your solecism. I witnessed the broadcast myself. In terms of our general and combined strategy I hardly think it will have helped.

It might be as well to let things lie low for a while.

Be it said, that I personally, had every sympathy with both what you were saying and the word that – inadvertently I suspect – you used. But, I did find the occasion quite, quite the wrong one.

This was indeed a serious setback to my television career from which it never recovered. Henceforth I appeared from time to time as an occasional participant in many different programmes. But having earned myself a reputation for unreliability, no top-class regular television work ever came my way.

But what really hurt was the collegiate cold-shouldering in the office itself. I still find this very difficult to explain. If being seen associating with me had carried some kind of danger, then a certain reluctance to do so would have been sensible enough. But of course the *Telegraph* was not remotely that kind of office – in spite of Brian Roberts' attempts, more absurd than frightening, to behave like a gauleiter. So why that sudden withdrawal of the normal comradely civilities? I am sure the answer has more to do with embarrassment than fear. Just as friends, out of embarrassment, avoid the company of the recently bereaved, so do colleagues, out of embarrassment, avoid the company of one of their number under a cloud. Or was there something more to it than that? In using a four-letter word on television I perhaps really had revealed myself as a disloyal member of the team who genuinely deserved to be pushed out beyond the pale. I wish I knew the answer. All I do know is that only one colleague, Ronnie Payne, rallied to my defence. He wrote a letter to Roberts and Berry to say that he (unlike them) had actually seen the programme and taken in context my use of the four-letter word was entirely justifiable. Unfortunately one friendly colleague's letter of defence was no match for the many hundreds of readers who wrote to the *Sunday Telegraph* cancelling their subscriptions.

Other indiscretions followed, all of them pretty trivial, but more than enough in the 1970s to earn one a reputation for 'flamboyance'. In earlier times what journalists got up to was not judged worth reporting by other journalists. Moreover there was a rule, laid down by newspaper proprietors for newspaper proprietors, that 'dog doesn't eat dog'. By the 1970s, however, *Private Eye* had successfully defied that convention and demonstrated beyond doubt that there was a market for Fleet Street gossip, as part of an enormously increased public interest in the media generally. Very largely this was due to television. A print journalist who might have been writing signed articles for decades without anybody recognising him in the street could become temporarily a minor celebrity overnight after making a single appearance on prime-time television. When this happened to me I must confess to having quite enjoyed being asked for my autograph on the Underground and hearing building-site workers call out, 'Watcha, Peregrine'. But there was a price to pay for this higher profile. Quite suddenly the names of even print journalists joined those of aristocrats and politicians in the gossip columns.

Thus it was that shortly after the four-letter word incident, Londoner's Diary in the *Evening Standard* carried a paragraph about an unidentified deputy editor of a national newspaper causing a sensation in a crowded Brighton restaurant in the middle of another Tory Party conference. According to the report, Tory grandees and their ladies looked on goggle-eyed as this unnamed deputy editor and Vanessa Lawson, the beautiful wife of Nigel Lawson, then a Tory MP, swapped shirts, stripping off to the waist to do so. Something of the sort had indeed happened. Vanessa had been going on all evening about how much better my striped shirt would suit her than me and eventually, in a fit of chivalry, I decided to put her theory to the test which it passed, it has to be admitted, with flying colours. No name having been given to the deputy editor and no mention made of the *Telegraph*, the item would have escaped Michael Berry's attention had not Patrick Hutber, a successor of Nigel Lawson as *Sunday Telegraph* City editor, chosen to raise the matter at one of those Saturday editorial lunches which still continued in spite of their begetter's disappearance from the scene. Patrick Hutber was an immensely talented financial journalist who made his name and his fortune working for John Bloom. Soon after his appointment as City editor my Canadian friend Jim Paterson, by now a director of RTZ, had expressed an interest in meeting him. Over the lunch I arranged for this purpose, Jim asked Hutber about some particular share dealings, at which Hutber went sheet-white in the face and excused himself from the table on the grounds that he was suddenly feeling sick. When he didn't return I asked Jim what had upset him. Jim replied, 'Hutber goes in for insider trading and from my question he realised that he had been rumbled.' Whether this was the case I do not know. All I do know is that after that lunch Hutber became an implacable office enemy. So I was not all that surprised when, in front of Michael Berry, he turned to me and asked, 'Oh Perry, have you any idea who the deputy editor was who changed his shirt with Vanessa Lawson?' His interest immediately aroused, Michael Berry wanted to know what Hutber was referring to. Hutber then told him the *Evening Standard* story, which Michael hadn't seen, and once again asked me if I had any idea who the culprit was. When I confessed, Michael said nothing. Knowing him, I would imagine that he was much more

226

shocked by Hutber's behaviour at this lunch than by mine at that dinner. Even so, it can hardly have failed to be one more black mark against me.

Finally there was the George Melly business. Contributing to a book, edited by George Macdonald Fraser, about schooldays, I mentioned very much *en passant* that I had been seduced at Stowe on a sofa in the art room by George Melly. Unfortunately for me the *Guardian* chose to serialise my chapter, highlighting this incident, which was then taken up quite prominently in the tabloids. Once again Brian Roberts called for my resignation, accusing me of bringing the paper into disrepute.

By his lights this was a fair complaint. Coming from a family with strong Church of England connections – his brother was Chaplain to the Queen – he not only thought my behaviour unbecoming to a *Telegraph* executive but also intrinsically disreputable. Any editor of his age – late sixties – would probably have felt something of the same. But in the case of Brian Roberts, these feelings were accentuated by the exceptionally sheltered life he had led before becoming editor. Cursed from birth by a bent back, he had always eschewed the social life of journalism, preferring to make a virtue of being the backroom type who stayed in the shadows minding the nuts and bolts – unlike the new breed of younger journalists, of which I was a particularly bad example, who thought more of their own careers than the good of the paper. In fact, Roberts was a man of great charm when he chose to show it – and also of great intelligence – and I would like to think that in different circumstances he might have had more time for me than he did. As it was, however, our relationship went from bad to worse. Increasingly convinced of my unreliability, he cut back my responsibilities even more than had his predecessor – a course of action which only served further to accentuate my frustrations and bloody-mindedness.

Providentially, at about this time, my literary agent, Brigadier David Higham, invited me to lunch at L'Etoile in Charlotte Street to discuss a book project. These lunches had been taking place annually ever since my early *Encounter* articles had persuaded Higham that I might have a book in me. On earlier occasions, nothing had come of them. Although it was very flattering to be courted by such a prestigious literary agent, who always sat at the window table, I did not really want to write a book, being far too preoccupied with my journalistic work. But with life at the *Sunday Telegraph* so unsatisfactory, the thought of a new challenge was much more attractive. What is more, on this occasion Higham for once came up with a project that really did seem up my street. Cassells, he said, was looking for a book which would explain why socialist policies would always fail – a fresh version of Professor von Hayek's famous book, *The Road to Serfdom*. The inevitable failure of socialism was not nearly so much a glimpse of the obvious in the 1970s as it is now. For although Harold Wilson's first Labour administration had just been defeated, his Conservative successor, Mr

Heath, was already in difficulties which would shortly lead to the return to power of Mr Wilson's second Labour administration. The book proposed, therefore, was by no means a matter of beating a dead horse. What is more, I felt I had something fresh to say. Whereas Professor Hayek had emphasised all those aspects of socialism which were bound to lead to excessively strong government I wanted to emphasise those elements, much more relevant to Britain, which would lead to excessively weak governments.

Cassells approved of my synopsis and a contract was signed. For the next nine months or so all my energies went on the book and there was no time for further indiscretions. Having become accustomed to the hundred-yard sprint of column writing, I found it exceedingly difficult to adapt to the mile-long slog of book writing. In fáct I never did adapt. Just as my columns were long on assertion and short on facts and examples, so, much less forgivably, was the book. Nevertheless, it got finished on time and reviewers, for the most part, were kind. Robert Skidelsky, in his *Guardian* review, summed up its argument as follows:

> A planned society requires a communal spirit much more than does a capitalist society which relies on self-interest. This communal spirit can arise either from the masses, fired with revolutionary or patriotic zeal, or from a public-spirited governing class able to command the deference of the masses, as the old aristocracy used to do.
>
> Unfortunately the Labour party can achieve neither. It cannot fire the revolutionary zeal of the workers because it is not revolutionary enough; at the same time it cannot appeal to their patriotism – beat the national drum – because patriotic themes are a monopoly of the Right.
>
> Equally, its egalitarian ethic prevents it from creating a new governing class or using the existing one. Meritocratic elites based on the intellect are no good as governors because intellectuals are basically critical and have no contact with the people. At the same time socialist taxation policies prevent the irresponsible plutocrats becoming responsible aristocrats as in the nineteenth century; prevent in other words, the Clores becoming the Alec Douglas-Homes.
>
> The result is a fatal contradiction in democratic socialism. Its collectivist economic policies require a markedly hierarchical system of status and rank, while its egalitarian social policies are aimed at producing the opposite. Paradoxically, Tory paternalism is far more applicable to the needs of the socialist economy than is Labour egalitarianism. The party of the Right alone has the instincts and the prejudices needed to manage the economic society demanded by the party of the Left.

C.P. Snow in a lead review in the *Financial Times* also took the book seriously, praising it for its 'genuine insights', albeit 'destructive insights that can't be reconciled with liberal hopes'.

The *Wall Street Journal*, under the headline 'Mr Worsthorne versus the egalitarians', described me as a 'Right wing J.K. Galbraith'.

Enoch Powell was also very flattering in the *Spectator*, particularly about my views on race, praising me for 'saying the unsayable with a precision, a prescience and a candour I have never seen elsewhere'.

The review I liked best was by Jonathan Meades who described the book as 'sceptical, sensible, unemotional, realistic and generally right'.

Although most of the other reviewers said nice things about me personally ('a splendid English eccentric' according to the *TLS*), they tended to assume that my emphasis on the importance of upper classes generally was no more than romanticism or even snobbery. David Watt in the *Observer*, for example, patronised me as 'an authentic voice from the past, the only political journalist in the country to interpret political events in the great romantic, high Tory, Burkean tradition'. In fact my thesis was much more prosaic. Socialists worried so much about the quality of life of bottom dogs, I argued, that they quite overlooked the even more important problem of the quality of life of top dogs. How under socialism, I asked, could society make sure that the man from Whitehall really did know best; that socialist planners, officials, administrators would be able to live up to their new responsibilities. By all means get rid of Eton, Winchester, Oxbridge and the old traditions of noblesse oblige, I conceded. But what kind of new upbringing more likely to produce a civilised élite would socialists put in its place? Again, if socialists got rid of the *rentier* class – out of which, incidentally, sprang so many of the most effective nineteenth-century radicals, not to mention Keynes and most of the intellectual founding fathers of the Labour Party – from where else would the necessary cultural leaven be likely to come? Manifestly a planned society required planners. But if inheritance was ruled out, and everyone at the top had to struggle to get there, might not Britain end up with an even more insensitive meritocracy than the insensitive aristocracy under which it had suffered in the bad old days? Contrary to what many of the reviewers assumed, I was not interested in preserving the old order out of nostalgic or romantic affection for the past but as a method of civilising the planned society of the future.

For the old order was, I insisted, more an ally of socialism than of capitalism. A capitalist economy did not need a ruling class since it could rely on the invisible hand of market forces to do its dirty work. But a socialist economy could rely on no impersonal forces to do its dirty work. The success or failure of the whole socialist system depended on the quality of the *people* at the top. In the past the class system had produced gentlemen for these jobs. The Labour Party, however, was too egalitarian to tolerate that. But it was also too liberal to replace gentlemen with commissars. In fact it left a vacuum of authority at the top. Hence its failure.

Unless a journalist produces a book, he can go on for ever without his work ever coming in for serious criticism. When he is young and junior, his editor may say something chastening or encouraging. But that situation had long ceased for me. I do not recall Brian Roberts ever commenting on any of my columns. Occasionally a colleague might say, over a drink, 'nice piece,' but never anything more specific or analytical. Certainly readers do let themselves go with blessings or curses, addressed either to the columnist in person or to his editor. But it is seldom that these reactions, often surprisingly intense, are more than expressions of agreement or disagreement about a particular article. Anyone producing a novel or a play or a work of history or a picture – not to mention all other performers and entertainers – can expect to be told where they go right or wrong, since the whole critical apparatus exists for this very purpose. But no such critical apparatus exists to keep the journalist up to the mark. The nearest thing to a regular forum of critical comment is Granada's *What the Papers Say*, which is not very near.

Publication of *The Socialist Myth* certainly made good this deficiency so far as I was concerned. About me as a journalist there was a lot of encouragement. 'The most imaginative and talented Conservative journalist in Britain today', wrote Brian Walden. 'A polemicist of the first rank', said William Davis. Tim Raison even called me the Conservative answer to Richard Crossman, and many others wrote in a similar vein. But about the political thinker there was much less ground for comfort. My friend Alan Watkins was devastatingly scathing, as was another friend, Wayland Young. But taking the rough with the smooth I was well pleased and never again was I to receive such sweet praise. It had been a good time for me to bring out a book since there were still reviewers around from an earlier generation, such as C.P. Snow, Jo Grimond and Enoch Powell, predisposed to be generous and encouraging to a younger writer. As for the other reviewers, they were contemporaries, most of whom were friends even more than they were rivals. Ten years later, with my next book, *Peregrinations*, I was much less lucky. For by then the reviewers were mostly from a generation younger than myself, and more eager, understandably, to draw attention to their own literary merits rather than to those of the ageing author. Neither Michael Berry nor Brian Roberts ever referred to the book. Almost certainly they never read it. Possibly, however, they would have read the reviews, most of which would have confirmed them in their judgment that I was a bit of a maverick. To some extent they even convinced me that this was the case. How do we know what we are, except by listening to the views of our peers?

In any case, I began to doubt whether I was cut out to be an editor, which was just as well. For it was at about this time that Roberts brought John Thompson on to the paper. I ought to have smelt a rat since there was no vacancy for him to fill. Even more suspicious, Roberts felt it necessary to invite me to lunch at the United University Club to inform me of this new appointment. Never before had he asked me to lunch or consulted me about anything. Roberts had a most engaging smile, and it was much in evidence on this occasion. In the middle of the meal he told me of his decision to recruit John Thompson from the *Spectator* – where he was deputy editor – and seemed quite inordinately pleased when I raised no objections. Why on earth should I have raised any objection? Then as now I admired John's journalism, particularly his marvellously civilised Nature Notes. What, of course, Roberts omitted to say was that he was being recruited as the next editor of the *Sunday Telegraph*, which in due course he became.

Thenceforward, more and more, Roberts encouraged me to undertake foreign travel which suited me privately as well as professionally. For I had fallen in love with a woman whose work often took her abroad for longish periods and it was usually quite easy for me to find a reason to be in roughly the same part of the world. For the next twenty years or more this relationship was at the very centre of my life. She was married and there was no more question of her leaving her husband than there was of my leaving Claudie. Claudie knew of the relationship which she reluctantly came to accept because it posed no threat to our marriage, and also – I like to think – because she understood how supremely much it meant to me. In a memoir such as this it might be better not to mention this relationship at all than to mention it once and then pass on. But after much thought I decided otherwise. Great as must be the dominion of discretion, it cannot absolutely deny the demands of truth. Nothing in my life has meant more to me than this relationship, into which I put so much loving care and out of which I drew so much joy and inspiration. Had my duties on the *Telegraph* been more demanding during those years it would have been much more difficult to follow my heart's desire. As it was, I could do so, not only to distant places but also on journeys into emotional realms which, without her, I would have never reached.

Rereading my cuttings for this period, I can find no evidence that the expensive air travel and four-star foreign hotels produced much copy of which I am the least proud. What it did produce were interviews with high-level statesmen – notably Presidents Johnson and Nixon – which could be advertised and promoted as *Sunday Telegraph* exclusives in spite of their containing nothing which the two presidents had not said on the record very often before. Knowing no big names himself Roberts was exaggeratedly impressed by any member of the staff who did. When the splendidly fly diplomatic correspondent, Gordon Brook-Shepherd – with whom, after Douglas Brown's retirement, I now shared a room – returned from long foreign trips without much copy to show for them, he only had to mutter something about having had two hours with Otto von Hapsburg or forty minutes with Dag Hammarskjöld to have the editor, if not a news editor, goggle-eyed with admiration. My presidential interviews, by the same token, gave even more satisfaction. But it is doubtful whether they should have because my access to these great men owed little to journalistic talent and much to my political views. I was one of the very few journalists, either inside or outside the United States, who went on supporting the American war in Vietnam long after it had ceased to be easily defensible (Joe Alsop was another).

My attitude was simple. Effective Western defence against the Soviet Union depended on a strong and confident United States and since a defeat in Vietnam would weaken America, that defeat must be avoided at any price. I didn't believe that if South Vietnam fell to communism the rest of South-East Asia would follow suit. But I did believe that a Vietnam defeat would demoralise America, as indeed it did.

It was the same with the other great foreign issue of the period, Rhodesia. Pretty well alone among the world's journalists I had easy access to Ian Smith, Prime Minister of Southern Rhodesia, again because of ideological affinity rather than journalistic talent. Here, too, my views rested on one very simple proposition: namely that white supremacy was the necessary condition of any progress in Southern Africa. Demoralise the whites or take away their power, and retrogression would follow as surely as night follows day. Lee Kuan Yew, the Singapore Prime Minister, was another excellent contact for similar reasons. Whereas most of the world's journalists criticised him for disregarding human rights, I took the view that in the conditions of South-East Asia this admirable ruler was justified in using any methods to stay in power. So not surprisingly he would give me the red carpet treatment when I visited him in Singapore and seek me out when he visited London. He would even telephone me sometimes in the office to ask advice and when one such top-priority call was put through in the middle of the editor's weekly conference, Roberts' face quite glowed with pride at having his telephone used for such a high-level communication.

Was I, then, simply a propagandist and not a true searcher after truth in any way? This is not an easy question to answer. If one assumes – as many now do – that the only truths proper for a journalist to seek out are ones that those in authority want to hide, then I was not a truth-seeking journalist. But should journalists aim only at doing that? Are the truths that those in authority want to hide the only ones that need to be searched after and exposed? Possibly that was so under the old order. But increasingly in recent years there has been another lot of hidden truths which need to be searched after and exposed: the truths that opponents of authority choose to ignore or brush under the carpet. The Vietnam War was very much a case in point. By the late 1960s scarcely anybody any longer understood the American government's reasons for continuing the war, so successful had the critics been in covering up the consequences of defeat and, indeed, in lying about the motives for intervening in the first place. Certainly the American government was misleading the public about the war. But so, much more successfully, were the critics of the government.

The same could be said about South Africa. By the 1970s nobody was unaware of the evils of white minority rule, the truths about which had been exposed ad nauseam. But about the evil consequences of establishing black majority rule most people remained in happy ignorance – another example of how nowadays the critics of government are often much more successful at brainwashing the public than are governments themselves. The reason for this is very simple. Whereas newspapers and television see it as their duty to expose governmental propaganda, and to remain resolutely sceptical about any official statements, they feel no comparable obligation to treat the protest industries' propaganda in the same way.

Rather the opposite. The great bulk of journalists, even more in broadcasting than in print, tend to identify with the adversarial culture, to the point where they are quite incapable of exposing its propaganda because they believe in it themselves. This is why most of the media fell for the global warming scare and the rest of the environmental lobby exaggeration. On these kinds of fronts the media cannot be relied upon to ask the awkward questions because so many of those who work in it are even more gullible and credulous than the public itself.

This would not matter if the adversarial culture was a negligible part of the whole culture or if the media were poor and powerless. But it does matter given the fact that the adversarial culture is now so massive and the media so powerful. It matters because for the first time in history the cultural and intellectual critics challenging orthodoxies, subverting authority and generally weakening the instincts and prejudices that support governments, have recently grown quite as strong as those doing the opposite and today, unlike in the past, it is the critics and subversives who have the media cheering them on.

According to traditional principles a journalist should eschew the propaganda of both radical and conservative camps and expose the duplicities of the one as much as those of the other. Some giants, such as Walter Lippmann, have even succeeded in living up to this ideal. But at the risk of special pleading I would like to suggest that during my lifetime these traditional precepts ceased to apply. For with such an overwhelming preponderance of fellow professionals making propaganda for one side it almost became a duty for a few of us to become equally uncritical apologists for the other.

Not that uncritical supportiveness of conservative causes generally has ever precluded me from a certain amount of journalistic mischief-making. For example, at the end of a long and highly sympathetic interview with

President Nixon I did not hesitate to tell a story which his ambassador in London, Walter Annenberg, regarded as an inexcusable breach of trust. It happened like this. Quite early in President Nixon's first term he wrote to congratulate me on a series of articles I had written about Vietnam. Some presidents would have found my thesis less than wholly welcoming. For I had written that with the inauguration of Mr Nixon, Ho Chi Minh had at long last come up against a man in the White House as ruthless, and as uninhibited by liberal sentiment, as he was himself. 'If Ho Chi Minh is relying on campus unrest driving this president out of office, as it drove his predecessor, Lyndon Johnson,' I wrote, 'he had better think again.' Nixon's letter ended by inviting me to keep in touch. This I did, and during the following eighteen months we kept up quite a correspondence. Eventually, in a postscript, I suggested that it might be a good idea if I visited the White House to give him my views in person. To my surprise and gratification, he replied to say that this was a good idea and in no time at all I got a letter from Patrick Buchanan, then a junior press aide, fixing up the details.

The plan was that I should spend a week being briefed by the White House staff before meeting the President on Friday morning. This was an extraordinary mark of presidential favour since at that time Nixon was even reluctant to hold regular press conferences, let alone to meet individual journalists. Taking advantage of Garrick Club exchange facilities, I arranged to stay at Washington's Metropolitan Club – within a stone's throw of the White House – and was further gratified, on arrival there, to find a note from the President's national security adviser, Henry Kissinger, proposing himself for breakfast the following morning. Henry I knew from old, having first met him at a party in London given by Wayland Kennett to publicise his new book on nuclear strategy which I had reviewed enthusiastically. We must have got on well since I remember asking him to lunch at Boodle's where he was embarrassed by having to eat a grilled sole with two Georgian silver forks, thanks to the club's obstinate refusal to adopt Queen Victoria's new-fangled invention of fish knives. In his letter of thanks Kissinger joked that any social loss of face Boodle's caused an unsophisticated American Jewish boy was more than made up by the opportunity given an aspiring American historian to learn more about England's strange social customs. If Henry had wanted to get my visit off to a flying start, he could not have devised a better way than to arrange to be seen breakfasting with me at the Metropolitan Club. The effect was instantaneous. By the time I got back to my room the telephone was buzzing with calls from Henry Brandon, Joe Alsop, Rowland Evans and others eager to arrange drinks. Even Kay Graham asked me to dinner, seating me next to Alice Longworth, than which in those days there could be no greater mark of social favour. One might have guessed, I suppose, that an interview with the media-hating Richard Nixon would make one the celebrity of the week.

But nowhere else does this kind of thing happen as uninhibitedly as it does in Washington. The great and the good, like George Will, who normally would not even return a telephone call, suddenly become one's closest friends and equally suddenly cease to be so when next you are in town.

For three days, I had the run of the White House with unrestricted access to all the presidential aides, some of whom, like Haldeman and Ehrlichman, were later to become so notorious. Much to my regret, however, I can't remember much about any of them. Unlike Henry Kissinger himself, whose conversation is a columnist's dream, Haldeman and Ehrlichman were wholly uncommunicative and scarcely even friendly. When I complained about this, Kissinger defended them warmly, saying that they were 'doers not thinkers, fixers not conceptualisers'. With the benefit of hindsight, he was obviously trying to warn me not to underestimate their importance – a warning, I regret to say, that I foolishly ignored. Apart from Henry himself, Patrick Buchanan was by far the best value. But because of his comparative youth I did not do him justice either.

Finally came the interview itself in the Oval Office which lasted from 11.00 a.m. to 1.00 p.m. Nobody else was present, not even the customary stenographer. At the time I took this to be another mark of trust, which it wasn't, since that very week the President's taping system had been installed. Certainly this tape contained no expletives, or much else besides. It was an unrevealing interview, even by my low standards, only redeemed at the end by a revealing 'happening' which brings me to the point of this story.

At about 12.45 p.m., fifteen minutes before the interview was due to end, an aide rushed in with a message, only to be dismissed by the President with an impatient wave of the hand. A few minutes later another even more frantic aide received the same treatment. Then Kissinger himself came bustling in looking distraught. 'The astronauts have just splashed down, Mr President, and the networks are waiting for you to greet them back to earth.' Still the President refused to be rushed. 'Is it in the schedule?' he asked and on being told that the return to earth was an hour ahead of schedule, adamantly insisted on completing the interview. That was obviously fine by me and in my account of the interview the following Sunday I made great play of the President having got his priorities right. The trouble was, however, that my account of why the President had failed to appear on television to greet the returning astronauts flatly contradicted the official White House version which stated that: 'The President and Mrs Nixon watched the splashdown in their private apartment.' Pressure was put on me to adjust my account to fit in with the official version, and Ambassador Annenberg regarded my refusal to comply as a vile breach of trust. I argued that whereas I would never have blown the gaffe on the Nixon White House for telling black lies in pursuit of victory in Vietnam, I saw no need to be a passive accomplice in their telling of silly white lies for no good purpose. To be indiscreet about Vietnam – that, I argued, would indeed be a breach of trust since my access to the President was conditional on my being a supporter, not a critic. But by the same token, the White House was breaking its side of the contract by expecting me to cover up about anything else.

Very similar complaints of betrayal followed an article I wrote from Southern Rhodesia shortly after Ian Smith's declaration of independence (UDI). Basically all my sympathies lay with Ian Smith and the white minority, as I made clear in a column on the Sunday following the coup.

> Just as in the light of history Lord North has been judged wrong for refusing to give independence to the white slave owners in America, so will Mr Harold Wilson be for refusing to give it to the white supremacists of Southern Africa. If black majority rule had proved a success in the other parts of newly independent Africa, then there might be a case for insisting on it as a precondition for South Rhodesia's independence. But since it has been a tragic failure wherever tried in Africa, why cavil at white minority rule which is no less democratic and much more efficient?

Since this article had been prominently reproduced in the *Rhodesian Herald* my welcome in Salisbury was even warmer than usual. Indeed my old Cambridge friend, P.K. van der Byl, one of Ian Smith's classier and more intelligent ministerial colleagues, even had me to stay. That was where the trouble began. For I was accused of revealing home truths. First I told the story of the missing dinner jacket. Having assumed that in a colony in rebellion against the crown, dressing for dinner would not be obligatory I had arrived without one. Far from taking this solecism in his stride, it seemed to cast a far more serious cloud over P.K.'s horizons than any of the angry threats emanating from Number 10 Downing Street. Recounting this story in my despatch was accepted as just within the bounds. My reference to finding an open copy of *Mein Kampf* in German on his drawing room table, however, was not. How could a guest and friend let him down in this way? he protested. Again I took refuge in the same somewhat sophistical defence. Yes, my presence in a Rhodesian minister's house was indeed due largely to my well-known sympathy for Rhodesia's white supremacists but that broad political sympathy did not necessarily involve remaining mum about their deplorable literary tastes.

To tell or not to tell, it is never an easy question. It was not only President Nixon who sought me out because of my support for his policies in Vietnam. So also, at an earlier date, had President Johnson – twice. The first occasion was in Manila where he was attending a council of war with South Vietnam's President Thieu. The interview took place in the penthouse suite of L.B.J.'s hotel. Although it lasted from about 6.00 to 8.00 p.m. nothing of note was said and I was in despair about having come so far for so little. As I got up to go, however, L.B.J. led me across the room to the balcony which had a magnificent view of the neon-lit city sprawling out below. He stood there for some moments looking down and I thought that perhaps at last he was about to say something quotable about the future of Asia. Instead he said; 'Christ, Mr Worsthorne, I sure wish I could join you down there for a night on the tiles.' Before I had time to think of what to say in reply there were loud rustlings and bangings from the suite's bedroom where the President's wife, Ladybird, was changing for that night's banquet. A broad smile then passed over the President's face and he put an avuncular arm round my shoulder. 'Tell you something, Mr Worsthorne,' he said, 'I don't truly envy you your night on the tiles one little bit. For I've the nicest little lay in town right next door.' At this point Ladybird herself came into the room which was just as well because never before or since have I been so lost for words.

To tell or not to tell. Certainly the temptation to tell was very great. For not only was the story highly revealing of L.B.J. the man but exactly the kind of leaven to help lighten the stodge of the interview itself. Nor indeed was it a damaging story, more touching than anything else. For once, however, I didn't tell, and even now that L.B.J. is dead I still feel slight qualms about recounting such an intimate exchange in the public prints.

Not so about another 'happening' in the second President Johnson interview which took place in the Oval Room of the White House shortly before he announced he was not going to run for a second term. By this time his conduct over the Vietnam War had incurred such unpopularity that he scarcely ever left the White House except by helicopter. No sooner had the interview begun than the President got a buzz on his mobile telephone. Important unexpected guests had arrived, he explained, whom he would have to see at once. Naturally I jumped to my feet and offered to withdraw. Not at all, the President insisted. It would be good for me to see in person the kind of pressure he was under. Naturally I was agog with expectation. What fascinating presidential encounter was I about to witness? Suddenly the double doors were flung open and in raced two grandchildren of about ten and eight. Nor did the charade end there. After much romping around the children eventually climbed into the vast chair behind the presidential desk over which the great Seal of Office hung. Then the inevitable happened. They started to play with one of the telephones on his desk. 'For Christ's sake, don't touch that one,' bellowed the President. 'It's the hot-line.' All this I did report. Possibly I was meant to. At least it gave the lie to the rumours that the President was sunk in gloom, even if it risked the rather more damaging impression that he was off his rocker. On my way out a photographer in the antechamber presented me with a complimentary picture which Brian Roberts blew up to illuminate my feature. It showed the President on one side of a sofa listening intently to me holding forth on the other. Apparently it is always possible to get one such shot, even if it is only – as in this case – of the visitor saying, 'Yes, Mr President'.

It is not only American presidents who play such tricks; so do British prime ministers. Harold Macmillan's was to pretend that he was keeping the American Ambassador waiting while he preferred to carry on talking to the British journalist – a truly flattering order of priorities. This first happened to Henry Fairlie who was very chuffed. He told me how Macmillan had repeatedly ignored the Downing Street butler's announcement that His Excellency was waiting downstairs. Henry being Henry, it seemed quite possible. This was how prime ministers did treat Henry. Only when exactly the same prime ministerial performance was put on for my benefit did scepticism begin to rear its ugly head.

Prime Minister Heath didn't play tricks. But his very awfulness sometimes helped one to make bricks without straw. One particularly striking interview I had with him would have been a complete journalistic washout had not he been so characteristically crass. It happened like this. He was seated in the middle of one side of the cabinet table and I on the other. At some point the butler brought in a giant silver teatray which was placed in front of the Prime Minister. It sat there for some time before Mr Heath deigned to take any notice. Then he snorted, 'You chaps prefer whisky, don't you?' the clear implication being that all journalists are alcoholics. On my saying that I was dying for a cup of tea with milk and no sugar he reluctantly poured the same. But that seemed to exhaust his hospitable energies. For the cup that should have cheered remained on the silver platter on his side of the table, well out of my reach and although he appreciatively sipped his own the interview ended without him ever bothering to pass me mine.

To tell or not to tell. No hesitation at all with this one. It was played for all it was worth. If I had been more professional about asking the right questions I would not have had to rely so much on these little incidents to justify the great expanse of feature space allotted to these interviews which were always promoted as either 'unique' or 'exclusive'. But never really being able to master those techniques, they were more often than not my only way of making journalistic bricks without straw.

Thus the 1970s and early 1980s passed. Mine was an enviable working life. When in England I wrote my column. But for much of the time I was travelling, to China, Australia, Chile, Argentina, India, South Africa (many times) and, most often of all, the United States. During these often quite long journeys I would keep a diary which on my return would be serialised in five-thousand-word chunks over four or sometimes even five weeks. In 1980 George Weidenfeld published a collection of these pieces entitled

Peregrinations, which prompted one reviewer, Anthony Howard, to write that at long last my unusual christian name had come in useful. Another managed to get in a dig by way of a compliment. 'Although Mr Worsthorne fancies himself as a political philosopher, he has at last come into his own as a first class travel writer.' My private life had also settled down. Claudie was working for Michael Wharton, author of the *Daily Telegraph*'s Peter Simple column, and found that coping with such a tormentedly difficult genius made living with me relatively painless. They sat face to face across the same narrow desk in a little office, locked in a love-hate relationship which lasted twenty years. According to Claudie, Michael – not the most generous of men – would provoke a terrible row every Christmas so as to escape having to give her a present or even a drink. About pretty well everyone else such a story would be implausible. But unlike some of Claudie's marvellous inventions, this one rang true. What Michael dreaded was that Claudie might get a little credit for the column, about which he was desperately possessive and protective – much more so than about any human being. One couldn't blame him since such was Claudie's black humour and original way with words that she very likely did make a far greater contribution than he ever had the grace to admit.

During these years we would spend most weekends at the little Essex port of Wivenhoe in a house on the quay bought so as to be near Pat and George Gale whose stormy marriage also made Claudie's and mine seem relatively plain sailing. Part baronial hall and part gin palace, Ballast Quay, their house on the hill, came to dominate this uniquely classless village which must be the only one in England where George and Pat could plausibly pass for Squire and Lady Bountiful. Because of Wivenhoe's famously good light, artists abounded, notably our fascinating and endlessly helpful next-door neighbours Dennis Wirth-Miller and Dicky Chopping who drove off gaily to consult the Colchester marriage guidance counsellors whenever their highly charged emotional relationship became strained beyond breaking point by the over-frequent visits of Francis Bacon who eventually bought a house of his own in the village. They made a remarkable trio whose goings-on with the local youths might have scandalised other villages. But not Wivenhoe, where they were accepted as part of the natural order, like the occasional floodings. Another famous resident was Joan Hickson whose years of practice pottering around Wivenhoe, nosing out its secrets, may well have helped her to portray Miss Marple so convincingly on the television screen. A mile down the river towards Colchester was the new University of Essex, in Wivenhoe Park, which also supplied a few rum characters, to the list of which must be added the former head of the Boilermakers' Union who conferred at least one idiosyncratic touch of class by eventually becoming Lord Hill of Wivenhoe.

For Claudie and me, however, Wivenhoe mainly meant the Gales.

Scarcely a weekend passed without there being a wild party at Ballast Quay. Not only was it the social centre of the village but also – it often seemed – of Fleet Street as well. Claudie described it, not altogether benevolently, as 'El Vino's-By-The-Sea'. Politicians would also visit and even the least social of them, like Ted Heath and Tony Crosland, would become quite human under Pat's bewitching influence. Cambridge dons, however, dominated the guest (or cast) list, being drawn to Pat like bees to honey. In the early years there were Michael Oakeshott and Brian Wormald, from Peterhouse, and then later Maurice Cowling, John Casey, Roger Scruton and a host of lesser fry. Writers, too, were in plentiful supply, although in the case for Kingsley Amis, George – the ideal drinking companion – was very much more the attraction than Pat. One became accustomed, when visiting Ballast Quay, to strange and wonderful sights – Antonia Fraser washing up and Paul Johnson in bathing trunks (to name only the two requiring least bowdlerisation) but the one I remember most fondly was the first arrival of Vanessa Lawson, looking like Nefertiti, followed by her children Nigella and Dominic dressed in beautifully ironed and snow-white sailor suits – perhaps because it was such a welcome insertion of exotic clarity into Ballast Quay's normal Bohemian blur.

Exactly what brought all these often ill-assorted guests to George and Pat's open door? Certainly not the meals which were as irregular as the sleeping arrangements. Of drink there was always plenty – George saw to that – but so visibly dusty were the glasses, particularly at night when the chandelier shone, that only hardened alcoholics were much tempted. No, we did not come for the creature comforts. Nor can it be said that we came for the talk, since nothing was more likely to drive George down to the pub or Pat to practise her singing than a guest who felt obliged – or tempted – to make conversation. Pat's admirable gift for befriending attractive unattached girls – as well as brilliant young men – certainly helped to make Ballast Quay a popular port of call with womanisers in search of erotic adventure, as did George's by now legendary reputation as a latter-day Dr Johnson do the same for intellectual masochists in search of verbal chastisement. But the biggest social magnet of all – than which there is no bigger – was the expectation, seldom disappointed, of some extraordinary 'happening'. Nobody was ever bored at Ballast Quay. Whatever else ran out, drama never did. That was Pat's doing. She was the most extraordinarily theatrical hostess imaginable, creating scenes of every kind – comic scenes, romantic scenes, violent scenes, absurd scenes, and even, towards the end, tragic scenes. I say scenes because that is what we took them to be – signs of fury signifying nothing. One went to Ballast Quay as one goes to the theatre, voluntarily suspending disbelief. It was all just excellent entertainment; nothing to do with real life; indeed a blessed escape from real life.

Instead of having to travel to distant parts for our minds to be broadened, or our lives rescued from the rut, all we had to do was walk up the hill to Ballast Quay.

Then one Christmas Day it all ceased to be Grand Guignol with rubber swords and red ink, in which the cast never got hurt. Some thirty of us sat down for lunch, with George standing four-square at the head of the refectory table patriarchally carving two giant turkeys, one of his best and favourite roles. He was scowling and speaking gruffly, but there was nothing unusual about that; nor anything unusual about Pat showering him with recriminations and abuse, even at the height of the season of goodwill. That too was part of the act. As for the presence of Maurice Cowling, that also had long ago become part of the *mise en scène*. Drunks falling off chairs and other guests insulting each other, there was a lot of that but, again, Ballast Quay would not have been Ballast Quay without those kind of traditional rituals. Only with the Christmas pudding did we notice something untoward. George had gone absent. Again, this in itself was not unusual since he very often 'buggered off' to the pub in the middle of lunch or dinner, leaving desolation on either side. But never before on Christmas Day, if only because the pubs were shut. Hours later when Claudie and I were back home a distraught Pat called. George had 'buggered off', this time for good, to an Irish lady love whom he eventually married, only to die all too soon thereafter. It was a terrible shock. Always before when the curtain came down after a night of mayhem, it had risen again next day as if nothing had happened. This time, however, it had come down for good.

Claudie and I continued to weekend at Wivenhoe where we had good friends apart from the Gales – notably Ted and Hally Palmer. Ted was the local doctor and a great ornithologist who would teach me about birds, and much else, on our regular Sunday walks down the estuary. But with the Gales gone it was never glad confident morning again. For Pat and George, as a couple, were very much founding members of our group, if not – after Henry's death – the catalyst. The crack-up of any marriage of old friends is an ominous sound. But for Claudie and me this particular one reverberated most dreadfully. A spell was broken. In the life of most of us there is someone who keeps reality at bay; in whose company there is so much vitality and animation, so much hope and promise, that shadows can never fall. The Gales as a couple played that invaluable role for us, and it was soon much needed.

For unfortunately, at roughly the same time, our London life had also suffered a great shock. Selwyn College, Cambridge, for a long time the landlord of 14 Airlie Gardens, sold the building, without warning, to a property developer who then refused to renew our lease. Claudie urged me to assert my rights as a sitting tenant which, it turned out, I could have easily done had I not listened instead to the elderly family solicitor who, ignorant of some recent change in the law, advised that there was no alternative but to get out. It was a terrible mistake. With no lease to sell, and house prices rocketing up, we had the greatest difficulty in raising enough capital to buy anything else and eventually had to settle for a small house near Fulham Broadway which was not only miles away from Claudie's beloved Kensington, but also far less commodious than 41 Scarsdale Villas where we had begun our married life some thirty years before. Although a good friend, Beverley Cohen, helped Claudie with the move, its strains and sorrows affected her health which never properly recovered. For the first time her spirit began to falter. I did not realise that the next few years were to be her last, made unnecessarily painful by my irresponsible improvidence.

15

On Being Editor

My first meeting with Andrew Knight was in Dublin at the end of President Kennedy's chaotic visit to Ireland in search of his hibernian roots. It was a Saturday morning in a hotel foyer and just as I was coming to terms with the bad news that all planes to London were fully booked until Monday, this highly personable young man, many years my junior, introduced himself as Andrew Knight of the *Investors Chronicle*. He didn't actually say 'at your service, sir' but that was very much what his manner implied. His actual words were, 'Isn't it awful about the plane situation. I have a hired car and if you have nothing better to do, why don't we drive into the country and do some sightseeing?' The offer was made in such a friendly and helpful way that it never occurred to me to refuse. In any case, I certainly didn't have any better plans and was only too happy to be rescued from a weekend killing time on my own.

Andrew was an excellent companion, flatteringly attentive but not awkwardly so. We must have got on well since over a pub lunch I suggested that we propose ourselves for the night to the Claud Cockburns in Youghal – a suggestion indicating considerable trust on my part in his savoir-faire, tolerance, good nature, discretion, sense of humour and above all alcoholic resilience. My trust was completely justified. Far from Andrew's head-boy presence inhibiting the old monster it encouraged him to be even more scurrilous than usual and on the rare occasions when our host seemed to be running out of steam, Andrew would come up with just the right question to get his memory – or imagination – firing again. I was very impressed. If being friendly to, and appreciative of, such an obviously sad and drunken burnt-out fraud as Claud Cockburn is a test of something or other, Andrew certainly passed it with flying colours. Then returning to Dublin on Sunday night we went our separate ways, and I did not see Andrew again until, about twenty-five years later, he slid into my room at the *Sunday Telegraph* trying very hard not to look and sound like my new boss which in fact he was.

The news of the *Daily* and *Sunday Telegraph*'s acquisition by Conrad Black, a relatively unknown Canadian financier, had just been announced and Andrew Knight, Black's new chief executive, was making himself known to the staff. It was an awkward meeting for me, since, on hearing of the takeover, I had immediately expressed doubts about a Canadian financier owning the two *Telegraphs* and also scepticism about Andrew Knight, until recently editor of *The Economist*, not wanting to interfere with editorial policy. Why I had written so imprudently is difficult to say. Partly, I fear, to attract attention to my *Spectator* diary – another example of ill-judged exhibitionism. But partly too – and this is the explanation I prefer – out of quixotic loyalty to Lord Hartwell who had been so cruelly deprived by Black of his birthright. Hartwell's humiliation had happened so quickly and so unexpectedly. The house the Berrys built had seemed so utterly secure. Rumours of financial trouble had certainly been heard but I, for one, never believed them. Only a week before the takeover was announced Michael had come to our Saturday lunch, and although he and the City editor, Ian Watson, discussed other City dramas, with Michael showing his customary appetite for every crumb of scandal and gossip, not a word was said about the *Telegraph*'s impending disaster. About the takeover itself, not only were his senior editorial colleagues – some of whom had worked for him for over forty years – not consulted but they were not even informed, being left to hear of it, like everybody else, on the news. In a way, therefore, there were plenty of grounds for welcoming a new and less secretive owner. But instead of feeling exasperated and even indignant about what Michael had done to his – dammit, *our* – company, we felt irrationally defensive and resentful of Black for taking advantage of our old proprietor. Or at any rate, I did. Hence my impulsive – and potentially self-destructive – article in the *Spectator*.

Andrew Knight, it has to be said, handled what might have been an embarrassing reunion very disarmingly. His first words, after shaking hands, were that he hoped he would have had the guts to write something similar if an unknown financier had taken over *The Economist*. 'You're quite wrong about Conrad,' he went on, 'but it will be up to us to prove it.' It was a brief visit; he was doing the rounds.

The next I heard from him was an invitation to lunch on New Year's Day. Brooks' Club being closed, he proposed the Ritz. Again he scored with me. I love the Ritz and have been going there for many years and he could not have chosen a more comforting venue for what might still, I feared, be an awkward and even possibly painful meeting. As soon as we sat down he ordered a bottle of champagne which also promised well as did the pointed way in which he wished me a *happy* new year. It was a long lunch. When the first bottle of champagne was finished he ordered another. Only over the coffee – long after his notebook had been put away – did he touch lightly on the subject of possible new editors, very much implying, I thought, that he felt free to do this only because my hat was no longer in the ring. Whom I suggested I cannot remember. But I do remember feeling a bit irked that my non-eligibility was so much taken for granted. Clearly I couldn't admit this in so many words. But I did hint at it indirectly by passionately arguing the case for the *Sunday Telegraph* to be given a writing editor. 'Whereas daily papers are news driven,' I argued, 'Sundays are opinion driven.' Then I added, as a punchline, 'Of course it's too late now but I still think I could make that paper sing.' As I say, Andrew had put his notebook away by then and the lunch had long since ceased to be anything resembling a working session. In fact, both of us must have been slightly drunk. Clearly after this lunch there was no more cause for me to fear the sack and even some cause to expect to enjoy working for my new boss. But nothing more. So when next Friday evening – soon after I had finished my column – I got a call to go up to see Andrew, his offer of the *Sunday Telegraph* editorship came as a complete and thrilling surprise.

Overwhelming excitement, however, immediately gave way to intense anxiety. For the offer, Andrew explained, was conditional on my making a good impression on Conrad Black who wanted me to fly out immediately to see him at his home in Toronto. Much more worrying still, Andrew went on, was the need to get Lord Hartwell's approval. For it had been agreed that the old proprietor should stay on for the transitional period as editor-in-chief and although, in the last resort, he no longer had the power to block my appointment, his opposition would be very awkward. The plan was to take him by surprise. If there were any speculation about the appointment in advance, he would have time to dig his toes in. So secrecy was absolutely essential until the crucial board meeting in a fortnight's time. Because of this paramount need for secrecy Andrew thought it would be a wise precaution for his former *Economist* secretary to arrange the ticket for my flight to Toronto and back, preferably on a Sunday or Monday – my day off – so that my absence did not arouse suspicions among colleagues. Andrew also confided that Max Hastings was to be appointed editor of the *Daily*. They were expecting some opposition to him on the grounds that he was unknown to Lord Hartwell; but nothing like the storm that my name would provoke. All in all it was going to be a tricky fortnight, said Andrew, and I had best keep my fingers crossed, as well as my mouth shut.

Tricky it was. Max went out to be vetted in Toronto first and briefed me on his return over dinner at Brooks', where we were spotted by Ludovic Kennedy who, fortunately for us, is not one of those journalists who betray club secrets to the gossip columns. According to Max the ordeal had been fairly painless except for the proprietor's almost obsessional preoccupation with abstruse points of nineteenth-century British political history. 'By the way,' warned Max, with one of his sheepish schoolboy grins, 'you'd better mug up a bit before it's your turn because I got out of answering difficult questions by saying that I didn't want to steal your thunder.'

In the event Conrad had other preoccupations on the day I flew out since that very morning his wife, Shirley, had given birth to their second child. Perhaps because of all the excitement surrounding this happy event nobody had remembered to unpadlock any of the gates into the grounds, and after the airport taxi-driver had despaired of gaining access I had no choice but to climb over the fence and make my own way up to the mansion on foot. This was no easy stroll and I spent at least fifteen minutes stumbling through snowdrifts before eventually reaching the front door, my shoes ruined and soaked to the skin. Nor was there any time to improve my pathetic appearance because Conrad answered the door himself, distractedly showing me into a splendid library before rushing back upstairs to help with the new baby. By then I had developed a most fearsome headache, almost certainly through nerves, and it was so bad that when Conrad returned in half an hour's time I felt compelled, most reluctantly, to ask for a painkiller. More confusion ensued because the Conrad Black medicine cupboard did not run to such things and one of the estate's security guards had to be despatched downtown, blue lights flashing, to buy a bottle. No, it was not a good beginning. Not only had the aspirant new editor arrived looking like a drowned rat but also shown signs of collapsing with influenza.

Once we did get down to talks, however, all went swimmingly. My friendship with Bill Buckley and good relations with Richard Nixon stood me in good stead, as did my right-wing views with many of which Conrad Black agreed. He wanted to know how I would change the paper and I said that it didn't need fundamental change; only a general brightening up, 'replacing forty-watt bulbs with sixty-watt ones, that kind of thing'. Only towards the very end of the interview did we get around to nineteenth-century British political history, about which he was far too knowledgeable to give me any opportunity to expose my ignorance. I liked the man and it has to be assumed that he reciprocated, since on my return to London the following day Andrew Knight said that the only remaining obstacle to my appointment was Lord Hartwell.

This less than wholly reassuring good news was imparted over lunch in the Fortnum and Mason restaurant – the one place in London, according to Andrew, where we could be absolutely certain not to be seen by any prying eye that mattered. The London Library in St James's Square, however, where I went afterwards, proved much more dangerous territory and I very nearly gave the show away to A.N. Wilson, the novelist, who happened to pass the pay-phone box in the hall just at the very moment when I was unsuccessfully trying to force it to take Canadian coins. 'Can I borrow a 10p?' I asked. 'These Canadian coins won't fit.' Those must still have been the distant days before A.N. Wilson became Fleet Street-wise since I don't think he twigged. But it was a close shave.

In the office and Fleet Street generally everybody was speculating on Andrew Knight's plans and any uncharacteristic reluctance on my part to join in would have immediately aroused suspicion. Apart from Claudie (and one other) I told nobody. But the necessary deception of close colleagues went much against the grain. On the Friday of the crucial board meeting – scheduled to start at 2.00 p.m. – I wrote my column as usual, finishing it at 6.00 p.m. As was the custom I took it in to John Thompson, the editor, who offered no comment, which was also the custom. By 6.30 p.m. I was back in my room, distinctly worried. No news must be bad news since clearly the tactics of stampeding Hartwell into a quick agreement must have failed. Then, just as despair was settling in, Andrew Knight called me up to the fifth floor. All was well, he said. It had not been easy but the appointments had finally gone through. That was all he said at that time, mercifully concentrating on the happy ending rather than overshadowing my moment of triumph with details of just how fierce and almost hysterical Lord Hartwell's resistance had been, beyond anything I had feared even in my most pessimistic moods.*

By the time I came downstairs from the fifth floor, the news was all over the office. Naturally I had made hypothetical plans, one of which was to hang on to my incomparable and invaluable secretary Sue Small, and another to appoint Alexander Chancellor, then a columnist on the paper, as my deputy. Aping Harold Macmillan who, on becoming Prime Minister, rushed his Chief Whip off to Bucks for a dinner of port and partridge, I rushed Alexander off to the Garrick for a celebratory glass of champagne. Then I rushed home to take Claudie out for a celebratory dinner. Never before in my life have I felt so elated.

I didn't sleep much that night. Thinking about what I was going to do as editor was too exciting. For now, unlike during the previous twenty-five years as deputy editor, I could make plans which did not have to depend on the agreement of colleagues. This, I found, made a tremendous difference. In recent years I had got into the bad habit of strangling difficult or controversial ideas at birth. For long experience had taught me that trying to argue for them at conference was usually more trouble than it was worth. This was not in the least because editors and colleagues were obstructive or unimaginative. It was because most journalistic hunches are difficult to communicate. The author may be convinced that they would work. But the thought of having to convince a lot of sceptical colleagues is

---

*For an account of the board meeting see Appendix, page 275.

more than enough to deter him from pressing ahead with them. Now, for the first time in my professional life, there was no such deterrent. Intriguing ideas could be made welcome, rather than turned away. At first, out of habit, I started dozing off exhausted by thinking about all the objections old so-and-so would make to a new idea that crossed my mind. But then would come the galvanising realisation that I didn't need to defer to old so-and-so ever again. I was editor and could do what I wanted. A sense of power is an enormous stimulus to thought. Quite suddenly all the cul-de-sacs were transformed into freeways. Later, of course, the many frustrations and limitations peculiar to being an editor made themselves felt. But during that first night, with these still in the future, and the limitations of being a deputy in the past, my mind suddenly became indefatigable, rather as years earlier, when leading route marches as a newly commissioned young army officer, my body had done the same.

I suppose the most important decision reached that night was to write a signed leading article every week; something which no editor had done since the end of the war. Ever since the paper had begun in 1961 I had written a weekly signed article on the leader page and usually the anonymous leader as well. Sometimes under the hat of anonymity I would disagree with what I had written under the columnist's hat. Now that I was editor, however, this arrangement no longer made sense since henceforth my ideas and those of the paper were going to be one and the same thing. One choice would have been simply to drop my name from the signed article and print it instead as an unsigned leader. But there seemed little point in doing that. By now my style and views were familiar to *Sunday Telegraph* readers and even without my name on the leader it would be easily recognisable as my own work. Alternatively I could have stopped writing regularly and concentrated on editing instead. This idea I dismissed out of hand. First, I wanted to demonstrate to Lord Hartwell that it was possible to do both. Second, however – and vaingloriously – no more than Winston Churchill had become Prime Minister to preside over the disintegration of the British empire, had I become editor of the *Sunday Telegraph* to preside over a leader page without my name on it. In fact, far from seeing the editorship as a reason for adopting a lower polemical profile I saw it as a reason for adopting an even higher one – and not only on the leader page. From time to time I would insert leaderettes, with my initials at the bottom, on the front page if some event requiring editorial comment broke on Saturday after it was too late to make changes on the leader page. Two things I was clear about from the start. News alone can't give the necessary lift to a Sunday paper since most weeks there isn't enough of it – even for the front page. The yeast of opinion is indispensable everywhere, except possibly on the sports pages. Equally indispensable was strong, vigorous and forceful writing which, in my experience, few unopinionated journalists are able to command. Unlike Lord Hartwell, who recoiled from viewy journalists, and liked to surround himself with safe pairs of hands, I could not wait to recruit more risk-takers. My calculation was simple. Since the *Sunday Telegraph* was never going to be able to compete with the greater journalistic muscle of the *Sunday Times*, our best hope was to outwit them, not only with superior brains, but with higher spirits, as well.

Absurd as it may seem, I remember rehearsing the famous Danton phrase, '*de l'audace, et encore de l'audace et toujours de l'audace*', not so much meaning by this more audacious investigative journalism aimed at all the traditional targets – wrongdoing in Westminster, Whitehall, and the City – as at all those malefactors in high places who spread false values, many of them, of course, in the media itself. Times had changed. Perverse cultural influences were now even more dangerous, in my view, than political misconduct, and people needed protection nowadays more from the teachings of idiotic academics and journalists than from the evil machinations of ministers or financiers. Therefore over and above having a staff knowledgeable enough and motivated enough to nose out political chicanery, commercial fraud and diplomatic double-cross, a contemporary newspaper worth its salt must also have one equally skilled and adept at nosing out intellectual fraud, ethical double-cross and moral phoniness. It was in this spirit that my first act on becoming editor was to refuse to join my new peers in demanding a reform of the Official Secrets Act, on the grounds that the most harmful things said and done in contemporary Britain were not plotted secretly behind closed doors in the corridors of power but openly propagated in most schools and universities, preached from most pulpits and asininely echoed in every television studio in the land.

Nothing that Andrew Knight did in those early days was more helpful than seconding James MacManus from all other journalistic duties to be my personal assistant. For although James was not himself a natural *Sunday Telegraph* journalist, he immediately understood the type I was looking for. In particular he recommended that I see Graham Paterson who was then a young junior on the 'Peterborough' column. At first sight Graham looked like any run-of-the-mill fat schoolboy, but it didn't take long for one to realise that inside this Billy Bunter there was a Just William – or even a Flashman – struggling to get out. Whether Graham shared his father Peter's left-wing politics I never discovered. What he did share to the full, however, was his father's sense of fun and mischief. In any case I was not looking only for Tories, still less Thatcherites, but rather for people wholly untainted by political correctness and on that account Graham scored bull's-eye after bull's-eye. Without a moment's hesitation I appointed him news editor with a remit to recruit more young talent. This he did with a vengeance. In no time I had interviewed and taken on Peter Millar, Walter Ellis and Simon O'Dwyer Russell.*

Another of my early appointments was Derwent May as literary and arts editor. For years I had been meeting him and his enchanting wife Yolanta at Margot Walmsley's incomparable salon and seldom came away from the encounter without having my wits sharpened and spirits raised. Endlessly intriguing, too, was the contrast between Derwent's meek and mild manner and the steely toughness of his taste. I don't think we had often discussed politics but from the way he discussed everything else – particularly people – I could see that his heart was in the right place. Before accepting the job he made only one easily agreed condition: that he should be allowed to continue contributing his regular miniature Nature Notes to *The Times*.

A more dangerous appointment was that of Bruce Anderson as political columnist. In his case there was no contrast between appearance and reality or inner and outer man. He looked a brute which is what he was. But he was immensely well informed, formidably intelligent, well read, witty, scabrous and, most enjoyable of all, unashamedly reactionary. His only previous journalistic experience was as a television researcher on the Brian Walden programme which is where I had first met him. But whereas most TV researchers are instantly forgettable, Bruce was outstanding even in that humble, not to say humiliating role.

In Lord Hartwell's day Bruce would have been regarded as too flagrantly partisan even for a columnist, let alone a political reporter, and indeed it was one of his early articles that provoked Lord Hartwell to have another go at exerting his authority. Although deprived of all power, he was still nominally editor-in-chief and would come into the office on Saturday exactly as usual. That it was now a ritual without any substance did not seem to worry him. He would sit in his room reading the proofs just as he had done in the old days of his glory and out of politeness, after lunch, I would visit him, as all the previous editors had done, to tell him the plans for tomorrow's paper. Always a man of few words, he had now become virtually silent and would simply hand me back the proofs with a nod. Bruce's first effort, however, proved too much for him. It was, he protested, straight Conservative Party propaganda and by printing it I would reduce the *Sunday Telegraph* to a laughing-stock. In the old days that would have

---

*O'Dwyer Russell, in his early twenties, was appointed defence correspondent more on the basis of enthusiasm than of experience. Coming from a service family he knew lots of young officers who tipped him off about all the mess rumours and gossip. In no time at all the Defence Ministry, assuming him to be the beneficiary of high level leaks, were bombarding me with protests and eventually the Secretary of State for Defence, Kenneth Younger, even went to the unprecedented lengths of inviting me out to dinner *à deux* at Simpson's specifically to ask for his dismissal. Sadly, this most engaging and enthusiastic young man died suddenly on the eve of his departure for the Gulf War. His army medical examination showed up a heart complaint requiring an emergency operation from which he never recovered.

been that. The article would have been spiked without more ado. But these weren't the old days. I was now in charge, with Andrew Knight's express authority to defy Lord Hartwell if need be. Even so, it wasn't easy. Habits of subservience formed over nearly forty years don't change in a few weeks. So there was a long pause as I summoned up my courage to contradict. Bruce's article, I said, was far too intelligent and far too brilliantly argued to be Conservative Party propaganda. No Tory Party hack could write like that. This was the kind of writing that made readers sit up and take notice and I was certainly going to print it. The earth didn't open up. Lord Hartwell finished reading the other proofs and handed them back to me without another word. This was not only the first time I ever contradicted Lord Hartwell but also the last, since he never sought to interfere again.

Not that there was much else, I imagine, that he wanted to interfere with, even if he still had the power to do so. Apart from Bruce Anderson's partisanship, the rest of the paper showed no signs of going overboard for Mrs Thatcher. In fact one of my early signed leaders received much notice precisely because of its critical tone. In it I coined the pejorative phrase 'bourgeois triumphalism' to describe her style of governing and for some time thereafter the *Sunday Telegraph* and its new editor were very much out of favour in Downing Street. Circulation, however, was going up and as a result of Graham Paterson and his lively team there were now frequent news exclusives on the front page. It had not been a bad first year and even the management were showing signs of satisfaction. This took the form of Stephen Grabiner, a public relations and advertising whizz-kid brought in by Andrew Knight, starting to look in quite often for an evening drink. At first I saw nothing significant about these friendly visitations which I enjoyed. Only much later, however, when they abruptly ceased, did I realise that their beginning and end, and frequency in between, corresponded disturbingly closely with the ups and downs of the circulation graph.

Throughout all this period Lord Hartwell continued to put in an appearance every Saturday. Increasingly it became almost a ghost-like presence, except that it was more sad than frightening. Only when the move to the Isle of Dogs was fixed did he let it be known that he was going to call it a day. I remember that last Saturday in the Fleet Street office very clearly. In the morning we all lined up for a memorial photograph on the fifth-floor balcony outside what in the old days had been the heavily guarded palatial apartments of the Lords Camrose and Hartwell. This was before Lord Hartwell arrived. Then there was the last lunch which he attended, with the usual exchange of City gossip between him and Ian Watson who had by then replaced Alexander as my deputy. If Lord Hartwell felt emotional he did not show it; rather less so than some of us for whom the move must have been much less of an agonising wrench than it was for him. After lunch I made the customary visit with the proofs which he studied so closely and at such length that I thought he had gone into a trance. Then, still looking down at them, he started to mutter and I had to lean forward to catch what he was saying. 'Just wanted to tell you, Perry, I was wrong. You are doing a good job.' Because he was speaking so indistinctly I will never be certain that I did not dream those words. But, if so, it must have been a very realistic dream because there was nothing imaginary about my having to rush out of the room before breaking down in tears.

Editing a national newspaper must be one of the least boring jobs imaginable. For as soon as you reach the office there is a queue of colleagues outside your door with a strong professional motive to succeed in arousing your interest. For without the editor's support their own projects may fall by the wayside. And whereas reporters and specialist writers are loath to share their secrets with each other, they are eager to do so with the editor, if only to demonstrate how much their important contacts trust them. Nor is it only a matter of the editorial staff having to make great efforts to interest the editor with their ideas and projects. Even more pleasurable, from the editor's point of view, is the interest the staff are compelled to take in his ideas and projects. When an editor throws out an idea, however far-fetched, it does not fall on stony ground. When the editor asks questions, they do not go unanswered. Not for him the frustrations of never finding his enthusiasm shared or his vendettas pursued. Also the editor has an excuse – indeed a duty – to trespass far outside the particular field where he himself is most at home, in my case politics. Before becoming editor, for example, I would never have dared – so little do I know of the game – to invite the *Sunday Telegraph*'s enormously distinguished cricket correspondent, Tony Lewis, to lunch. Almost as soon as I did reach the chair, however, this is what I did, taking along Geoffrey Wheatcroft, who is omniscient, as a fig-leaf to disguise my ignorance.

Not all my forays into unfamiliar territory, however, were so enjoyable. At one editorial conference I demanded to know why our music critic never wrote about a contemporary British composer called Ramsbottam whom on my way to work I had heard described on Radio Three as a latter-day Edward Elgar. Shocked by, for once, getting no response, I waxed ever more lyrical about the genius of Ramsbottam, even to the point of demanding a profile on him next Sunday. Only after the conference was over did Derwent, very discreetly, come back into my office to enquire whether by chance I was confusing Ramsbottam with Birtwhistle.

Derwent proved a most game and supportive colleague; arguably on one occasion too game and supportive. For he was an enthusiastic accomplice in a journalistic *jeu d'esprit* which later came to be seen as the first sign of my editorial loss of touch. Long before becoming editor I had noticed, when staying away with friends for the weekend, that people seldom spent much time reading Sunday paper front pages – at least not those of the broadsheets. This wasn't in the least surprising. Because there is so little hard news on Saturday, most lead stories have a fairly ersatz flavour which puts the reader off. So as soon as possible I introduced an innovation. We started carrying an off-beat human interest strip across the top of the front page, as a kind of appetite-whetter for the lead story proper immediately below. A few colleagues, hard news purists, thought this was a waste of front page space; not, however, Graham Paterson who saw the point and cooperated enthusiastically. But on this particular Saturday he had to confess that the newsroom cupboard was bare. I was in despair. For those resisting the innovation had warned us about the difficulty of finding enough suitable stories and it now looked as if they were about to be proved right.

Suddenly I had a brainwave. Over lunch at the Garrick Club earlier in the week Kingsley Amis had shown me his exchange of letters with the director of the National Portrait Gallery, angrily rejecting an invitation to sit for a joint 'conversation piece' with his son Martin. In those days I was writing the *Spectator* diary and Kingsley thought this exchange might make a good paragraph. Why not inflate it a bit, I thought, and use it instead for the *Sunday Telegraph* strip. Derwent agreed and we both spent a hilarious hour hyping this little storm in a teacup into a great literary and artistic row. 'Not since Dr Johnson attacked his patron Lord Chesterfield has the art of epistolatory vituperation reached such peaks . . . ' In my judgment the strip just got by. Certainly it didn't deserve such prominence but beggars can't be choosers. For some reason or other, however, several media correspondents – perhaps they too were hard up for a story – saw fit to question my sense of proportion and when, in two years' time, my editorship came to an abrupt end the critics wrote that this absurd incident was the seed from which my downfall stemmed.

This seems unlikely. Certainly Andrew Knight made no complaints at the time. But then after the move to the Isle of Dogs I was seeing much less of him. In the old Fleet Street office days Max and I breakfasted with Andrew every Tuesday at 9.00 a.m. I used to enjoy these occasions. For although Andrew only ate yoghurt and the occasional mango, the Berry family's tradition of hospitality was still strong enough to ensure that his guests received the full panoply of a proper Edwardian repast served by a butler, chafing dishes and all.

The purpose of these breakfasts was to keep the editors informed of what the management were up to – something Lord Hartwell had never bothered to do – and for us to keep Andrew informed of what we were up to. On only one occasion do I recall Andrew playing the heavy-handed proprietor. It was over a critical leaderette I had written arguing that since *Sun* readers would never punish Rupert Murdoch's excesses by cancelling

their subscriptions, might it not be a good idea for readers of *The Times* –
which is also owned by Murdoch – to punish him by cancelling theirs? It
seemed a safe enough suggestion, particularly as *The Times* was the *Tele-*
graph's main rival. Andrew did not find it so, and the only order he ever
gave me – also the only one I ever ignored – was never again to criticise
Murdoch without his express authorisation. Unfortunately, such were the
difficulties of getting to the Isle of Dogs in time for breakfast that these
sessions soon began to lapse. This was a loss. A countervailing gain from
the move – at least for me – was the acquisition of a chauffeur. In the
Hartwell days only senior managerial executives had chauffeurs. Under
the new dispensation, and thanks to the inaccessibility of the Isle of Dogs,
henceforth editors were to be equally privileged. Nor was this the only
immensely valuable perk now showered upon us. We were also given
generous share options. At the time, in my ignorance, I had no idea just
what a boon these share options were going to be. After working for Lord
Hartwell for so long any hope of not ending up a poor man had long since
disappeared. So I signed the forms sent to me by Anthony Rentoul, the
company secretary – not even bothering to read the figure which would
have meant little to me anyway – and thought no more about it until the
same company secretary explained three years later that as a result of
having signed that document I was nearer to being a millionaire than any
journalist of my generation would have thought possible, or even, in a
funny kind of way, proper.

Those were enormously busy and fulfilling years. I don't think my
writing suffered, although it did mean rising early on Friday morning so as
to get the signed leader at least started before reaching the office in good
time to take the main news conference at 11.00 a.m. That was my favourite
conference. For as editor I was now able to make sure that the news and
comment sides of the paper reinforced each other, instead of operating as
separate and even hostile empires. On a Sunday paper this is absolutely
essential. For in the already much mentioned absence of hard news, it is
often necessary for an editor to invent it. By invent it I don't mean make it
up but rather imagine what might be happening and then ask reporters
and foreign correspondents to follow up these hypotheses or hunches.
Here knowledge of history is an enormous advantage. German reuni-
fication, for example, has happened before. Empires have disintegrated
before. Devaluations have happened before. Reporters and foreign correspondents, with their noses properly glued to the ground for clues about
what is going to happen tomorrow, cannot be expected to spend time
reading up all the historical precedents. But an editor, and his ideas team,
can. That is part of their job. Obviously this shouldn't mean delivering long
history lessons at the news conference. But a Sunday paper's news conference on Friday doesn't have to be as hurried as a daily's news conference.
Discursiveness should be encouraged, and unquestionably a Sunday

paper's coverage of great developments can be given an extra dimension by learning lessons from similar grand developments in the past and I saw it as very much part of my job to encourage my more academic colleagues to range far and wide, even if this did sometimes cause Graham Paterson – and others concerned to get the paper out on time – to rustle papers with impatience.

Writing grew easier rather than more difficult. Before becoming editor I had often suffered from writer's block. Now that curse never descended. In fact by 4.00 p.m. I would usually be in a bouncy mood, refreshed by the relief of having finished my leader and therefore more rather than less keen to read the mass of other people's copy that had by now accumulated in my in-tray (I use the word figuratively because there was no such thing). At about 6.00 p.m., Ian Watson, my splendidly Scottish deputy, on whom I could and did rely absolutely, would look in for a drink, usually accompanied by Richard Sykes whose job it was to advise about libel, starting always with my leader. Mercifully Richard is more reactionary than I am. So on matters ideological he was more *agent provocateur* than moderating influence and on the very few occasions when he did have to cut out my or Bruce's attacks, for example on the Labour Party, the excisions really did seem to be hurting him more than us.

It was on one such occasion that I showed him my leader criticising Andrew Neil and Donald Trelford for cavorting in public with Pamella Bordes. How I enjoyed writing that leader. There is no denying it. Vituperation can become an addiction. Once one starts exercising the art of mockery all concern about consequences, about damaging reputations, goes up in smoke. Hilary Mantel in her marvellous historical novel about the French Revolution, *A Place of Greater Safety*, describes a Jacobin editor thus: 'A kind of sweet venom flowed through his veins, smoother than the finest cognac; quicker to make the heads spin. Laudanum might quicken the senses but a good editorial put a catch in the throat and a skip in the heartbeat. Writing's like running downhill; can't stop if you want to.'

Not that I did want to. The headline on that leader was also mine. 'Editors as Playboys'. Even now I can remember the intense satisfaction of writing that line. Richard Sykes did warn me that there was a risk of libel, but both of us agreed that neither of the editors would be silly enough to sue. Even if Sykes had warned me much more vehemently I doubt whether I would have paid attention. In this sense writing editors can indeed be a liability. For having finished that leader, and decided on the headline, I was no more restrainable than any wild animal which has once smelt blood.

In the event Andrew Neil demanded an apology, which I refused, and then went on to sue for libel. But because the wheels of justice grind so slowly, that was something that could safely be put out of mind for the time being. In any case a more dramatic preoccupation intervened in the form of an operation for acute appendicitis which put me out of action for about ten weeks. Convalescing in the Seychelles – at the *Sunday Telegraph*'s expense – I received a telephone call from Ian Watson conveying the marvellous news that the *Sunday Telegraph*'s circulation the previous Sunday had at long last overtaken that of the *Observer*. Buoyed up by this achievement and by a fortnight's sunshine, I returned to London fighting fit. This was the highpoint of my editorship and I couldn't wait to get back to work.

Then things started to go wrong. Renewed doubts about my editorial judgement were raised, for example, by my sacking of the *Sunday Telegraph*'s much admired – except by me – and long serving City columnist, Jock Bruce-Gardyne. I found his column flip, offhand, insubstantial and facetious – a view shared by my City editor James Murray. Since Jock also wrote regularly for the *Daily Telegraph*, where he was the economics leader writer, and for the *Spectator*, it never occurred to me that he would greatly object to being removed from his additional outlet on the Sunday which he often dashed off in a hurry as late as Friday afternoon. But object he did, with all the affronted dignity of one of Mrs Thatcher's former treasury ministers and a recently ennobled (by Mrs Thatcher) peer of the realm.

What he especially objected to was the manner of the sacking and here he had a point. By mistake he learnt of it from the City editor, before he learnt of it from me. This was a miserably unfortunate piece of bungling, for which I apologised abjectly. But to no avail. In Jock's eyes, and those of his many influential friends at Westminster and in the City, I was irredeemably damned as a callous butcher. Andrew Knight, in particular, took up the cudgels on behalf of Jock and sent me a censorious letter, handwritten and delivered at my home by special messenger. Its charge was that I had behaved high-handedly and insensitively to a distinguished public servant and old colleague. What part this played in turning Andrew Knight against me is difficult to say. But it certainly deserved to play some part. For there can be few more unforgiveable irresponsibilities in an executive than a botched sacking, made all the more lamentable, in this case, by the discovery, not long afterwards, of Jock's terminal illness from which he died, after the most gallant struggle.

Andrew may also have been concerned about my having incurred the wrath of the Prince of Wales. Along with the editors of *The Times* and *The Economist*, I was invited to lunch at Kensington Palace to advise him on how to improve his relations with the Press. This was long before his marriage problems. His concern at that time was with papers only reporting his recreational activities, like polo and skiing, and not his serious good works. In the informal discussions after the Lucullan working lunch I ventured to say, half jokingly, that it was idle for him to suppose that he would ever get the Press that he deserved. Some papers might responsibly decide to concentrate more on his good works. But their efforts would always be overshadowed by the great mass of media attention which would never resist the temptation to trivialise and vulgarise. If he really wanted to avoid being trivialised and vulgarised, the only sensible course was to adopt a lower profile, distance himself and his family from the media generally, and recreate the barriers which had once protected the royal family from the public's prying gaze; in other words put the clock back to the good old days before the royal family had been bamboozled by modernisers into trying to be just like any other celebrity.

To my dismay the Prince reacted to this advice with passionate resentment. Did I want him to spend the rest of his life unveiling monuments and so on, he asked. He could not bear to envisage such a retrogression. All his life he had been struggling to escape that fate. It was an extraordinary outburst. Clearly the Prince was under considerable strain. At one point he even put his head in his hands.

Where I went wrong was to mention this incident – not for attribution – to the London correspondent of the *New York Times* who came to interview me for an article he was writing on the royal family. Although the resulting article in the *New York Times* did not sensationalise this angle, the British tabloids, picking it up the following morning, most certainly did. It was front-page news. No particular editor was named as the source of the leak. But since the other editors of the lunch categorically denied responsibility, the finger of blame pointed inescapably at the editor of the *Sunday Telegraph*.

Andrew, a close friend of the Prince, issued no formal rebuke. In fact he did not refer to the matter at all until we ran into each other by chance at a social gathering some weeks later. 'Oh Perry', he said, taking my arm, 'I thought you might like to know that I may just about have succeeded in smoothing down the Prince of Wales' ruffled feathers'. This was said with a smile. But it was a pretty autumnal smile which left the air distinctly cool.

Most troubling of all, circulation began to drop, a process which was calamitously accelerated when the management transferred our colour magazine to Saturday's *Daily Telegraph*. Paul Johnson privately and publicly urged me to resign rather than to let them do this. Without a fully fledged colour magazine, he warned, the *Sunday Telegraph* would lose readers by the drove. Arrogantly and complacently I dismissed his warnings. Having never regarded the *Sunday Telegraph* colour magazine as much of an asset, I could not believe that its removal would prove much of a liability. Arguably the transfer of the colour magazine from the *Sunday* to the *Daily* was good from the point of view of the company as a whole. Sales on Saturday certainly zoomed up. But for the *Sunday* it was a crippling blow from which it has never recovered.

It took me quite a time to realise that I was no longer the blue-eyed boy. First, there were no longer friendly calls from Stephen Grabiner; then the tone of Andrew Knight's memos subtly changed from enthusiastic support to gentle admonition. The book pages, for example, which previously had received nothing but praise, were now said to be far too highbrow. Complaints, too, began to come from the management about the rowdiness of my staff. Apparently two of the best reporters, Peter Millar and Walter Ellis, both robust Ulstermen, were mislaying their passes now needed to get into the building and instead of waiting patiently for the security men to check their identities, would leap over the turnstile and storm on regardless. Other similar misdemeanours were alleged. Not only was I no longer the blue-eyed boy but in no time at all I had become the Lord of Misrule.

Soon the straws in the wind thickened. Rumours began to circulate in the trade magazines about the *Sunday Telegraph* ceasing publication; then of it being merged with the *Daily*. One day, out of the blue, I got a letter from Lord Hartwell inviting me to lunch. He, too, had heard rumours about a merger between the *Daily* and *Sunday* and wanted to offer me his assistance in opposing such an ill-judged plan. Still I refused to believe that there could be anything afoot. But if only to reassure colleagues, whose morale was suffering, I asked Andrew specifically what was going on and received a letter from him which put my mind entirely at rest. On its basis, I circulated a memo to the staff telling them that there was nothing to worry about. Likewise I sent a message to Lord Hartwell thanking him for offering to help avert a threat which I was now confident had never existed.

Rereading Andrew Knight's letter I see that I was wrong to have been reassured by it. For although it specifically stated that the management 'has no wish to, intention of, or interest in diminishing the *Sunday Telegraph*, let alone, as we are oddly accused, selling it,' it also went on to say, more ominously, 'rather we wish to take it to a position of success on Sunday comparable to that of the *Daily* on weekdays'. Again I was guilty of complacency and arrogance. Having been told not long previously by Conrad Black that the *Sunday Telegraph*, under my editorship, was now 'the best Sunday newspaper in the world', the idea that Andrew Knight was seriously planning any radical changes never crossed my mind. One Friday evening, however, I ran into him in the lift and he asked, quite casually, whether I would like to have breakfast on the following Tuesday, not on the Isle of Dogs but at Claridge's. He had just returned from holiday and from a visit to the United States and seemed in the best of spirits. Nothing in his manner or expression gave me the slightest cause for anxiety. Rather the opposite. The invitation to resume our pleasant breakfast meetings seemed a return to normalcy rather than any dramatic innovation. So did the choice of venue. How could anything nasty ever happen at Claridge's?

Sidney, my chauffeur, picked me up at 8.30 a.m. and although I arrived early Andrew was already at the table reading the papers. Not until we had ordered our breakfast did he tell me his plan to make the *Sunday* a seventh-day edition of the *Daily*, under Max Hastings' editorship. My role in future would be reduced to editing a four-page Sunday Comment section, with no further say in any other part of the paper. Some months later, in a *Spectator* diary, I described the exact moment when this blow hit me.

It was when the waiter had just served two perfectly poached eggs on buttered toast – a dish of which I am inordinately and insatiably fond. In my mind I knew that the information just imparted was paralysingly painful; pretty well a professional death sentence. But for some reason this sense of acute shock did not get through to my taste buds or palate or whatever part of the nervous system or anatomy controls the appetite, and I continued eating the eggs with as much pleasure as usual; and also, a bit later, the rolls and marmalade as well. Even while doing so I was surprised and even shocked at my quite indecent insouciance. Surely an editor, on hearing that his beloved paper is about to be killed, should not calmly continue to eat a hearty breakfast. How can you? I thought to myself. Would not anyone with the slightest sensitivity have his appetite cut clean away, choke on his food, on hearing such unwelcome news? Only later did I recall all those wartime testimonies of how on being shot, men can feel no pain for quite a while and even carry on as if nothing had happened. Could it be that deeply wounding words have the same delayed impact, temporarily anaesthetising the victim? I don't know the answer. All I do know is that, at the time, I enjoyed that Claridge's breakfast and only began to feel sick with indignation and shame some hours later.

Sidney Bore was the first person to hear the news while driving me from Claridge's to the Isle of Dogs. Andrew had said that there was no question of my perks being reduced, along with my status, and I wanted to assure Sidney that however many other jobs would be affected by Andrew's radical reorganisation, at least his would be safe, at any rate for the time being. Later in the day Andrew came down to my office to explain his plans to a gathering of the *Sunday Telegraph* staff. It was an angry and emotional meeting and the *Evening Standard* that afternoon carried a Londoner's Diary story about my having broken down. In a way that was true. That is to say, I did shed a few tears. But not because of being demoted. It is never the big things that make adults cry, and in fact I had got through the painful business of listening to Andrew Knight explaining his decision to the staff without excessive or uncontrollable emotions. What set me off happened a few minutes after the meeting was over when a relatively junior colleague, whose copy I had sometimes spiked and who had no reason to thank me for anything, came in to offer me his sympathy. Most people can cope, at any rate in public, with personal disasters without breaking down. For we are all steeled not to give way to self-pity. Much more difficult to cope with, however, are those unexpected small gestures of human solidarity which succeed in penetrating the thickest emotional armour-plating. So the truth was this: I did not weep out of hurt at the nastiness of the world but out of wonder at its niceness.

In the event, Andrew Knight's plans for a seven-day *Daily Telegraph* never began to work. Conrad had been talked into it against his better judgment, Max Hastings thought it a mad idea from the start. Some of the best of the *Sunday Telegraph* staff, including Graham Paterson, Walter Ellis and Peter Millar, upped sticks and found jobs elsewhere, most of the old team eventually reforming on *The Times*. I was half inclined to resign myself, and entertained several tempting offers, including one from Andrew Neil on the *Sunday Times* who wanted me to become their star columnist. These negotiations even went to the extent of my seeing Rupert Murdoch. No mention was made throughout these negotiations of the Andrew Neil libel action pending against me which, if I had agreed to join his staff, would presumably have been dropped. As it was, I didn't agree, and the libel action wasn't dropped. But more of that in a moment. Of all my colleagues, the one who suffered most from Andrew Knight's ill-fated and short-lived merger was my deputy, Ian Watson. For when a few months later, the merger was aborted and the *Sunday Telegraph* given back its own separate identity, Max Hastings seized the opportunity to make one of his own men, Trevor Grove, editor of everything except my Comment section, leaving Ian little option but to join the exodus. Here mention must be made of Frank Johnson, a brilliant writer and most loyal of colleagues, with strong conservative views, whom I had enticed on to the *Sunday* from a senior job on *The Times* not long before the merger. In his mind as much as in mine there had been the unspoken assumption that in due course he might hope to succeed me. Now, however, as a result of all the changes brought about by the merger, any such prospect was pretty well ruled out. But instead of feeling resentful at my having lured him to the *Sunday Telegraph* on a false prospectus, Frank chose to look on the bright side of things and it was almost entirely due to his enthusiasm and encouragement that I came to regard editing a four-page comment section, with him as my number two, and Bruce Anderson as another founder member, as likely to be a lot of fun, as indeed it turned out to be.

For Andrew had given me a three-year contract under which my four pages were an independent editorial entity entirely under my control. From the point of view of the paper itself the arrangement made no sense at all since the *Sunday Telegraph* became, as Max Hastings put it, a pantomime horse with the front legs and the rear legs functioning separately and sometimes even at odds. But this was Andrew's doing, not mine, and after initial misgivings I settled down happily, and not a little defiantly, to make the best of a bad job. If an independent comment section was what they wanted, then by God that was what they were going to get with knobs on.

Ironically, one of the new Comment section's first opportunities to show its mettle came when Andrew Knight announced that he was departing from the *Telegraph* – with £14 million worth of share options in his pocket – to take charge of the Murdoch newspapers which included the *Telegraph*'s main rivals. It would have been an odd decision at the best of times. But to go over to the enemy, so to speak, so soon after crippling his own side with this disastrous merger made it all the odder, and I decided, without consulting anybody, to carry a vicious profile of this strange and mixed-up character. Under the heading 'Constant Smiler With the Knife' the profile made no attempt to be fair or judicious. We weren't writing Andrew's obituary. We were writing in the heat of the moment. Unquestionably there is more virtue in Andrew than our profile allowed. It could even be argued that Black owed Knight so massive a debt of gratitude for past services that he should have forgiven, rather than recriminated over, the untimely and unseemly manner of his parting. Certainly, so far as I was concerned, making me editor in the first place did me far more good than demotion did harm. None of this favourable side, however, was reflected in our profile and its omission made me feel very guilty when, on the Saturday afternoon before publication, Andrew rang to say he knew his reputation was safe in my hands. Such confidence was misplaced, just as my confidence in him had been misplaced. Rereading the profile now, with all passion spent, I still think that its partial, unbalanced, *parti-pris* tone caught the truth about the man better than some fairer, blander and more objective profile – in the style favoured by the *Independent* – which would have missed the truth altogether.

Although the mills of justice normally grind slowly, they can on occasion grind with alarming rapidity. This is what happened in the libel case. As the result of some unexpected cancellation in the Royal Court of Justice lists our case was suddenly brought forward for hearing in a week's time. Until Richard Sykes rang to tell me this news I had not really expected it ever to come to court. Not only had Andrew Neil offered me that job after the alleged libel appeared, but he had also invited me to his annual Christmas party where we had been photographed together in friendly conversation. True, for months past Auberon Waugh, at parties, had always eagerly enquired about the progress of the case, and speculated as to the size of the possible damages; but these joshing exchanges – which were usually either followed or preceded by similar enquiries about my hypothetical knight-hood – served only to remove it even further from the realms of reality into the realms of fantasy. Now for the first time, however, it had to be taken seriously.

Just how seriously became clear when Patrick Milmo, QC, my counsel, whom Richard and I visited in his chambers, read out the leader in question very slowly, occasionally stopping to look over his spectacles and ask me exactly what I had meant by certain of the potentially libellous passages. In truth the whole leader was intended as a piece of social commentary. Once upon a time, editors of quality newspapers were dignified figures like Garvin and Dawson who spent their evenings dining at All Souls in the company of scholars. Now they were figures like Andrew Neil and Donald Trelford, who spent their evenings in nightclubs in the company of Pamella Bordes. My point was not that Neil's and Trelford's behaviour had been such as to make them unsuitable to edit newspapers today but that it would have been regarded as such in bygone, and by implication, better days. In other words, it was much more the contemporary world I was disparaging than Neil and Trelford personally.

But listening to Mr Milmo, QC, reading out my prose, I could see that certain sentences, taken out of context, could be read as meaning these two editors were not fit to hold their jobs in the here and now. Both Milmo and Sykes, however, seemed pretty confident that even these were fair comment and there was no need for me to worry – much more confident than I was myself. A milling crowd of reporters and photographers was waiting outside the Courts of Justice when Claudie and I arrived on the first day of the trial. Having over the years watched on the television so many scores of other people being mobbed in this way, it was almost impossible not to put on a bit of an act now that one was experiencing the same treatment oneself. Claudie pushed ahead looking very stern and dignified but I smiled, thinking it best to appear at ease and confident. Once inside the Courts of Justice, however, it became much more difficult to appear at ease and confident since everything about the neo-Gothic building is designed to impress and overawe. Walking up the steps pursued by photographers one could imagine oneself a central figure in a great drama. But inside the echoing building itself, amidst the throng of other bewildered litigants, and with begowned and bewigged lawyers stalking to and fro, no such delusions of grandeur long survived. One was a mere cog in a great judicial wheel, powerless and utterly insignificant. In the outside world it was Neil versus Worsthorne. But sitting side by side down in the well of Court 13, where the trial took place, with serried ranks of lawyers rising up behind us and the judge on his raised dais in front of us, and the jury on their elevation to the side, we were just appellant and defendant on whom everybody – including the public in their gallery and the court reporters in theirs – could, metaphorically and literally, look down.

The case lasted eight days, two of which were given over to my cross-examination by Andrew Neil's QC, Michael Rampton. Some of this was almost enjoyable. But towards the end it got rough and it was a strange and disquieting experience to find a professional man ranged against one and ranged against one, not over some trifling argument, but in a matter involving one's very reputation. Surely he must be joking, teasing, only pretending to want to do one down? Would he not break into a smile any minute, or at least give a friendly wink? Normally professional people almost never raise their voices, let alone their fist. We tell each other what we think the other would like to hear, and even disagreements are almost always softened by a smile. Never is a spade called a spade. Of course rivalries and hatreds exist but they are buried beneath a beautifully re-assuring surface of civilised cordiality. In Court 13 that safe world of middle-class cordiality was turned upside-down. 'I submit, my lord, that the defendant' – i.e. me – 'is a hypocrite and a humbug, pompous, sancti-monious and malicious.' Mr Neil's counsel was not joking. There was no smile on his face. Nor was the allegation made in passing. It came as a conclusive climax of hours of detailed denigration. This was no mugging at the hands of a thug in a dark alley. For that nowadays one is all too prepared. It was a mugging by a highly well-spoken gentleman who looked and sounded just the type who outside Court 13 could be relied upon to defend rather than attack.

Once up against the law you are on your own. During the trial there was much talk of the Garrick Club mafia. For the judge, like me, was a Garrick member. In fact in the middle of the trial I got a note from him to ask me not to use the club that night because he and his wife were planning to dine there. It was a chilling note. While the trial lasted, said the message between the lines, even the camaraderie of the Garrick must needs be suspended. Never have I felt more certain that pulling strings was a total waste of time. At school one felt the same. That, too, was a world of its own from which there was no escape. Aged sixty-six, I had foolishly assumed that I would never again feel that awful sense of isolated vulnerability which is the schoolboy's lot. In Court 13, however, I had the same sense of powerlessness, expendability. It was demoralising, certainly. But also chastening.

In the event the jury found for Andrew Neil and the *Sunday Times*. But by awarding only £1,000 damages to Neil (roughly the price of a party at Tramps) and a mere 60p to the *Sunday Times* (the price of a single copy) they indicated pretty eloquently that the libel, in their view, did not amount to much. Long before the jury's verdict the newspaper commentators had rightly reached the same conclusion. As far as they were concerned the trial was less a legal battle than a social one. Andrew Neil was described as representing classless New Britain, and I as representing fuddy-duddy, class-ridden Old Britain. Neil himself seemed to concur in this view since after the trial was over he explicitly referred to the outcome, not as a victory for justice, but as a victory for New Britain. Victory it may have been, but not at all a decisive one. For the war between New Britain and Old Britain is still being waged in the columns of the *Sunday Times* and the *Sunday Telegraph*, where it most properly belongs.

Why Andrew Neil felt the need to have recourse to the courts I shall never understand. All he needed to do was to answer my rude leader criticising him by writing an equally rude one arguing, all too plausibly, that nowadays playboys spending their time at Tramps made much more successful editors than snobs spending their time at the Garrick Club. As it was, by going to court, he made fools of us both, as well as saddling the *Telegraph* with £200,000 of costs.

For me personally, this ridiculous case also had a far more serious consequence. Because so much of the legal argument had to do with my criticism of Andrew Neil's private life, the tabloids had a perfect excuse to enquire into mine which they did with vengeful thoroughness. Even schoolboy and youthful crushes of fifty years ago were hunted down and ludicrously interviewed. As for more recent and serious friendships the foot-in-the-door lengths gone to were inexcusably odious. The fault was mine, of course. Before writing as I had I should have thought through all the possible risks, not for myself but for others close to me. There was no excuse. Unfortunately once the ink begins to flow a certain intoxication takes over. Journalism makes monsters not just of tabloid journalists but also of quality ones. That is the trouble. In some ways, the better the journalist, the greater the temptation to transgress. For the most part, however, we transgress with impunity, seeing no more of the havoc we create than do air force pilots who drop different kinds of bombs from a great height. A libel action, however, does give one pause. Andrew Neil himself was not in the least on my conscience. The article had done him no harm. But others, one in particular, caught up in the cross-fire, most certainly were harmed. And if I had thoughtlessly harmed her, how many other unintended casualties – of a very different kind – had there been as a result of ill-judged words of mine, over the years, in other columns and articles? Being a defendant in a libel action knocks the smile, and still more the sneer, off a journalist's face. It makes him think more deeply about the consequences of his words, both intended and unintended. How different the clever phrase sounds when read out at the Bar of Justice than when tried out at the bar of El Vino's. As it happens, the Andrew Neil libel article still strikes me as relatively justifiable. So many ruder ones, if picked upon for litigation, would have given me much more cause for shame. This thought made me feel quite sick. Never again, I vowed, would the sweet venom of vituperation be allowed to take possession of my soul. But all too soon it did. Just as diplomats are born to pacify, journalists are born to incite. It is in their nature and at sixty-six I was far too old a dog to learn new tricks.

After the trial was over Claudie and I went to stay with my old Oxford friend Borys and his Norwegian wife, Angelita, in their house on Lanzarote in the Canaries. For some reason I always went there to recover from demeaning experiences, the precedent having been set by a wonderfully cleansing holiday on this volcanic island after a week spent inspecting strip-clubs in Copenhagen as a member of Lord Longford's pornography commission. It was heaven on earth for the first few days. Then Claudie began to develop backaches and a temperature. Such was her passion for the sea and the sun that I knew something must be seriously wrong for her to stay in bed when the golden beaches beckoned. Since the brain tumour fifteen years earlier, she had been successfully operated on for breast cancer, and only recently been given an encouraging report after one of her regular three-monthly check-ups. So we felt reasonably confident that these new back pains were not a recrudescence of that old and dreaded trouble. But as day after sunny day passed, with Claudie still unwell, doubts began to stir, if not in Claudie's mind, then certainly in mine.

On the day before we were due to return home she decided to come to the beach, not to swim – there was no question of that – but to lunch at Borys's favourite fish restaurant. This was a mistake. For as soon as we had sat down Borys was joined by lots of his local Spanish drinking companions whose rowdy presence helped to prolong proceedings. This was by no means an unusual occurrence. These lunches usually went on longer than suited Claudie and me at the best of times and there was almost always very great difficulty in persuading Borys to call it a day. Just as he was getting up one of the Spanish cronies would order another bottle of immensely expensive champagne and honour would require Borys to sit down again. Normally, of course, as guests of the most generous host in the world, we grinned and bore it. But acutely conscious of Claudie's discomfort on this occasion, my patience suddenly snapped. Borys must take Claudie home now, I shouted. How dare he be so cruel and insensitive. The Spanish cronies, who didn't speak English, looked completely stunned at having their festive lunch ritual suddenly interrupted by a ferocious Englishman whose glass they had so recently and so lavishly replenished. Borys, outraged by my peremptory order, continued talking. Claudie, too, was indignant that I should be making such a spectacular scene. What on earth had come over me, she protested. Why hadn't I asked our always solicitous hostess quietly to take us home, which, once appraised of the problem, she immediately did.

It was true. I had behaved hysterically. At the time even I was surprised by my behaviour which wasn't at all in character. Normally I didn't play the part of an over-protective husband. Perhaps something in Claudie's expression at that lunch had warned me that it was about time to begin to do so since if I didn't start now it would soon be too late.

Back in London a string of specialists found nothing wrong. Months went by when she felt only slight discomfort. Then the back pains would start again in earnest. Pleurisy was suspected and appropriate treatment and drugs seemed to have done the trick. But not for long. Cancer was obviously at the back of our minds. But repeated tests kept on ruling out cancer. Then one didn't. I think we must have had some warning that there was bad news because I accompanied Claudie to our GP when the blow finally fell. 'I am sorry to tell you that this time the results are positive.' Claudie remained quite calm. 'How long?' she asked. 'You can never be sure,' he replied. 'It could be three months or three years.' Sidney was waiting outside and as he drove down Sloane Street we told him the dire news. 'Oh my God, Mrs W,' he said, miraculously expressing sympathy through the back of his dear head. The plan had been to buy a new sofa after visiting the doctor and then to call on Margot Walmsley for a drink, and Sidney wanted to know whether there would be a change of plan. There wasn't. We carried on as before. Far from making Claudie feel in more discomfort than usual, she seemed strangely cheerful with more colour in her cheeks than for many months.

Dominique immediately came to stay. By now she was married to Jim Keeling, the distinguished potter, and living in Whichford in Stratford-on-Avon with her five children. Although Claudie and her daughter had an intensely close relationship, this did not normally prevent them quarrelling hotly when under the same roof. This weekend, however, was different. Both of them were in complete agreement about the need for us to move out of Kempson Road which had lots of stairs, into a flat, and that the location of this new flat should be in Kensington, near Claudie's old haunts. Jim and Dominique would help find the flat and take care of the move. It was an unusually peaceful weekend. Dominique confided that Claudie's real reason for wanting to move was less to simplify her own domestic arrangements now than to simplify mine when she was gone. Not only was Dominique movingly tender with her mother but also with me. Without a word being said she and I knew that the next few months – or as long as it took – we were joined in a cruelly painful responsibility that would test our love, not only for Claudie, but also for each other.

Claudie's condition deteriorated with grim regularity, almost week by week. By an iron effort of will she kept herself mobile long enough to supervise the move to a ground-floor and basement maisonette in 74 Kensington Church Street. From then on she was in and out of the Lister Hospital, growing ever weaker. Even so, there were some respites. One such was Claudie's last visit to her beloved native land. Our doctor friend in Wivenhoe, Ted Palmer and his wife, Hally, drove us to Wimereux, near

Boulogne, where they have an apartment. Claudie and I stayed in a convenient downstairs room in an expensive hotel. Although moving around was out of the question, simply being in France was a pleasure for her and one incident in particular provided us with a last great laugh. It happened when the time came to pay the hotel bill before departure. First, after what seemed an endless wait, the patron returned from some inner sanctum complaining that my credit card was out of date. After much searching in her bag Claudie found one of hers which she duly handed over. To the patron's evident relief this one was valid, and in due course he returned again from his inner sanctum to get Claudie's signature on the required form. Then, horror of horrors, Claudie simply could not grip the pen tight enough to be able to sign, hard as she tried. The patron was incredulous; then suspicious. Was this some new Anglo-Saxon trick? First the husband presents his invalid credit card, and then his wife can't sign her valid one. Instead of looking upset Claudie's face was wreathed in smiles. 'Beauvallon,' she said. It was enough. Instantly both our minds went back nostalgically to our honeymoon when an equally suspicious and horrible French hotel manager physically restrained us for non-payment of his bill. Claudie was now too ill to enjoy most jokes but the thought of our last visit to France together ending up in the same humiliating fashion as had our first, forty years earlier, was black enough to raise even her deeply sunken spirits. Fortunately the Palmers arrived to sort matters out. But not before Claudie and I had added one more detail to the long list of other shared vicissitudes, the full richness of which only the two of us could ever hope to understand.

Friends – oh, the undeserved blessing of such fond ones – were a great support: in particular Phil and Val Goodhart, the Lubbocks, the Letwins, the Knoxes, Euan and Caroline Graham, Margot Walmsley, and Beverley Cohen. The last outing was a weekend in the Gower peninsula staying in Pat Gale's flat where Claudie felt most at home. But even in the company of close friends there was not much comfort to be found. David and his family flew over from the United States and Dominique would visit as often as possible, often staying with me when Claudie was in hospital. Then the end came suddenly. It was on a Friday morning. When I had left the Lister late on the previous night there had been no particular cause for worry. But arriving at about 10.00 a.m. the next day, on my way to work, I found Claudie so worryingly weak that I sought out her doctor in his room on the floor below. He said there had been new complications and just as he was starting to explain them a nurse came in to call him away. Returning in a couple of minutes he told me Claudie was dead.

I had only been away three minutes at the most. How could it have happened so easily? I wanted to shout and scream. Grief came later. Initially there was only shock at the insulting uneventfulness of death.

Rushing back to the floor above I found the nurses going about their business as if nothing had happened. In my responses, weeks later, to letters of condolence I was to write 'Claudie died peacefully in hospital' as if this were cause for relief which in a way, of course, it was. But it was also, for the first hour or so, a cause of despair. How could an event of such terrible finality, dreaded for so long and so bravely struggled against, be such a monstrous anticlimax? 'Don't bother with the forms now,' said the kind doctor. 'Come back later.' Sidney drove me to the office where I left my leading article written earlier that morning. My dear secretary, Sue's stricken face, when told the news, helped beyond all measure. In olden days lamentations began instantly at the deathbed. All the protracted ceremonials designed to dignify death came into play without a moment's delay. Not so nowadays. Nowadays, initially, there is nothing, nothing at all, to protect one from death's annihilating insignificance.

After Claudie's funeral, at which Colin Welch gave a moving address, I wrote about her death in the weekly diary which I was then contributing to the *Daily Telegraph*. I hadn't intended to write about Claudie at all; in fact I had warned the *Daily Telegraph* not to expect a diary that week. It seemed indecent to exploit my personal sorrow for journalistic purposes. Then at Dominique's home, where I was staying for the weekend, I read a report in the *Sunday Times* criticising the Bristol Cancer Centre to which several of Claudie's friends had urged her to go. Rightly or wrongly this seemed somehow to give me an objective journalistic peg. Not only did the diary I wrote help to relieve my own feelings but it also helped to bring comfort to others. No piece of mine on any subject has ever received such a large response from readers, many of whom had themselves suffered a recent bereavement. This, in part, is what I wrote:

> When urged to go into the Bristol Centre, my wife said that she did not intend to spend the last months of her life, eating shredded carrots to the sound of Prince Charles blowing his own trumpet. At the time we thought she might be making a mistake. The Bristol Centre was still thought to have a better record for holding cancer at bay than does orthodox medicine. Now we know better. It seems that orthodox medicine is incomparably the more effective of the two. For my own part, I am glad that my wife remained cynical about the benefits of dieting to the very end – as much in sickness as in health. Her view was that, once you were certain that your illness was terminal, it was better to concentrate on making a good death than to waste precious energy on staying alive.
>
> Precisely what she meant by making a good death I shall never know. We never talked about it. Not talking about it was probably part of what she meant. But from the point of view of her family, friends and, above

all, husband, she certainly succeeded in making a death which we found good.

Instead of concentrating on her illness, to the exclusion of us, i.e. hiding away in a clinic, measuring out what remained of her life in health food-filled teaspoons – she concentrated on us to the exclusion of her illness. By concentrating on us, I do not mean doing things for us. Obviously, in the physical sense, bone cancer makes that impossible. By doing things for us I mean allowing us to do things for her. This was a new experience for me. During the previous forty years of marriage she had cared for me rather than the other way round. Only in the last six months did I have a redeeming incentive to correct the balance, however ineptly.

How difficult it is to write about these things without striking the wrong note, either too mawkish or too matter-of-fact. Of course terminal cancer is unspeakably awful. That aspect needs no emphasis. More difficult to imagine is the blessedness which is the corollary of the awfulness. If music is the food of love, so are the cries of anguish. I think my wife learned more of our love during those dreadful months than she did at any other time, and we of hers, too. Going quickly in one's sleep, or in a sudden accident, or peacefully in the fullness of years – all these deaths minimise suffering, and that is one blessing. But the suffering of a long and terminal illness is not all waste. Nothing that creates such tenderness can be all waste.

Perhaps I am trying too hard to make some sense of cancer, to find a silver lining that exists only in an imagination disordered by grief. If that is what I am doing, it is nothing to be ashamed of. But I don't think that that is what I am doing. I truly believe that the way my wife coped with her cancer was a form of love in that it brought out the best not only in her but in us as well. As a destroyer cancer is second to none. But it is also a healer; or an agent of healing. I believe my wife felt this, and drew satisfaction from this, as she lay dying; conscious that she made the best of the last few months. That is why I am thankful she did not spend them in the Bristol Centre or any of the other places given over to distracting the mind from death by vain efforts to purify the body. Nor indeed did she waste much time with orthodox medicine either, accepting at the very end only the minimum of chemotherapy. She had better things to do with her remaining time on earth than indulge in false hopes about getting well; things as precious to me now as are the memories of the good times. Indeed, in a way, these last months were the good times.

One small extra footnote also deserves mention. In addition to the many friends who sent messages of condolence there was a particularly touching one from Andrew Neil. 'Having sat next to your wife for several days in

Court 13,' he wrote, 'I just hope that one day I will be lucky enough to find a girl who will show me the same devoted loyalty as she showed you.'

As the result of Claudie's death, I found myself spending far more time with my close Comment section colleagues, two of whom, Frank Johnson and Geoffrey Wheatcroft, were also members of the Garrick Club. Once a week we would hold a large luncheon party in the office to which congenial politicians and dons were invited. Being isolated from the rest of the *Sunday Telegraph* staff and operating very much as a self-contained unit, our high-profile little group soon began to arouse notice, not all of it favourable. The phrase 'Worsthorne College' was coined at about this time and its suggestion of an ivory tower was not wholly inappropriate. Not allowed to have anything to do with the news and forced to interest ourselves only in ideas, our proceedings did have something in common with an Oxbridge high table, albeit of a reactionary and somewhat eccentric kind.

Although never specifically defined, my aim was to produce a four-page section every week filled with articles certain to give maximum offence to the great and the good. *Epater les bien pensants*, that was both our duty and our pleasure, and the only *infame* we wanted to *écrase* was political correctness. For me this became an obsession. I had a certain idea of the kind of people responsible for bringing England to its present parlous condition – not socialists or radicals or subversives, for all of whom I have respect – but rather high-minded, liberal middle-of-the-roaders who preferred running Covent Garden to fighting on the barricades in the class war. Edward Boyle, who had died in 1981, was such a one. Had he fought to defend the grammar schools? Not at all. Indeed, his enthusiasm for comprehensives had been no less great than that of Shirley Williams or Anthony Crosland. Had he, or his ilk, battled to uphold even the minimum of sexual taboos and repressions necessary for the survival of monogamous marriage? Had they fought against pornography side by side with Lord Longford at Copenhagen? Had they ever risked popularity by upholding the exercise of authority in any shape of form? Had they ever spoken out boldly against the scandalous misuse of trade union power or in support of Enoch Powell's struggle to stop mass coloured immigration? On none of these fronts had they made an effective stand. Even against the IRA they had only battled half-heartedly, reserving their real contempt far less for the cruelties of the terrorists than for the intransigence of the Orangemen, just as in the Cold War they had reserved their fiercest ire not for the communists but for the anti-communists. Although, for the most part, nicely cushioned by hereditary wealth and moving easily in the Wiltshire world of country houses, never for a moment, in the bad days when socialism ruled the ideological roost, had they risked confronting the egalitarian Zeitgeist with bold arguments in favour or rank and hierarchy. God, how I hated their lack of guts. Unlike Mr Major's Tories, who know no better than to talk nonsense about a classless society, they did know better, but chose to keep their heads below the parapet. Nothing mattered – so long as Covent Garden survived. Nor was this lot willing to fight shoulder to shoulder with Mrs Thatcher when in the 1980s she struggled to undo the social evils which their tolerance had allowed to flourish. Did they sing her praises, for example, for putting an end to progressive taxation? Oh no. Although few sections of society benefited more, all we heard from them was yet more bleating about the cuts in the Arts Council subsidy.

Pillorying the great and the good is high-risk journalism. Investigative journalism exposing anti-social 'nasties', such as the makers of thalidomide is risky enough. But exposing do-gooding 'nicies', as the *Sunday Telegraph* Comment section sought to do, was, in many ways, even riskier. For whereas an editor who exposes anti-social 'nasties' only hears from their lawyers, one who exposes do-gooding 'nicies' hears from their friends. Nor was it only I who heard from their friends; so did Conrad Black. Almost without exception, he gave me his full backing both in public and in private. For example, one of our targets was Elspeth Howe about whom we published a splendidly rude profile. I had had her in my sights for quite a long time, ever since she sent out all the wrong Tory signals by joining the Equal Opportunities Commission. Then one evening at Sue Baring's sixtieth birthday I heard her, not for the first time, abusing Mrs Thatcher loudly to, on this occasion, Mark Bonham Carter of all people, and this when her husband Geoffrey was still deputy Prime Minister. Geoffrey was outraged by our profile and used the occasion of the *Spectator*'s Parliamentary Awards of the Year Luncheon, attended by Conrad Black and myself, to accuse the *Sunday Telegraph* Comment section of having taken the safe course of getting at him by attacking his wife. An absurd charge, of course. Attacking Geoffrey would have been far less risky than attacking Elspeth. As soon as Geoffrey sat down, however – to much sympathetic applause from the assembled hacks – Conrad came over to where I was sitting and put a protective arm around my shoulder.

Another popular heroine among the liberal establishment to get a hostile profile was Heather Brigstock, the much acclaimed headmistress of St Paul's. Her offence, in my book, was to flatter the great and the good. At dinners of Lord Goodman, and on other comparable high-minded social occasions, she could always be relied upon to mouth any fashionable liberal trendiness that happened to be around. Of all forms of inauthenticity, being too good to be true is the most difficult to detect and one of the uses to which we put our profile columns was to search it out in the most respectable places.

Sometimes, however, our aim was a bit wild, and I do rather regret having been so rude about John Julius Norwich. Up to a point he was a friend. For years I have admired – even envied – his charm and his cultivation. Never did a Christmas go by without Kenneth Rose in Albany waxing lyrical about the wit and wisdom of his famous greetings cards. Nobody could be nicer or more inoffensive than John Julius Norwich. But that was what stuck in my throat. How could anyone so genuinely civilised living in Britain during the last forty years have made so few enemies? How could anyone have remained so bland while living in a country going to the dogs? Judged in this light his virtues became vices and his innocence, guilt. Flaubert, in a letter to George Sand in 1871, made the same complaint about her. 'Ah, chère bon maître, if you could only hate! This is what you lack: hate. Despite your great sphinx eyes, you have seen the world through a golden haze. That comes from the sun in your heart. But so many shadows have loomed that you no longer see things for what they are. Come now! Shout! Thunder!' John Julius himself took the criticism in good part. But his friends didn't and his friends happened to include sizeable numbers of the *Telegraph*'s board of directors. This time Conrad Black was not amused. I had gone too far. The Comment section, he said, was beginning to sound bad-tempered, if not malicious. There was truth in this complaint. A stench of misanthropic reaction was beginning to infect its columns. When I had edited the whole paper this flavour had been spread much thinner. Now it was much more concentrated. Possibly this put off some young readers. But it certainly switched others on. Worsthorne College was much noticed. The *Guardian* even carried a two-page-spread feature about us. But in the office there were rumblings of discontent. Bruce Anderson put up a serious black which I should have spotted but didn't. Perhaps my grip was slackening. Alternatively perhaps the Comment section was attracting so much attention that others on the *Telegraph* began to resent its prominence. For whatever reason I again began to feel slightly under threat. Conrad Black made Max Hastings editor-in-chief, and although in fact he did not interfere, in theory he now could if he wanted to. This was a straw in the wind; quite a large straw, as it turned out.

Not that I worried. For something then happened which was an enormous morale-booster. It happened just before the final ballot for the Conservative Party leadership which resulted in Mrs Thatcher's resignation as Prime Minister. I was told of her intention to recommend me for a knighthood in the New Year's Honours List. The news came in a most unusual, if not unique way: over the telephone. A Miss Simper from the patronage office rang to ask me whether I had received a confidential letter sent, three weeks earlier, to my home address. On learning that the letter had been sent to a defunct address, and had never been forwarded, she read it over the telephone, asking for an immediate reply as they needed to send the completed list to Buckingham Palace without further delay. My first reaction was to suspect a practical joke. The voice claiming to be Miss Simper speaking from Downing Street must be some practical joker speaking from Combe Florey or from the offices of *Private Eye*. In spite of

Auberon Waugh's campaign to get me knighted, I had never supposed for a moment it would actually happen. This wasn't modesty. I rather prided myself on being a cut above the kind of journalist on whom prime ministers smile. So I asked for a number to ring back. Sue checked it and it was authentic. Only then did I feel immensely gratified. Sir Peregrine, indeed. What better way of postponing the obscurity that awaits all journalists, accustomed to the limelight, on approaching retirement. Journalists are only as good as their last article. Once they stop writing, their names are quickly forgotten. In no other profession are reputations so ephemeral. A knighthood offered a chance of a slightly longer shelf life. It was, if you like, a bit of an insurance. I would no longer need to worry so much about the twists and turns of office politics. For what the Queen was minded to confer, not even Conrad Black or Max Hastings could take away.

Only after accepting the knighthood did I realise how compromising its timing would look to anyone not aware of the precise circumstances. For it was bound to look as if it had everything to do with my passionate espousal of Mrs Thatcher's cause in the current leadership struggle. No part of the media had been more supportive than the Comment section in general and my leading articles in particular. In truth, however, the two were in no way connected. They might have been, if the patronage secretary's letter had gone to the right address and arrived before the leadership crisis broke. But it didn't. I only learnt of the recommendation when the crisis was almost over, and such help as I could give had already been given. She made the recommendation for a knighthood before I became her champion, and I became her champion before knowing of her recommendation. Unquestionably, journalists should not accept honours in return for services rendered or render services in return for honours given. In my case, however, contrary to appearances, that didn't happen. Although often inconsistent and erratic, and at times irresponsible and even unprincipled, I have never consciously been a journalistic hack.*

In the patronage secretary's letter a grave warning was given that any premature publicity about the honour could cause it to be withdrawn. So once again it was necessary for me to put a tight rein upon my tongue, this time over the entire Christmas season. In the case of the editorship I had shared the good news with two loved ones. With the knighthood, sadly, it was only one.

---

* In the hiatus between her resignation as prime minister and her departure from Downing Street I received a call in my office from Bernard Ingham indicating that Mrs Thatcher wanted to see me to say goodbye. The time suggested was 5.00 p.m. Unlike on the only two previous occasions when I had been summoned into the presence for a rebuke, no length was mentioned for the duration of the visit. After half an hour I rose to my feet, wrongly assuming there to be the usual long queue waiting for their turn, but was encouraged to stay. How quickly the current of power gets cut off. Twelve hours earlier Mrs Thatcher was the most sought after woman in the world. Now her faithful Bernard Ingham was almost begging me, with his eyes, not to leave her alone in her hour of need. In the event I stayed well over an hour and on the way down the staircase from her room on the first floor passed her daughter, Carol, on the way up, carrying a string bag with a cold chicken in it for her mother's supper. Seldom have I witnessed a sadder scene.

Postscript 1991

The year 1991 was a remarkable one for me. Pretty well everything changed. I fell in love with Lucy Lambton and married her; retired from the *Sunday Telegraph* and went to live in the country where these memoirs have been written. It all happened very quickly. Lucy and I met at a party of Cynthia Kee's and were engaged within a month. Three years earlier I had been much struck by her television programme, *The Great North Road*, and asked Geoffrey Wheatcroft to interview her for the paper. Arising out of this, she was invited to one of the Worsthorne College lunches where she not only arrived over an hour late but also, most inappropriately, delivered a rip-roaring denunciation of the upper classes. No further meetings occurred until the chance encounter at Cynthia Kee's.

The wedding took place in May.* It was anything but quiet. We had the string section of the Northern Orchestra (by courtesy of my brother Simon) playing at the Hedgerley church blessing, the village doctor Alistair Reece playing the bagpipes from the church tower, a brass band at the reception in the garden and a Cajun group for the dancing. On the day of the wedding the *Daily Telegraph* announced that I would be retiring on 1 September. The retirement was not by my choice. I had written to Max Hastings asking for a three-month sabbatical and received a reply,

---

* It would have taken place earlier but was postponed because of my mother's death in April. Her last years, passed in the Convent of St Nicholas in Holland Park, had been overshadowed by a stroke which severely damaged her speech. But she fought back with superb courage, displaying the same strength of will in her decline as she had in her prime. The nuns, for example, were constantly upbraided for passing so much time on their knees in the chapel praying to God which would have been more usefully employed reading or talking to her. Shortly before her death I took Lucy to the convent to meet her. By then my mother was very weak and not taking much in. Lucy sat on her bed while I rattled away reminiscing about old times. In the middle of one particular reminiscence – about Kathleen Ferrier's concerts at Thorpe Lodge in the 1950s – Lucy suddenly began to sing Ferrier's favourite aria from Gluck's *Orfeo ed Euridice*, 'Che Faro Senza Euridice', and my mother, who had not moved for months, sat bolt upright, her eyes aflame, clasping Lucy's hand. That was her last real sign of life. Right to the end, however, she remained a formidable personality whom it was easier to admire than to love.

delivered by special messenger on the same day – none the less painful for being understandable – that at my age it might be best to call it a day. This I have done, with no hard feelings, and now only write a weekly column, largely about the activities of our four dogs, which I fax to Canary Wharf from the country. Party politics now seem unworthy of notice. Although all political journalists probably rationalize their loss of a ring-side seat in this way, seldom has it been so easy to do as in the 1990s.

Ours is an idyllic life. At the time I signed the contract to write these memoirs, shortly after Claudie's death, my idea was to spend time remembering the past, for want of very much to hope for in the future. It had seemed a sensible undertaking under the circumstances to fill in the blank spaces in existence, 'the nullity', as the Italian writer Charles Magris puts it, 'which suddenly yawns wide open in the hours and the days, and appears between the objects in the room, engulfing them in unending desolation and insignificance'. As it has turned out, however, there was this whole wonderful new existence to experience. When the winds of change in life suddenly blow so strong, there are uprootings which leave the old familiar landscape dismayingly bereft. Haunting memories and regrets return and will never cease to do so. But new, never dreamed of vistas also open up. How lucky I am, beyond all measure and desert.

Appendix

An account of the *Telegraph* board meeting where the decision to appoint Max Hastings as editor of the *Daily Telegraph* and Peregrine Worsthorne as editor of the *Sunday Telegraph* was taken. From *The House the Berrys Built* by Duff Hart-Davis (Hodder & Stoughton, 1990) pages 415–16:

Andrew Knight came to the *Telegraph* boardroom on 25 February. His tactics were to give Hartwell no warning, and so bounce him into acceptance of the nominees. The meeting was carefully timed: the new share issue had gone through the day before, and Hartwell no longer had the power to block innovations.

The result was an explosion, or rather several. In a preliminary meeting held at 2.00 p.m., Hartwell 'blew his top' (his own words) at Frank Rogers and Andrew Knight, for trying to fling a *fait accompli* in his face. 'Surely, if I'm still Editor-in-Chief, I control these appointments?' he cried. 'Why didn't you tell me what you were doing?'

'Well,' replied Knight coolly, 'I didn't think you'd agree.'

At the main meeting, which began at 2.30, Hartwell let fly again. Not wanting to discuss the matter in front of the executive directors, he sent them away, and then had 'an up-and-down for half an hour' with the remainder of the Board. For the first time in the experience of those present, he quite lost his self-control. Far from muttering, as he usually did, he remonstrated loudly and passionately. In Knight's phrase, his reaction was 'very violent'. Hastings he did not know: he would have liked to meet him before a decision was taken. The choice he could not swallow was that of Worsthorne. 'He couldn't edit his school magazine, let alone a national newspaper!' Hartwell cried. 'He's a brilliant writer, but terrible with people. It would be a disaster. You're mad!' He brought up the famous television gaffe, citing it as evidence that the man was unfit to take charge. So angry did he become that David Montagu feared he was going to pass out on them again, and to reduce the tension he took Hartwell off to another room for a recess, together with Lord Rawlinson, hoping to talk him round. 'You don't know anything about these people, David,' said Hartwell bitterly. 'How can you sit there and accept them?' Montagu replied that the papers now belonged to Conrad Black and that if he wanted to appoint editors who turned out to be useless, that was his lookout.

Back in the boardroom Adrian, loyal as he was, spoke out with honesty and courage. He was, he said, the only person present with personal experience of Worsthorne in action. He had often been at editorial conferences when, with John Thompson away, Perry had taken the chair. The meetings had always been most stimulating, for Perry encouraged debate and the development of ideas. He would, Adrian thought, make an excellent editor.

Eventually, as a last throw, Hartwell asked if they could put the matter to a vote. The first man round the table was H. M. Stephen, who said, 'Of course, I vote with the Chairman.' But when it came to Adrian he said, 'Well, Father, I will not vote against you, but I will abstain.' No full account was taken and Hartwell accepted defeat with great dignity.

Index